Work
Requirements

WORK REQUIREMENTS

RACE, DISABILITY, AND THE PRINT CULTURE OF SOCIAL WELFARE

Todd Carmody

Duke University Press *Durham and London* 2022

Designed by A. Mattson Gallagher
Typeset in Adobe Caslon Pro and Knockout
by Westchester Publishing Services

Library of Congress Cataloging-in-Publication Data
Names: Carmody, Todd, [date] author.
Title: Work requirements : race, disability, and the print
culture of social welfare / Todd Carmody.
Description: Durham : Duke University Press, 2022. |
Includes bibliographical references and index.
Identifiers: LCCN 2021044991 (print)
LCCN 2021044992 (ebook)
ISBN 9781478015444 (hardcover)
ISBN 9781478018070 (paperback)
ISBN 9781478022688 (ebook)
Subjects: LCSH: Public welfare—United States—
History. | Welfare recipients—United States—History. |
Work—Social aspects—United States. | African
Americans—United States—Social conditions. | People
with disabilities—United States—Social conditions. |
Minorities—United States—Social conditions. |
BISAC: SOCIAL SCIENCE / People with Disabilities |
SOCIAL SCIENCE / Ethnic Studies / American / African
American & Black Studies
Classification: LCC HV91 .C376 2022 (print) | LCC HV91
(ebook) | DDC 361.973—dc23/eng/20220120
LC record available at https://lccn.loc.gov/2021044991
LC ebook record available at https://lccn.loc.
gov/2021044992

Cover art: Time-lapse photograph of an industrial
motion test conducted at Aleksei Gastev's Central
Institute of Labor, ca. 1924.

Duke University Press gratefully acknowledges the
Bates Faculty Development Fund, which provided
funds toward the publication of this book.

CONTENTS

INTRODUCTION
SIGNS TAKEN FOR WORK

In the fall of 2016, Dale McGlothlin went to a busy intersection near his home in southwest Virginia and held up a sign that read, "Need donations to help to feed my family God Bless." McGlothlin was an unemployed white man in his fifties who had lost the full use of his right arm in a mining accident years earlier. What happened to him afterward was a common enough story in this part of Appalachia, a region hard hit by the collapse of the coal industry and the broader economic downturn. It is a story of disability, unemployment, public assistance, addiction, and jail time—a contemporary portrait of poverty in the United States. McGlothlin was soon joined on the side of the road that day by a man named David Hess, who also carried a sign: "I offered him a job and he refused." It is unclear how long the two men, evidently already acquainted, stood together or how the drivers passing by responded. But before the day was over, Hess posted a photograph of himself and McGlothlin, signs in hand, on social media (figure I.1). The image quickly stirred an outpouring of ridicule and anger, but also pity, and in time local and national media took note.

To many observers, the photograph of McGlothlin and Hess captured a growing split in rural America between "those who work and those who don't."[1] At once somber and provocative, the image seemed to corroborate a spate of recent reporting on how a jobless economic recovery was transforming disability benefits into a de facto public assistance program while still leaving many people in dire need. And yet it doesn't take much digging to see that McGlothlin's experience troubles easy distinctions between working and not working. Not only could McGlothlin make more money on the street than in a low-paying job, he told reporters, but he did

Panhandling Post: A Social Media Post Out of Tazewell County Goes Viral

1.1 Homepage of CBS/Fox59 in Ghent, West Virginia, November 22, 2016. https://www.wvnstv.com/archives/panhandling-post-a-social-media-post-out-of -tazewell-county-goes-viral/.

his best to keep things aboveboard. He had permission to stand on private property and put in regular hours there.[2] McGlothlin, it would seem, approached soliciting like any other job. Unsurprisingly, Hess saw matters differently. He argued that "begging" was the opposite of productive work and that anyone who turned down a "real job" forfeited the right to ask for help in the first place.[3] Hess also flirted with racist caricatures of the "welfare queen," hinting that McGlothlin was jeopardizing his whiteness by seeking a "handout." "I work. You bums should try it." For all his bluster, however, Hess's straight talk seems rather more tortuous when we consider the position he offered McGlothlin: promotion work that required "standing on the side walk twirling a sign on the model of other businesses."[4] To condemn McGlothlin as Hess and his allies did was thus to see a world of difference between twirling a sign for someone else and holding one's own. The former was work; the latter was not. But this criticism also obscures the obvious. Given McGlothlin's limited range of motion, twirling any sign—no matter whose it was or what it said—was out of the question. Not only could he not have accepted the job even if he had wanted it, but the moral chasm separating work from idleness amounted to just a few degrees of rotation.

Writing more than a century before McGlothlin was forced to defend his work ethic on the side of the road (and online), the Black educator Martin A. Menafee described his experience at Booker T. Washington's famed Tuskegee Institute in strikingly similar terms, though with a rather more upbeat conclusion. Menafee begins an autobiographical essay titled "A School Treasurer's Story" (1905) with a recollection of childhood injury. As a boy, he writes, "I had had one of my shoulders dislocated in an accident and have been able to use but one arm since."[5] This impairment prevented Menafee from attending the local college but not from enrolling at Tuskegee. Once on campus, he was assigned to work in the brickyard, a rite of passage at a school that prided itself on teaching cadets the value of hard work for its own sake. This posting soon proved unmanageable, however, and Menafee, unable to cover his fees, was forced to leave Tuskegee after less than a week. Not a full year would pass before he returned for a "second trial." This time Menafee lobbied for stenography work in the front office, an assignment that allowed him to finish his studies on time and launch a successful career in educational administration. At Voorhees School, Menafee worked with founder and principal Elizabeth Wright to help build an institution that would survive, if not always thrive, in the difficult years to come. "A School Treasurer's Story" does not dwell on these hardships or anticipate the rocky road that lay ahead for what is now Voorhees College. Once he moved from the brickyard to the front office, Menafee would have readers believe, the rest simply fell into place.

It would be easy to assume that McGlothlin and Menafee share little more than a personal history of injury and impairment. There is no direct comparison to be drawn, of course, between the social circumstances that shape life for a working-class white man in the deindustrializing present and those encountered by Black professionals in the early twentieth century. Nor does the public attention these men garnered seem at all similar. For a brief moment in the news and outrage cycle linking social, local, and national media, McGlothlin was drawn into a morality tale of two Americas—"makers" and "takers." Menafee's story, by contrast, published in a volume commemorating Tuskegee's fifteenth anniversary, is presented as a triumph of Black industrial education—an ableist tale of overcoming adversity, equal parts Washington's *Up from Slavery* and Helen Keller's *The Story of My Life* (1903).[6] As with the job McGlothlin turned down, however, things seem different when we consider what Menafee actually did

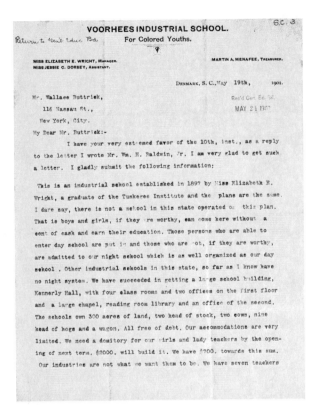

I.2 Letter from Martin A. Menafee of Voorhees Industrial School to Wallace Buttrick of the General Education Board, May 19, 1902, box 122, folder 1110, General Education Board Records, Sc 3 Voorhees Normal and Industrial School, 1902–1920, Rockefeller Archive Center.

at Voorhees. While he was indeed the school's treasurer, Menafee did not spend most of his time balancing the books or doing the payroll. Rather, his primary responsibility involved asking donors and philanthropic foundations for money. Menafee did not take to the street to do this, to be sure. But the letters, applications, and reports he mailed out by the hundreds did proleptically take a page out of McGlothlin's book (figure I.2). Menafee's task was not only to present Voorhees as a worthy cause but also to assure potential benefactors that he was a professional fundraiser and not a beggar. Armed with business English, Menafee thus also set out to show his work.

Taken together, the stories of McGlothlin and Menafee illustrate what probably remains the most widely held assumption about US social welfare provision, a catchall term I use for government and private initiatives to support people in economic need.[7] Today it passes for an unassailable truth that only people who work or are willing to work deserve help. This idea is hardly new. From colonial poor laws to twentieth-century workfare, the social safety net has long been woven of a resolute commitment to the labor market as the only legitimate arbiter of economic resources. From this truism follows another: that it is easy to tell what counts as work and what doesn't. In many contexts this statement would seem all but irrefutable; either goods are produced or services rendered, or they aren't. The issue is thornier, though, with social welfare provision. Whether in the antebellum poorhouse or under Temporary Assistance to Needy Families (TANF)—known today pejoratively as "welfare"—the labor required of beneficiaries usually has far greater noneconomic or moral value than economic value. It matters less that anything particular is made or done than that recipients persuasively perform their potential for self-reliance.[8] What persuades in one context, however, may not in another. In the early nineteenth century, alms seekers could demonstrate their deservingness by breaking rocks or chopping wood but not by selling handicrafts. The work requirements created by 1990s welfare reform can be met by caring for someone else's children—even one's nieces and nephews—but not by looking after one's own.[9] Such arbitrary distinctions suggest, centuries of social policy and custom to the contrary, that not all work is inherently meaningful. In fact, because the noneconomic meaning of work is defined by an ever-shifting set of political, social, and cultural priorities, social welfare provision requires ceaseless acts of representation and interpretation. Recipients strive to make their work legible as such, and those on the other end of the exchange—whether charity organizations or federal agencies—assess the results. Work may be the cornerstone of social welfare provision, in other words, but it is not a self-explanatory or universal truth. Work is a sign to be held just so.[10]

The Dignity of Labor, or Four Ways of Looking at a Field

Why should we assume that all work is inherently meaningful? And why are people on the economic and social margins so often on the hook for assuring us that it is? Implicit in the stories told by and about McGlothlin and Menafee, these questions are rooted in the broader constellation of ideas and institutions that theorists call the work society. As the philosopher André Gorz notes, work societies consider work at once "a moral duty, a social obligation and *the* route to personal success. The ideology of work assumes that the more each individual works, the better off everyone

work society : work has value as contribution to society

will be; those who work little or not at all are acting against the interests of the community as a whole and do not deserve to be members of it; those who work hard achieve social success and those who do not have only themselves to blame."[11] In work societies, in other words, the value of work is not only or even primarily economic. Work is the means by which individuals find recognition in the overlapping social, political, and moral communities that constitute the broader collective. Though it might not always feel this way, we never dedicate ourselves to work out of raw necessity alone. Social and political norms also tell us we should. Recently, thanks to dramatic advances in productivity and automation, this contradiction has become hard to overlook. As the political scientist James Chamberlain has observed, "The value of employment in contemporary society far exceeds its function in distributing material rewards and enabling us to satisfy various needs and wants."[12] For the feminist theorist Kathi Weeks, the conclusion at hand is clear: work produces not only goods and services but also social and political subjects.[13] And in so doing, it crowds out other possible modes of political, social, and cultural community. In work societies, we become a *we* first and foremost as workers.[14]

work is never purely economic

work produces people

work defines society

Only those whose activities are recognized as work, however, can join this *we*. As such, many people whose lives are consumed by labor are nonetheless excluded from full participation in the work society. As we know from a robust body of scholarship—in disability studies, Black studies, and gender and sexuality studies but also history, political science, and sociology—these exclusions have historically provided a foil for the ideal US worker-citizen, typically figured as white, male, and able-bodied.[15] The economic segregation of people with disabilities, for instance, has long served to justify their social and civic disenfranchisement. As disability studies scholars such as David T. Mitchell, Sharon L. Snyder, Sunaura Taylor, and Jasbir K. Puar have shown, global capitalism assigns value and care to laborers who adhere to ableist and eugenic ideals of properly "useful" and "productive" bodies.[16] Race and ethnicity have also played a crucial role in determining whose work deserves the name. The racialization of low-wage and low-status sectors in our own moment, for instance, is rooted in both antebellum efforts to bolster the whiteness of free labor and the overlapping histories of African American inclusion and Chinese exclusion after Reconstruction.[17] Similar exclusions abound in social policy and critical theory. Just as the 1935 Social Security Act wrote Black agricultural laborers out of the US welfare state, orthodox Marxism often presumes a white working class.[18] In Cedric Robinson's phrase, historical materialism too often consigns "race, gender, and history to the dustbin."[19] More recently, Frank Wilderson has argued that work itself "is a white category." Wilderson's point is not that Black people have never worked but that the ontological project of white supremacist capitalism never intended for Black people to be workers. They were instead "meant to be accumulated and die."[20] Like disability and race, ideas about gender and sexuality are also leveraged to determine what counts as genuinely meaningful work. As feminist scholars like Linda Gordon, Barbara Nelson, Alice Kessler-Harris, and Jennifer Mittelstadt have shown, traditionally feminized practices of social reproduction have long been subordinated to the masculine ideals of capitalist production—from nineteenth-century ideologies of separate spheres to the twentieth-century denigration of domestic and home health care services.[21]

The burdens of life in the work society, it is thus clear, are not shared equally. But given the coercion experienced by even the most privileged, questions remain: Why do we prioritize work above all else? And how have the most economically and socially vulnerable people been made to do the heaviest ideological lifting? In asking these questions, it is helpful to recall that work was not always the center of social life in the West. For much of antiquity, in fact, work was considered a curse. Plato, for instance, equated manual labor with slavery, whereas Aristotle complained that work distracted people from the cultivation of virtue, life's truest purpose.[22] Work continued to be seen as an onerous burden into the Middle Ages, though the monastic tradition lent it the additional freight of religious penance.[23] All of this dramatically changed during the Reformation, when Martin Luther brought the Benedictine mantra of *ora et labora* (prayer and work) out of the monastery and into society at large. No longer a cloistered practice of atonement, a lifetime commitment to labor in God's name became the basis for a universal work ethic. The spread and secularization of this ethic is Max Weber's famous subject in *The Protestant Ethic and the Spirit of Capitalism* (1905). There Weber argues that the "coming of the modern economic order" evacuated the Protestant work ethic of its religious ethos and reduced it to a "worldly morality" of rational conduct. By the twentieth century, this "joyless lack of meaning" was fully "in the saddle" and no longer needed the "transcendental sanction" of the Reformation.[24] "The Puritan wanted to work in a calling," Weber concludes. But "we are forced to do so."[25]

As a psychological justification for why we work so much, the Protestant work ethic has proven surprisingly resilient. By the mid-nineteenth century, as Daniel T. Rodgers notes, industrialization and the factory system rendered Weber's theory functionally obsolete. Even as a "rhetorical shibboleth," however, it remained authoritative enough to provide nakedly exploitative industries with a steady labor force.[26] In the Fordist era, the work ethic's anachronistic hold only grew stronger, the increasingly fragmented nature of industrial production notwithstanding. Given recent developments in global political economy, we might well wonder whether the work ethic has finally run its course. As Annie McClanahan argues, there is good reason to suspect that workers tolerate "the austerity of low-waged life" only because they have to.[27] But the work ethic retains its force even today, due in no small measure to progressive reappropriations by feminist, antiracist, and unionist initiatives. As Weeks notes, these projects have sought "to expand the scope of the work ethic to new groups and new forms of labor." But in so doing they inevitably reaffirm the power of the work ethic itself.[28] A similar dynamic is at stake in the blurring of work and personal life that has become a familiar touchstone in the neoliberal present. To "discover oneself" in work is not to escape the logic of the market, but instead to embrace economic rationality as the truest measure of individual authenticity. From Wages for Housework to the creative class and the gig economy, the work ethic lives on.[29]

In addition to the Protestant ethic, work societies also find a conceptual touchstone in the labor theory of value. The subject of considerable debate, both historically and among contemporary scholars, at its core the labor theory of value maintains that only labor can produce economic value. As Adam Smith states in *The Wealth of Nations* (1776), labor "is alone the ultimate and real standard by which the value of all commodities can at all times and places be estimated and compared."[30] From Smith and other classical economists, most genealogies of the labor theory of value turn to Karl Marx, who is said to have sharpened these insights into a critique of the commodity form. We must first understand how capitalism expropriates economic value, this narrative cautions, before we can abolish the structural conditions that alienate laborers from their labor. The conceptual legwork would seem well worth it. In reclaiming their labor, workers regain nothing less than their very humanity. In arriving at this conclusion Marx combines British classical economics with Hegelian idealism, from which he learned to grasp labor as both the source of all economic value and the "self-confirming essence of man."[31] Demystifying capitalist exploitation, it thus follows, allows workers not only to enjoy the fruits of their labor but also to experience work as self-realization. As Erich Fromm noted in his 1961 preface to Marx's newly translated *Economic and Philosophical Manuscripts of 1844*, labor "is the self-expression of man, an expression of his individual physical and mental powers. In this genuine activity, man develops himself, becomes himself; work is not only a means to an end—the product—but an end in itself, the meaningful expression of human energy; hence work is enjoyable."[32]

This is a familiar Marx: the materialist philosopher who transforms the labor theory of value into an attack on the economic structures that alienate us from the very wellspring of our humanity—our labor.[33] But this might not be the only or even the real Marx. Indeed, theorists and activists have in recent years begun to reimagine the Marxist project by questioning the pride of place usually attributed to labor. Although grounded in disparate political and intellectual traditions—from Italian workerism to German *Wertkritik*, US feminist theory, Black studies, and disability studies—these writers share a provocative point of departure. They argue that labor in Marx is not an anthropological constant or the essence of humanity but a historically embedded ideology maintained by capitalism itself.[34] The historian and political economist Moishe Postone is a particularly influential voice in this discussion. In *Time, Labor, and Social Domination*, Postone contends that a different Marx comes into view when we read *Capital* not as a blueprint of the capitalist edifice but as the unfolding of an immanent critique—an argument that derives its terms from the object it criticizes. Marx, in other words, initially inhabits the capitalist concepts he goes on to attack. As such, it is no surprise that we can point to any number of moments in *Capital* when Marx seems to celebrate "living labor" as the universal truth of human life. For Postone, Marx is here not endorsing but rather working through the labor ideology that sustains capitalism. Marx's own position, stated most succinctly in the third volume of *Capital*, is that there is no there there. Any transhistorical notion of labor as "the productive activity" of humans in general or the "externalization and confirmation of life" is a "mere specter." The ideal of living labor, Marx concludes, is "nothing but an abstraction and taken by itself cannot exist at all."[35]

Displacing orthodox Marxism's focus on living labor, Postone concludes, is no minor course correction. Doing so requires rethinking the emancipatory aims of the Marxist project itself. Instead of struggling to make work meaningful (once more), a pursuit that is not only bound to fail

to be anticapitalist is to work less

but actually perpetuates the structures of domination it means to subvert, we should endeavor to work less—and to organize social life around something other than work. Culminating as it does in this rejection of the work society, it is clear why Postone's argument has found traction across the full spectrum of what Weeks calls "antiwork politics and postwork imaginaries," from economic crisis theory to universal basic income.[36] But there is reason as well to linger on Postone's method, which sheds light on a crucial feature of the work society often neglected in these conversations—namely, the role of representation in shoring up the noneconomic value of work. Indeed, for Postone, Marx's point is not only that work is not the essence of human life but also that capitalism goes to such great lengths to convince us that it is. This insight is another and perhaps less likely payoff of Marx's immanent critique: by inhabiting its key terms and rhetorical moves, Marx shows us how capitalism makes work seem inherently meaningful. Whether through the "mysterious character of the commodity form," vis-à-vis the obfuscating explications of classical economists, or in the cultural realm, the work society depends on representation to shore up belief in the noneconomic value of all work. For Postone, there is little doubting Marx's endgame—to have us abandon our commitment to work and remake social life anew. But we should also heed Marx's argument about representation. Before we can dispense with the threadbare social fiction that holds the work society together, Marx warns, we must first learn to read it.

Following Postone's lead, we can thus turn to *Capital* to unpack the role of representation in making work seem innately meaningful. Consider a passage usually thought to underscore how little the consumption of a commodity tells us about the conditions of its production. This notably literary aside follows a more schematic discussion of the "labor-process" in which Marx seems to suggest that all work is essentially the same. Labor, we read there, is at base the "appropriation of natural substances to human requirements" and "the everlasting Nature-imposed condition of human existence." Marx then turns to reflect on why making this point did not require much in the way of specifics.

> It was, therefore, not necessary to represent our laborer in connection with other laborers; man and his labor on one side, Nature and its materials on the other, sufficed. As the taste of the porridge does not tell you who grew the oats, no more does this simple process tell you of itself what are the social conditions under which it is taking place, whether under

the slave-owner's brutal lash, or the anxious eye of the capitalist, whether Cincinnatus carries it on in tilling his modest farm or a savage in killing wild animals with stones.[37]

The taste of our breakfast, Marx reminds us, teaches us nothing about how it came to market. We do not know whether the oats were harvested by enslaved people, waged laborers, or the Roman dictator Cincinnatus on his hobby farm. At first glance, these examples would seem to suggest the variety of ways that the labor process manifests itself in real life. Each would seem to be a particular instantiation of the universal "appropriation of natural substances to human requirements" that defines the essence of work as such. A different conclusion presents itself, however, if we read immanently, bracketing what Marx seems to be saying in order to focus on how he says it. From this vantage, we are struck less by how the pictures Marx conjures differ from one another and from his taxonomy of the labor process than by what all of these ways of imagining work share: they are all representations. This is not to suggest that these distinct modes of labor are at root the same. It is rather to point out how Marx here models the interpretative moves that capitalism makes to convince us that they are interchangeable. Instead of the fungibility of Black bodies or the hypocrisy of ruling-class relaxation, capitalism sees only (and everywhere) "the everlasting Nature-imposed condition of human existence." Marx, in other words, is concerned in this passage less with revealing the truth of labor than with showing us how capitalism looks at a field and makes that truth—in and through representation.

Though Marx's immanent critique of living labor is buried in a rather arcane passage on the labor process, the practice of looking he models here and across *Capital* is far from uncommon in the work society—and nowhere is it more apparent than in social welfare provision. This connection is not as arbitrary as it might seem. For just as Marx turns to the limit cases of slavery and hobby gardening to illuminate how capitalism makes work of any kind seem like work as such, the work society looks to the economic margins and to the make-work demanded of social welfare beneficiaries for much the same purpose. If onerous work that yields little or nothing in the way of profit or satisfaction can be made to seem inherently meaningful, can't all labor? Consider another field, this one at the Craig Colony in upstate New York, a custodial institution that championed farm work for people with epilepsy. In 1896, the colony superintendent declared that "outdoor life is best for the epileptic." In the fields, "the main thing is labor—labor that demands a real use of muscular force; labor that is systematically performed; labor that opens the pores of the skin, quickens the circulation, brightens the eye, and brings about a healthful, physiological fatigue; labor that has a place in the world of economics; labor that conquers all things."[38] This description unwittingly resembles Marx's conceptual account of the labor process. Like Marx, the author invites us to watch from across the field but soon beckons us closer—so close, in fact, that we seem to enter the worker's body. We note how the "muscular force" of labor "systematically performed" radiates across organ systems to the skin before resolving into a "healthful physiological fatigue." This latter sensation marks the laboring body coming into perfect harmony with the labor at hand, but it also announces the worker's snug fit in the broader "world of economics." The conclusion we are to draw is clear: labor is as natural as human physiology. When we read this passage alongside the photographs that often accompanied the Craig Colony's printed materials, however, a different interpretation seems possible. Not immediately legible as the essence of human life, the labor captured in the image in figure I.3 is disorganized and chaotic. We might be at a loss as to how to read this scene, in fact, were it not for the figure in the middle of the field. Wearing a black jacket and a white hat, the overseer is physically in charge of directing the inmates. But as the compositional center of the image, he also guides our reading of the photograph, providing a focal point to which our eyes return after surveying the haphazard goings-on around him. Transforming the superintendent's proclamation into an interpretative mandate, the overseer thus shows us how to look at a scene of disorganized milling-about and discern there the revitalizing force of labor as such.

To take our cue from an immanent reading of Marx is thus to recognize how capitalism seeks to persuade us that work is naturally meaningful by obscuring the vagaries of representation. We may need to look beyond Marx, however, to thinkers like W. E. B. Du Bois and the disability activist Marta Russell, to grasp how the universality of labor requires particularized forms of social marginalization. As Russell points out, work societies leverage the idea of disability "to permit a small capitalist class to create the economic conditions necessary to accumulate vast wealth."[39] The inmates at Craig Colony may usefully embody the redemptive promise of free labor, in other words, but they will never share its profits. Black Americans found themselves in a similar situation at the turn of the twentieth century, a moment when white reformers could declare that labor "conquers all things" while still assuming white supremacy to be all but impenetrable. As Du

I.3 Promotional photograph of Craig Colony in Sonyea, New York. Printed in William Pryor Letchworth, *Care and Treatment of Epileptics* (1900).

Bois trenchantly reflected on his famous prophecy a few decades after the publication of *The Souls of Black Folk* (1903), the "problem of the color line" was also the "problem of allocating work and income in the tremendous and increasingly intricate world-embracing industrial machine which we have built."[40] As Du Bois knew, Black labor could become legible in the post-Reconstruction US work society only if it could also signify Black subservience. This necessity is aptly captured in a photograph of a Black woman at work published in Booker T. Washington's "Chapters from My Experience" (figure I.4). Flirting with a common racist trope, Washington appears to suggest that newly emancipated African Americans were in danger of mistaking white-collar work for idleness: "The colored people wanted their children to go to school so that they might be free and live like the white folks without working." While probably meant to curry favor with white readers, Washington's troubling quip nonetheless acknowledges an incisive truth. The point is not that Black Americans do not work, but that Black Americans know it is not enough for them to work; they must also appear to be working.[41] Black labor must be visible and measurable, irrefutable evidence of both economic advance and racial humility. Such is the knowledge this woman ultimately performs. Whatever her labor might yield in material terms, it is meaningless unless her work can be read as a capitulation to white supremacy.

From Marx to the Craig Colony and Tuskegee, it is clear that labor performed on the economic margins is valuable not only for the goods or

I.4 Photograph accompanying the serial publication of Booker T. Washington's autobiography "Chapters from My Experience" in the *World's Work* (November 1910).

[handwritten margin notes: capitalism claims ≠ work has meaning; work needs to be done + the satisfy of logic of capitalism]

profits it produces. This labor is also meant to uphold the constitutive exclusions of capitalist society by persuading us that all work is at base meaningful. Moving from field to field, we get a sense of how widespread this representational project was and remains. But we might also wonder what (make-)work performed on the edges of the market shares with another mode of endeavor whose value is also generally imagined in noneconomic terms, namely aesthetic practice.[42] Consider a final field, this one overseen by the performance artist Chris Burden (figure I.5). In 1979, Burden was invited to be an artist in residence at the Emily Carr College of Art and Simon Fraser University in Vancouver. Burden initially declined but soon countered with a proposal of his own. He later recalled:

> Rather than meet with students to present and discuss my past work in a teaching context, I requested that I be provided with a wheel barrow, a shovel, and a pick ax. On the first day of my visit, I immediately began, in a vacant lot that had been provided for me, to dig a straight ditch about 2 1/2 feet wide and 3 feet deep. Each following day, students could find me digging from 9 a.m. until 5 p.m. I did not have a specific length or goal, except that I would be digging during the times that I had designated. Occasionally, someone would offer to dig for me, but after trying it for a few minutes they would return the job to me.[43]

Art historians tell us that the resulting performance piece, *Honest Labor*, was very much of its moment. When in the 1970s and '80s a broad economic shift from manufacturing to service began to transform traditional

1.5 Chris Burden, *Honest Labor* (1979). Printed in Helen Molesworth, ed., *Work Ethic* (2003).

definitions of work, artists across a variety of media set out to interrogate the peculiar nature of aesthetic labor.[44] Burden and other self-declared "art workers" invited audiences to draw comparisons that were at root analogical: art is (like) work. Determining how exactly art is (like) work, of course, was part of the provocation, the open-ended question that Burden and others put to audiences. To grapple with this question is to recognize, at least implicitly, the formal structure of analogy. As Janet Jakobsen notes, analogies bring two terms into a relation of equivalence but require that the first term is less well known than the second.[45] To suggest that art is like work is to imply that work needs less explanation than art but also that our grasp of art changes in light of what we know (and presume to be unchanging) about work. From this vantage, *Honest Labor* invites us to extrapolate from what we know about digging ditches to better understand what might puzzle us about art. There is nothing to prevent us, though, from reading in the other direction. Indeed, from this perspective *Honest Labor* becomes a powerful meditation not on the institution of art but on the work society itself. To suggest that work is like art, after all, is not only to suppose we know more about art than we do about work. It is also to imply that we can only make sense of work using the tools we use to make sense of art. Just as we can only know the truth of art in acts of interpretation, so too is the meaning of work always up for grabs—legible only in and through acts of representation.

At first blush, the labor performed at Tuskegee and the Craig Colony would seem a far cry from Burden's conceptual provocations. There was clearly much less at stake for an established artist dictating the terms of a paid fellowship than for Black and disabled workers laboring under conditions they had no hand in shaping and for wages we can assume were less than fair, or nonexistent. But if we look at these fields as Marx looks at his, a shared representational project nonetheless comes to the fore. We recognize that each of these images telegraphs the inherent dignity of all labor, while also pulling the curtain back to reveal how that dignity exists only in and through representation. Taken together, these fields thus underscore how people on the economic margins have historically shouldered the burden of shoring up the work society—a representational project that, like the aesthetic more generally, at once belongs to and lies outside of the market.[46] But these fields also suggest that the representational effort that goes into making work seem self-evident might also be used to rather different ends: to rethink both what counts as work and why work should count for so much in the first place.

Showing Your Work

This book is about how we came to assume that all work, even the most patently debasing and plainly unproductive, is inherently meaningful. More particularly, it is about how the Sisyphean task of shoring up the noneconomic value of work is outsourced to people on the economic margins and mediated by institutions of social welfare. From the early republic to the neoliberal present, this representational project has long been crucial to US social life. But it is rarely recognized as such, and with good reason. Acknowledging that work requirements are at base formal requirements—that beneficiaries are tasked above all with performing their commitment to the "dignity of labor"—exposes a contradiction at the heart of the work

But all sorts of work is rendered meaningless — e.g. care work?

society: that the noneconomic value of work, not a universal given, is an arbitrary sign whose meaning must continually be shored up. Critics of the welfare state thus only get it half right when they argue that welfare reform holds poor people hostage "so that the rest of us behave."[47] The goal is not only to deter would-be idlers with the threat of hard labor but more fundamentally to affirm the moral value of all work, coerced or otherwise. The poor are held hostage to make the meaning of work legible. Someone has to hold the sign straight.

Work Requirements explores the history and stakes of this unacknowledged representational project. In so doing, it parts ways with conventional works of political, social, and legal history.[48] I focus less on particular policies or programs than on the formal strategies used to make work seem inherently meaningful across a range of institutional, disciplinary, and cultural contexts. As with any history of the present, the story of how social welfare practice has given representational and ideological cover to the work society could be told in a number of ways. A broad sweep might begin with the spectacle of the "wheelbarrow men" in eighteenth-century Philadelphia—vagrants and criminals whose heads were shaved before they were forced to repair public roads—and conclude with the interpretative authority wielded today by the "street-level bureaucrats" who administer contemporary workfare policy.[49] My approach is narrower with regard to both historical chronology and representational medium. Rather than sketch out a comprehensive account of the knotty interweaving of representation, discipline, and performance across the long history of US social welfare provision, I explore how social welfare became a specifically textual undertaking at the end of the nineteenth century. My reasons are both practical and substantive. Focusing on a discrete moment in the longer representational project at the heart of social welfare provision lends the chapters that follow a sense of coherence they might otherwise lack. More important, though, is how this particular moment allows us to grapple with the representational project at the heart of social welfare tout court. Indeed, as transformed by industrial print culture and by the forces of modern bureaucracy, the textual practice of social welfare at the turn of the twentieth century laid bare the vagaries of representation and the conceptual work of disability and race more clearly than ever before and perhaps ever since.

Work Requirements is thus a book about US social welfare provision that begins before the advent of the US welfare state proper. Historians usually date that development to the New Deal, an era in which the state-based programs established by Progressive reformers were gradually expanded and federalized, culminating in the Social Security Act of 1935.[50] For most of US history prior to the New Deal, social welfare provision was a patchwork of relief initiatives inherited from or implicitly modeled on English poor law. In this tradition, local community members—families, church brethren, charitable organizations, and municipal governments—were responsible for determining how best to provide for (or discipline) anyone in need of economic assistance.[51] These practices varied from town to town and remained largely ad hoc. All of this changed in the latter half of the nineteenth century. In this dawning era of industrial print technologies, expanding communities of literacy, and widespread professionalization, negotiations of social need and deservingness that had once taken place in person were increasingly mediated by the printed word.[52] Reformers and institutions devised new modes of bureaucratic documentation to determine who had genuinely earned the aid they sought, while applicants navigated a tangle of print genres to prove their commitment to self-help. Although novel in both form and production, these industrial print genres gave new shape to an old ambition. The goal was now to capture the inherent meaningfulness of work on the page.

I call this forgotten archive the print culture of social welfare. This phrase might seem too broad to have any real purchase. Turn-of-the-century US public life, after all, was shaped by a dizzying array of reformist agendas, most of which made use of print culture in one way or another. Names like Jane Addams, Jacob Riis, and Du Bois come readily to mind in this regard. When I use the term *print culture of social welfare*, however, I mean to focus more narrowly on print forms used not to disseminate information, expose corruption, or debate best practices but to actually do the work of social welfare. In this book, then, the print culture of social welfare refers collectively to the documentary genres created by charity organizations, municipal agencies, settlement houses, and reform-minded academics to shore up belief in the inherent value of work as such. The most prominent of these is social casework, but the print culture of social welfare includes a host of other genres used to mediate between individuals and institutions, from invalid pension claims to affidavit blanks and photography. Like the photographs produced at the Craig Colony and Tuskegee Institute, these materials most often fall into one of two categories: documents that surveil the work performed by others, and self-representations of one's own labor. To be sure, the print culture of social welfare is not literary in any conventional sense. But we can nonetheless sharpen our grasp of what it was and did by looking to the nineteenth-century rags-to-riches tale. Today, of course, the name Horatio Alger is synonymous with the rewards of hard work. Like the penniless bootblack in *Ragged Dick* (1868), however, many of Alger's heroes actually make good thanks only to the generosity of strangers.[53] This is not to say that these characters don't earn their keep, but rather that familiar paeans to self-help obscure the particular kind of work they do: presenting themselves as someone who deserves help—someone, that is, whose capacity for economic citizenship is immediately legible. Much the same kind of representational labor is at stake in the print culture of social welfare. Although they often document specific acts of labor, these genres were intended first and foremost to capture an individual's capacity to embody the dignity of work.

Formally speaking, the wide-ranging print culture of social welfare was shaped less by the era's dime novel than by the narrow concept of disability inherited from the poor law tradition. As disability studies scholars have shown, there are countless ways to approach disability as such, whether as lived experience, cultural identity, political minority, or medical diagnosis, to name but a few.[54] But from the colonial era onward, disability in US social welfare provision was defined as an "incapacitation" for manual labor." To be disabled meant to be exempted from the obligation to work, although not from the stigma of dependency. In this way, as Deborah Stone argues, the disability category served a crucial sorting function. It determined who belonged in the work-based system of economic distribution (the labor market) and who could access the need-based system of social welfare.[55] In early America, deciding who counted as disabled was usually a matter of communal consensus. As the print culture of social welfare emerged in the late nineteenth century, however, bureaucratizing institutions set out to rationalize the process with a range of new documentary genres. These documents would distinguish more accurately and efficiently—or so it was believed—between those who "could not" and those who "would not" work. The goal, however, was to define disability as narrowly as possible and to penalize anyone who did not submit to the market. Ultimately, even people who (were) identified as disabled, as the historian Sarah F. Rose demonstrates, had "no right to be idle."[56] As such, the disability category was both the exception that proved the rule and a tool of social coercion. It marked the limits of the market's reach while also sustaining the fantasy of expanding that horizon infinitely to incorporate everyone, no matter why they were on the economic margins or how they understood their own bodies, capacities, or relation to work.

So broad was the disability category's explanatory power, in fact, that it shaped how the print culture of social welfare made sense of the volatile relations among citizenship, race, and labor created in the social ferment of the late nineteenth century. As Evelyn Nakano Glenn notes, the abolition of racial slavery and ongoing histories of industrialization, urbanization, immigration, and imperialism upended the labor market in the United States and globally. As a consequence, new mechanisms of economic discipline and disenfranchisement emerged to manage people of color the world over.[57] In a parallel development, many of these people were also conscripted into the vast networks of writing that charity officials, reformers, government agencies, and academic researchers had begun to compile in the name of social welfare. At base, these documents adapted the questions at the heart of the disability category: Would formerly enslaved people, imperial subjects, and immigrants work for wages? And how could they be integrated into the labor market? Racial and ethnic difference thus entered the print culture of social welfare as barriers to productive citizenship—under the sign of disability. It is no coincidence, then, that many of the same representational strategies and genres were used by urban charity organizations, philanthropic backers of Black industrial education, and boosters of US imperialism. This shared representational project ultimately sought to reconcile the structural expansion of the global market with the moral economy of the work society. Even as capitalism created ever-new ways to sharpen and profit from racial difference, these particularized modes of labor were still expected to embody—and make legible—the universal meaningfulness of labor as such.

The role of the disability category, however, was not uniformly coercive. To many people caught up in the print culture of social welfare, in fact, it provided an idiom of connection across disparate experiences of economic marginalization. *Disability*, after all, named a structural position that could be inhabited by people with physical and/or intellectual impairments and by those whose precarity was (also) bound up with race, gender, sexuality, or class. To be sure, being lumped together as disabled— in danger of falling through the economic cracks—meant being targeted for discipline and even violence in the name of social welfare. But the print genres that facilitated these categorizations also fostered unexpected collaborations and deeply intersectional solidarities. The strange career of the Civil War invalid pension claim explored in chapter 1 is a case in point. While it would be easy to assume that injured veterans were awarded pensions based on the evidence of their bodies alone, the process relied extensively on personal affidavits. Veterans were called on not only to narrate the details of their service and injury but also to prove that they had truly earned a pension. The ideological work of the invalid pension claim was thus to transform wounds into compensable labor and to ensure that honorable veterans were not reduced to taking "handouts." The pension claim's surprising prominence in public life led to widespread misgivings about this narrative alchemy, but also to a history of generic borrowing that spawned the earliest movement for reparations. For the Black activists at the forefront of the ex-slave pension movement, the administrative genre created to redress the wounds of war offered a powerful means of demanding payment for stolen labor. But the pension claim also fostered wide-ranging meditations on the relations between and among different kinds of physical, psychic, and social injuries.

The various genres that constituted the print culture of social welfare could also be repurposed to interrogate the very foundations of the work society. Here as well, the disability category played a key role. For the arbiters of social welfare, as we have seen, the fiction of disability designated the limits of the market's reach. It marked a boundary to be rigorously policed but also pushed infinitely outward—toward an imagined horizon of full economic participation. Many would-be beneficiaries, by contrast, recognized in the disability category a conceptual language with which to gesture toward or even reclaim a space of endeavor entirely outside of the market. As the unlikely presence of the African American work song in the print culture of social welfare suggests, many of these reclamations implicitly leveraged the disability category's conceptual proximity to the aesthetic. Strange though it may sound, between the Civil War and the early 1930s—before, that is, the well-known efforts of John Lomax—white social welfare workers took it upon themselves to collect and transcribe Black vernacular work songs. Many of these welfare workers saw this project less as an exercise in cultural preservation than as a contribution to ongoing debates about prison and asylum labor. As explored in chapter 4, however, the efforts of social welfare professionals to make vernacular work songs embody the redemptive value of work were often contested by the people they surveilled. To many Black laborers, the work song was most valuable insofar as it could be used to resist the moral economy of labor it was so often made to embody.

The textual project of representing work as the truest sign of social deservingness thus began with the new industrial print genres that emerged to mediate between individuals and institutions in the latter half of the nineteenth century. These genres were in turn shaped by the overlapping histories of economic discipline that the disability category brought into relation. From the criminalization of poverty to the rise of Jim Crow and US imperialist expansion, *disability* provided a language with which to identify people thought to be in danger of becoming "socially dependent" and thus in need of being forcibly returned to the work-based system of economic distribution. But while the documentary genres that constitute the print culture of social welfare originated in particular institutional and social contexts, they rarely stayed there. The forms used to reinforce the moral self-evidence of work in one milieu or discourse were just as often taken up in another, crisscrossing ostensibly discrete fields like public administration, economic planning, social science, and even literature and the arts. Tracking these circuitous trajectories across the turn of the twentieth century reveals the effort that went into making work seem naturally meaningful. But doing so also suggests that the print culture of social welfare was not always a top-down affair. Official genres also provided prompts for vernacular improvisation, creating a bureaucratic fake book with which people on the economic and social margins might rethink, remake, or even refuse the model of economic citizenship they were offered. Such is ultimately the value that the print culture of social welfare holds for us today: an object lesson in how to imagine social being and belonging beyond work. We can most easily take this lesson to heart by first asking how the print culture of social welfare built on earlier histories of social welfare and earlier practices of representation.

From Work Test to Paperwork

As even a cursory overview makes clear, the industrial print forms that emerged in the late nineteenth century continued a representational tradition rooted in the poor law system inherited from England. In colonial and early America, this project was guided above all by the bonds of family and religion. Although community members who fell on hard times through no fault of their own were cared for as a matter of course, anyone deemed physically able but unwilling to work faced a biblical ultimatum: "If a man will not work, he shall not eat."[58] Such "sturdy beggars" might be "sold" (auctioned to a neighbor who agreed to care for them at the lowest municipal cost), "contracted out" to a family on similar terms, or placed in the almshouse or other local institution ("indoor relief").[59] These arrangements disciplined would-be shirkers into the labor market, but they also stressed the community's role in interpreting the work extracted in the process. Under the vigilant eye of one's neighbors, even the most brutal forms of coerced labor could be made to signify the mutual obligations of Christian kinship. Beginning in the nineteenth century, poorhouses, reformatories, and other custodial institutions came to dominate the practice of social welfare. Here as well, though, the labor performed by beneficiaries was valued less for what it produced than for what it signified. Indeed, Jacksonian reformers championed institutions such as Philadelphia's Colored House of Refuge as an antidote to the upheaval wrought by industrialization and the market revolution. When everything else seemed so dangerously in flux, the "principles of hard work and solitude" that structured institutional life stood as proof that work's redemptive promise still held good.[60]

There was, to be sure, great variation across the disparate initiatives spearheaded by reformers, religious organizations, and municipalities in the early United States. But whether carried out for one's neighbors or for the overseers of the poor, the work required of relief seekers served a common purpose. Whatever product or profit might result, this labor created a ritualized space of performance in which nonmarket exchanges—that is, charity or relief payments—could be made to bolster the primacy of the market. (These performances also naturalized the ideological underpinnings of the particular work society in question, from the reciprocal obligations of Christian community to the coherence of the agrarian *Gemeinschaft* and the ontological erasure of Black humanity.) In the late nineteenth century, the hermeneutic sleight of hand that had long shaped US social welfare practice was given an apt name: the work test. As popularized by charity organization societies and municipal agencies, work tests required "beggars" and "tramps" to chop wood or do laundry in return for food or lodging (figure I.6). It was clear to everyone involved that there were always less expensive and more efficient ways to do the work at hand. As a sorting mechanism that enforced the bounds of the disability category, though, the work test was unrivaled. As one municipal board of charities underscored in 1894, the work test was the most effective means of "preventing those who are able to work, but unwilling, from securing a livelihood by misrepresentation and beggary."[61] Just as important, these closely choreographed spectacles of social discipline made beneficiaries and benefactors into formal collaborators. In what was by no means an equal partnership, these parties endeavored together to make the inherent value of work manifest.

THE WORK TEST.

Everybody seems to be agreed that the best way to get rid of tramps is to apply the work test.

I. WHAT IT IS.

The first question, therefore, is, What is the work test? The essence of the work test is the giving of good food (supper and breakfast) and good clean lodging in exchange for a certain specified amount of hard work.

II. HOW IT WORKS.

The reason the work test is effective is that the tramps do not care so much for good food and lodging as they do for avoiding work. Experience has shown that where the two go together the tramps do not go.

III. CONDITIONS OF SUCCESS.

1. It is an absolute condition of the efficacy of the work test that it shall not be possible to avoid it by going elsewhere in the town. It is therefore necessary : —

(*a*) That public opinion in the town shall support it ; that is to say, that the women of the town shall refuse to give food at the door, and shall refer all applicants to the place where the work test is applied.

(*b*) That the police shall refuse lodging without work in the police stations.

(*c*) That cheap lodging houses shall not be allowed to become tramp resorts.

2. One town by itself, however, cannot succeed with the work test, because tramps can easily avoid passing a night in any particular town, and may, in spite of a good work test, infest the neighboring towns, and to some extent also the town where the test is applied. So long as there are in the State towns without a work test, which may serve as stepping-stones for the tramps, these will continue to infest the State. The starting of an efficient work test in Springfield, for instance, has from the first been rendered of less than its normal value by the absence of such tests in the neighboring towns of Westfield, Holyoke, and Chicopee.

Any efficient action, therefore, must necessarily come from some

I.6 *Annual Report of the Massachusetts Civic League for the Year Ending November 30, 1903.* Frances Loeb Library, Harvard University. VF NAC 22 M 1938, 1940.

I.7 Sheet of "Investigation Tickets," Philadelphia Society for Organizing Charity, 1880s. Library Company of Philadelphia.

The turn of the twentieth century did not put an end to either the performative logic or the physical brutality of the work test. The influence of both remains unmistakable today in the punitive authority wielded by the welfare and carceral states, which scholars often describe as "a single policy regime."[62] But we are also heir to a late nineteenth-century development that recast the work test as a specifically textual undertaking in the name of what came to be called "scientific charity." Inaugurated by a decentralized group of reformers, researchers, and community leaders, scientific charity was born of a desire to modernize and professionalize the largely ad hoc practices of traditional social welfare.[63] In theory, making charity scientific meant following the prominent example of the social sciences, which sought to transform social life into an object of rational, scientific inquiry. In practice, however, scientific charity was defined chiefly by a proliferation of new print genres by social welfare institutions of all stripes. Negotiations and assessments that would previously have taken place in person were now mediated by the authority of bureaucratic protocol. No single genre better encapsulates this broad shift from the work test to paperwork than the "investigation tickets" issued by charity organization societies (figure I.7). If in previous generations poor people might be given a hammer and instructed to break rocks, they could now be issued slips of paper telling them where to report to make sure that their files were up to date. No longer a matter of direct oversight and assessment, social welfare provision aimed to commit the meaningfulness of work to the page.

The emergence of scientific charity and with it the print culture of social welfare was part of a wider transformation of late nineteenth-century public life. In a narrative that has become a touchstone in media studies, historians describe how the social changes of the era—from the growing complexity of manufacturing and distribution to the disruptive forces of urbanization, nationalization, and postwar reconstruction—gave rise to both a "crisis of control" and a variety of compensatory responses. The consolidation of modern bureaucracy was fundamental to this latter "control revolution," as were new communication technologies like photography, telegraphy, telephones, transatlantic cables, and film.[64] More recent media historians have also added industrial print culture to the list. As Carl Kaestle and Janice Radway argue, the era's crises could not have been managed without new print technologies and genres. Just as the transportation and communication networks that modern firms depended on would have been inconceivable without printed timetables and rate schedules, the modern state could not have expanded its increasingly bureaucratized reach without a host of printed manuals, reports, and forms.[65] As civic groups and social institutions began to take advantage of inexpensive commercial job printing, moreover, industrial print culture gradually came to remake daily life itself.[66] As Lisa Gitelman argues, individuals came to use printed materials to negotiate "their everyday relationships to and amid many institutions and institutionalized realms at once."[67] The spread of industrial print culture was thus not a one-way street. The same genres developed to consolidate institutional authority also created differentiated sites of identification from which to call that authority into question.[68] As mediated by industrial print, late nineteenth-century public life was "one part Max Weber's iron cage and another part a conflicted jangle of aspirations, allegiances, and demands."[69]

This jangle echoed especially loudly through the print culture of social welfare. As we have seen, the documentary genres created to mediate between social welfare institutions and beneficiaries could be and often were used to rather different ends. In time, the widespread circulation of these genres gave rise to equally widespread doubts about the use of print and writing more generally to do the work of social welfare. Many of these concerns, in fact, came to coalesce around the idea of the literary. This is not to say that alms seekers began to think of themselves as novelists— though many did and were—or that philanthropic foundations started soliciting poetic self-reflections.[70] Rather, public fixation on the literariness of the print culture of social welfare reflected a dawning awareness—at once fleeting and begrudging—of textual effort necessary to make work as such seem inherently meaningful. To many skeptics, the literary connoted above all a failure of documentary rigor. In this regard, the same anxiety about fraud that shaped canonical nineteenth-century US literature in Lara Cohen's retelling also informed attitudes toward the print culture of social welfare.[71] What, after all, was to prevent wily applicants from mastering a given genre or modeling their stories on what they knew to be a winning formula? Other observers doubted whether bureaucratic objectivity was possible under even the best of circumstances. Who was to say whether a particular documentary genre could in fact capture the truth of labor? Perhaps the entire enterprise was itself merely a literary exercise.

As proponents of scientific charity sought to replace the work test with paperwork, questions about the representation of work thus often gave rise to questions about the work of representation. These anxieties about the economic status of writing were at once much older than the print culture of social welfare and very much of its late nineteenth-century moment. Just as philosophers as far back as Aristotle have contemplated whether writing is productive, canonical writers from Thomas Carlyle to Herman Melville and Frederick Douglass struggled to define the nature of their work and its relation to the work performed by others in the wake of the market revolution.[72] In the print culture of social welfare, however, questions about the work of representation were tied to the professional ambitions of social welfare practitioners. Like many other late nineteenth-century fields of endeavor, industrial print culture offered social reformers and institutions a means of transforming what had traditionally been a community-based volunteer undertaking into a specialized profession with its own methods of inquiry and intervention. Unlike other professionalizing fields, however, social welfare practitioners turned to writing and industrial print culture more particularly not only to shore up their own productive bona fides but also to pass judgment on the work performed by others. The abundance of new print genres and bureaucratic procedures was thus also a response to the difficulty, if not impossibility, of capturing the inherent meaning of work as such. When one genre or method was found to be lacking, it was soon replaced by another. A refusal to acknowledge the representational project at the heart of social welfare practice, that is, led to the creation of ever more industrial print forms.

For people on the other side of the exchange, writing often meant something altogether different. To be sure, demonstrating one's mastery of the bureaucratic genres and protocols that gradually came to govern the practice of social welfare was a powerful means of showing one's work. But these genres and protocols could also be used to renegotiate one's place in the work society and thereby to assert what the disability scholar Jacobus tenBroek termed "a right to live in the world." By the same token, the print culture of social welfare could also be leveraged to opt out altogether and thus to assert what the artist, writer, and disability scholar Sunaura Taylor calls "the right not to work."[73] Indeed, given the role of the disability category in the print culture of social welfare, it might make sense to speak of this archive in the broadest strokes as disability writing. Scholars usually use this term to refer to writing that dispenses with well-established traditions of metaphorical and allegorical representations to account for lived experiences of disability.[74] To speak of the print culture of social welfare as disability writing, by contrast, is to underscore how this body of writing is shaped by the intersectional histories of economic marginalization and disenfranchisement policed by the disability category. Approaching the print culture of social welfare as disability writing also foregrounds how the disability category afforded disenfranchised people unlikely opportunities for imagining a life outside the market. In this regard, the literariness of the print culture of social welfare marks the frisson of possibility—by turns unsettling and electrifying—that arises when seemingly incommensurate economies of language and value collide and new ways of imagining the social become legible.

From Paperwork to Literary Labor

Describing the print culture of social welfare as literary might seem to contradict both common sense and scholarly consensus. Just as we are unlikely to mistake an insurance claim for a novel, scholars have historically distinguished documents from literature more or less absolutely. In this familiar narrative, literature is formally meaningful, of interest not only for what it says but for how it says it. Documents, by contrast, are transparent, their form self-explanatory and ultimately beside the point. More recently, scholars in media and paperwork studies have pushed back by asserting what now seems obvious: that documents are formal artifacts with material histories. Rather than collapse the documentary into the literary, these critics explore the specificity of each. One influential line of inquiry asks how material, cultural, and institutional histories shape how documents are used. The goal, as Ben Kafka riffs, is to "put the bureau back in bureaucracy."[75] A related body of scholarship theorizes the document as such. Beginning with its Latin roots in *docere* (to teach or show) and later uses in Old French and English of *documentum* (written instrument), *document* has historically connoted evidence and inscription. Documents present information, but they also certify or document the existence of that information.[76] Gitelman calls this the document's "know-show function," a self-reflexive epistemology in which "knowing is all wrapped up with showing and showing wrapped with knowing."[77] Documents, in other words, prioritize communication over persuasion, stripping away detail in order to improve efficiency. And yet, as John Guillory cautions, documents bear no inherent relation to knowledge as such. Unlike science, which aspires to the condition of knowledge, or literature, which fosters a complex and "ultimately indeterminate relation to knowledge—the *fictional relation*," the document is only ever a "carrier of information."[78] It is an empty form with no specified content. A corollary returns us to the distinction between literature and documents, albeit with a twist. Documents do not have readers, much less interpreters, in any conventionally literary sense. They have users.[79]

Persuasive though this argument is, in the print culture of social welfare the line separating the documentary from the literary (and using from reading) is not always bright. This archive's peculiar literariness, in fact, raises fundamental questions of method—about how we approach a body of writing that is at once resolutely interdisciplinary and irreducibly formal, beholden to the ideal of bureaucratic efficiency but also the disruptive affordances of the "merely literary."[80] For the most part, the chapters to follow bracket definitional distinctions—between the literary and the documentary or among the practices of formal analysis rooted in literary studies, history, and sociology—in favor of tracing how genres that emerge in one social or institutional context find traction in another. In this regard, my own literary labor takes its cue from the New Historicist tradition, broadly speaking. In particular, the book attends to what Stephen Best terms the "subtle mode of causality" by which cultural forms constrain expectations, organize uses, and channel meanings across disparate historical milieus and discourses.[81] With regard to literary history, tracking how the print culture of social welfare circulated across turn-of-the-century public life shifts our approach to reform literature. Instead of focusing on the advocacy work of elite white writers and the literacy programs administered by settlement houses, civic societies, and other institutions, *Work Requirements* explores how writing was actually used to do the work of social welfare itself.[82] Just as important, the book's archive reveals the forgotten role that informational genres created under the banner of scientific charity played in what Elizabeth McHenry has called "the complexity of the history of African American literacy and literary interaction."[83] Indeed, the writing that Black administrators, educators, and civic organizations exchanged with the arbiters of social welfare deepens our understanding of Black print culture by asking us to grapple with the kind of work it performed. Given the outsized contribution made by disabled writers of color, moreover, the print culture of social welfare is also an important and unacknowledged archive of Black disability writing.

In addition to literary, cultural, and media studies, *Work Requirements* also draws on historical and theoretical scholarship on the US welfare state that spans from the early republic to the New Deal and contemporary workfare. The book's archive is indebted to interdisciplinary social histories of the charitable, philanthropic, religious, and carceral practices that defined welfare provision prior to the twentieth century. In reading this material, however, I ultimately take my cues from the rich and immensely important body of feminist scholarship on how gender, race, and class have shaped the welfare state as it exists today. From the male-breadwinner model to the National Welfare Rights Organization, Wages for Housework, and more recent reclamations of the "welfare queen," feminist writers and activists have incisively interrogated how the "putative" universality of work sustains hyperparticularized forms of inequality and violence.[84] *Work Requirements* aims to bring these theoretical and historical conversations into dialogue with the methods of close reading rooted in the humanities. The book's guiding premise is that we cannot understand how the practice of social welfare has served to bolster the work society and the gender-, race-, and ability-based exclusions on which it relies without understanding the representational effort required to make work as such seem meaningful. Building on the groundbreaking insights of feminist scholars, *Work Requirements* explores how people precluded from economic citizenship are nonetheless made to embody its promise.

 The expansive and interdisciplinary body of scholarship on racial capitalism is also a touchstone in the chapters that follow. Sidestepping the distinction orthodox Marxism draws between capitalism and slavery, studies in this vein examine how capitalism relies on the elaboration, reproduction, and exploitation of racial difference.[85] Key sites of inquiry in recent years have included transatlantic slavery, settler colonialism, and mass incarceration. Social welfare provision belongs on this list as well. Indeed, from the racial exclusions codified in the New Deal to the cultural bogeyman of the welfare queen and the disproportionate burdens that contemporary workfare places on people of color, the social safety net has long perpetuated what Lisa Lowe calls the "captivity, expropriation, disposability, and fungibility of Black communities."[86] Needless to say, the print culture of social welfare was also an instrument of racial capitalism. To read this body of writing as an archive of racial capitalism means asking not only how people of color are subjected to harsh forms of discipline and oversight but also how they are saddled with the representational effort of shoring up the noneconomic value of work as such. And yet, given that the print culture of social welfare was a space of both bureaucratic control and vernacular co-optation, this archive also attunes us to what for Du Bois was an antiwork politics of Black emancipation. "There can be no doubt," Du Bois noted in *Darkwater*, "that we have passed in our day from a world that could hardly satisfy the physical wants of the mass of men, by the greatest effort, to a world whose technique supplies enough for all, if all can claim their right." It remained an open question, though, whether the solution was to claim a "share in the future industrial democracy" or to overturn "the world of work" as such.[87]

The critical genealogy of racial capitalism that extends from Du Bois to Robinson—and from Angela Davis to Robin D. G. Kelley and Ruth Gilmore—does not generally make disability an explicit concern. But contemporary work in disability studies leaves no doubt that capitalism's cultivation and exploitation of racial difference is deeply intertwined with material histories of disability. As Nirmala Erevelles and Andrea Minear note, the critical conversation about race and disability has in recent years moved beyond vexed issues of analogy to engage with "the historical contexts and structural conditions within which the identity categories of race and disability intersect."[88] From the slave pen to the popular stage, the voting booth, and special education, the history of disability is inseparable from the history of racial capitalism.[89] Building on an expansive body of scholarship by Rabia Belt, Cynthia Wu, and Leah Lakshmi Piepzna-Samarasinha, among many others, *Work Requirements* focuses more narrowly on the intersectional histories rooted in the economic category of disability that emerged from the poor law tradition. Where disability is defined as the incapacity for work, as we have seen, it serves as both a sorting mechanism (for determining who could eke out a living outside the market) and a cudgel with which to discipline anyone on the economic margins—for whatever reason—back into the workforce.[90] Across the long nineteenth century, in other words, both people who might have thought of themselves as disabled and those who might not were brought together under the umbrella of disability. For this reason, the history of social welfare provision marks a space of intersectional encounter, solidarity, and even collaboration from which to connect critical conversations about race and disability to broader inquiries into racial capitalism and the work society.[91]

Taken together, the book's four chapters do not offer an exhaustive or a strictly representative accounting of the print culture of social welfare. The story told here is less a comprehensive portrait of social welfare provision at the turn of the century than an effort to parse a representational project that reaches across a range of disciplines and genres and extends from that earlier era into our own. In addition to the Civil War invalid pension claim and the African American work song, the subjects of chapters 1 and 4, chapters 2 and 3 focus on social casework and industrial motion studies.

Like the former, these latter two genres demonstrate how the burden of shoring up the noneconomic value of work falls to people on the economic margins. But to read with and across the print culture of social welfare is not only to understand how work became a textual sign at the end of the nineteenth century. It is also to ask how we might hold that sign differently today, or perhaps let go of it altogether. It is this possibility that the anachronism of the book's title is meant to suggest. When we contemplate work requirements today, of course, we do not usually think of ephemeral documents produced a century ago, much less the vagaries of genre. Bill Clinton's 1996 promise to "end welfare as we know it" is far likelier to come to mind. This book assumes that neoliberal workfare—not as new as Clinton and other partisans declared—builds on older histories of work-based welfare provision. Ultimately, though, *Work Requirements* argues that we cannot "know" welfare, then or now, without coming to terms with the representational project at its core. Only by understanding how work is made meaningful, both on the backs of people on the economic margins and through their representational labor, can we begin to imagine social welfare apart from—and even in opposition to—work.

THE PENSIONER'S CLAIM

The history of Civil War invalid pension policy is byzantine. But even a brief overview clarifies why a program created to encourage volunteer enlistment in the Union army became a flashpoint in turn-of-the-century debates about social welfare.[1] The earliest piece of Civil War pension legislation was the General Law of 1862, which granted pensions to veterans disabled in the line of duty and to the widows and orphans of fallen soldiers. Initially, claimants could receive up to $8.00 per month, a sum roughly equivalent to 30 percent of the earnings of an unskilled laborer. This amount rose by leaps and bounds over the next two decades, and by 1883 a claimant deemed "totally disabled" could receive $30.00 per month, almost completely replacing the average worker's income.[2] As rates of pay increased over the years, eligibility requirements were likewise relaxed. Among the most significant revisions were those wrought by the Dependent and Disability Pension Act of 1890, which opened the program to all veterans who had served ninety days, had been honorably discharged, and were now incapacitated for manual labor. Crucially, claimants no longer had to prove that their disabilities resulted from the war; any disability not caused by intemperate or otherwise "vicious habits" was covered.[3] An even more significant milestone was reached in 1904, when veterans were invited to file on their sixty-second birthday regardless of health or employment status. With age now a compensable disability, the Civil War invalid pension system had reached a turning point. What began as a limited program of income maintenance for wounded veterans and their dependents had become a comprehensive system of disability, old-age, and survivor benefits that accounted for nearly 40 percent of the federal budget.[4] Initially, given the respect commanded by wounded veterans and deep-seated convictions about the moral debt they were owed, the liberalization of pension policy found broad public support. Before long, though, worries about interlopers, imposters, and idlers became difficult to ignore, as did gut-level misgivings about a program that seemed to encourage would-be laborers to leave the workforce.

This is the story that social scientists and historians tell about the rapid growth of the Civil War invalid pension system across the turn of the twentieth century. It is a peculiarly American tale in which certain social needs are deemed legitimate and others are not. As Theda Skocpol argues, the expansion of veterans' pensions into a sweeping program of disability and old-age provision created a "precocious" US welfare state that predated the New Deal and shared little with the welfare systems emerging in Europe. Whereas countries like France and Germany awarded benefits to those in greatest need, the US system supported those who "by their own choices and efforts as young men had *earned* aid."[5] In later years, social reformers and trade unions endeavored to transform the Civil War pension system into a universal program of publicly funded benefits for all workers. These efforts never found traction, however. Nor did invalid pensions survive in the armed forces. In the first few decades of the twentieth century, reservations about the expense of providing for wounded veterans gave way to dire warnings about the ethical peril involved in doing so. Building on this momentum, Progressive reformers and military officials successfully lobbied to replace invalid pensions with mandatory physical and vocational rehabilitation.[6] At once more economical and morally up-to-date, advocates promised, these programs would help disabled veterans rely on their own wage-earning capacities instead of federal largesse. Before long, the Civil War invalid pension would be remembered as little more than a blunder of extravagance and a costly affirmation of what still remains a truism of US social welfare policy: that only those who work deserve help.

A different legacy of the Civil War pension system comes into view, however, when we focus not on the benefits won by disabled veterans and their dependents but on how those benefits were administered. This story is still about work and who can be honorably exempted from the obligation to work. But told from this perspective—strange though it might sound—the story is also about narrative, textual, and even literary labor. We might well expect that evaluating a pension claim was a more or less straightforward affair, so prominent are visual images of injury and maiming in the cultural memory of the Civil War. Either an applicant was wounded or he was not, we might suppose. Only rarely, though, was the merit of a given claim decided using medical or military documentation alone. Not only were records commonly lost or damaged during the war, but physical exams were often far from conclusive. As a result, personal narratives were the primary source of evidence used by the Pension Bureau. These documents included first-person statements from claimants—stories about their bodies before, during, and after the war—and affidavits from friends, family, and comrades. All told, it was not uncommon for claims to run one hundred pages and more. A narrative construction of the most literal kind, disability was thus for the Pension Bureau a bureaucratic status granted not to particular bodies but to bodies about which particular stories could be credibly told and sufficiently corroborated.[8]

Given the bureau's reliance on personal affidavits, it would be tempting to describe the pension claim as a kind of life writing. Considering the substantial sums of money that hung in the balance, it may have been the most profitable mode of autobiography in the postbellum era. But most veterans and their dependents, of course, turned to the pension claim as a bureaucratic necessity first and as a vehicle for individual expression only second, if at all. And in public culture at large, the genre was best known not as an exercise in self-portraiture or an exploration of "what it's like to have or to *be*, to live in or *as*, a particular body," but for the social fiction it propped up. The pension claim assured an anxious public that disability benefits were not gratuitous alms or "handouts." They were earned entitlements akin to back wages or the disbursement of a contributory retirement plan.[9] The peculiarly narrative genre of the pension claim, in other words, was defined above all by how—on paper—it transformed pain or suffering into compensable labor. To claim a pension was to assert not only "I have been wounded" but also "I have worked," which amounted to the same thing. The success of this narrative alchemy depended less on how a given claimant's story was told than on public faith in the bureaucratic state. And when that faith faltered, public attention focused anew on the textuality of the pension claim and the pride of place it gave to narrative evidence. Hardly transforming injury into compensable work, a growing chorus argued, the pension claim was an exercise in merely literary labor that threatened the sanctity of real work.

Bureaucratic necessity or literary indulgence, ideological cover for the work society or ticket out of the labor force: as the Civil War pension claim became a fixture of postbellum culture, debates about the genre's narrative status reflected deeper disagreements about the means and ends of social welfare provision. At base, the thorny questions about work, injury, and writing that shaped reception of the pension claim were freighted with the difficulty of reconciling society's compassionate desire to help people in need with its ideological commitment to the labor market as the only legitimate arbiter of deservingness. But like other genres in the print culture of social welfare, the pension claim emerged to mediate between individuals and institutions—here the federal Pension Bureau—while also circulating promiscuously across the culture at large. Indeed, to map the trajectory of the pension claim is to chart a history of formal encounter that blurs the boundaries between the documentary and the literary and interrogates the relation between and among seemingly incommensurate experiences of injury. Whether as a foil for proponents of Black industrial education or a sourcebook for the formerly enslaved people who inaugurated the reparations movement, the pension claim sutured postbellum racial politics to the disability history of the precocious welfare state. Across these disparate discourses and social milieus, the genre fostered a wide-ranging meditation on how suffering becomes (a sign of) work, as well as on how social welfare—and social justice—might be imagined beyond the compensatory logic of the market.

As such, the forgotten history of the Civil War invalid pension claim reveals how the industrial print genres created to mediate between individuals and social welfare institutions across the turn of the twentieth century were never merely bureaucratic. On its face, this insight is not new. But by building on foundational scholarship in media and paperwork studies, this chapter explores how taking stock of the pension claim's peculiar metaphysics helps us reframe ongoing debates about liberal citizenship and the politics of pain. As scholars from Wendy Brown to Jasbir Puar and Alexander Weheliye maintain, progressive efforts to find redress for social injury within the liberal state inevitably reinforce many of the practices, discourses, and ideologies that cause social injury in the first place.[10] These conversations elaborate compelling new ways of articulating the relationship between pain and politics, suffering and solidarity. But they often neglect the fundamental role that ideas about work and productivity play in what Lauren Berlant calls "the epistemology of state emotion."[11] If the liberal state only recognizes social injuries that affirm the ideal of white, heterosexual, able-bodied citizenship, any redress offered must bolster the productivist ideology of the work society. In this regard, the social fiction at the heart of the pension claim illuminates how the liberal politics of pain—though often couched in the language of moral obligation—is at root an economic transaction. By the same token, however, that genre's unlikely prominence across turn-of-the-century public culture marks a history of vernacular efforts to rethink the work of redress and even to rethink redress beyond work.

The Anatomy of a Claim

Looking back at the expansion of the pension system in 1907, some forty years after the end of the Civil War, Mark Twain reached a conclusion shared by many of his generation. The system originally created to repay the nation's wounded veterans had given way to a corrupt scheme of depraved charity seeking. "At first we granted deserved pensions," Twain observed, "righteously, and with a clean and honorable motive, to the disabled soldiers of the civil war. The *clean* motive began and ended there. We have made many and amazing additions to the pension list, but with a motive which dishonors the uniform and the Congresses which have voted the additions."[12] That unclean motive, as Twain saw it, was greed pure and simple, and with plenty of blame to go around. While deceitful claimants and their attorneys hoped for an easy payday, politicians sought to secure votes with targeted expansions. Twain and other critics pointed to the Arrears Act of 1879 as a watershed for all parties. In addition to their monthly checks, with the passage of this measure enrollees could receive immediate and generous lump sum payments.[13] Claims skyrocketed, as did the program's costs. In the ensuing outcry, the pensioned veteran was scorned as never before. As one observer noted, "every Union soldier is 'a suspect' in the eyes of his countrymen. He is regarded as a pension-grabber, and as a patriot who desires to commute his military glory for a stipulated sum in cash."[14]

Though intended as an insult, the idea of the "pension-grabber" aptly captures the cultural logic of the pension system. To claim a pension was indeed to translate (or "commute") injury (or "military glory") into cash. But in suggesting an act of physical theft, "pension-grabber" obscures the specifically textual concerns that fueled public misgivings about Civil War pensions.[15] The widespread suspicion that it was easy to "add one's name to the pension rolls" is closer to the mark. Here, though, writing is imagined as a singular event and not the almost ceaseless production of documentary materials that the process usually entailed. Rather than inscribing names on a scroll—as the phrase *pension roll* would suggest—the Pension Bureau maintained a vast archive of printed and written documents that until 1913 were folded and bundled for storage (figure 1.1).[16]

These materials were initially housed in the Patent Office Building, but the need for more room led to the construction of the Pension Bureau Building in 1877, then the largest such structure in the world. This massive edifice was a monument not only to the nation's commitment to Union veterans but also to the bureaucratized social order of the postbellum United States. To be sure, the use of documentary records to administer military pensions was not new in itself. But in the wake of the Civil War, the Pension Bureau—like many other government agencies, private corporations, and civic organizations—adopted new methods of record keeping and bureaucratic management. In this dawning era of rapid technological change and economic consolidation, the pension claim took its place alongside other novel forms like the death certificate, the report, and the memo.

The prominence of the pension claim in public life was also rooted in the late nineteenth-century rise of job printing and the ubiquity of preprinted forms or blanks, which reshaped how individuals interacted with institutions. As Lisa Gitelman argues, "preprinted blank forms help[ed] triangulate the modern self in relation to authority: the authority of printedness, on the one hand, and the authority of specific subsystems and bureaucracies on the other hand."[17] The blanks included in a pension claim were printed by the federal government but also by job printers for attorneys, claims agents, and other clerical go-betweens. Many of these were used to solicit discrete pieces of information, from the dates of a claimant's military service to the number of children in the charge of a widow. Other blanks were prompts for narrative elaboration. Lined sections invited veterans and witnesses to describe how an injury was sustained or whether a claimant had avoided "vicious habits." It was not uncommon for these responses to continue on a separate sheet of paper or for narratives to be submitted on unlined stationery. The visual contrast between printed and handwritten text might suggest an epistemological contest between institutional and individual knowledge. In practice, however, the pension claim folds the handwritten contributions of veterans and witnesses into the "authority of printedness," giving them a gravitas they might not otherwise possess—as if mirroring the physical creasing and accordion-style folding together of all the documents, printed and handwritten, into a single package, with the outermost sheet serving as a jacket.

The first piece of writing a claimant filed was the "Declaration for Original Invalid Pension," a blank that recorded the veteran's name, age, place of residence, dates of military service, physical description, circumstances of injury, and medical treatment received (figure 1.2). The declaration

1.1 Accordion-fold jacket for an invalid pension claim. National Archives, Washington, DC.

1.2 Declaration for Original Invalid Pension, filed on behalf of Amos Boyden on August 13, 1885. National Archives, Washington, DC.

also included a more or less abbreviated personal statement by the claimant, a narrative that would be augmented over the course of the review process, typically in response to bureau requests for further information. In a handwritten affidavit updating his original declaration, for instance, Henry Moore admitted that he was wounded while "rest[ing] under the shade of a large tree" in a training camp near Nashville but insisted that "was as much in the line of duty as if [he] were drilling" (figure 1.3). Statements from family, friends, and comrades were also part of the initial submission, and many veterans seem to have created informal affidavit-writing networks to support their claims and reciprocate favors. The letters exchanged by Will Eastman and Ziba Roberts, for instance, both of the Twenty-Eighth New York Infantry Regiment, convey how elaborate these collaborations could be: "Where is Aron Southworth? I Believe he would help you. You can get his address by writing the commission of pensions.... If you can't do any better, get up some special affidavits and send me a copy and I'll [be] strong in your case and we will punch them up. I did that in Will Lever's case, and he got his pension."[18] In other instances, particularly where veterans used pension agents, notary publics, or other clerical intermediaries, writerly collaborations were not always entered into intentionally. John Douglass, for instance, who joined the Massachusetts Fifth Calvary after escaping slavery in West Virginia, described his background in rather straightforward terms. A later insertion to his "General Affidavit," however, presumably made by a pension agent, transformed his statement into a slave narrative of sorts: "I was born a slave in ..." (figure 1.4).

An original pension claim also included narrative affidavits from physicians, which were often treated like any other narrative affidavit. The Pension Bureau, in fact, distinguished between just two kinds of evidence, "record" and "parol." The former included the files of the War Department and the certificates of disability issued by military hospitals during the war. Parol evidence, by contrast, was submitted by a witness ("lay evidence") or by a physician ("medical evidence").[19] If not exactly interchangeable, these two kinds of parol evidence supplemented each other during the bureau's review of "testimony of any character, other than record," regardless of whether an affidavit was processed. To be sure, every claim included a "surgeon's certificate," complete with a line drawing of the human form, front and back, on which ailments and injuries were noted (figure 1.5). But even bureau surgeons recognized that physical examinations were subjective and the standard formula used to rate disability as a percentage

1.3 First page of a supplementary personal affidavit submitted by Henry Moore on January 31, 1889.

1.4 A general affidavit sworn to by former slave John Douglass of Portland, Maine, in support of his own pension claim.

of incapacitation was arbitrary. One veteran seen by ten doctors might receive ten different disability ratings. Many physicians, moreover, relied heavily on personal recollection when drafting their own affidavits.[20] The ledger book kept by Dr. Nathan Smyth also suggests that many physicians wrangled personal reflections into formulaic language that varied little from one affidavit to the next. Of three hundred affidavits Smyth wrote from 1890 to 1893, almost all reproduced the same narrative template.[21] Facing such boilerplate, Pension Bureau officials would certainly have read Smyth's affidavits alongside those filed by other acquaintances to flesh out their understanding of the claim at hand. As field manuals note, statements by classmates or childhood friends "with whom [the claimant] bathed" were of particular interest.[22]

For claimants and witnesses, as for the Pension Bureau itself, the effort involved in bolstering the documentary value of narrative evidence could not help but point in the other direction as well—to mounting public discomfort with the bureau's methods and to misgivings about the social fiction the pension claim was meant to sustain. In time, many of these concerns came to coalesce around the idea of the literary and literariness as such. To many skeptics, there could be no way of knowing for sure whether the personal narratives the bureau solicited were not in fact simply works of fiction. Given the conventionality of the stories told by veterans, dependents, and witnesses, after all, what was to prevent undeserving or duplicitous claimants from learning how to game the system—or from soliciting help from attorneys and claim agents whose business it was to master these narrative forms? All of the effort that inevitably went into submitting a pension claim—from drafting or dictating a personal statement to soliciting corroborating affidavits and records to answering the questions raised by bureau officials—also cast doubt on the whole enterprise. Would disabled veterans and their dependents not be better off investing this time in something productive? Far from transforming battlefield injury into respectable back wages, critics argued, the pension claim was a literary ruse—a farcical but nonetheless regrettably effective means of writing one's way out of the obligation to "really work."[23]

Public mistrust of the Pension Bureau's reliance on narrative evidence often focused on the complicity of family and friends but also the paid services of lawyers and claims agents. As one writer for the *Century* observed in 1884, "Men asked to do the neighborly act of witnessing a pension paper are always compliant, and seldom particular as to what they certify to."[24] Congressman John De Witt Warner fretted that affable collusion

1.5 The schematic rendering of the body in the "Surgeon's Certificate"—a single sheet, front and back, in pension claims that could encompass hundreds of pages—raises the question of whether medical testimony supplemented lay affidavits, or vice versa. National Archives, Washington, DC.

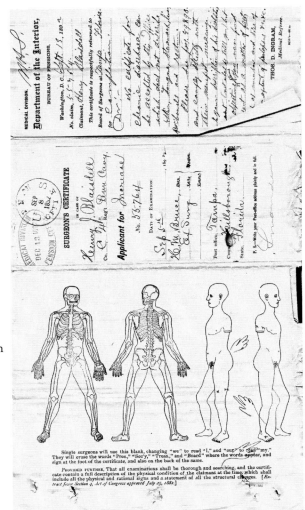

had long since given way to a cottage industry of counterfeit affidavits. "Any one can now have a seal manufactured for two or three dollars," he cautioned, "bearing his name or an assumed name, and, to his heart's content either forge affidavits or certify to false ones—all of which will be accepted by the Pension Office—without even giving a clue to his own identity, and with perfect confidence that no one executing an affidavit before him can be convicted of perjury."[25] Not only did many Americans fear that the bureau's reliance on narrative affidavits opened the system to abuse, but many also complained that these procedures made it impossible for the honorable veteran to claim a pension without jeopardizing his reputation.[26]

Shared by bureau officials and veterans alike, this latter criticism found expression in prominent fraud trials, such as the 1893 prosecution of William Newby. After calling 150 witnesses to the stand, the court concluded that the real Newby died on the battlefield decades earlier and that the man drawing his pension—evidently with the willing collusion of Newby's wife and family—was a ne'er-do-well from a neighboring town. The Newby case became synonymous with pension fraud of the most flagrant sort but also with the bureau's procedural failings. Well after the trial's conclusion, many Americans continued to believe that the condemned man was the real Newby, a soldier who had fought bravely for his country only to fall victim to the Pension Bureau's red tape. Like G. J. George, author of *William Newby, alias "Dan Benton," alias "Rickety Dan," alias "Crazy Jack," or The Soldier's Return; a True and Wonderful Story of Mistaken Identity* (1893), Newby's champions put the Pension Bureau itself on trial. The system stood accused of providing deserving veterans no means of distinguishing themselves from the tricksters and cheats whose lucrative ploys required but a narrative sleight of hand.[27]

Criticism of its methods did not go unheeded at the Pension Bureau. Some of the earliest warnings about the dangers of its reliance on narrative testimony, in fact, came from within the bureau. Commissioner J. A. Bentley led the charge by declaring that the "cumbersome and expensive" method of evaluating narrative affidavits provided "an open door to the Treasury for the perpetration of fraud." The corporate attorneys who processed most of these claims "gave themselves little concern as to the character of the affidavits they gathered and presented," which as a consequence had "the same appearance to the officers of the Bureau, whether true or false."[28] After several proposals for revamping the claims process were abandoned in the face of opposition from veterans' organizations and attorneys, however, in 1881 the bureau created a new regulatory system that answered the problem of narrative with more narrative. Dubious claims were now to be handled by the Division of Special Examination, which sent agents into the field to assess the credibility of individual claimants and witnesses. The process of special examination could last several weeks, depending on how many interviews were necessary and where the interviewees lived. Once their inquiries were complete, special examiners compiled their conclusions in narrative and tabular form.[29] These files then served as reading guides when the original claims were returned to Washington for final review.

Special examination was thus at root an exercise in fact-finding, as agents sought to resolve inconsistencies flagged during a claim's initial evaluation. But special examination could also become an exercise in writerly collaboration, essentially blurring the lines between the documentary and literary that the bureau was otherwise concerned to police. As one examiner described his work in the field:

> A soldier's statement when his initial examination was finished contained from one thousand to ten thousand words and sometimes more, and the special examiner in several instances, on finishing his statement and reading it over to him, made him feel so proud, if his history had been honorable throughout, that he ventured to state that he would give a liberal sum for a copy of it, that he might have it printed in pamphlet form, or a booklet, to leave with his family, as it was the only correct record of his life reduced to writing.[30]

The outcome of special examination was certainly different for veterans whose histories were less than honorable. A negative report could cause a claim to be put on hold or dismissed altogether, and veterans already on the pension roll could have their benefits revoked or face criminal charges. Nonetheless, as agents' memoirs and bureau guidelines attest, special examination was not simply a punitive project. In addition to reducing fraud, examiners were also tasked with distinguishing the deserving claimant from the canny manipulator of documents. The former, it was believed, should be able to claim a pension without being subjected to the shame and scorn rightfully visited upon the latter. As such, special examination was at base an effort to redeem both the Pension Bureau and the disabled veteran by curating—or coauthoring—a set of personal narratives that were irreproachable in their authenticity and honesty. Indeed, these narratives rethink the relation between the literary and the documentary such that the perfectly accurate personal statement itself becomes a thing of beauty.

Literary collaborations of this sort were less common when agents investigated claims filed by ex-slaves. In this regard, the Division of Special Examination reproduced the structural biases of the Pension Bureau itself. For although federal pension law granted the same disability benefits to every soldier, bureaucratic procedure and the attitudes of individual officials created unique difficulties for Black veterans.[31] The relative scarcity of official documentation was foremost among these challenges. Lacking birth and marriage certificates as a matter of course and often appearing only intermittently in War Department records, Black veterans were disproportionately dependent on witness testimony to substantiate their claims. And because affidavits as such were widely associated with fraud, the claims filed by Black applicants were especially suspect and subject to inordinate scrutiny. Illiterate claimants were also deeply reliant on the clerical services of claim agents, notoriously profit-driven middlemen. Rather than investigating the facts at hand, many claim agents contrived false cases for Black claimants by using what one official aptly described as "ready made affidavits."[32] Once discovered by the bureau, such practices compounded the already pervasive mistrust of Black claimants and witnesses. Voicing a belief probably shared across the bureau, one examiner stated his reservations: "The reputation for truth of all witnesses who are colored cannot be rated higher than 'fair.'" Those who could "be counted reliable and absolutely truthful" were allegedly fewer still—"a rarity indeed."[33]

As a consequence of both structural racism and individual bigotry at the Pension Bureau, Black claimants were disproportionately targeted for special examination. Blackness as such became a marker of the pension claim's suspect literariness. At the same time, however, the mixed messages that special examiners received about ex-slave testimony could also lead to collaborative investigations in which the literary served as an index of white supremacy. Bureau field manuals, for instance, acknowledged the lack of material evidence available to Black claimants and urged examiners to be mindful of how life was organized under slavery. The timing of events, for example, might be established by asking informants about holidays or memorable storms rather than calendar dates.[34] Because marriages among enslaved people were rarely documented, moreover, agents were advised to consult local opinion to determine whether a given relationship should be recognized as marital. Special examiners were also told, however, never to give Black claimants or witnesses the last word. "More accurate and satisfactory" information could be found, the bureau assured, in the testimony of "former owners or members of the owner's family."[35] These instructions give the lie to the race-neutral wording of federal pension legislation. But they also make clear that the bureau's antifraud mandate coincided with postbellum racial politics. By subordinating the affidavits of ex-slaves to the memories of ex-slave owners, special examiners reproduced the pervasive skepticism about both Black autonomy and Black participation in the Civil War. These, of course, were the very stories told in the pension files of Black veterans. Special examiners thus rewrote the pension claims of Black veterans not as the valorous boutique memoirs they crafted for white veterans but as "romances of reunion" often coauthored with former slave owners.[36]

In response to what were perceived as the intertwining threats of blackness, literariness, and fraudulence, the Pension Bureau set out to establish ever more robust systems of narrative checks and balances. Public discourse, on the other hand, ginned up the same racist fears in order to call for the program's outright elimination. Like Thomas Fleming's *Around the Capital with Uncle Hank* (1902), works of popular literature commonly made their case by marshaling the tropes of blackface minstrelsy (figure 1.6). Fleming's book is a boisterous send-up of "the foibles and vagaries of public life in Washington" as observed by a salt-of-the-earth white veteran from rural New England whose rural dialect is meant to underscore his no-nonsense moral clarity. After sniping at the lavishness of the Pension Building, a common target during the postbellum era, Hank comes upon two Black veterans struggling to decipher a sign hanging in a claim agent's window: "Pension Vouchers Executed." Pausing over the last word, the man engaged to testify for his friend about their experiences during the war wonders whether he will be put to death for his statement, which readers are led to believe may not be entirely truthful. Relishing his exegetical authority, Uncle Hank settles the matter of the sign's import: "Et means thet they'll hang ye ef ye don't tell th' truth when ye 'pply fer a penshun."[37] Featuring a white interlocutor flanked by two pension-seeking end men, this scene retools minstrel iconography in order to lampoon disabled veterans. The warning to white readers is clear: to submit a pension claim is not only to blacken up, it is also to commit a crime of writing by monetizing one's honor. Uncle Hank, who was injured in the war but never sought a pension, is by contrast truly white both because he earns his own living and because he prefers folksy satire to groveling autobiography.

Another strand of popular condemnation invoked plantation mythology, not to satirize the extravagance of federal pension legislation but to imagine counterfactual alternatives to a mode of social provision dependent on narrative affidavits. These critics commonly contrasted the easily gamed pension system with the compassionate accountability of Southern paternalism. The latter, it was supposed, could better accommodate Black veterans and their dependents. Such is the argument at stake, for example, in the *New York Times* coverage of the 1893 trial of William H. Taylor,

1.6 Uncle Hank amusing himself at the Pension Building. (The figure with the top hat at lower right is Uncle Hank.) Thomas Fleming, *Around the Capital with Uncle Hank, Recorded Together with Many Pictures* (1902).

a case that "brought up a vanished phase of American life and history and filled the courtroom with figures from antebellum days."[38] Accused of pension fraud and imposture, the defendant is described as "a modern negro, one of the coarse commonplace types so familiar in the slums of Northern cities." More surprising than these pedestrian slurs against working-class Black culture is how they shade into misgivings about the Pension Bureau's bureaucratic procedures. Taylor is dubiously "modern" not only because he lives in the "slums," but also because he traffics in counterfeit affidavits. The witnesses who testify against him, on the other hand, embody the honesty of a bygone era. These include "the typical 'mammy' of the South" and a "southern Colonel of fiction."

The most damning indictment, however, comes from an elderly man whom the *Times* identifies as the "real" William Taylor—"a venerable colored man of the old house-servant type of the days 'before the war.'" "As the two men faced each other it seemed like the contrasting of two periods of American history. The old negro spoke softly, gravely, in the deliberate speech and with the unconscious dignity on which Southern writers of plantation days delight to dwell. He had still something of a soldierly bearing, and looked venerable with his white mustache and beard. His mild, serene speech and mellow Southern dialect contrasted wonderfully with the aggressive modernity of the claimant."[39] This encounter between defendant and star witness is a confrontation between two modes of Black testimony. The real Taylor is a man of "unconscious dignity" whose "serene speech" is scripted by the "Southern writers of plantation days." While his testimony garners trust from the court and the *Times*, the witness ultimately reveals more about "the old South, past and gone," than about himself. The fake Taylor, by contrast, has become a narrative subject in his own right by manipulating the Pension Bureau's review process. For the *Times*, there can be no valor in this act of self-creation; the fake Taylor is doomed to fail in his subterfuge, much as he had failed to meet the competitive demands of industrial modernity. Indeed, the only hope that the *Times* entertains for the younger man is that he might follow the example set by the older. The latter has gone back to work for the man who used to own him rather than claiming the pension that would be his legal due. This decision, of course, is but further evidence for the *Times* that the elder Taylor is indeed the real veteran.[40]

The fears of pension fraud that consolidated around the specter of the scheming Black claimant in popular culture are clearly cut from the apologist cloth of postbellum racial politics. The idea that the nation was equally indebted to all disabled soldiers, whether white or Black, assumed a shared national identity or even a shared humanity that ran counter to the rising tide of both anti-Black sentiment and anti-Black violence. That Black veterans were in theory invited to take up the same narrative genre with which white veterans proved that they had truly earned their pensions, moreover, was for many skeptics but further evidence that the social fiction at the heart of the pension claim was unsalvageable. What more convincing evidence could there be, this line of argument went, that suffering and pain were not compensable as back wages and that pensions were not earned entitlements but degrading charity? If blackness came in postbellum culture to signify narrative's dubious evidentiary value, in other words, it also became shorthand for the pension system's inconsistency with the labor market. The subsequent cultural history of the pension claim, however, suggests that these oppositions—between blackness and truth, between writing and work, and between injury and back wages—were far from settled. Whereas critics of the pension system turned to the iconography of Black industrial education and to the writings of Booker T. Washington to make the case against exempting veterans from the workforce, ex-slave activists returned to the specifically literary labor of the pension claim to place the injuries of slavery both within and beyond the market.

Booker T. Washington Does the World's Work

It is not surprising that Booker T. Washington and Tuskegee Institute would become signposts in the backlash against the expansion of the Civil War pension system. Washington's had been a household name since 1895, the year of his celebrated address before the Cotton States and International Exposition in Atlanta. In that speech, Washington famously told Black Americans in the South to "cast down your buckets where you are" and join forces—though hardly on equal footing—with white-led agriculture and industry. From that point onward, Washington and Tuskegee were synonymous with "the dignity of labor," a concept as equivocal as the notion of industrial education itself. In white contexts industrial education could mean vocational training or preparation for the skilled trades or engineering. Tuskegee's pedagogy of dignified labor, on the other hand, was carefully calibrated to the racial politics of the day. In an era that witnessed the rise of Jim Crow, the terrors of lynch law, and the subordination of Black labor to sharecropping and debt peonage, Tuskegee cadets were to learn "how to work," as an early catalog put it.[41] In light of the extraordinary productivity of Black labor under slavery, a less relevant pedagogy is scarcely imaginable. But Washington's was of course a strategic choice that reflected his reluctance to upset the racial status quo even as he promoted a modest agenda of Black progress. And although Washington's work at Tuskegee is often disparaged today as "schooling for a new slavery," for turn-of-the-century critics of the Civil War pension system, there could be no better spokesperson for both the value of industrious self-help and the dangers of government handouts.[42] If learning the dignity of work had helped formerly enslaved people make such tremendous social progress, then might not disabled veterans make similar strides?

Critics of the pension system were also drawn to Washington's prominence as a memoirist. Famously told in *Up from Slavery* (1901), but also in countless newspaper articles, magazine articles, and even children's books,

Washington's personal history was for millions of US readers an allegory of Black self-help. Across these various genres, Washington and his ghost-writers were careful to emphasize the modesty of his ambitions, which reflected a desire for economic opportunity rather than social or political equality for Black Americans. In this regard, Washington's writing shares more with popular rags-to-riches memoirs such as P. T. Barnum's *Struggles and Triumphs* (1869)—after the Bible the best-selling book of the later nineteenth century—than with the antebellum slave narrative tradition.[43] If slave narrators took up the pen in order to prove their humanity, as William L. Andrews has noted, then Washington and other postbellum Black memoirists wrote to demonstrate their readiness to contribute to the economic life of the nation.[44] Such pragmatism also made Washington's memoirs a welcome rejoinder to the increasingly disreputable pension claim. A skeptical public disparaged dissembling veterans for embracing the literariness of the genre to write themselves out of the labor force, but Washington's paeans to the dignity of work assured readers that he and other Black Americans sought only to work their way in. And unlike the invalid pension claim, the postbellum uplift memoir was little concerned with the social fiction that injury and suffering could be transformed into compensable labor. Rather than seek redress for the wounds of slavery, Washington and other postbellum memoirists seemed to suggest that the peculiar institution had been an apprenticeship for modern wage labor.

To be sure, Washington and his team were far more self-conscious in how they told his story than were most of the disabled veterans who submitted personal narratives to the Pension Bureau. But throughout his career as a de facto professional writer, Washington nonetheless remained ambivalent about the economic status of writing as such and had little patience for anything that smacked of the "merely literary." In *Up from Slavery*, for instance, Washington conceded that he often found himself compelled "to read a novel that is on everyone's lips," the better to maintain social and philanthropic relationships. But his "greatest fondness" was always for biography and autobiography. "I like to be sure that I am reading about a real man or a real thing," he quipped.[45] For Washington, though, the reality of biography and autobiography had less to do with the faithful representation of a life than with writing's proximity to genuinely productive labor. On the one hand, this proximity could be a question of subject matter, insofar as stories of industrious self-help in turn inspire readers to work hard themselves. On the other hand, however, writerly productivity can be measured more directly by asking what it creates in the world. In Washington's case, the answer was clear. As we will see in more detail in chapter 2, the vast network of educational and political operations that Washington directed from Tuskegee were financed directly and indirectly by his writing. From formal autobiographies to the strategically placed magazine and newspaper profiles, Washington's life writing was as productive as the work done in Tuskegee's wheelwright shop or brick kiln.

Opponents of Civil War pensions thus found in Washington the embodiment of dignified work and a productive model of literary labor. It was through his relationship with Walter Hines Page, editor of the *Atlantic Monthly*, that Washington's story would contribute directly to the fight. An early supporter of Washington, Page was seminal in seeing *Up from Slavery* into print and urged its author to make the most of his prominence in the service of a nation still divided by sectional loyalties.[46] As Page wrote to Washington about an earlier essay slated for the *Atlantic*:

> My notion is that if you will strike out from the shoulder, broadening the application of the principle that you have worked out so as to show . . . that this principle which has made a success of Tuskegee is really the proper principle for education in the whole south without reference to race—this I am sure will meet a very hearty response, and will throw your work where it properly belongs, among the great forces of our time and not simply the force of work done at a single institution.[47]

The lesson to be learned from Tuskegee, Page and other liberal Southerners believed, was about work first and race only second, or perhaps not really at all. It was not fifteen years later that, with Page's help, the story of Washington and his "single institution" would help bring this message about the universally redemptive power of labor to bear on another social upheaval of the early twentieth century, the turning of public opinion against the Civil War pension system. Now directed at disabled veterans, the message was to be promoted in Page's newest venture, a Progressive journal fittingly called the *World's Work*.

In October 1910, the *World's Work* published a six-part series by journalist William Bayard Hale titled "The Pension Carnival" that laid out the consensus opinion of its Progressive readers: the extravagance, expense, and corruption of the pension system had reached the point of absurdity. This argument was by itself far from novel. But in pairing each installment of Hale's sensational exposé with an excerpt from Washington's forthcoming memoir, *My Larger Education: Being Chapters from My Experience*

(1911), Page introduced a provocative new comparison to drive the case against the pension system home. The progress made through self-help and industrial education at Tuskegee was to stand as proof that soldiers disabled in future wars should be given physical and vocational rehabilitation rather than income maintenance. If industrial training of this sort had helped Black Americans make such remarkable advances after slavery, wouldn't disabled veterans also embrace the dignity of labor? In printing "The Pension Carnival" back-to-back with Washington's "Chapters from My Experience," the *World's Work* made this argument by contrasting the deceitful veteran with the diligent Tuskegee cadet. Whereas the former operates behind the scenes to game the system for his own benefit, the latter labors in plain sight. And while both write autobiographies, the stories they tell differ in substance and purpose. The scheming veteran masters the formal conventions of the pension claim in the hopes of being exempted from real work. Washington's students, by contrast, prefer narratives of industrious achievement to spectacular woe. Crucially, Bookerite memoirs have little truck with the social fiction maintained by the pension claim: instead of transforming past suffering into compensable labor, this writing inspires others to embrace the hard but meaningful work ahead.

Before proposing the uplift memoir as a riposte to the invalid pension claim, the first article of "The Pension Carnival" sets the stage by tracking the origins of the crisis to the Arrears Act of 1879. As we have seen, with this piece of legislation veterans who had not yet filed for a pension could receive lump sum payments extending back to the date of their initial discharge. When word got out, Hale writes, "thousands of old soldiers searched their bodies for some twinges that might be attributed back to war-time." Thus began the pensioner's steep decline in public esteem: "To-day, unpleasant as it is to say, the pensioner is a suspect. The common presumption is against his being a hero. The presumption, cynical perhaps, but not unjustified is that he is as likely to be a cook or a hostler or a peddler, who has perjured himself, a thrifty patriot who has no objection to receiving an annuity of a summer's episode of half a century ago."[48] What follows is a selection of choice outrages. Hale writes of veterans receiving multiple pensions, of lawyers suing to overturn dishonorable discharges, and of civilians scouring graveyards for the names of deceased soldiers whose benefits might yet be claimed. Like many of his contemporaries, Hale blames the Pension Bureau and its reliance on narrative affidavits for this rampant fraud. But rather than adding his voice to the chorus of demands for more rigorous and exacting medical examinations, Hale notes that physicians' statements are easily counterfeited and often no less subjective than the affidavits submitted by claimants and their witnesses. Nor do medical exams ever tell the whole story. "It is questionable," Hale writes, "whether 'veterans' shot trying to run away should be allowed to draw allowances for wounds of cowardice."[49] Only honorable wounds, in other words, are genuinely remunerable.

"The Pension Carnival" rehearses a well-known critique of the Pension Bureau's methods, but like earlier writers Hale also finds in the plantation mythos an expedient iconography of fraud. Much like Fleming in *Around the Capital with Uncle Hank*, Hale adopts a minstrel pose to condemn another landmark pension law, an appropriation act that authorized payments to war widows retroactive to the date of their husbands' deaths. "Probably no single piece of pension legislation," he writes, "has been more productive of bogus pensioners." In its wake, "gangs of swindlers" went from town to town rustling up accomplices to pass off as dead soldiers' wives. "The government had no chance; the game was safe, the prizes big." Nowhere was this scam easier to pull off, Hale notes, than "in the South among the Negroes, where willing witnesses would glibly swear at a moment's notice to having attended the wedding of Sambo and Dinah on the 'back po'och ob de big house jes''fore de wah.'"[50] Such minstrel tropes would seem to be a gesture of solidarity with Southern critics of the Pension Bureau. But rather than summon Sambo and Dinah as cherished relics of a bygone era, Hale scorns them as anachronistic throwbacks out of place in the Progressive present. Not only is the pension system as outmoded as these plantation conventions, Hale suggests, but it also threatens the social progress brought about by the Civil War. The amity that many bureau officials and special examiners seem to have imagined between themselves and former slave owners is for Hale nothing to celebrate.

In pairing "The Pension Carnival" with Washington's "Chapters from My Experience," the *World's Work* turns from the farce of minstrel caricature to the solemnity of industrial education. The conversation begins with a set of photographs depicting narrative production and custodianship that are printed on facing pages (figures 1.7–1.8). On the first page, two photographs present the Pension Bureau as a site of secrecy and textual excess. Overrun with paperwork, bureau agents file away from public scrutiny ream after ream of pension claims, many of which, we are given to understand, are probably fraudulent. These images show the bureaucratic apparatus at work, categorizing some bodies as normal and others as aberrant according to arbitrary standards that are soon naturalized.[51] But these photographs also reveal the ultimate futility of any endeavor to define disability. In place of crisp classifications and clear guidelines, the bureau's methods can only capture the conceptual blurriness that dooms their efforts from the start. As such, the Pension Bureau's reliance on narrative evidence points up the historical intertwining of disability and deception. As Deborah Stone notes, because no single condition of disability has ever been universally recognized, the concept "has always been based on the perceived need to detect deception."[52] These images thus picture a conceptual tautology. In seeking to establish the "truth" of the bodies described in the dossiers they catalog and assess, pension officials can only ever get at the truth of disability—that it is an arbitrary classification. The only way out of this conundrum, it seems, is to sidestep it altogether by providing all veterans with the care and training they need to rejoin the workforce. Once implemented, a program of mandatory rehabilitation would obviate both the narrative ruses that the pension system invites and the elaborate but finally ineffectual mechanisms of narrative detection it requires.

The photograph on the facing page, of Washington and his secretary, Emmett J. Scott, could not be more different—either in its composition or in the relation it draws between labor and narrative. Seated at his desk, Washington exudes confidence and honesty. His program of industrial education embodies the rehabilitative power of work in contrast with the dependency fostered by the pension system. The scene of writing has also changed. Washington's is a simple tale of self-reliance that requires but a few sheets of paper to get down. Nor is it particularly original; unlike the wildly fabricated pension claims that go on for hundreds of pages, Washington's narrative is brief and typological, made for easy copying and rapid distribution. Although he has a marginal place in the image's composition, Washington's secretary is central to its overall meaning. Scott's presence underscores not simply the efficiency of Washington's style, but more so his literary productivity. Washington is a professional writer not only because his publications finance the empire he directs from behind his desk at Tuskegee, but also because he employs others in the process. The caption under this photograph further specifies that Washington's managerial duties extend to the work of image making: "I have never at any time asked or expected that any one should forget that I am a Negro." These sentiments echo a point that Washington often made in response to accusations that he delivered different messages to white audiences in the North and mixed audiences in the South. But in an essay responding to and ginning up mistrust of the fraudulent veteran, this caption also does

SOME OF THE HUNDREDS OF THOUSANDS OF FILES IN THE PENSION OFFICE
Evidence in these cases and even the names of the pensioners are scrupulously withheld from the public which pays the bills

for twenty-seven years. With what justice does Katie V. Kellogg draw $12 a month from the Government?

Helen L. Fitch lives with a son by her first marriage in his comfortable home, and owns a tract of land; but she is given a dollar a day by the Government of the United States because she took a veteran as a second husband, seventeen years after the close of the Civil War.

Mary Ann Shirey, the widow of Jacob Shirey of Companies D and G, 83d Pennsylvania Infantry, failed to secure a pension when her husband died, though a special examiner of the Pension Bureau was assigned to help her prove that his death was attributable to his service. So, in 1902, she married another veteran, David Hoover, once of Company F, 134th Pennsylvania Infantry. She now receives a pension on account of Hoover's nine months' service forty years before she married him.

Surely, enough has been said to justify the suspicion that this matter of pensions deserves looking into. A sum sufficient to support all the colleges and universities of the country for two years or to run its public schools for six months

must not every year be spent in ways so criminally careless as these. The honor of the veterans' roster must not be suffered to remain thus ignobly blotted.

The Remedy? Yes, indeed, there is one. Yes, indeed, it is possible to apply the awakened common-sense of the nation to a task even so delicate as the reform of the Pension Office.

What that remedy is will appear later on as this series of articles progresses. But here it may at least be said that reform will at the outset demand:

That the records of the Pension Office and the War Department be open to public inspection;

That no further extravagant pension legislation be enacted;

That no private-pension bill be passed till the name of the beneficiary and his claim shall have been published in the community in which he lives.

The pension snowball has rolled up into a burden ten times as big as it was forty-five years ago. It is time to stop it; time, first, to blow the hot breath of publicity upon it, and then to try those more drastic measures which wise men apply even to a beautiful and necessary thing that has grown too big.

Figure 1.7
William Bayard Hale, "The Pension Carnival," *World's Work* (October 1910).

CHAPTERS FROM MY EXPERIENCE

THE FUNDAMENTAL PRINCIPLES OF MY LIFE—HOW I HAVE DEALT FRANKLY WITH SOUTHERN WHITE MEN, WITH NORTHERN WHITE MEN, AND WITH MY OWN RACE, AND HOW I CAME TO KNOW THE HEARTS OF MY OWN PEOPLE

BY

BOOKER T. WASHINGTON

["*Up from Slavery,*" which has been translated into almost all living languages, even into some of the languages of India, is mainly the story of Mr. Washington's life up to the time that he began his career at Tuskegee. In these articles he continues his autobiography, in a broader way and into his wider career as the leader of his race and as a national figure in American life.— THE EDITORS.]

ONE of the first questions that I had to answer for myself after beginning my work at Tuskegee was how I was to deal with public opinion on the race question.

It may seem strange that a man who had started out with the humble purpose of establishing a little Negro industrial school in a small, Southern country-town should find himself, to any great extent, either

MR. WASHINGTON AND HIS SECRETARY, MR. EMMETT J. SCOTT
"I have never at any time asked or expected that any one should forget that I am a Negro"

1.8   Booker T. Washington, "Chapters from My Experience," *World's Work* (October 1910).

something more. It answers the epistemological slipperiness of disability with the ontological certainty of race. Disability is a fraught and a flexible social category, prone to deception but also amenable to rehabilitation. Racial difference, by contrast, is absolute and easily verified. Notwithstanding the progress made since Emancipation, Washington assures white readers, blackness itself cannot be "overcome."

The binary between the truth of race and the fraud of disability structures Washington's recollections throughout "Chapters from My Experience," as denunciations of deception become something of a refrain. "I learned long ago," he repeats, "[that] nothing but honest hard work lasts; fraud and sham are bound to be detected in the end."[53] Even Washington's sense of his own leadership is informed by a reluctance to be anything other than himself, a position exemplified by his decision not to emulate Frederick Douglass. The latter's death in 1895 left "the place of the 'leader of the Negro people'" conspicuously vacant.[54] "After thinking the matter all over," Washington observes, "I decided that, pleasant as it might be to follow the programme that was laid out to me, I should be compelled to stick to my original job and work out my salvation along the lines that I had originally laid down for myself."[55] Profiting from a legacy one hasn't earned is as bad as claiming someone else's pension. The same moralism informs Washington's portrait of an Ivy League graduate who fails to make a living by lecturing on "The Mistakes of Booker T. Washington." For Washington, this man's failure brings the value of industrial education into sharper relief while also illustrating the common ground shared by elite Black politics and misguided pension policy. Had he learned the "dignity of labor," Washington implies, his critic would have ceased trying to live by his wits alone. But like the disabled veteran and his allies in the cottage industry that sprang up to meet the clerical formalities involved in filing a pension claim, "a certain class of race-problem solvers don't want the patient to get well, because as long as the disease holds out they have not only an easy means of making a living but also an easy medium through which to make themselves prominent before the public."[56]

For his part, of course, Washington was eager to persuade readers that there is no "easy means of making a living" and that being "prominent before the public" is no measure of success. But it is likewise clear that Washington's warning is not only about the lure of celebrity but also about the spectacle of injury. The comparison at stake here, in other words, is ultimately between the handout-seeking veteran and the backward-looking Black leader who, to Washington's mind, prioritized "special pleading" and the wounds of slavery over the obligations of racial self-help. In "Chapters from My Experience," Washington thus flips the racial script created by the (white) backlash against the Civil War invalid pension system. That discourse, as we have seen, associated blackness with fraud and with the literary deception inherent in the idea that injury might be transformed into compensable labor. Washington and his allies, by contrast, took blackness to exemplify both the self-evident dignity of all labor and the particular kind of productivity to which writing should aspire. By these lights, disability—and not blackness—represents the threat of duplicitous shirking and literary conniving. Washington, of course, also had other reasons for keeping pensioned veterans at a distance. Like other racial uplift projects of the early twentieth century, Washington's program of industrial education promoted the health and capacities of the Black body in order to defuse the racist canard of Black inferiority.[57] Expressions of solidarity between African Americans and disabled white veterans or full-throated support of disabled Black veterans would have been a precarious proposition.[58] But in stressing the self-evident value of Black labor, Washington also sought to sidestep a dangerous comparison—that, like injured soldiers, African Americans were owed back wages for generations of chattel servitude. Such would be the basis for the first modern campaign for slave reparations, a movement that embraced the genre of the pension claim that Washington and his accommodationist allies eschewed.

The Literary Labor of Reparations

Not long before Washington rose to prominence, the Civil War pension system became a touchstone for a radically different agenda of post-Reconstruction Black politics. Indifferent to industrial education and impatient with gradualist approaches, a network of ex-slave activists saw in the expansion of the pension system not an ideological straw man but an unprecedented opportunity. There, ready at hand, was a working bureaucracy with which to articulate the grievances of formerly enslaved people against the state and with which to seek appropriate remuneration. Thus was the first modern movement for slave reparations born in the 1890s as the ex-slave pension movement, a national campaign in support of a congressional bill to make former slaves eligible for the income maintenance programs created for disabled veterans. Although no ex-slave pension bill would ever be put on the books, historians have celebrated the movement as a decisive first step in what remains an unfinished and urgent social justice project. The role of narrative in this endeavor, however, has been largely neglected, as has the pressure that formerly enslaved people put on the social fiction at the heart of the Civil War pension system. The genre of the pension claim was tasked with transforming the physical wounds sustained by Union veterans into compensable labor, and the ex-slave pension movement leveraged this narrative form to pose a related question: what kind of compensation were formerly enslaved people owed for the physical, psychological, economic, and even ontological injuries of slavery? The genre of the pension claim and the constellation of ideas about injury, disability, work, and writing that it set in motion is thus a crucial but largely untold part of the story of reparations.

Given the notoriety of the Civil War invalid pension system in the 1890s and the concomitant resurgence of anti-Black sentiment in US public culture, it is unsurprising that activists faced an uphill battle in their efforts to have formerly enslaved men and women added to the pension rolls. But if the ex-slave pension movement was at odds with late nineteenth-century popular opinion, the movement's use of the pension claim also contradicts the consensus that has emerged in more recent conversations about the means and ends of slave reparations. Contemporary writers from a range of fields and with disparate political commitments have argued that the social ideal of reparations cannot be realized through economic compensation or legal restitution alone. Reparations must instead be conceptualized in terms that are more capacious and more contingent. Emphasizing the "incommensurability between pain and compensation," Stephen Best and Saidiya Hartman have championed the open-endedness of grief over the pragmatic resolution of legal grievance.[59] Robin D. G. Kelley argues that the reparations campaign "was never entirely, or even primarily about money." It is instead motivated by "social justice, reconciliation, reconstructing the internal life of Black America, and eliminating institutional racism."[60] Alexander Weheliye's assessment of how political liberalism makes pain "the only price of entry to proper personhood" also challenges legal and economic models of reparation. Rather than dispensing with suffering, however, Weheliye seeks to reclaim the "atrocity of the flesh" without reinforcing the structures that cause social injury and harm to begin with. Such a politics of pain, Weheliye concludes, would be irreducible to the laws of the liberal state.[61]

In the light of these conversations, the Civil War invalid pension claim adopted by ex-slave activists would seem at best a compromised and at worst a counterproductive choice. Not only does the genre by definition seek to translate suffering and pain into compensable labor, but the pension claim was itself a product of the liberal state. To address the grievances of formerly enslaved people via the bureaucracy created to administer benefits to wounded Civil War veterans, moreover, is to flatten out grave differences of personal and structural circumstance. Ex-slave activists, however, were hardly unaware of these pitfalls. Not only did they both underscore and problematize commonalities across disparate experiences of injury, but they also used the pension claim for their own ends. In particular, the ex-slave pension movement embraced the genre's narrative instability and the literariness that made it suspect in US culture. While detractors argued that the pension claim offered the least deserving a reliable means of writing their way out of the workforce, to ex-slave activists the documentary and the literary were not necessarily mutually exclusive. Indeed, the social fiction fostered by the pension claim—that pensioned veterans had earned the benefits they received—created room for interrogating work's relation to suffering in an entirely different context. Embracing the genre of the pension claim thus did not mean constraining the ambitions of formerly enslaved people to the modes of recognition offered by the liberal state. It was a means by which to begin the literary labor of reparations.

The campaign for ex-slave pensions was actually initiated by a white Southerner named William R. Vaughan, who in 1890 began circulating a pamphlet titled *Vaughan's "Freedmen's Pension Bill"* in Black communities and among legislators in Washington. The proposal called for arrears payments and monthly stipends to ex-slaves, with rates of pay determined by the number of years a claimant had lived under slavery. At base, Vaughan made a bluntly economic case for extending the Civil War pension rolls "to include the millions of people who were held aforetime in the bonds of servitude."[62] As was the case for the injured veteran, ex-slave pensions were "reasonable recompense for the years of toil" and unpaid labor.[63] Vaughan's proposal, however, was also intended to appease white Americans who worried that the South was paying far too dearly for a federal pension system that until 1924 excluded Confederate veterans. Each pension check cashed, this argument went, transferred funds from Northern to Southern coffers. Adding to their woes, many white Southerners evidently felt obligated to care for the "old, maimed and decrepit ex-slaves" that the United States had freed but never provided for. Barring what Vaughan suggests would be a fortunate return to slavery, putting ex-slaves on the federal pension rolls was the surest means of guaranteeing both the economic survival of the South and the welfare of freed people. For

The South furnishing revenue for the Nation with a liberal hand, contributing millions for the pension of Union soldiers at the North, while supporting their old, maimed and decrepit ex-slaves, who have been freed by the Government!

1.9 The costs of Civil War pensions to the South, as part of a proposal for pensioning "old, maimed and decrepit ex-slaves." Walter Vaughan, *Vaughan's "Freedmen's Pension Bill"* (1890).

this reason, Vaughan promoted his ex-slave pension bill as "a Southern tax-relief bill" that would also greatly benefit the North (figure 1.9). "A proper recognition of the claims of former slaves for pensions by the government," he argued, would "obliterate the last trace of enmity that has resulted from our sad civil commotion and terrible appeal to arms. The North and South will be a unit again."[64]

In promoting his bill among freed men and women, Vaughan naturally spoke more often of restitution than of tax relief. He also established grassroots organizations like the Ex-Slave National Pension Club Association and Vaughan's Justice Party to collect initiation fees and monthly dues from ex-slaves that could be used to finance a national lobbying campaign. Vaughan's model quickly proved successful, and a number of Black-run offshoot groups soon followed. The most effective challenge to Vaughan's direction came from the Ex-Slave Mutual Relief, Bounty and Pension Association, founded in 1897 by Callie D. House and Isaiah Dickerson. After enrolling 34,000 members in five years, House and Dickerson nearly succeeded in consolidating the entire movement under their leadership.[65] Like Vaughan, House and Dickerson argued that ex-slave pensions should be administered like Civil War invalid pensions. And like Vaughan,

House and Dickerson often compared racial servitude to military service. But unlike the white Southerner, these Black activists also conceded the difficulty—and even the counterproductiveness—of distinguishing too sharply between the wrongs of slavery and the duties of war. As Dickerson observed, "If anyone who's been anywhere near the army can get paid for a lifetime," there could be no good reason not to pension "the old ex-slaves who worked unpaid all their lives and then helped the Union digging ditches at the forts, washing the soldiers' clothes, cooking for them, and nursing the injured."[66] In another typically protean argument, Dickerson declared that his organization "advocate[ed] the rights of the Negro as citizen of this government, and, especially the right of the ex-slave to a compensation for the wrongs perpetuated under the existence of slavery that were not in accord with the Declaration of the Independence of the United States."[67] In the space of one sentence, Dickerson pivots from a universalist plea for full Black citizenship to intimate that the best proof of the ex-slave's eligibility for a pension is the founding document of the American Revolution itself.[68]

Rarely coalescing into a unified theory of reparations, the arguments made by the leaders of the ex-slave pension movement are best understood as prompts to more writing—as invitations for other ex-slaves to submit their stories and further democratize the literary labor of reparations. With some variation across different organizations, ex-slave pension associations established application processes that closely resembled those used by the Pension Bureau to administer the claims filed by disabled veterans and their dependents. New enrollees were promised both that they would be kept informed of the bill's progress and that they would be first in line once it became law. To ensure a seamless transition, in fact, claimants submitted personal accounts of their lives under slavery, affidavits that often read like clerical revisions of the traditional slave narrative. Some ex-slave pension groups even had "I was born a slave in …" included in their preprinted application blanks (figure 1.10). In addition to their own testimony, applicants also submitted corroborating narratives from family, friends, and even physicians—the latter not because disability or a particular health status was a prerequisite for receiving a pension in Vaughan's plan, but because disabled claimants would be entitled to higher levels of pay. Dossiers thus compiled, it was hoped, would become the basis for as many successful pension claims once the pension bill became law. In the meantime, these claims served as proof of the movement's strength and legitimacy. It was perhaps to underscore this point that many ex-slave

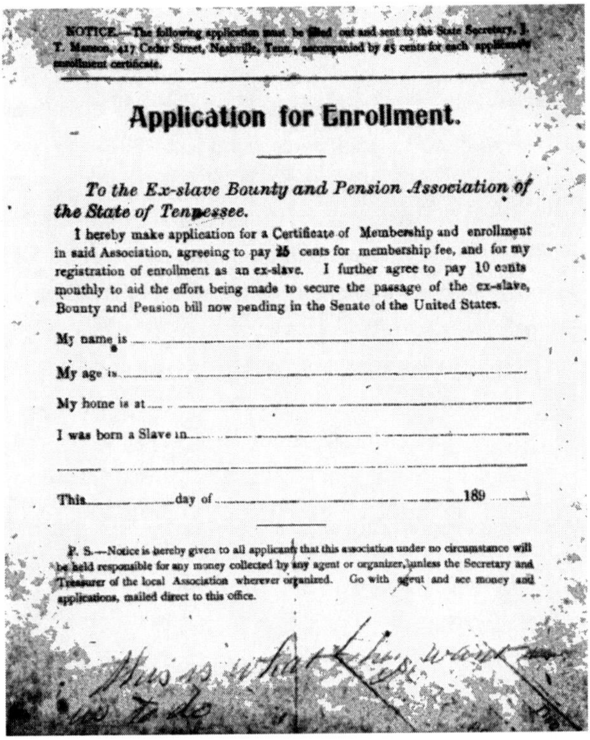

NOTICE.—The following application must be filled out and sent to the State Secretary, J. T. Manson, 417 Cedar Street, Nashville, Tenn., accompanied by 25 cents for each applicant's enrollment certificate.

Application for Enrollment.

To the Ex-slave Bounty and Pension Association of the State of Tennessee.

I hereby make application for a Certificate of Membership and enrollment in said Association, agreeing to pay 25 cents for membership fee, and for my registration of enrollment as an ex-slave. I further agree to pay 10 cents monthly to aid the effort being made to secure the passage of the ex-slave, Bounty and Pension bill now pending in the Senate of the United States.

My name is ____________________

My age is ____________________

My home is at ____________________

I was born a Slave in ____________________

____

This ________ day of ____________ 189 ____

P. S.—Notice is hereby given to all applicants that this association under no circumstance will be held responsible for any money collected by any agent or organizer, unless the Secretary and Treasurer of the local Association wherever organized. Go with agent and see money and applications, mailed direct to this office.

1.10 An application for enrollment in the Ex-Slave Petitioner's Assembly, a Black-run organization modeled on Vaughan's Ex-Slave National Pension Club Association. National Archives, Washington, DC.

organizations staged a "great show" of "making out and carrying away full records of the ex-slaves."[69]

The disdain and mistrust that ex-slave activists anticipated proved inevitable. In time, the entire movement was reputed to be a scam perpetrated by treacherous "agents" on their vulnerable brethren. Anyone claiming to represent a national organization could, of course, pocket enrollment fees and dues before skipping town. And because the chances of Vaughan's bill passing were slim, hucksters had good reason to believe they would never be caught. Thus, stories of fly-by-night confidence men abound, as do reports of deceitful orators passing themselves off as representatives of reputable ex-slave organizations or the Pension Bureau itself. As with Civil War pensions, there is no way of knowing the real extent of the fraud committed. But ex-slave pension organizations fell into disrepute nonetheless. In popular culture, the movement was satirized with songs like "'Jes' Hurry Up De Penshun': The Old Time Darkey's Appeal for a Pension" (1903), which restages the activists' demands for reparations in the farcical realm of play (figure 1.11).[70] Nor was the Black press any less dubious of the ex-slave pension movement, though its criticism was more measured on the whole. Until Vaughan's bill became law, a chorus of voices argued, Black organizations that collected dues, compiled dossiers, and presented themselves as friends of the ex-slave only worsened the situation of all Black Americans.[71] Clearly, the most systematic opposition to the ex-slave pension movement came from the Department of the Interior. The federal government's concerted campaign began with cease-and-desist letters and ended with broad postal bans and prison sentences for both Dickerson and House.[72] The Department of the Interior justified its actions by claiming to have the interests of formerly enslaved people at heart. "While there is no objection whatever to exslaves organizing for the purpose of attempting to secure legislation believed to be advantageous to them," one of these letters reads, "it is the earnest desire of this Bureau that they shall be protected from the swindling schemes" of imposters.[73] Federal agents also sought to make informants of formerly enslaved people and solicited letters with firsthand information on the movement's goals and methods.

Ultimately, the federal government's campaign of intimidation, harassment, and censorship spelled the end of the ex-slave pension movement. When House was jailed for fraud, the prospect of achieving monetary reparations through the pension system—a possibility that once felt realistic if not probable, given previous expansions to the program—seemed but wishful thinking. The documentary record of the ex-slave pension movement is no less ephemeral. The claims that formerly enslaved people submitted to ex-slave pension organizations have unfortunately been lost, and the writings that survive remain with us primarily because they were deemed to contain potentially valuable intelligence by the Pension Bureau and the Department of the Interior. In addition to documentary records of their own surveillance operations and movement literature (job-printed pamphlets, broadsides, and forms), these agencies collected hundreds of letters written by formerly enslaved men and women to inquire about the status of Vaughan's bill. Now housed in the National Archives' Ex-Slave Pension Correspondence and Case Files, these letters remain an important resource for historians of the movement. But to mine these documents for empirical data is not only to risk reproducing the relations of power that ensured their preservation, it is also to obscure how these letter writers took their correspondence with federal agencies as an opportunity to reflect on the idea of reparations.

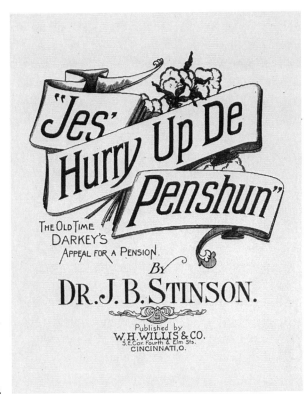

1.11 J. B. Stinson, "'Jes' Hurry Up de Penshun': The Old Time Darkey's Appeal for a Pension," 1903. Lester S. Levy Sheet Music Collection, Sheridan Libraries, Johns Hopkins University.

Indeed, while these reflections speak to the particulars of the legislative process and Pension Bureau procedures, they also engage more speculatively with the question of how reparations might be realized outside of state bureaucracy and beyond the market. In this way, the National Archives' collection of Ex-Slave Pension Correspondence and Case Files shares a great deal with the "epistolary archive" that literary scholar David Kazanjian has examined. Like the letters written by Black settler-colonists in Liberia and by Mayan rebels in Yucatan, the inquiries that formerly enslaved Americans made of the federal government are at once detailed descriptions of everyday life and "theoretical reflections on the ongoing, volatile *concrescence* of a free life."[74] But whereas Kazanjian is careful to tease out how his archive is shaped by its canny negotiation of traditional letter writing, the formerly enslaved men and women who corresponded with the federal government engaged directly with the conventions of the pension claim. To wit: although they were at base requests for information, most of these letters also pass along details of their authors' biographies and gesture at the evidence that family and friends might be able to provide. Some letters also feature lists of everyone in a given community, with information about each individual's experience under slavery. Beyond these and other generic hallmarks, however, letter writers also interrogated the social fiction at the heart of the Civil War pension claim. Their speculative reflections on reparations, in other words, rethink the relations between and among injury, writing, and compensable labor. Not just documents of surveillance or ephemeral repositories of everyday life, the vernacular pension claims made by former slaves appear as so many speculative reflections on what it means to make a claim on the state by means of writing.

Like Anderson Dillon, who addressed his correspondence with the Pension Bureau in November 1898 to President McKinley, many of these men and women wrote to inquire whether there was "any such a thing as old slaves getting anything" (figure 1.12).[75] Rumors were unavoidable in small towns, where self-identified "agents" were seen "going around and getting people to sign and spending money on that." As Dillon put his question to the president, no one knew just what to believe: "I want to know from you to be sure for if there is any one [who] could need help—I do for I am old and cannot work now and no one to help me and cripple with the rheumatism and I am 84 years old now."[76] Dillon goes on to ask about McKinley's health and to inquire if the president might have a few dollars to spare while the matter is being settled. His sentimental appeal to McKinley's conscience notwithstanding—"you are a Christian man and I know you would not suffer to know of one getting along so poor [with] you doing so well"—Dillon's letter shrewdly points out that he meets each of the yardsticks the Pension Bureau used to establish a disabled veteran's eligibility. If pensions were initially awarded on account of a claimant's physical incapacitation for manual labor and subsequently to anyone who had reached the age of sixty-two, Dillon was qualified on both counts. His inquiry also conveys a clear understanding of the role pensions played in patronage politics. "I have done all in my power to get you elected," Dillon tells the president, "and will do all I can again if I am living untill [sic] then for times is hard and I think if the democrats gets in it will be worse and I don't want to see any harder times then they are now." As with his age and disability, Dillon's political sympathies likewise made him as well suited a candidate for support as any of the hundreds of thousands already on the pension rolls.[77]

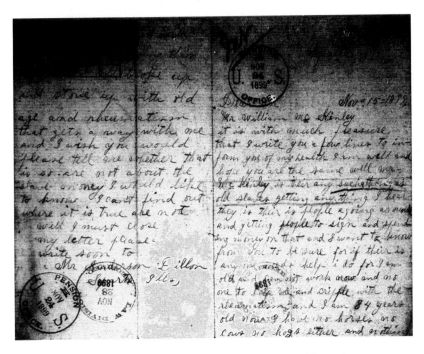

1.12 Letter from Anderson Dillon to President McKinley, November 1898. National Archives, Washington, DC.

Other letter writers, knowing that pensions were not granted to veterans whose disabilities were caused or exacerbated by "vicious habits," sought in correspondence with the government to emphasize their respectability. Such was the tack taken by Reverend T. Parker and Marry Parker in a letter of September 1899 addressed to Henry Clay Evans, US commissioner of pensions. Writing on behalf of the Ex-Slave Club of Warsaw, North Carolina, the Parkers inquired about the "bill to provide pensions for Freedmen, etc. We has been informed that there is something for us[.] If so we ask you to please identify it."[78] The members they represented were trying to live Christian lives and to keep from "disobeying the laws," the Parkers continued, but were in "a quite needful condition" and largely unable to work. The bureau responded to the Parkers that it was indeed persuaded of their club's respectability, but that it viewed respectability in this case as a sign not of deservingness but of vulnerability. Answering the Parkers' first question, a bureau official declared in no uncertain terms that "an ex-slave may not be pensioned as such, nor is there any legislation to that end now pending."[79] But this official then advised the Parkers of a dangerous person in their area, "an agent of one of these ex-slave associations" who had been recently released from prison. "His personal description is as follows: 'age, 34; height, 5 feet, 8 inches; weight, 160 lbs; well built, eye hair and complexion black. A good talker.'"[80] The nature of the bureau's obligation to respectable clients, it would thus seem, was sharply divided along the color line. White veterans received aid, whereas ex-slaves were awarded paternalist protection from criminal types masquerading as ex-slave activists, protections they hadn't asked for.

Even the men and women who corresponded with bureau officials in order to defend the ex-slave pension movement and to stake a more direct claim to federal subvention found it difficult to escape the terms of deservingness established for disabled veterans. Like Alfred Latham, many of these writers responded negatively to the government's efforts to gather information on ex-slave pension organizations from community members and to intimidate those it believed to be involved in the movement. The representatives of the Ex-Slave Petitioners' Assembly who visited his town, Latham wrote to the bureau in 1897, "induced us to come together as a race and ask this great commonwealth to grant us a pension for our past services to help us care for our old and infirm parents. I do believe it would be God's will if we could get such."[81] In appealing to divine right, Latham strikes a far more defiant note than many of the ex-slave authors who addressed themselves to representatives of the federal government. But here as well the argument for pensioning ex-slaves is made with reference to "past services," just as Latham dutifully notes that the money would allow him and others to care for their disabled parents. So routinized, in fact, were many of the letters ex-slaves wrote to the Pension Bureau and other governmental agencies that some seem to have been produced collaboratively. Letters from Margaret Thompson and Synthia Shelby addressed to the Pension Bureau on December 21, 1897, for example, report hearing that "they were speaking of giving the old slaves so much money to help them along for we are getting along in age." Each woman then records her own age, notes that "I thought that I would write to see if it was so," and closes with a prayer: "I hope that the blessing of God will abide with you all hence forth and forever. Amen."[82]

Many ex-slaves who inquired about the fate of Vaughan's bill thus told stories about themselves that exemplified the eligibility criteria that the Pension Bureau established for invalid pensions—disability, old age, patronage, and respectability. Others, however, equated pensions with compensation not for injury or expropriated labor but for the work of writing itself. When R. J. Lowry wrote to the Secretary of Pensions in January 1898, what began as a simple inquiry about the status of Vaughan's bill soon became a brief on both the economic status of literary endeavor and the belated work of emancipation (figure 1.13):

> Will you be so kind as to send me the proper information as to the "Pension bill" for ex-slaves.
>
> There is a lot of persons out down South, calling themselves agents for the government, going around organizing Clubs, charging twenty-five (25) cents a head, claiming that they are authorized by the government.
>
> Now, sir, I know if there is such a thing in fact, why of course, you ought to know something about it. You know again that my people have been frauded enough since the "Emancipation" by such humbugry.
>
> Of course, I know, the old "ex-slaves" need a pension and all the help we can get, but we don't want to be frauded by "so called 'agents.'["]
>
> They claim that Congress has requested the ex-slaves to ask for it in order to obtain a bill.[83]

In what would appear a matter-of-fact request for information, Lowry emphasizes just how much he already knows. Lowry knows how the swindlers identify their marks and carry out their schemes, just as he knows who would be in charge of an ex-slave pension bill, were one on the books. Lowry, however, also suspects—in the same way he suspects that the "agents" touting new "Pension bill[s]" may not be entirely truthful—that "Emancipation" may not be the full story of Black freedom. From the vantage of more than thirty years after the end of the Civil War, in fact, "Emancipation" appears another instance of the very kind of "humbugry" perpetrated in the popular imagination by "so called 'agents.'"

For Lowry, it is ironic not only that the truth about Emancipation is disclosed by the very "agents" that the government takes for confidence men but also that these agents lay out what he sees as the clearest course of action. "Ex-slaves," Lowry reports, have "to ask for it in order to obtain a bill." Such is precisely the work Lowry undertakes in writing to the Pension Bureau. More than a request for information, his letter is an effort to rethink the compensatory logic of justice. Compensation is usually understood as a relation of exchange that requires an equivalence between two objects or practices. To compensate is literally to weigh one thing against another.[84] Lowry's vernacular pension claim, by contrast, seeks justice not as the equitable payment for work performed or debts incurred but as something which might be attained only by writing. The end of his literary

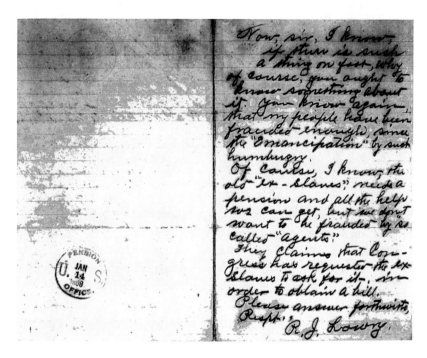

1.13   Letter from R. J. Lowry to the Secretary of Pensions, January 1898.
National Archives, Washington, DC.

endeavor is thus not—as Washington and critics of the Civil War pension
system might have charged—to exempt himself from manual labor, but
rather to attain that which can be neither created nor destroyed.

The vernacular pension claims addressed to the federal government
and preserved by the same as part of a broader campaign of surveillance,
containment, and intimidation thus elaborate a narrative transformation
that draws inspiration from but ultimately parts ways with the bureaucratic genre of the Civil War invalid pension claim. We might also say that
the vernacular pension claims written by R. J. Lowry, Anderson Dillon,
Margaret Thompson, and Synthia Shelby, among many others, literalize
the social fiction that sustains both the pension claim and the precocious
welfare state it helped to bring into being. This is not to say that the letters
of these formerly enslaved people actually transform pain into work, were
such a thing possible or even imaginable, but rather that their writing embraces the very literariness that made the pension claim so controversial.
By taking up the pen to inquire about ongoing efforts to enact reparations

by legal means, these men and women rewrite reparations as an improvisatory practice that answers the familiar humbug of Emancipation with the possibility of an unsettled future. Indeed, these speculative sorties suggest that ex-slave pensions—as a mode of reparations—may well be humbug, fraudulent in the sense of not yet true, or realizable only in the act of writing. Inhabiting the social fiction that pain is compensable only as work means putting in the literary labor necessary to think reparations beyond the market.

Contributory Fantasies

The passing of the last beneficiaries of the Civil War invalid pension system marked a turning point in military history. Soldiers injured in future conflicts would be given mandatory physical and vocational rehabilitation rather than monetary compensation. Not long after the government stopped paying out the "debt" owed to Union and (after 1924) Confederate veterans, moreover, the pension system's ad hoc role in establishing an expansive program of disability, old-age, and survivor benefits—the basis of Skocpol's "precocious" welfare state—was replaced by the systems created during the New Deal, many of which formalized the racist exclusions that were improvised on the fly by Pension Bureau agents and other intermediaries. From this vantage, the genre of the Civil War pension claim, the cause of such strife at the turn of the century, would seem but an outdated relic of an earlier generation's idea of bureaucratized social welfare provision. The cultural need met by the pension claim, however, remains as pressing as ever. Today, as in the wake of the Civil War, public benefit programs are tasked with balancing a collective obligation to help those in need with the economic, social, and moral priority of the labor market. A century and a half ago, the federal Pension Bureau relied on narrative affidavits to square this circle and thus assure an increasingly anxious public that beneficiaries had indeed earned what they received. In our own moment, the analogy of social insurance serves the same function, and nowhere more explicitly than in the disbursement of Social Security benefits.

From the 1930s onward, US public culture has tended to embrace the range of welfare programs overseen by the Social Security Administration as earned entitlements rather than public assistance. At the core of this popularity is the conviction that Social Security—an umbrella category that names a number of different initiatives—is an insurance program that only pays out to those who have paid in.[85] This conviction holds, in broad strokes, for both old-age or retirement programs and the federal cash benefit for workers who acquire long-term disabilities, Social Security Disability Insurance (SSDI). To be eligible for these benefits, claimants must meet prior work requirements, a provision designed in theory to ensure that Social Security remains solvent. Such requirements also bolster public support by ensuring that Social Security "is not a handout; it is not charity; it is not relief. It is an earned right based on the contributions and earnings of the individual."[86]

Historically speaking, however, the benefits paid out by the Social Security Administration have tended to far exceed the revenues taken in. Indeed, as Jacobus tenBroek and Floyd Matson underscore, "there is only the most casual relationship between the benefits and premiums, premiums and wages, wages and past productive activity or work; and accordingly there is little foundation for the claim of benefits as a matter of earned right."[87] But though the "whole insurance concept thus becomes only a remote analogy rather than an operative reality," it nonetheless wields enormous power in public discourse. The insurance analogy provides moral cover for certain social welfare programs while subjecting others to scrutiny, scorn, and ultimately defunding. These latter programs, generally the so-called noncontributory public assistance programs known collectively and pejoratively as welfare, are perceived as a threat to the sanctity of the market and stigmatized as such. Beneficiaries of programs such as Temporary Aid to Needy Families are viewed not as respectable citizens cashing in their retirement plans but as pathological malingerers.[88] And as a distinguished body of scholarly literature and a long history of grassroots welfare rights activism attests, this stigma has been disproportionately borne by people of color.[89] Like late nineteenth-century pension skeptics, contemporary critics of social welfare programs that fall outside the protection of the insurance analogy commonly associate blackness with shirking, laziness, and unproductivity.[90]

Against this backdrop, it is unsurprising that conservative commentators in the ongoing debate about slave reparations argue that "black people have already received billions of dollars of aid through welfare and poverty programs."[91] These arguments not only wish away ongoing histories of anti-Black violence, systemic racism, and white supremacy, but they also stigmatize the very idea of reparations by casting it as a noncontributory public assistance program. From this vantage, the strategic use that the postbellum ex-slave pension movement made of the Civil War invalid pension claim seems more relevant than ever. That bureaucratic genre, like the contemporary social insurance analogy, allowed ex-slave activists to suggest that they were seeking no more than what they had earned. In likening the injuries of slavery to those of war, members of the ex-slave pension movement argued that they had met the prior work requirement—and already paid into the system. By the same token, though, inhabiting the narrative instability of the pension claim allowed formerly enslaved people to rethink the social fiction whereby pain and suffering become recognized as compensable labor. Rather than using this social fiction as ideological cover for a mode of social welfare that threatened to run afoul of the market, these writers embraced the equivocal literary labor of the pension claim to contest the nature of compensation itself.

writing as a means of dignified labor "

2
THE BEGGAR'S CASE

As we saw in chapter 1, opponents of the Civil War invalid pension system drew a bright line between veterans who received federal benefits and those who rejoined the labor force. But it should not surprise us that these distinctions were hardly cut and dried, or that pensioned veterans often worked. Many veterans, especially those with lower disability ratings, had trouble making ends meet with their pensions alone. Getting by was especially difficult immediately after the war, when benefits were in fact rather modest. It was only after years of lobbying that rates of pay rose to the lavish levels that enraged pension skeptics. Consequently, many disabled veterans returned to the jobs they held before the war. Others discovered they could neither live on their benefits nor find work for which they were suited. To top off their pensions, many of these latter appealed not to the state but to strangers. On streets across the nation, they were joined by comrades whose claims had been outright rejected, but also by people thrust out of the labor force for any number of reasons during the decades of economic tumult that followed the Civil War.

A conspicuous presence in public life, these "beggars" were often regarded as lazy, deceitful, and worse, even by those who gave them money.[1] Many street operators no doubt shrugged off these insults and attacks, seeing pity and disgust as two sides of the same coin. Others, though, insisted that they were working—not as manual laborers but as writers. As Susan M. Schweik and Ann Fabian have shown, in the postbellum era poor people commonly solicited donations in return for broadsides, handbills, or whole books of their own composition (figure 2.1).[2] "Mendicant literature" did not originate in the late nineteenth century, of course. But the rise of inexpensive job printing made it easier than ever for people without means to bring their writing before the public. As Schweik notes, mendicant literature of the era runs the gamut from brief lyric poems to multivolume prose narratives.[3] Ultimately, though, the genre was defined less by a given set of formal conventions than by how these ephemeral texts were used—namely, to "transform" begging into work. Where mendicancy was outlawed or unwelcome, poor and disabled people could point to their writing as a visible means of support and perhaps avoid arrest or violence. Where begging was tolerated, mendicant literature fundamentally changed the nature of the charitable exchange along similar lines. What might otherwise appear a pathos-laden encounter between donor and supplicant became an economic transaction between buyer and seller. That this transformation was never complete or entirely persuasive only added to its appeal. Rapt but circumspect donors could convince themselves they were paying for someone else's labor while luxuriating in romantic fantasies of selfless compassion. And even the mendicant writers most seriously committed to their craft knew what they stood to gain by keeping up sentimental appearances: steady business.

In the annals of literary history, mendicant writing often appears as a colorful footnote to more canonical developments or a transgressive inspiration for better-known writers.[4] Thanks in large part to Schweik's research, the genre is now recognized as a crucial archive of vernacular disability culture. But the sleight of hand with which turn-of-the-century mendicant writers transformed begging into work also finds an unlikely parallel in the era's changing attitudes toward charitable and philanthropic giving. For much of US history, charity was seen as a necessary evil. Even when guided by the best of intentions and the noblest of sympathies, a common refrain went, charity too easily fosters idleness, the root cause of pauperism. Better to let the poor learn the value of self-reliance, no matter the hardships they might encounter along the way, than to subsidize their moral failures. This diagnosis remained persuasive well into the postbellum period (and continues to find traction today). But if in previous eras outrage over indiscriminate almsgiving led to forceful (if soon forgotten) calls for self-restraint, in the latter half of the nineteenth century reformers set out to purge charity of its emotional charge once and for all. To do so, advocates of so-called scientific charity endeavored to shift the scene of charitable exchange from the street to the page, thus replacing the vexed immediacy of personal encounter with the rational mediation of the document.[5] Though manipulative beggars and reckless pedestrians

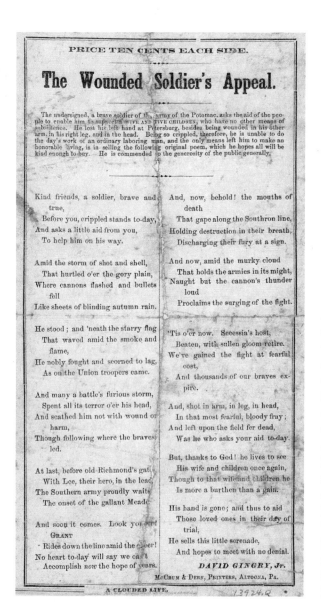

2.1 "Being so crippled, ... he is unable to do the day's work of an ordinary laboring man, and the only means left to him to make an honorable living, is in selling the following original poem." David Gingry Jr., "The Wounded Soldier's Appeal," 1865. Library Company of Philadelphia.

might indulge in the pleasures of arbitrary giving, charity workers prided themselves on being white-collar professionals. Perhaps unsurprisingly, reformers oversold the novelty of scientific charity and the strength of their own resolve. But they also overlooked how much their methods shared with the practices and people they aimed to police. In becoming scientific, modern charity took a page out of the mendicant writer's book.

To be sure, scientific charity's genre of choice was not mendicant literature. The movement turned instead to the novel mode of bureaucratic documentation and evaluation that would come to be known as social casework. As practiced today by social workers, case managers, and many others, social casework encompasses a variety of methods and goals. But as a "little tool" of professionalization in the late nineteenth century, social casework served a narrower purpose: ensuring that decisions about giving money to a particular individual (or cause) were rooted in objective facts and not gut feelings.[6] Doing so meant at base affirming the incommensurability of work and emotion, a touchstone for the emergent regime of bureaucratic rationality but also for older ideologies of gender and sexuality. Bureaucracy, as Max Weber observed, requires "the successful exclusion of love, hate, and all purely personal, irrational, and emotional elements to which calculation is alien, from the process of discharging official business."[7] In order to assert their professional bona fides, charity workers thus had to hold the vagaries of emotion at bay. But making the business of charity official also meant rejecting the field's historical association with women and the feminized excesses of pity and compassion. Armed with the protocols of social casework, charity workers—men and women alike—would subject poverty and social need to the rational (and hence masculine) intervention of bureaucratic documentation. Only then could charity work become work.

Formally speaking, social casework at the turn of the century was a peculiar and peculiarly collaborative exercise in life writing. Compiled from documents and records composed by both charity workers and charity seekers—the people whose lives were to be rationally parsed and committed to the page—casework belongs to the longer cultural genealogy that contemporary scholars often theorize simply as "the case." Etymologically speaking, *case* derives from the Latin word *casus* and the Middle English *cas*, meaning a fall, as in something that befalls someone.[8] Cases involve specific individuals and events, but they can only be understood comparatively. To say "this is a case," in other words, is to generalize. It is to say "this is a case of *that*."[9] This tension between the general and the particular defines the case (and the case study) across the disciplines. As Lauren Berlant argues, the case "hovers above the singular, the general, and the normative." It is "any irritating obstacle to clarity" that, in its call for resolution, reveals more about the "conventions for folding the singular into the general" than about the singular itself.[10] André Jolles puts the matter more concisely: the case is not a record of fact but a prompt for decision:

is this a case of that?[11] For turn-of-the-century advocates of rational charity, the question was whether someone could meet the responsibilities of economic citizenship in the future and was thus a deserving recipient of aid in the present. Crucially, answering this question meant deciding on an applicant's work ethic in order to reduce even the most singular of lives to a single word—deserving or undeserving.[12]

This theory of the case, as it were, is not hard to substantiate. One does not have to spend long in the records of the New York Charity Organization Society or the Carnegie Corporation to see how casework rewrites the messy parataxis of lived experience into prompts for objective decision making. But neither is it uncommon in the archives of scientific charity for cases to feel less than resolved or still mired in the purely personal. Especially in dossiers that incorporate a variety of materials—from first-person affidavits to transcribed interviews and field notes—casework is often a muddle of competing voices and agendas. In some instances, this cacophony stems from the difficulty of nailing down a sequence of events or verifying a set of details, the inconsistencies in one document calling for the proliferation of ever more. And yet, the casework amassed by turn-of-the-century charity workers also registers the contingent and often contradictory efforts of applicants to contest how their life stories entered the file. Many applicants challenged how casework accounts for the particular through the general, arguing, "I'm not this—I'm that." Others set out to trouble the foundational distinction that officials drew between work and emotion. Indeed, not only are tales of misfortune and woe hardly uncommon in the case files of scientific charity, but these stories often interrogate the cultural work of emotion and its relation to writing. Charity workers, this history of generic reckoning and reclamation makes clear, were not alone in borrowing from mendicant writers at the turn of the twentieth century. Charity seekers did as well.

This chapter explores how the rationalization of private giving at the turn of the twentieth century produced a counterarchive of the case rooted in vernacular disability culture. Focusing on the philanthropic funding of Black industrial education, my own case studies are drawn from the files of the Rockefeller-backed General Education Board (GEB), one of several corporate philanthropies that came to dominate the educational landscape of the rural South after the Civil War. Committed to the large-scale implementation of scientific charity, the GEB joined a wave of Northern philanthropy that sought to reconcile the reformist aspirations of elite whites in the North with the white supremacy of the New South. Instead of following their hearts, as sentimental abolitionists had a generation earlier, Northern reformers were to be guided by data. Only verifiably deserving Black schools would be funded—that is, those that adopted orthodox industrial curricula and could demonstrate their commitment to churning out well-disciplined workers unlikely to upset the delicate racial balance of the New South. The GEB and other philanthropic outfits relied on meticulous casework, record keeping, and investigation to hold up their end of the bargain. Black industrial schools played no less important a role. Teachers, administrators, and even students worked in a variety of print genres to transform their schools and even themselves into cases. But this ephemeral archive of (institutional) self-representation also pushed back against the conventions of social casework—not least of all against the rigid distinction the genre was meant to preserve between emotion and work.

The story told here thus builds on the history recounted in chapter 1, broadening our sense of the print culture of social welfare by turning from public provision to private giving.[13] The invalid pension claim mediated between individuals and the "precocious welfare state" of the post–Civil War era, and social casework played a similar role in the evolution of charitable and philanthropic practice.[14] To sketch out this story, I draw on a rich body of interdisciplinary scholarship that traces how scientific charity paved the way for foundation philanthropy and, more recently, the evidence-based project of effective altruism.[15] In focusing less on legal or social history, however, than on the documentary genre of social casework, this chapter ultimately asks how people caught in the clerical networks of scientific charity negotiated an ideological truism equally binding on either side of the public/private divide: only those who work or are willing to work deserve help. The ephemeral traces of these negotiations reveal that the disciplinary ambitions of charitable and philanthropic institutions did not go uncontested, least of all by Black educators who found themselves beholden to Northern capital. Indeed, the textual record of scientific charity represents a forgotten repository of African American print culture and Black disability writing, an archive in which advocating for oneself also meant interrogating how and why causes become legible only as cases.

In this regard, the vernacular history of the case sketched out here also speaks to efforts across the disciplines to reimagine the relation between work and emotion. From feminist reclamations of "the unfinished business of sentimentality" to labor histories of the freak show in disability studies and generative elaborations of Afro-pessimism, Black optimism, and "wake work" in Black studies—across a range of critical traditions, scholars have begun to rethink what work emotion can do and how it might bring about structural, even utopian, change.[16] At first glance, the circulation of social casework in the print culture of social history—and especially in the philanthropic funding of Black industrial education—might seem decidedly less ambitious. Given the asymmetrical power relations at the heart of the charitable enterprise, after all, even the most dissident reappropriations of social casework usually aim less at escaping than at gaming the system. And yet, the counterarchive of the case explored in this chapter, particularly in its relation to the genre of mendicant literature, may point these ongoing conversations about the "cultural work of emotion" in a new direction.[17] The question to ask is perhaps not only how emotion can become genuinely productive, but rather how we can accord emotion social value or even social utility without putting it to work.

The Science of Begging

To grasp the idea of social casework, we might imagine laying hold of an individual applicant's dossier. Pressed between thumb and forefinger, the feel of the outermost folder—of heavier stock than the files within—augurs a sense of resolution. It is a tactile reassurance that all relevant details have been gathered, but also that these details matter only because they can be generalized into a clerical directive: this or that pile. Indeed, our folder first becomes a case not when we press it closed but when we place it atop others. We have the sense, moreover, that no emotion was involved in this operation, as if the decision had been taken out of our hands entirely. It is a matter not of intuition, that is, much less compassion, but a rote and almost automatic following-through after a rational process of elimination has run its course. By the same token, we also have a feeling of accomplishment. Coming to a decision on this or that case is evidence of productivity—or work having been done. This thought experiment, of course, bears all the hallmarks of wishful thinking. The case is defined, after all, as much by the nagging detail that can't quite be ignored as by the promise of abstract clarity. And try though we might to follow bureaucratic best practices, depending on what exactly is in the folder we would will into a case, there is nothing to say that we haven't actually been following our sympathies or even our desires all along.

The case, in all of its ambivalence and irresolution, first became part of US social welfare practice in the charity organization society (COS) movement, which popularized the paradigm of scientific charity. Founded in England in 1869 and soon spreading from Buffalo, New York, to hundreds of US cities, the COS movement pledged to eliminate "indiscriminate almsgiving" of any kind.[18] Charged encounters between beggars and pedestrians were to be made a thing of the past, as was the aid arbitrarily given by civic and religious groups. Most donors, COS officials conceded, were inspired by pity and benevolence. But behind such sympathy was a desire for emotional gratification that was too easily sated and brought little genuine benefit to those in need. "Relief is easy to give," reformers argued. "Permanent improvement is slow and hard."[19] Charity organization societies thus aimed to create an objective bulwark against the sentimental status quo, not by disbursing funds of their own but by coordinating resources among various benevolent societies and donors—and ensuring that generosity was balanced with self-help. The latter almost always took precedence over the former. Not only did COS agents pride themselves on giving the poor only what they earned, but in returning clients to work they hoped to end the need for charity in the first place. For this to happen, wealthy Americans would have to follow the "well defined principles" of scientific charity and give with their heads rather than with their hearts.[20] Charity seekers would have to learn that "honest employment, the work that God gives every man to do, is the truest basis of relief."[21]

The novel rhetoric of scientific charity notwithstanding, the COS movement initially shared a great deal with earlier benevolent traditions.[22] When the first charity organization societies opened in the 1880s, in fact, investigations were carried out not by credentialed specialists but by socially minded middle-class women who volunteered to go "friendly-visiting" among the poor. These amateur agents collected information and conducted interviews, but their chief task was to lead by example and teach poor people the habits of middle-class respectability. These practices were rooted in the assumption that poverty was a moral failing and could best be remedied by contact with one's "social betters."[23] By century's end, more dynamic and less moralistic ideas of social need came to prominence. As a result, charity workers gradually began to professionalize.[24] Crucial to this process was the formalization of the ad hoc methods of friendly visiting into a specialized and exhaustive regime of investigation and record keeping. Indeed, municipal organizations aimed to compile files on anyone who applied for assistance from any organization in the city.[25] The information collected was to be filed in "registration bureaus" that were available to both private donors and charitable organizations to consult when evaluating new applicants. When COS agents were asked about someone who did not yet have a dossier, in many cases a "special examination" would even be launched on the spot to fill the gap.[26]

No one played a more important role in professionalizing the investigatory work of scientific charity than Mary Richmond, with whom the term *social casework* originates. In her writing and from posts at the Philadelphia COS and the Russell Sage Foundation, Richmond standardized the training charity workers received and systematized the paperwork they produced. Social casework, Richmond maintained, was "a comprehensive method of inquiry and treatment" that began with the gathering of "social evidence." Of relevance were "all facts as to personal or family history which, taken together, indicate the nature of a given client's social difficulties and the means to their solution."[27] These facts often came directly from clients themselves, whether in the interview process or in personal letters and affidavits. After compiling these materials, charity workers consulted with the COS board to determine the right "social diagnosis" and create an appropriate plan of "social treatment." The latter varied from client to client.[28] The goal, however, remained the same: economic self-support. In many instances, the solutions proposed reflected the male breadwinner model, but at other times labor ideology trumped normative gender politics. As Emily K. Abel has shown, COS reformers often sought to institutionalize ill or disabled working-age men so that their wives, unburdened of their care, could join the workforce themselves.[29] The oft-remarked uniqueness of every alms seeker notwithstanding, social casework thus inevitably subordinated the details of personal history to casework's generic raison d'être—deciding whether the individual in question was willing to work.

The story of "how a crippled man became a shoemaker," as told by the Associated Charities of Atlanta, exemplifies how charity officials set out to transform personal histories into social casework. "On the first day of December, 1909, as this man walked along the street upon his crutch," he came upon "a gentleman" striding in the opposite direction. Not the pathos-laden exchange we might expect, what next happened bears out that gentleman's commitment to the ideals of scientific charity and his mistrust of traditional almsgiving. "Noting his crippled condition," the gentleman "stopped long enough to tell [the disabled pedestrian] to go to the Associated Charities."[30] This the latter did, thereby beginning the formal process of investigation, documentation, and individualized assistance that would return him to productive wage labor:

> A kindly interview brought out the facts that he was thirty years old, and had a wife and three small children. Until a year previous he had worked on a farm, when he lost his leg by an accidental gun-shot wound. Coming into town, for he could no longer support his family in the country, they were all living in one small room, rented from his wife's sister, herself a poor dressmaker. The wife worked in a factory and was earning $4.50 a week. The husband took care of the children.
>
> "Why couldn't your wife stay at home with the children, do the sewing, and let you find some light work?" He was asked.
>
> "She can't see to sew, and it makes her eyes hurt," was his reply.[31]

With the facts of the case established, the "rest of the story" unfolds as a sequence of coordinated interventions undertaken by various agents in the community. One by one, the barriers to economic participation are removed. The intervention is ultimately deemed a success, however, not only because it helps the disabled man rejoin the workforce but also because it reaffirms the economic prerogative of husbands and fathers:

> An oculist examined the wife's eyes.
>
> An optician gave her the glasses.
>
> An institution supplied temporary employment to the work at which he proved his willingness to work.
>
> Relatives cared for the children while both parents worked.
>
> A shoemaker agreed to take the man in his shop and teach him the trade.
>
> A Sunday-School class provided money equivalent to the wife's earnings so that she might care for the children while the man served his apprenticeship in the shoemaker's shop.
>
> A public hospital treated both husband and wife during temporary sickness.
>
> The same Sunday-School class guaranteed the cost of a shoemaker's outfit for the man and paid rent while he was building up a business.
>
> Numbers of individuals were found to give him work.
>
> The result has been that this man paid for his outfit and is now making three times as much as his wife formerly earned. The oldest child is in school, and has done so well that he has been advanced in his grade. In short, a hovel has been made into a prosperous home.[32]

There is certainly no reason, of course, to believe that the plan of "social treatment" created for the disabled shoemaker was as effective as this account suggests. But in its brief and evenly punctuated progress from precisely defined problem to perfectly managed solution, this succinct rendering of the shoemaker's personal history exemplifies the case method that originated with organized charity. A "kindly interview" yields a plentitude of "facts" about the client's circumstances, only the most relevant of which are recorded in the initial narrative summary. As if to illustrate visually how these details are then streamlined into a logical sequence of issues to be addressed, the list that follows is a compendium of resources identified and actions taken. The successful conclusion of this process—a "crippled" man's redemption as a productive shoemaker and a hovel "made into a prosperous home"—in turn bears out the tension between the particular and the universal that defines the case as such. The client's personal story, in other words, is reduced to the case of a potentially and then demonstrably productive citizen and male breadwinner.[33]

In practice, however, social casework was rarely this straightforward. Nor was it always objective, the efforts of Richmond and others to professionalize the field notwithstanding. Historians who work in the archives of the New York Charity Organization Society, for instance, often note that applicants regularly relied on conventional representations of misfortune and direct emotional appeals. As David Huyssen suggests, this fact may well reflect a central power imbalance. Whereas charity workers "bore the perquisites of inquiry, judgment and most importantly record keeping," applicants were left instead to their own devices and "individual powers of persuasion."[34] At times this meant stressing one's work ethic above all else. As Abel writes, charity seekers were under enormous pressure to couch their appeals in the idiom of productivity and self-reliance. At the same time, however, many also wrote and spoke (in interviews transcribed for the file) "the language of emotion and intimacy."[35] With these kinds of appeals, Abel notes, charity seekers endeavored not only to engender sympathy in the charity workers with whom they interacted but also to "[maximize] their autonomy by asserting an alternative set of values."[36] These assertions could take any number of different forms, of course, and often ask to be read between the lines. At other times, charity seekers struck out more directly against the narrative discipline of social casework. Huyssen recounts the story of a woman who stormed into the New York COS office carrying a written "Synopsis of My Life," a letter seeking vindication for the "lies" that the COS investigator had written about her "on your long Postal Cards," or the memorandum blanks used by the charity officials.[37] Whatever result this protest might have yielded, both the "Postal Cards" and the "Synopsis of My Life" they inspired were placed in the applicant's file—but further evidence to be considered in deciding on the woman's case.

The contestations that mark the fissure between casework in theory and in practice are all the more pronounced in the records compiled by early twentieth-century philanthropic foundations. Financed with the fortunes amassed during the Gilded Age and made possible by sweeping changes in federal law, the philanthropic foundation was heir to the philosophical ethos and documentary protocols of the COS movement. Indeed, Andrew Carnegie and other industrialists proudly acknowledged how the earlier assault on indiscriminate almsgiving had inspired them to approach philanthropy with the same managerial detachment that had made them rich.[38] Instead of investigating and evaluating individual charity seekers, modern philanthropic foundations set out to solve intractable social problems. But the tools they used to do so were nonetheless grounded in the casework methods first developed by charity reformers a few decades earlier. Each organization, institution, or initiative that applied for funding was rigorously investigated with an eye to determining both its operational efficiency and its potential for social utility. Even more so than applicants swept up in the rational bureaucracy of organized charity, however, the institutions that sought philanthropic foundations took on much of this documentary burden themselves. As such, the casework that documents these exchanges pushes at the genre's limits, contesting not only the terms on which foundation philanthropy sought to fold the particular into the general but also the too-fine distinction it drew between work and emotion.

As twentieth-century philanthropic foundations continued the shift to bureaucratized and rational giving inaugurated by the COS movement, they took on a range of social issues. Education was a consistent concern, especially in the South, as it had been since the end of the Civil War. Indeed, the earliest substantial philanthropic foundations in the United States were created after the war to support Southern education, on a segregated basis. The first philanthropic foundation that addressed itself solely to African American education was the John F. Slater Fund for the Education of Freedmen. Created in 1882, the Slater Fund set two lasting precedents for the philanthropic support of Black education. First, only schools with industrial (rather than classical or liberal arts) curricula were upported.[39] Second, as early as the 1890s the Slater Fund brought the businesslike methods and documentary rigor of scientific charity to bear on an altruistic project historically associated with the sentimental politics of abolitionism and, after the Civil War, dominated by Protestant efforts to "elevate the Freedmen."[40] Broad enthusiasm for the Slater Fund's methods and priorities among wealthy whites led in 1902 to the establishing of the GEB, a Rockefeller-funded trust that would gradually come to monopolize the philanthropic funding of Black education in the South.[41] The GEB administered grants of its own, but it was also an umbrella organization that oversaw smaller foundations such as the Slater Fund, the Peabody Fund, the Jeanes Foundation Negro Rural School Fund, the Phelps-Stokes Fund, and the Julius Rosenwald Fund.[42]

The foundation era of philanthropic support for Black industrial education ushered in by the GEB was at once a turning point and a natural progression for the reformist project of scientific charity. To be sure, COS reformers in the North rarely concerned themselves with the needs of Black communities. And for their part, African Americans in the South knew that applying for charity would do little good and probably a great deal of harm. White Southerners would almost certainly use these appeals to justify the race's further disfranchisement.[43] As such, foundation philanthropy was most Black Americans' first exposure to the doctrine of scientific charity, tailored though that doctrine was to the racial dynamics of the Jim Crow South. Indeed, the labor ideology and investigatory methods used to discipline would-be beggars in the North dispensed with any but the barest semblance of objectivity below the Mason-Dixon line. Instead, the economic coercion of the market was explicitly deployed to enforce the social subordination of Black Americans. Racism became scientific anew, we might say, approximating less the rigor of positivist physiology than the precision of bureaucratic rationality. Scientific charity thus ensured that the philanthropic support of Black education did not disrupt the racial politics of the postbellum South. As such, decisions made about the productivity and deservingness of particular schools were not isolated judgments. Rather, in deciding the case of any given Black industrial school, philanthropic foundations were in effect making a pronouncement on the viability of the only path of social advancement that turn-of-the-century racial capitalism could imagine for African Americans—collective progress through market-based manual labor.

The stakes were thus high for the countless Black industrial schools founded across the South toward the end of the nineteenth century, the so-called Little Tuskegees. At a minimum, qualifying for philanthropic support meant verifying that one's curriculum was thoroughly industrial, often more difficult than might be assumed.[44] Schools were also forced to negotiate the bureaucratic protocols of scientific charity. To be sure, the paperwork submitted to grantors like the GEB was only one part of a broader fundraising project that often included door-to-door campaigns in Northern cities and benefit concerts of various kinds.[45] The most common method of fundraising, however, involved printing ephemeral promotional materials, typically on the school press. These documents included fact sheets, annual reports, institutional histories, student-run newspapers, and reprinted lectures. As Laura Wexler and Allyson Nadia Field have shown, photography and film also played a crucial part in this work.[46] Across these different genres, schools sought not only to put themselves in the best possible light but also to demonstrate a mastery of the formal conventions of scientific charity. Pathos-laden appeals were to be avoided in favor of taking stock of past industriousness and future potential. Schools also adopted the cultural logic of the case by abstracting the particulars of institutional experience into a generalized portrait of deservingness. This latter strategy was not as obscure as it might sound and could be easily accomplished by returning the genre of the case to its roots in biography. Accordingly, the fundraising materials produced by Black educators and students told the story of their school's merit by recounting the personal history of a prominent representative, often the school's principal or founder.

Booker T. Washington's *Up from Slavery* exemplified this genre of (auto)biography as case; it was enormously successful in raising money for Tuskegee Institute, including an unheard-of one-time donation of $600,000 from Andrew Carnegie.[47] But *Up from Slavery* is representative for another reason as well, namely the animosity it engendered among less sympathetic members of the public for whom the fundraising that sustained Black industrial education amounted to little more than shameless begging. Washington was routinely scorned for having "never done anything except to demonstrate his skill as a beggar in raising a million dollars from Northern sentimentalists."[48] For his part, Washington seems to have greeted slander of this sort with humor. In *Up from Slavery* he even playfully refers to fundraising as "the science of what is called begging," a strange phrase that conjures both the rhetorical tricks of the mendicant's trade and the rational aspirations of charity reformers.[49] Ultimately, however, Washington left little doubt that he sided with the rigorous methods of objective investigation and documentation pioneered by COS agents and later taken up by foundation philanthropies. Nor was his allegiance in spirit only. Washington recruited members of the New York COS for Tuskegee's board and was himself a trusted adviser of the GEB. In that capacity, he offered candid assessments of schools seeking funding and made what were often make-or-break recommendations. Unlike Washington, however, many of his protégés were far less concerned about the specter of "begging" that shaped public opinion about Black fundraising. And many drew on their own experiences of disability culture and mendicant literature to transform themselves and their schools into cases.

Embodying Institutional Authorship

It is perhaps surprising that disabled writers, much less disability culture, had a hand in shaping the self-representation of Black industrial education. The "postbellum, pre-Harlem" era in African American cultural history is punctuated by forceful affirmations of the normative health and ability of the Black body intended to counter popular conceptions of Black inferiority. We need look only to the promotional materials produced at Tuskegee, however, to see how the labor ethos that industrial education shared with scientific charity created both institutional and rhetorical space for people with disabilities. A case in point is *Tuskegee and Its People* (1905), an anthology of autobiographical essays by prominent alumni commemorating the school's fifteenth anniversary. The contribution by William J. Edwards, who experienced chronic pain and impaired mobility as a result of childhood tuberculosis, is representative. In "Uplifting the Submerged Masses," Edwards describes founding Snow Hill Normal and Industrial Institute in 1894 and soberly surveys the challenges that lay ahead. He is more succinct when writing about himself. "I need not tell of the hard times and suffering that I experienced before I entered [Tuskegee]," Edwards observes. "But knowing that I was without parents and being sick most of the time, my hardships can be imagined."[50] Edwards's measured tone creates a sense of decorum and respectability; nor does he spell out what readers likely suspected—that in his youth Edwards had been a "beggar."[51] Opting instead to abstract the particulars of his history into a few lines of schematic prose, Edwards encourages readers to make the caseworker's "social diagnosis": he was an "orphaned invalid" who went on to become a productive citizen.

Such a gloss is in keeping with the bootstrap message of *Tuskegee and Its People* as a whole. But Edwards's essay did not find its earliest readership in Washington's lavish promotional volume. Rather, "Uplifting the Submerged Masses" first appeared as a cheaply printed booklet that invited sympathetic readers to tear off one of the perforated "coupons" on the last page and return it with a donation (figure 2.2). This essay was one iteration of a career-long project that found Edwards endeavoring to translate the story of Snow Hill and his own biography into the idiom of the case, while also drawing on his mendicant roots. In 1918, Edwards did publish a formal memoir titled *Twenty-Five Years in the Black Belt*. But most of his writing during the period recounted in that book appeared in forms closer to the coupon than to the codex: pamphlets, newsletters, annual reports. Across these and other genres, Edwards's practice was to redraft and recycle as the occasion required. Though careful to telegraph his mastery of the protocols of bureaucratic administration, Edwards also embraced a peculiarly embodied mode of institutional authorship in which his disability features prominently. Such a strategy would seem to flaunt the antimendicant politics of scientific charity and the ableism of Bookerite discourse but also to undercut the subordination of the particular to the general at the heart of the case. Frequent allusions to Edwards's disability, however, are not meant to draw out the specificity of his personal experience. Instead, staging the obstinacy of his body allows Edwards to redirect the emotional spectacle fostered by the mendicant exchange in order to draw attention to the material conditions of Black industrial education.

Beginning in 1899, the documentary materials produced at Snow Hill typically recount some version of the following story, quoted here from a 1908 pamphlet titled *Some Results of the Snow Hill Normal and Industrial Institute* (figure 2.3): "From 1881 to 1888 might be considered as the sick period of my life, for during this time I was of but little use to myself and nothing but a burden to others. Instead of getting better, I gradually grew worse until it was with difficulty that I could move about. I used two sticks in trying to walk. My bed during this period consisted of a few ragged quilts spread upon the floor of the cabin at night."[52] Readers who consulted *Some Results* for statistics on Snow Hill's industrial and academic performance might have been surprised to encounter a personal statement like this on the first page. But Edwards's narrative serves here less to supplant the information later provided in charts and tables than to create room for thinking about how experience is abstracted into evidence and at what cost. Edwards goes on, for instance, to describe the extraordinary

COUPONS.

Pamphlet No.   Coupon No. 12.

........................., of ...., State

of ...., sends herewith .... dollar

for the support of Snow Hill School, Snow Hill, Alabama. The

pamphlet with the remainder of the coupons has been passed on to

..............................., of...........................,

...............State.

Date.

- -

Pamphlet No.   Coupon No. 11.

........................., of ...., State

of ...., sends herewith .... dollar

for the support of Snow Hill School, Snow Hill, Alabama. The

pamphlet with the remainder of the coupons has been passed on to

..............................., of...........................,

...............State.

Date.

- -

Pamphlet No.   Coupon No. 10.

........................., of ...., State

of ...., sends herewith .... dollar

for the support of Snow Hill School, Snow Hill, Alabama. The

pamphlet with the remainder of the coupons has been passed on to

..............................., of...........................,

...............State.

Date.

- -

Pamphlet No.   Coupon No. 9.

........................., of ...., State

of ...., sends herewith .... dollar

for the support of Snow Hill School, Snow Hill, Alabama. The

pamphlet with the remainder of the coupons has been passed on to

.........,..............................., of...........................,

...............State.

Date.

2.2 Fundraising coupons distributed with Snow Hill pamphlets, ca. 1910.

effort he put into making his experience at Tuskegee appear typical. Like Martin A. Menafee, whose story we encountered in this book's introduction, Edwards struggled most in the brickyard. "It was the only work that my physical condition would not allow me to do without suffering great pain," Edwards notes, "but I did not complain. Neither did I tell anyone of my physical handicap. During my four years' stay at Tuskegee, I did not make one complaint. Nor did any teacher complain of me."[53] It is perhaps not surprising that Edwards had to pass as nondisabled at Tuskegee; the school's admissions forms declared in no uncertain terms that "cripples were under no circumstances to be admitted to the night school."[54] But in a booklet distributed among potential donors, this anecdote tells us as much about the physical hardships encountered by disabled students at Tuskegee as about the writerly challenge facing Edwards as the principal of Snow Hill. Transforming oneself into a case involves rewriting individual experiences such that they pass for results. But though Edwards suggests that his career at Tuskegee can be neatly folded into the school's narrative of steady achievement, the lingering suggestion that his experience might be irreducibly singular is not without advantage. Noting that he did not measure up to his alma mater's physical ideal also allows Edwards to intimate that Snow Hill could no longer count on financial support from the Tuskegee machine.[55] As such, the analogy between his "sick period" and Snow Hill's financial health signals Edwards's keenness to pitch his appeal further afield and to cultivate a philanthropic network of his own.[56] From this vantage, the principal's disabled body is not the liability Bookerite doctrine would suppose but rather a proliferative nexus of new connections.

Photography was also integral to Edwards's efforts to reembody institutional authorship in the era of foundation philanthropy. Like *Tuskegee and Its People* and other works of Bookerite uplift, the mailers produced at Snow Hill often include studio portraits of teachers and alumni and staged images of students at work. These photographs serve most explicitly to convey the school's respectability and its embrace of orthodox industrial education. Particularly common are before-and-after images of students, school campuses, and neighboring communities. A favorite among Bookerite educators across the South, the genre was also a staple of late nineteenth-century reform culture more broadly. From Civil War–era cartes de visite that featured Black Americans prior to and following Emancipation to the intake and graduation snapshots produced at Carlisle Indian Industrial School and similar institutions, before-and-after

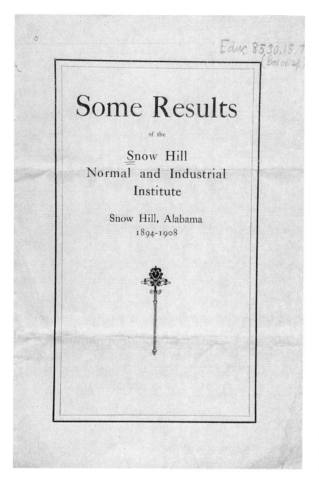

2.3 *Some Results of the Snow Hill Normal and Industrial Institute, Snow Hill, Alabama, 1894–1908* (1908).

photography harnessed the seeming self-evidence of the visual in order to make social transformations legible on the individual body.[57] Whether representing the movement from slavery to freedom, from "savagery" to "civilization," or from idle matriculant to self-supporting graduate, before-and-after images at once naturalize the identities at either pole and posit an impassible divide between them. What these images do not represent, however, is the means by which the transformation at hand was effected.[58] Viewers do not know or cannot see, that is, what exactly was done to make the before image into the after image. In the case of Black industrial schools, the absent motive force was nothing less than the work of industrial education as such. Viewers presented with photographs of entering and graduating students might well appreciate that a change has taken place. But they are left to imagine for themselves how the men and women pictured in the after column became so industrious.

The before-and-after images featured in Snow Hill fundraising materials are no exception. The paired photographs with which Edwards sought to capture the transformations his students underwent give us little sense of the actual day-to-day work they performed. In many of these publications, though, Edwards does use strategically paired images to bring his own labor as principal—above all the work of fundraising—to the fore. *Snow Hill: A Light in the Black Belt* (1907), for instance, includes before-and-after images of Edwards himself (figures 2.4–2.5): the first shows Edwards "as he appeared when he entered Tuskegee in 1888," and the second presents him as the esteemed principal of Snow Hill. At first blush, the rhetorical force of this comparison would seem to lie in the distinction it draws between the capable race man, recognizable by the sartorial trappings of middle-class respectability, and the shiftless teenager, whose ill-fitting garb of coarse material seems to bespeak a life of bare necessity. Already acquainted with Edwards's story, readers would likely have identified the young man as a beggar. This moral distinction between before and after is also shored up by the framing of each image. The oval portrait of "W.J. Edwards"—the principal identified by name rather than by the time and place of his photographing—is a study in Victorian propriety. The rectangular shape of the before image, by contrast, trades what Allan Sekula calls the "honorific" function of studio portraiture for the "repressive" function of surveillance photography.[59] Whereas the elder Edwards looks directly at the viewer, his posture calmly telegraphing self-possession, the younger man exposes as much of his face as possible to the disciplinary gaze of the camera. The resulting image resembles nothing so much as a police booking photo, as if for the crime of vagrancy or "unsightly begging." Whatever charge the viewer might imagine, the takeaway here would seem clear: Edwards before shares nothing with Edwards after.

Readers might come to a different conclusion, though, by contemplating the missing third term in this before-and-after pairing. How exactly, that is, did the unsightly beggar become the respected school principal? Given that *Snow Hill: A Light in the Black Belt* was intended to convince donors of the school's industrial bona fides, most readers would likely have assumed that the transformation here was wrought by the careful and methodical intervention of Bookerite pedagogy. But absent visual evidence of Edwards's education, we might also speculate that the distinction

2.4–2.5 Edwards before and after Tuskegee, from *Snow Hill: A Light in the Black Belt* (1907).

between Edwards before and after should be chalked up to the other mode of development implied by these images—namely, the natural progression of aging. Edwards, in other words, might have changed with the passage of time alone. A counterintuitive corollary would seem then at hand. The trappings of respectability aside, Edwards might not have been transformed in any meaningful way. Rather than document the dramatic change wrought by Bookerite education, from this vantage the paired images of Edwards bear witness to a more modest family resemblance of sorts—between the younger and the elder Edwards, to be sure, but also between the ostensibly different endeavors each pursues. If the first image invites us to imagine Edwards as a young mendicant, the second shows the revered principal making a similar if more respectable appeal. Both are ultimately engaged in the work of self-presentation. Crucially, this labor leads not to the creation of a wholly new identity but to the abstraction of the self into a form more immediately legible to the audience in question, whether pedestrians, wealthy donors, or charitable organizations.

From *Some Results* to *A Light in the Black Belt*, the fundraising materials produced at Snow Hill thus orchestrate scenes of seemingly sensational encounter to stress the labor of abstraction demanded of street mendicants and grant seekers alike in the age of scientific charity. As such, the intransigence of the body in these ephemeral documents is not an impediment to the generalizing logic of the case but a strategic means of its fulfillment. In addition to pamphlets and annual reports, printed on the school press and distributed to prospective donors, large and small, much of Edwards's writing on behalf of Snow Hill took the form of personal correspondence with individual caseworkers and bureaucrats. In these documents, typically written on school stationery and modeled loosely on the conventions of the business letter, Edwards likewise drew attention to his body. In this context, though, his interest turns to exploring the kinds of social relationships that constellate around personal narratives constructed as cases. Though the occasion for Edwards's writing was inevitably a grantor's request for information—an inquiry about Snow Hill's budget or enrollment, for instance, or its prospects for future growth—the letters he wrote to philanthropic organizations such as the GEB were usually addressed to particular caseworkers or bureaucrats and often adopted a tone of familiarity. To be sure, such formalities were in many ways par for the course, reflecting at once the deference that grantees were still expected to perform and the origins of the modern report in traditional epistolary forms.[60] For Edwards, however, blurring the individual and the institutional was not a gesture of simple politeness. It was also a means of reframing the nominally objective bureaucratic encounter as a case study in friendship.[61]

A case in point, as it were, is Edwards's decade-long correspondence with Wallace Buttrick, who became the GEB's first secretary and executive officer in 1903 and, after numerous other such roles, was appointed president in 1917. After years of limiting himself to discussing Snow Hill's financial and material needs, Edwards's letters suddenly took a strangely personal turn (figure 2.6). As if angling, in fact, for a return to the emotional encounters targeted for elimination by the COS reformers who paved the way for foundation philanthropy, Edwards started to address Buttrick as a confidant. "About twenty-two years ago," the first such letter in this vein begins, as Edwards was "partly recovering from an illness" that had left him all but "helpless to [himself] and made [him] a burden on others for seven years," he learned about an upcoming church meeting. Getting there was no small ordeal, particularly given that his neighbors did little to hide their disapproval of him. Edwards thus resolved to make his way there unseen:

> After all the other people had gone I would walk slowly behind and would wait a short distance from the church in the dark of the night until the service had begun, then I would creep up close to the rear of the church, where I could hear every word the preacher would say.... After the sermon in these country churches, the negroes usually take up as much more time in praying for sinners and collecting money, (taking up collection, it is called) as the preacher consumes in his sermon. At the beginning of this latter service, I would start on my return home getting there far in advance of those who remained until the service was closed.[62]

It was at this meeting, as he lay hidden from the scrutinizing gazes of his neighbors, that Edwards heard about Booker T. Washington for the first time. The seed was planted, Edwards suggests, and the details of his travel to Tuskegee and his subsequent academic career would work themselves out in due time. Framed in this manner, Edwards's backstory would seem predictable enough. But as communicated to a bureaucrat with whom he had corresponded for a decade without mentioning his illness, this anecdote gives pause. It is perhaps less important for the information it relays than for how it serves to disrupt philanthropic business as usual. Indeed, Edwards's unexpected recourse to the details of his childhood strain at the generic limits of the case by prompting Buttrick to reciprocate what amounts to Edwards's gesture of friendship. To be sure, Edwards and

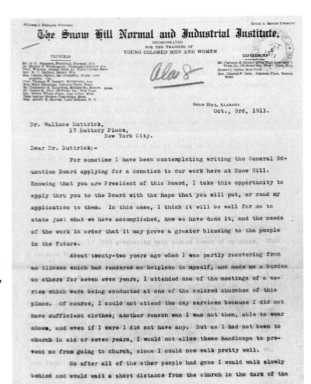

2.6 Letter from William J. Edwards to Wallace Buttrick, October 3, 1911, box 2, folder 17a, ALA 8 Snow Hill 1906–1914, General Education Board Records, Rockefeller Archive Center.

Buttrick are not friends in any conventional sense. But in strategically disclosing his disability, Edwards does give the lie to rational charity's blanket prohibition of emotion. He not only points out the obvious—that correspondents of such long acquaintance could not help but develop a mutual investment—but he also intimates that friendship itself is a case of sorts. There is to every friendship, of course, an intimate quality of the irreducibly personal and particular. But as a category of connection, friendship is nonetheless an abstract concept that some relationships fulfill and others do not. In this way, Edwards retools the conventional pathos that charity reformers likened to "indiscriminate almsgiving" by making himself into a very particular kind of case, a friend. As if repurposing, in fact, an earlier cos slogan—"Not alms but a friend"—Edwards works to convince his bureaucratic interlocutor, heir to that reformist movement, that he intends to return the favor.

Edwards's formal memoir, *Twenty-Five Years in the Black Belt*, is at once the culmination of and a departure from the earlier experiments in autobiography that fueled his fundraising on behalf of Snow Hill. Assembled largely from the pamphlets and circulars printed over the course of the prior two decades, this book recalibrates Edwards's ephemeral explorations of the tension between the particular and the general in part by blurring the lines between the informational and the aesthetic. He begins on familiar terrain, assuring readers that what follows is an objective account of an individual life that will nonetheless have much to say about the merit of the institution in question. But readers do not have to take Edwards's word; he calls on "George W. Keyser, M.D." to authorize his as a representative case: "[Edwards] had been sick for several months from scrofula and it had affected the bone of his left arm (hinneras) near the elbow joint, and the heel bone (os calcis) of his left foot. It was with much difficulty and pain that he walked at all.... The work of this pupil of Booker Washington—carried out under adverse circumstances—is worthy of emulation. He has, and is, now, doing much good work for his race."[63] The orthopedic surgeon, flaunting his Latinate vocabulary and diagnostic acumen, here replaces the abolitionist as the white authenticator of Black memoir. But Keyser's comments do more than validate the truthfulness of Edwards's autobiography. In attesting to how Edwards learned to walk, the physician also sanctions the allegorical leap that *Twenty-Five Years in the Black Belt* appears to demand. We have it on solid authority, that is, that Edwards's past achievements in the "work" of physical rehabilitation exemplify the "work" of racial uplift that Edwards advanced through the literary labor of fundraising. But exactly what kind of work does this latter autobiographical project perform? *Twenty-Five Years in the Black Belt* offers any number of answers—bring in philanthropic support, increase enrollment, and improve the output of student industries, for instance. Such, of course, are the quantitative benchmarks we would expect in any accounting of institutional efficiency. And from this vantage, Edwards's narrative of long odds and personal achievement would seem to transpose this numerical accounting of Snow Hill's circumstances into the allegorical mode of the rags-to-riches story. Much of *Twenty-Five Years in the Black Belt* is indeed dedicated to suggesting that Edwards's life story can be distilled into the facts and figures that quantify Snow Hill's institutional health.

At other moments, however, Edwards's autobiography takes a surprising turn away from such material measures of accomplishment. Instead, he explores how the authorial labor of self-abstraction demanded by foundation philanthropy might actually create a space of disinterested introspection and aesthetic experience. In one of these peculiar flights of self-reflection, Edwards describes convalescing after a particularly trying surgery: "The first few days that I was alone were the most miserable days of my life. I tried to walk, but fainted once or twice at these attempts, so I had to be contented with crawling. Soon, however, I began crawling about the yard. I found several ants' nests within about twenty or twenty-five yards of the house, and soon made friends of the ants. I would crawl from nest to nest and watch them do their work."[64] This is a striking, even strange scene. But Edwards makes it clear that he is not interested in the reader's pity. Rather than making a spectacle of himself, Edwards emphasizes his own agency as a spectator. As he crawls along the ground, Edwards watches how "the ants worked by classes," each in its own time and each with its own tasks: "One class would bring out the dirt, another would go out in search of food, another would take away the dead, another would over look those that worked, and still another class ... would come out and look around and then return."[65]

Breezy with delight, these remarks continue for the better part of a page. And in the pages that follow, Edwards describes his own experiences with the organization of labor, both on his family's farm and at Tuskegee. Readers are meant, it would seem, to extrapolate from the anthill to the industrial academy. A different allegory, however, seems in the offing if we focus on Edwards and not the scene he describes. Lying on the ground, Edwards takes no part in the efficient division of social labor playing out in front of him. Indeed, Edwards seems to be modeling the objective detachment that philanthropic officials brought to social casework. For Edwards, though, the decision at hand has less to do with work ethic than aesthetic experience. Is this performance (of labor), Edwards asks us to consider, something we like or not? This shift from bureaucratic decision making to aesthetic judgment is not as far-fetched as it might sound. The same tension between the particular and the general at the heart of the case is also crucial to conventional ideas of the aesthetic. As Kant argues, in judging a particular object to be beautiful, we are implicitly claiming that this beauty is universally apparent. Under ideal circumstances, everyone would agree that the object is beautiful and share in the aesthetic pleasure it affords.[66]

We might chalk up Edwards's turn to the aesthetic to writerly prerogative, the professional fundraiser momentarily dispensing with the bureaucratic templates to which he was usually bound. But this strange episode with the ants is also a tacit acknowledgment of how the autobiographical materials Edwards and his staff produced for donors and philanthropic foundations were read. The bureaucratic objectivity asserted by charity agents and philanthropic officials notwithstanding, Edwards underscores that these professionals also read for pleasure. To be sure, the casework compiled and assessed under the umbrella of the scientific charity did not offer the same enjoyment that one might find in a best-selling dime novel or even in mendicant literature. But nor, Edwards suggests, did these files traffic only in the maudlin pleasures of the sentimental decried by charity organizations and philanthropic foundations alike. Rather, for Edwards social casework can also foster aesthetic appreciation. It remains an open question, particularly when we turn from this peculiar episode in *Twenty-Five Years in the Black Belt* to Edwards's broader and often far more directly instrumental autobiographical project, just what kind of work appreciation does—or indeed whether it works at all.

Showing Your Work

An unflinching response to D. W. Griffith's *Birth of a Nation* (1915), Oscar Micheaux's *Within Our Gates* (1920) captures the racial violence of the post-Reconstruction era that is conspicuously absent from the portrait of Black life promoted by industrial schools like Snow Hill. Perhaps most famously, a flashback sequence at the end of Micheaux's film crosscuts the protagonist Sylvia's near rape at the hands of her biological father with the lynching of her adopted parents. For all its candor in exposing the gruesome anti-Black terror that held sway in the postbellum South, however, *Within Our Gates* shies away from representing the action that drives the film's parallel plot in the North—Sylvia's efforts to raise money for a struggling industrial school in Mississippi called Piney Woods. Not simply an oversight, the work of fundraising is purposefully obscured by means of an unlikely narrative coincidence. While in Boston about to start her rounds, Sylvia runs into the street to save a child from oncoming traffic (figures 2.7–2.12). When she is herself struck in turn, luck would have it that the owner of the car is a wealthy white woman eager to support Black industrial education. All that is left to talk about, it would appear, is the amount Mrs. Warwick would like to give to Piney Woods. This chance encounter gives pause, flagging as it does the film's reluctance to show Sylvia asking for money. To do so would evidently compromise Micheaux's investment in normative femininity and middle-class respectability. But the chain of happy events set in motion by the accident also registers an implicit skepticism about whether fundraising should count as work to begin with, a skepticism that Micheaux shared with advocates and detractors of Black industrial education alike.[67]

The historical school that may well have been the model for Micheaux's fictional academy did not harbor any such misgivings about fundraising. Nor were teachers, administrators, and even students at Piney Woods Country Life School in Braxton, Mississippi, reluctant to show the effort they put into keeping their institution—and themselves—afloat. Indeed, even more explicitly than Edwards at Snow Hill, principal Laurence C. Jones and his staff and students at Piney Woods interrogated the rational protocols of foundation philanthropy to persuade donors that fundraising was work. Whereas Edwards relied on a novel mode of institutional authorship to sharpen the blunt sensationalism of the mendicant encounter into a nimble analytic, Jones and his collaborators championed the productive value of sentimentality itself—the more mawkish the better. This they did by likening the bureaucratic genre of the case to the stock figure and the clerical work of philanthropic administration to the literary labor of abstracting complex personal narratives into broadly legible tropes of need and deservingness.

Constructing a stock figure, Jones and his collaborators argued, was as demanding as transforming one's story into a case. Both involved shifting the scene of philanthropic encounter from the street to the page in order to abstract the general from the particular and thus to pose a question to the reader: is this a case of that? Particularly in light of the role that disabled students played in this project, Piney Woods's fundraising methods were contentious from the beginning. Even before the school was designated Mississippi's sole institution for blind children of color in 1929, disabled children were integrated into both the academic and the industrial curricula.[68] Although, as we will see, many of these students played an active role in shaping how their stories were used to raise money for Piney Woods, the school nonetheless gained a certain degree of notoriety. As an officer of the Rosenwald Fund warned, "The Piney Woods people are notorious beggars" who "succeed in interesting a great many people who are simply sentimental about the Negro problem without trying to find out what will really meet his problems."[69]

Jones's fundraising venture began rather more conventionally, in much the same spirit of self-help and community-building on which the broader industrial education movement was founded. After graduating from the University of Iowa, Jones traveled to Braxton and approached the town's Black residents with the idea of founding a school.[70] The first practical

"Now that you are recovering,
can you tell me what troubles
you so?"

2.7–2.12 Oscar
Micheaux, dir.,
Within Our Gates
(1920).

step forward was a gift of forty acres provided by a former slave who had made a sizable sum in the North after the Civil War. Support then came from Black farmers and later from white business owners. With a stable cadre of local backers thus established, Jones sought funding from philanthropic organizations and donors in his native Iowa and in the North. In the tradition of Fisk University and Hampton Institute, he also sent musicians from Piney Woods on tour. In the years to come, the Cotton Blossom Singers and the International Sweethearts of Rhythm became an important source of revenue for their school and earned considerable acclaim along the way.[71] As with Snow Hill, however, most of Piney Woods's funding came from private philanthropic foundations and was of necessity procured not in person but on paper. Indeed, although Jones would recount the founding and funding of Piney Woods in two books of memoir and institutional history, *Piney Woods and Its Story* (1922) and *The Spirit of Piney Woods* (1931), like Edwards he spent most of his time writing to administrators and donors. And while Jones also took the bureaucratic conventions of scientific charity to heart, his writing—in mailers, reports, leaflets, and letters of application alike—was from the start of a decidedly more experimental nature.[72]

Much of the notoriety that Piney Woods attracted had to do with the use of photographs of and narrative by disabled students and alumni in fundraising materials. Many of these documents do indeed walk a fine line, often anticipating the worst impulses of the mid-twentieth-century telethon.[73] The scandal of Jones's methods, however, lay not only in how he ignored the foundation era's prohibition on sentiment and spectacle (at a moment when foundations and individual donors had begun to articulate their revulsion to disabled bodies as paternalist opposition to exploitation and manipulation). Rather, the sensational writings that Jones and his students produced were controversial because it was all too clear how much effort went into their production. Had these appeals seemed truly heartfelt, or been legible as unmediated bursts of emotion originating in a desperate need for compassion, they probably would not have met with such hostility. As one disillusioned donor in Boston complained, "These letters always make a very pathetic appeal—the boy is always crippled, is fatherless or motherless."[74] Less offense would be taken, it seems, if Jones and his students had not been at such pains to show their work.

Jones's earliest efforts to create stock figures representative of Piney Woods's deservingness did not directly involve students. After first struggling to transform himself into a case, as Edwards had done for Snow

Hill, Jones turned to a series of other surrogate figures on campus, beginning with the white women who taught at the school (figure 2.13).[75] These women were typically presented as sentimental figures of self-sacrifice and vulnerability, as in the mailer printed after a fire in 1921 that ruined the "largest and best building of the Piney Woods School," the boys' dormitory. The headline of this circular draws attention neither to the boys nor to their dormitory: "DISASTROUS FIRE / PINEY WOODS COUNTRY LIFE SCHOOL; TWO NORTHERN WHITE TEACHERS IN BURNED BUILDING."[76] Readers do learn that two Black students were in the building as well, but Jones evidently assumed that the danger they faced would speak less directly to donors. Jones likewise sought to instrumentalize the school's white teachers under less dramatic circumstances as well. These women were also called on to write to the school's most ardent supporters or to loan their likenesses to various fundraising mailers. In 1918, for example, Nellie T. Brooks wrote to a select group of donors "whose hearts [she] believed would cause them to respond favorably" to the story of how she "gave a year of her life" to further the work being done at Piney Woods. This letter, of course, draws on the familiar conventions by which white women could powerfully represent the vulnerability and deservingness of others. But as reprinted by Piney Woods students in a circular destined for wider distribution, Brooks's missive also became part of a fundraising agenda that showcased the labor involved in the creation of such a deliberately emotive persona. In this document, a studio portrait of Brooks appears adjacent to a photograph of the students she led in a "Class in Patriotism." A collaborative statement captions this latter image: "This Letter Head was Designed and Printed by the Boys and Girls of The Piney Woods Country Life School ... in order that the lady whose picture appears hereon, and who came from up North, can help us get an education by interesting others." The students seem to propose Brooks as an appropriate emblem of their school's accomplishments and needs. But they also make it clear that theirs was the effort that went into producing Brooks as a conventionally sentimental sign.

The literary labor of Piney Woods students is also showcased in a circular titled "Broadcasting Their Smiles to You" (figure 2.14). In this single-page form letter, Jones draws on the visual logic of before and after to represent the transformative power of industrial education at Piney Woods. If the disabled students pictured at the top of the page inhabit the rhetorical before, the posture of the Piney Woods alumnus whose image appears at the bottom clearly marks the rhetorical after. With an extended

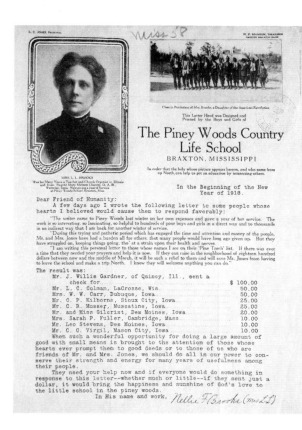

2.13 Promotional mailer distributed by Piney Woods Country Life School, February 1918, box 96, folder 863, Miss 58 Piney Woods School, 1909–30, General Education Board Records, Rockefeller Archive Center.

left leg figuratively accentuating his moral uprightness, Charles M. Shed embodies the past achievements and future promise of Piney Woods. But even as Shed offers a visual counterpoint to "those nine boys above," the comparison ultimately has less to do with the spectacular transformation of unsightly bodies than with the pursuit of employment for disabled students.[77] "Broadcasting Their Smiles to You" is remarkable, in fact, for the ordinariness of its ambition. Disabled students evidently shared the same goals harbored by all students at Piney Woods—to become "useful citizens." And even though Piney Woods was not officially a normal school, like Shed, many of its alumni did go on to become teachers. The transformation imagined here is thus not from disabled student to nondisabled worker but from disabled student to disabled teacher. And as a stand-in for Jones, Shed also embodies the primary duty of the Bookerite administrator: fundraising. The most evident sign of Shed's accomplishment, in other words, is that he orchestrates the rhetorical transformation of personal

2.14 Promotional mailer distributed by Piney Woods Country Life School, February 1918, box 96, folder 863, Miss 58 Piney Woods School, 1909–1930, General Education Board Records, Rockefeller Archive Center.

narrative into case history while also underscoring the productive labor involved in creating a stock sentimental caricature. The "nine boys above" also play their part in this orchestration. The brief descriptions beneath each student's name serve less to mark their bodies as aberrant than to stress their active involvement in the work of fundraising. Indeed, students' poses cut against the cheerful passivity promised by the document's title. Instead of having their smiles broadcast to readers, the students telegraph self-confidence and attentive readiness. Nor are the students exactly smiling, for that matter. These knowing looks communicate not helplessness but pride in the work of the student aid department.

It is precisely the work of fundraising so understood that Dean Carter, one of the nine students pictured here, stressed in the letters he wrote to

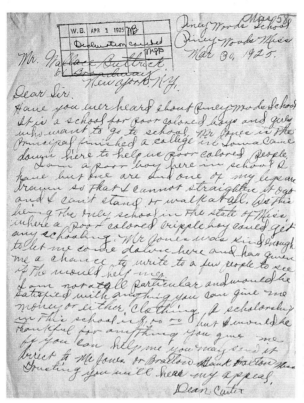

2.15 Letter from Dean Carter to Wallace Buttrick, March 30, 1925, box 96, folder 863, Miss 58 Piney Woods School, 1909–1930, General Education Board Records, Rockefeller Archive Center.

philanthropic individuals and organizations asking for donations to fund his scholarship. Carter addressed one of these letters to Wallace Buttrick, William J. Edwards's longtime interlocutor, who had in the years since been promoted to president of the GEB. The first of these letters opens gently, in a familiar tone, by asking whether he has heard of Piney Woods (figure 2.15). After then glossing the school's history and educational philosophy, Carter describes his own body: "I am a poor boy here in school. I have but one arm and one of my legs are broken so that I cannot straighten out and I can't stand or walk at all. As this being the only school in the state of Mississippi where a poor cripple boy could get any schooling, Mr. Jones was kind enough to let me come down here and has given me a chance to write to a few people to see if they would help me."[78] The analogy Carter draws between his body and financial need is clear. Carter, however, also specifies that he wrote these letters not as a favor to Jones or out of goodwill to the school but to earn his tuition fees, just as other students did in the industrial or agricultural departments. If Carter thus seems to embrace the popular begging letter and to transform himself into a stock sentimental figure, he also stresses the labor involved in doing so. As such, his literary practice productively confuses the sentimental caricature with rational case study by insisting that he has in fact earned the money he is requesting.[79]

The decades-long process through which Jones and his students perfected this balancing act finds its zenith in an unlikely mailer created in 1938 with the title "Abraham Lincoln and the Colored Man with One Leg" (figure 2.16). As if to substantiate the apocryphal lore that provided its conceit, this single-page leaflet also includes a mimeographed rendering of the check Lincoln made out to "colored man with one leg or bearer" in 1863. Now held by PNC Bank, the check was in private collections and out of circulation for most of the early twentieth century. Photographic reproductions, however, were hardly scarce. Readers of *Collier's* could in 1907 buy a "Fac-simile of Lincoln's check, payable to 'colored man with one leg'" for ten cents.[80] The check also appeared in later editions of Ida M. Tarbell's popular *Life of Lincoln*, which was first published in 1900. For Tarbell, Lincoln's kindness to the unnamed Black man was further evidence of the president's famed generosity, a story to echo the tales of compassion she recounts in an extensive chapter called "Lincoln and the Soldiers." There we read about the "scores of cases where [Lincoln] interfered personally to secure some favor or right for a soldier," whether for the ailing "Pittsburgh boy" seeking furlough or for the "crippled soldier" the president met outside of the White House. Lincoln assured the latter that he "used to practice law in a small way" and helped the veteran apply for a pension "at the foot of a convenient tree." Lincoln's encounter with the "colored man with one leg" also took place near the tree, and it is likewise a story of simple sympathy: "One day as he crossed the park he was stopped by a negro who told him a pitiful story. The President wrote him out a check for five dollars" (figure 2.17).[81]

As reprinted at the top of a fundraising circular seventy years later, the "Facsimile of [the] check given in charity by Abraham Lincoln to a colored man with one leg" would seem intended to produce much the same compassion for Piney Woods. But the mimeographed image cannot help but emphasize the difference between then and now—between the Black amputee's seemingly spontaneous appeal and Jones's mechanical form letter. The faded reproduction likewise suggests that the charitable exchange it honors may have fallen short of the sentimental ideal it seems

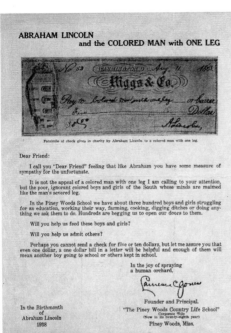

ABRAHAM LINCOLN
and the COLORED MAN with ONE LEG

Facsimile of check given in charity by Abraham Lincoln to a colored man with one leg.

Dear Friend:

I call you "Dear Friend" feeling that like Abraham you have some measure of sympathy for the unfortunate.

It is not the appeal of a colored man with one leg I am calling to your attention, but the poor, ignorant colored boys and girls of the South whose minds are maimed like the man's severed leg.

In the Piney Woods School we have about three hundred boys and girls struggling for an education, working their way, farming, cooking, digging ditches or doing anything we ask them to do. Hundreds are begging us to open our doors to them.

Will you help us feed these boys and girls?

Will you help us admit others?

Perhaps you cannot send a check for five or ten dollars, but let me assure you that even one dollar, a one dollar bill in a letter will be helpful and enough of them will mean another boy going to school or others kept in school.

In the joy of spraying
a human orchard,

Laurence C Jones

Founder and Principal.

In the Birthmonth
of
Abraham Lincoln
1938

"The Piney Woods Country Life School"
Corporate Title
(Now in its twenty-eighth year)
Piney Woods, Miss.

2.16 Promotional mailer produced by the Piney Woods Country Life School, 1938. Abraham Lincoln Presidential Library.

2.17 Lincoln offering to complete the paperwork for a Union veteran's pension claim. Ida M. Tarbell, *The Life of Abraham Lincoln* (1900).

to epitomize. As historians and humorists of the day were eager to point out, Lincoln made his check out to a type rather than to a person. One commentator noted, for instance, that Lincoln's phrase would have been "sufficient identification for the most careful teller at the meticulous Riggs Bank."[82] Although clearly pejorative, such invocations of minstrel typology nonetheless underscore the work performed by the Black amputee in becoming the "colored man with one leg." In Tarbell's account, in fact, this labor of self-fashioning distinguishes Lincoln's Black interlocutor from the white soldiers. Whereas the president instantly recognizes the white soldier's deservingness, the Black amputee must tell a "pitiful story" to win Lincoln's sympathy.[83] The "colored man with one leg" has no part of the effortless sentimentality that marks the president's exchanges with the white soldiers. The latter are the passive beneficiaries of Lincoln's fellow feeling, whereas the former earns what the president gives. From this vantage, "Abraham Lincoln and the Colored Man with One Leg" cites less an exemplary instance of sentimental identification than a knowing performance of deservingness that for Jones makes the work of fundraising socially legible as labor.[84]

Recognizing that Jones reproduces Lincoln's check in order to represent fundraising as labor helps us understand what is ultimately the governing conceit of "Abraham Lincoln and the Colored Man with One Leg" and Piney Woods's basic fundraising strategy. As Jones clarifies, "It is not the appeal of a colored man with one leg I am calling to your attention, but the poor, ignorant colored boys and girls of the South whose minds are maimed like the man's severed leg." On its face, this analogy would seem but a tendentious likening of physical disability to the economic and educational injustices of Jim Crow. But how exactly are the figuratively maimed students "like" the "colored man with one leg"? If we bracket the obvious spectacle of injury, it seems clear that both model the cultural conventions of deservingness even as they also show their work. Indeed, the students who transform themselves into sentimental objects are "working their way, farming, cooking, [and] digging ditches." The analogy drawn between the students of Piney Woods and the "colored man with one leg" is thus a comparison between what only appear to be disparate forms of labor—fundraising and the "actual" work performed at the school. In this way, "Abraham Lincoln and the Colored Man with One Leg" is the culmination of a history of formal experimentation defined above all by a strategy of both-and that encompassed mendicant practice as well as scientific charity: at once modeling sentimental conventions and attempting to demonstrate that these performances constitute a form of labor in keeping with the ideals of industrial education. If William J. Edwards negotiated this apparent contradiction by inhabiting the tension between the particular and general that defines the genre of the case, Jones and his students took inspiration from the "colored man with one leg" in underscoring the productive labor involved in creating stock figures that, in the end, were also cases.

The Poetics of the Case

The efforts of Edwards, Jones, and their students at Snow Hill and Piney Woods to repurpose the genre of social casework find an unlikely parallel in modern and contemporary documentary poetry. Whether by selective editing, paratactic rearrangement, or caustic fragmentation, this body of writing seeks to wrest new meaning and fraught intimacies from putatively objective and obviously coercive archives of all kinds. An important early touchstone is Charles Reznikoff's _Testimony_ (1934), which reworks turn-of-the-century legal cases into a harrowing meditation on systemic violence. A similar commitment to disrupting the authority of the law informs M. NourbeSe Philip's _Zong!_ (2008), a work at the center of recent conversations about poetry, affect, and the archive. In this book of "fugal antinarrative," Philip examines the paper trail created when the owners of an eighteenth-century slave ship filed an insurance claim for 150 Africans murdered en route to Jamaica. The poem attends to what the archive conveys and how, as Philip writes, but also to what it leaves unsaid and renders unsayable.

> My intent is to use the text of the legal decision as a word store; to lock myself into this particular and peculiar discursive landscape in the belief that the story of these African men, women, and children thrown overboard in an attempt to collect insurance monies, the story that can only be told by not telling, is locked in this text. In the many silences within the Silence of the text. I would lock myself in this text in the same way men, women, and children were locked in the holds of the slave ship _Zong_.[85]

Philip's task is twofold. In addition to dismantling the dehumanizing language of the case, _Zong!_ seeks to "conjur[e] the presence of excised Africans."[86] The poet is "both censor and magician," the poem an act of demolition and revelation. As such, we might also say that _Zong!_ combines documentary poetry's attention to the syntax of facticity with the recovery project that scholars have begun to associate with the genre of outsider writing. Building on the robust theorization of outsider art in visual studies, literary critics such as John Wilkinson use this neologism to collate a wide variety of work by variously marginalized, excluded, and institutionalized writers.[87] As the subgenre of prison literature makes clear, outsider writing is often shaped by particular discourses and practices of social discipline. But unlike documentary poetry, which begins with the textual substrate of institutional violence, outsider writing is an act of self-conscious representation first and foremost. It emerges in spite of the historical record, not because of it. Insofar, then, as documentary poems like *Zong!* seek to amplify the voices that history has silenced, they could well be called outsider writing. But given this literature's insistent recourse to the violence and absence at the heart of the archive, this ethos of recovery is inevitably the inverse of an often more forceful commitment to *"break[ing] the words open."*[88]

The line between documentary poetry and outsider writing that *Zong!* both brightens and blurs is also useful in understanding how the genre of the case circulated in the print culture of social welfare at the turn of the twentieth century. Indeed, asking how social casework shifted the scene of philanthropic exchange from the street to the page confronts us with a question as familiar to poets and literary critics as to social historians: how do we read in the archive? Where the ideology and institutions of scientific charity hold sway, it is clear that many applicants found no opportunity for self-expression in the protocols used to rewrite their lives as cases. Our approach to these materials might thus resemble that of the documentary poet: we trace the patterns of narrative, syntactical, and formal restraint that sustain asymmetrical relations of power in the hopes of chancing upon a break in the case, as it were—not a clue that reveals the truth of a given life but a crack in the iron cage of bureaucratic rationality that allows a glimpse of the irreducible specificity of individual experience. And yet, as this chapter has shown, in practice social casework was not the objective decision-making machine theorized by charity organization societies and foundation philanthropies. The print artifacts produced at Snow Hill and Piney Woods certainly do reflect the pressure that teachers and students felt to make their case as a case. But these writings also reveal how that same bureaucratic genre was far more capacious, and far more literary, than one might expect. From this vantage, in fact, the GEB case files demand to be read as outsider writing—a trove of forgotten African American personal narratives and vernacular disability writing that has meaning above and beyond the philanthropic transactions and acts of surveillance that originally brought them into being.

Mapping the formal distinctions between documentary poetry and outsider writing onto the print culture of social welfare, however, can also lead in the other direction—not to the literary as such or to the archive's relation to the canon but to more overtly clinical uses of the case. The bureaucratic mode of accounting for individual lives promoted by advocates of scientific charity, after all, also found purchase in pseudoscientific and eugenicist projects of the era that likewise aimed to eliminate beggars, malingerers, and other "social dependents." Reading the archives of scientific charity also requires making decisions about casework itself: is this case doing this or that? A book of experimental verse by an anonymous collective of poets, scholars, and activists identified only as the Blunt Research Group is instructive in this regard. *The Work-Shy* (2016) consists of two poetic sequences derived from the archives of various psychiatric hospitals, prisons, and reformatories joined by a brief reflection on poetic method—on "the obligation to seek permission to listen and the impossibility of obtaining it from a voice that cannot be reached."[89] The second of these poetic sequences reworks texts written by inmates, from diary entries to treatises, tabulations, rants, and undelivered letters, and would seem as such to fit squarely in the category of outsider writing. The first section of *The Work-Shy*, by contrast, presents a definitional, interpretive, and perhaps even ethical challenge. The poems in "Lost Privilege Company" are composed of phrases drawn from the case files of inmates in California youth prisons between 1910 and 1925.

Like Snow Hill and Piney Woods, these reformatories were funded in part by the Rockefeller Foundation. But unlike Black industrial schools, institutions like the Whittier State School were overseen by the Eugenics Records Office, a US organization instrumental in the international eugenics movement. As such, the casework compiled on inmates in reformatories across California—disproportionately young Hispanics and African Americans—was used primarily not to determine who deserved help but who should be recommended for sterilization. The young "wards" rarely speak in their own voices on this or any matter. The central conflict in "Lost Privilege Company" is thus whether an archive "originally compiled to justify the elimination of certain populations" can be the basis for poetry—no matter how virtuosic—that does not reproduce the violence visited upon those whose experiences have been all but excised from the historical record.

"Lost Privilege Company" engages this question directly and self-reflexively, beginning at the level of typography. Each of the poems in this section encodes two or more perspectives: italicized text indicates the voices of the young inmates; text without italics belongs to caseworkers; and passages in quotes convey the voices of the inmates, or their families and friends, as cited by caseworkers. What begins on the page as a visual contest between differently marked text then gives way, in the substance of these poems, to a semantic contest between statements made from subject positions we know to be irreconcilably different but which are nonetheless syntactically enjambed. The first of two poems titled "Pedro," for instance, is structured as a list of caseworkers' observations about an inmate (figure 2.18). The uneven left margin and irregular indentation evoke a page of handwritten notes and an associative scattering of impressions—not yet information—that seems at odds with the diagnostic imperative of the case file. Instead of adding up to anything definitive, that is, these reflections circle back continually to the same idea, as if to describe the inmate's indolence from every possible angle, even his own. Indeed, though we are told that Pedro "wants to do everything but / what looks like work," Pedro himself describes how, before becoming incarcerated, he did something that "looked" like work, namely "*acting as look out* for older boys." He and his friends operated outside of the formal economy, but theirs was still a rational division of labor.

Just as Pedro's voice is marginalized in his case file, however, so too is this work history illegible within the regime of forced labor in which he declines to participate. This question of what work looks like is thus also a question about what an authoritative voice sounds like, and in both instances the decision is clearly not Pedro's. Each poem in "Lost Privilege Company" could be met with similar reservations, so canned are the voices of the inmates and so uncannily eloquent the experimental reimagining of the bureaucratic files that document their mortification. As such, *The Work-Shy* would seem to stand as a monument to the violence of the case, even for those—like Edwards, Jones, and their students at Snow Hill and Piney Woods—who possess some modicum of textual agency and are not (immediately) facing compulsory sterilization. But the ephemeral print culture of social welfare may also help us to read *The Work-Shy* and to understand better how the Blunt Research Group approaches its more immediately troubling archive. Though there can be no doubt that the inmates' voices are effectively silenced in the files on which "Lost Privilege Company" draws, many of these poems nonetheless also register fugitive scenes

[handwritten margin note: reduction of personhood in case file]

shows nomadic trait

slept in old barn on pile of straw nights

wants to do everything but
what looks like work

P E D R O

acting as look out for older boys

shows displeasure at correction
by making unnecessary noises

at work

indolent in the extreme

2.18 Blunt Research Group, *The Work-Shy* (2016).

of writing—by turns abortive, failed, ineffectual, and imaginary. These moments suggest that inmates may have had a far more ambivalent relation to the genre of the case than we might assume. But they also illustrate what we stand to gain when we not only "close listen" to the voices that have been muted in these case files, as the Blunt Research Group describes its method, but also to close read the writing that has been excised from the record.

To be sure, these moments of writing are fleeting and few. In a second poem titled "Pedro," for instance, we learn that the subject of this case file—not necessarily the first Pedro—was punished for an outburst in the yard when the wards gathered together to drill. As transcribed on the page, this outburst—"*Ish gebibble!*," popular, probably polyglot slang for "Who cares?"—would seem a tragicomic but futile response to totalizing authority shared by both the drillmaster and the caseworker who reported this episode for disciplinary action. But after being transferred to solitary confinement, Pedro "wrote [a] four page letter / to the Superintendent stating that he was *not guilty* that / *it could not have been him.*" As if recognizing the inadequacy of his voice as an instrument of self-assertion, Pedro again

```
                                    E M M A N U E L
              a cold-blooded schemer
        he would undo everything I did

         July 4th he wrote a postal card from Catalina Island
                saying he was having a vacation

        the next day
           they found a fifteen page letter
              showing that he had been studying a code
                            of some sort

        if the boy can be reached

                       shoe pinched his own foot


        Stella Schreiber, cousin, living at 1021 Grand View Ave. Los Angeles
```

2.19   Blunt Research Group, *The Work-Shy* (2016).

took up the pen. The only details we have about his letter—that it was four pages in length—suggest both his intensity of focus and his eagerness to make himself legible in the idiom of the case, or indeed even to produce a document that could be physically inserted into his own case file. There is nothing to suggest that this letter made it into Pedro's casework, but neither is his the only memo of this kind in *The Work-Shy*.

At first glance, the story at stake in "Emmanuel" would seem to be about an attempted escape (figure 2.19). Emmanuel, identified both by his demeanor ("cold-blooded schemer") and by his social network ("Stella Schreiber, cousin, living at 1021 Grand View Ave. Los Angeles") evidently made his way to an island opposite Huntington Beach on July 4. From there Emmanuel sent school officials a postcard "saying he was *having a vacation.*" By splitting this statement between two voices, the caseworker's and Emmanuel's, the poem hints that the former might have meant to underscore the impertinence of the latter. The arrangement of these lines on the page also suggests that caseworkers misread Emmanuel's sharp wit as evidence of "cold-blooded" scheming. By the same token, however, when we consider that the ephemeral print genre of the postcard serves, among other functions, to place its sender at a certain place at a certain time, Emmanuel's joke may be parodic rather than simply cheeky. It reproduces the caseworker's desire to track his movements and place him in time and space, as evidenced by the insertion of his cousin's address into the file. This work of parody continues with the piece of writing that next turns up: "they found a fifteen page letter / showing that he had been *studying a code* / of some sort." Presumably hunting for clues about how Emmanuel has escaped or where he has gone, school officials find waiting for them a document that distills the information they are after into a "code" they cannot understand. They are left holding a case file that is of no greater use in understanding his motivation or even his whereabouts than the documents they themselves have compiled on Emmanuel. Both the last word and the last laugh are his: when inserted into his file, this document will become a decoder key of sorts, shaping how all the other writing produced about him will be interpreted in the future. His case will ultimately land in the pile marked "escaped."

3
THE WORK OF THE IMAGE

What does work look like? The question is more difficult than we might suppose. For even the most provisional of answers, given in good faith, is also a confession of ignorance. To say "I know work when I see it," after all, is to concede that others know work when they see it. And if such knowledge is indeed common, two corollaries are also true: first, that everyone knows how to appear to be at work; and second, that it might be impossible, at a glance, to tell who is and who merely seems to be working. This ambivalence is encapsulated in the notion of job performance. Productivity, this familiar turn of phrase suggests, is not only a matter of meeting a particular set of goals by a certain date. One must also give a credible performance of being at work in the moment. Which poses are to be struck and how—the worker's repertoire, so to speak—vary from one occupation to the next. But though productivity does not look the same for medical orderlies and corporate accountants, most workers are subject to some kind of scrutiny from above. Whether foremen or administrators, those higher up on the institutional ladder watch and assess the performances of workers below. To one degree or another, supervision is thus always an exercise in visual interpretation.

This truism would seem to resonate across a range of historical eras and modes of endeavor. All sites of labor, even or especially those we wouldn't dare call workplaces, share something of Foucault's panopticon. As photography and film entered public culture in the late nineteenth century, however, the inherently visual nature of all supervision took on more specific meaning. And because both media promised greater objectivity than even the most vigilant human observer could muster, a dream of long standing began to seem within reach: it might be possible to determine, beyond the shadow of a doubt, who was actually working and who was just going through the motions. Part of early cinema's popular appeal, for instance, was how it introduced viewers to the difficulties (and pleasures) of deciding what real work really looks like. From the demonstration films that Thomas Edison's laboratory produced for its peephole kinetoscope—titles like *Blacksmithing Scene* (1893), *Horse Shoeing* (1893), and *The Barber Shop* (1893)—to the Lumière brothers' *La Sortie de l'Usine Lumière à Lyon*, known in English as *Employees Leaving the Lumière Factory* (1895), consumers learned to read moving pictures in part by scrutinizing visual representations of work.[1] Images of labor were likewise crucial to the era's culture of social reform. But rather than analyzing the intricate skills required to perform a given task or trade, the tradition of social documentary photography associated with Jacob Riis and Lewis Hine zoomed in on spectacles of toil and abuse. One could not understand "how the other half lives," reformers argued, without seeing the misery that passed for work. Only a few decades later, a similar aesthetics of exposure came to serve a radically different social agenda under the rubric of scientific management. Updating F. W. Taylor's "stopwatch method," a new generation of labor consultants used photography and film to identify and discipline inefficient workers. The minutiae of technique and circumstance that had by turns enthralled and scandalized earlier viewers now encoded a hieroglyphics of corporate profit.

From early cinema to scientific management, turn-of-the-century visual archives of work run parallel to and overlap with the print culture of social welfare as I have defined it in this book—the interdisciplinary range of print genres that emerged to mediate between individuals and institutions at a moment of rapid bureaucratization and new developments in industrial print technology. Indeed, as we saw in chapter 2, photographs were often integrated into the casework compiled by charitable and philanthropic organizations. Unsurprisingly, many of these images traffic in the stoic iconography of dignified work that long predates the print culture of social welfare. Consider a 1902 photograph that the Calhoun School commissioned from Frances Benjamin Johnston (figure 3.1). In *Class in Manual Drawing*, students stand at the sturdy benches lining two of the workshop's four walls, each young man stretching one leg behind the other in a posture of focused concentration. The symmetry directs our attention down the right side of the room and up the left. Along the way, we recognize a figurative echo of the image's composition in the rectangular drafting tools hanging on the back wall. Preparing students to contribute

3.1 Frances Benjamin Johnston, *Class in Manual Drawing*. Printed in Brian Wallis and Deborah Willis, eds., *African American Vernacular Photography: Selected from the Daniel Cowin Collection* (2006).

to the race, we are to understand, demands the same kind of hard work on display here. We also note the watchful presence of the teacher, who with upright bearing and downcast gaze scrutinizes both what these young people produce and how they perform productivity. In addition to acquiring a trade, students must also learn the importance of always appearing to be at work. This truism may be universal, as we have speculated, but it held particular urgency for Black Americans in the postbellum United States. Indeed, the framing of *Class in Manual Drawing* foregrounds the omnipresent possibility of white surveillance—whether from townspeople passing by the open windows or from the potential donors for whom this photograph, with its open fourth wall, was intended.

Images like *Class in Manual Drawing* are not uncommon in the archives of twentieth-century foundation philanthropy. Nor are photographic variations on the theme of industrious concentration hard to come by wherever clients, applicants, or alms seekers engaged with bureaucratizing institutions. But what marks these images as belonging to the print culture of social welfare may have less to do with the still life of dignified labor than the visual logic of abstraction best exemplified in the ostensibly unrelated genre of the industrial motion study. Consider two more images. Produced in 1918 by Alexei Gastev, the Bolshevik poet who headed Russia's Central Institute of Labor, the first is a time-lapse photograph of an amputee laborer (figure 3.2). The woman's expression of rapt attention contrasts with the darting arcs of light traced by the bulbs attached to her prosthetic arm and hammer. The other hand here, however, extending through the right side of the frame with a calibration strip, makes clear that what matters most is not the worker's will or attitude—or her body itself. Rather, the image aims to represent work as such. This abstraction of worker into work is even more pronounced in the line drawings made by the German engineer Ludwig Ascher using a similar method (figure 3.3). Here we see how the motions of an experienced (*right*) and inexperienced (*left*) worker filing metal are reduced to either smoothly curved or squiggly lines. Likewise abstracted away are the particulars of each worker's embodiment, social identity, and working conditions. The fullness of experience thus gives way to the fundamentals of movement.

At first glance, neither Gastev's image nor Ascher's line drawing appear to share much with the self-conscious performance of productivity captured in *Class in Manual Drawing*. But while Johnston's photograph and others like it in the print culture of social welfare seem to underscore the irreducibly embodied and the irreducibly situated nature of all work, these images also aspire to much the same kind of abstraction more explicitly at stake in industrial motion studies. When engaging with an institutional interlocutor, it was not enough to show that a certain task had been accomplished or a particular goal met. One had also to demonstrate that the work performed was at base indistinguishable from any other kind of work. Beyond what one actually did or produced, one's work had to signify as work. A glance back at Johnston's photograph of the Calhoun School brings this point home. The students posing in *Class in Manual Drawing*, their legs straightened backward and shoulders arched forward, may be staging a static tableau vivant to commemorate their school's particular achievements in the field of industrial education. But they are also stepping into the universality of labor. As such, they ask institutional viewers to judge not whether they have met a particular benchmark of productivity, but rather whether the movements of their labor successfully arc toward abstraction. *Class in Manual Drawing*, in other words, asks to be read not as a solemn study in productive respectability but as an exercise in industrial motion study.

3.2 Industrial motion tests conducted at Aleksei Gastev's Central Institute of Labor, ca. 1924. Reprinted in René Fülöp-Miller, *The Mind and Face of Bolshevism: An Examination of Cultural Life in Soviet Russia* (1927).

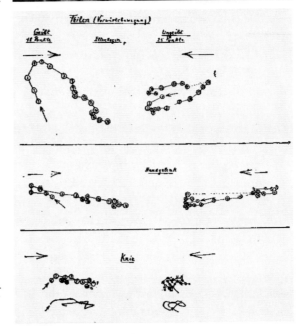

3.3 Ludwig Ascher, "Der Einfluss technischer Verbesserungen auf die Gesundheit des Menschen, insbesondere des Arbeiters" (1927).

In exploring the role of photography and film in the print culture of so-cial welfare, this chapter thus begins with a paradox. The fantasy that shaped how images could do the work of social welfare was elaborated most fully by a technology that was rarely, if ever, employed in this way. As such, this chapter marks a methodological departure. The previous two chapters, on the claim and the case, examine how institutional genres were taken up in a disparate range of noninstitutional contexts. This chapter, by contrast, is a chronicle of false starts, missed connections, and hypothetical collabora-tions. It tells the story of how motion study almost became part of the print culture of social welfare. This speculative or counterfactual history, however, reveals a fundamental truth about the print culture of social welfare that is easily obscured by the sheer volume and specificity of its textual produc-tion: the belief that—once shorn of the particularities of embodiment—the moral value of work is universally the same and can be made legible as such. What motion study renders visible, in other words, is the hermeneutic fan-tasy underpinning the print culture of social welfare. It also demonstrates, however, that there is more to universality than meets the eye. Indeed, the history of misfires and dead ends traced below underscores how the putative universality of motion study—and of the print culture of social welfare more broadly—is in fact rooted in specific ideas about particular bodies in partic-ular contexts. For this reason, the story told here is not as counterintuitive as it might appear. Rather, the material history of visual literacy I explore makes clear that we define the print culture of social welfare too narrowly when we overlook its connections to filmic and photographic practices associated with another agenda of social benevolence, namely empire.

In making these connections, this chapter charts a squiggly line of its own. I begin by tracking the origin of industrial motion study to the experimental methods that the French savant Étienne-Jules Marey de-veloped to record the movements of people with mobility impairments in the late nineteenth century. The visual syntax of what came to be known as *pathological locomotion* flags the first of two contradictions that shaped how motion study, despite a merely fleeting history of involvement with the print culture of social welfare, became that archive's visual unconscious. The same technique used to differentiate between normal and pathological movements would later be used to reveal the universality of all laboring bodies. A second contradiction follows from this first and, like Marey's heirs, forks off into two different directions: the same technology and vi-sual hermeneutics developed to document the universality of all laboring bodies were also used in the context of US imperialism and European colonialism to differentiate the laboring bodies of various racialized people. The chapter thus turns from Marey's influence on US scientific management vis-à-vis the labor consultants Frank and Lillian Gilbreth to the use of motion study in the popular cinema of the Spanish-American War and in the serial photography of colonized peoples in French visual anthropology. The chapter concludes by returning to the Gilbreths and examining what may have been the only use of motion study in the print culture of social welfare in the domestic United States. The Gilbreths took their cameras to upstate New York's Craig Colony, aiming to teach the institution's epileptic residents the ennobling power of work. But visual fantasies of abstract universality soon gave way to compensatory analogies. Though they set out to capture the moral value of all work, the Gilbreths ultimately succeeded only in documenting what work looks like.

Luminous Curves

It is a truism of film history that popular cinema was made possible by the serial photography developed by Étienne-Jules Marey in France and Eadweard Muybridge in the United States for the study of movement. The scientific cinema these figures helped to inaugurate took shape in the decades between 1870 and 1890.[2] In subsequent years, photographic apparatuses built in laboratories across the continent and in the United States gradually found commercial application, paving the way for the cinematic devices introduced in 1895 by the Lumière brothers and Thomas Edison, among others. Many European and American scientists, in fact, would have recognized these latter machines not as new inventions but as updated versions of the tools already in their workshops.[3] Popular cinema's debt to science, however, was both technical and formal. As Lisa Cartwright observes, the visual codes of the laboratory were as integral to the advent of cinematic discourse as those of narrative and spectacle. "Whether or not they convey 'scientific' subject matter," early films like *Fred Ott's Sneeze* (Edison, 1894) and *Photographing a Female Crook* (Biograph, 1904) "are evidence that the popular cinema at its origins was infused critically, if subtly, by the representational modes of experimental physiology."[4] For Tom Gunning, this continuity marks the persistence of the "gnostic impulse" across scientific and popular cinema. The syntactical codes of the former are grounded in the latter's efforts to redefine the nature of visual evidence and to reconstitute our relation to the visual world.[5]

Marey's first experiments in visual motion study took shape after he came across Muybridge's serial photographs of a galloping horse in the journal *La Natura* in 1878. Sharing in the wide excitement these images sparked among both scientific and lay readers, Marey hoped that Muybridge's methods might help him resolve a technical impasse facing his own graphic-inscription studies of animal locomotion.[6] After meeting Muybridge in person, however, Marey began to doubt the usefulness of the latter's techniques. Muybridge's famed photographs did reveal what the human eye could not see, most spectacularly that a galloping horse leaves the ground entirely for a brief moment during each gait cycle. But because each image was taken by a separate camera from a different vantage—and with no way to measure the time between exposures—Muybridge's serial photographs were of limited scientific value.[7] When the dust settled on Muybridge's celebrated European tour, Marey thus set out to create devices that could make successive images from a single vantage on a single plate. He eventually coined the term *chronophotography* to describe this work. Resembling a shotgun, Marey's first chronophotographic camera imprinted twelve images per second on a small rotating plate. After experimenting with several other prototypes, Marey's next breakthrough was a design he called the chronophotograph. This device used a slotted disk that rotated in front of a fixed-plate camera ten times per second, thereby recording images every 1/100 of a second. Marey continued to tweak the chronophotograph over the years and regularly brought new models into service. One of his most consequential innovations, however, had less to do with the technology in the camera than with broader questions of experimental design. In a method he named *geometric chronophotography*, Marey clothed human subjects in black and attached luminous reflectors to their joints and limbs. These men and women were then photographed against a black background, such that only the luminous material was visible (figures 3.4–3.5). The effect, Marey noted, was that of "artificially reducing the surface of the object under observation." In geometric chronophotography, in other words, the subject's body all but disappeared. What remained was movement itself.

As Marey refined the techniques of chronophotography and geometric chronophotography and developed new devices in the service of each, he trained his cameras on a broad range of subjects. From gymnasts and birds in flight to water and air currents, Marey scrutinized the hidden laws of human and nonhuman movement and sought "to give the subtle and fugitive phenomena of life a permanent and true expression."[8] For the most

3.4 A research
subject outfitted for
geometric chrono-
photography. E.-J.
Marey, *Movement*
(1895).

3.5 Geometric
chronophotography
of a runner in mo-
tion. E.-J. Marey,
Movement (1895).

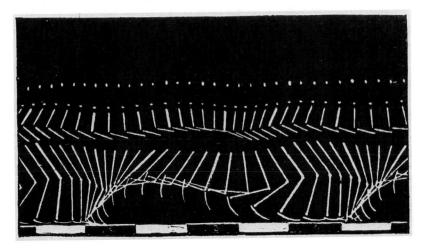

part, Marey left it to others to apply his research outside of the laboratory; he claimed to prefer objective and disinterested inquiry. Such distinctions, however, between objective inquiry and practical application are rarely tenable. This is all the more true when the task at hand is determining the natural course of a particular movement or reducing a certain activity—say, walking, jumping, or pole-vaulting—to its constituent gestural elements. After all, to trace the ideal trajectory of an object or person through space—to transcribe what Marey called "the language of the phenomena themselves"—is also to designate any deviation from that trajectory as improper or unnatural.[9] If the chronophotograph is a portrait of movement in all its hidden particularity, it is thus also a picture of aspiration. The stray observations that Marey did occasionally venture about the practical applications of his methods suggest that he recognized this didactic impulse. In *Movement* (1895), for instance, Marey notes that chronophotographs of prize-winning athletes might "betray the secret of their successes, perhaps unconsciously acquired," for the benefit of less successful competitors and lay spectators alike. Chronophotography could also be used to help novice workers learn the "movements necessary for the execution of various skilled industries."[10] In abstracting the body out of the picture of work, in other words, Marey transformed that picture into a blueprint.

These observations mark Marey's place in the wider efforts of scientists, physicians, and reformers in France and Germany to study and improve the efficiency of the laboring body. As Anson Rabinbach has argued, the "European science of work" conceived of the human body as a thermodynamic machine whose potential for productivity had yet fully to be realized.[11] Building on the self-consciously disinterested studies of intransitive movement and physiology conducted by Marey and others, applied researchers pursued an agenda at once pragmatic and utopian. On the one hand, these scientists sought to quantify the body's physiological capacity for work and thus to identify exactly how hard a worker could be pushed without jeopardizing either health or performance. Placed at the disposal of the state, advocates promised, these data could be used to determine the objectively best organization of industrial production and to end the conflict between labor and capital. On the other hand, though, advances in the physiology of work also spurred fantasies of making the laboring body perfectly efficient.[12] How might workers be trained to approach their physiological limits as closely as possible without exceeding them? Could fatigue and overexertion, now seen as the most pressing threat to industrial efficiency, be eliminated outright? This latter challenge, the elimination of fatigue, became a rallying cry for industrial scientists and government bureaucrats alike. But it was clear that the meaning of *fatigue* had changed with the times. If religious tradition had historically associated fatigue with a failure of the will and with the scourge of idleness, scientists and reformers now understood fatigue as a physiological mechanism. Fatigue ensued when the body outstripped its capacities; it was an avoidable consequence of inefficient labor. "The measurement of fatigue," Rabinbach observes, "thus promised to unlock the principles of the body's energies, to determine its economies of motion, and to reveal the most beneficial methods of organizing the expenditure of energy."[13]

To one degree or another, all of Marey's chronophotographic work was concerned with the efficiency of movement and with the elimination of fatigue. When contracted by the French military to study the physiology of marching, for instance, Marey set out to identify the most advantageous gait and the best distribution of weight in the soldier's pack. In so doing, his goal was "to diminish fatigue and use to greater advantage the bodily forces."[14] Marey's assistants used chronophotography to target fatigue even more directly. Charles Fremont, for instance, filmed blacksmiths at work to determine the most efficient path by which a hammer could be brought down on an anvil with the maximum of force.[15] The question of efficiency and fatigue was no less central, however, in Marey's abstract discussions of movement. Even, for instance, when he sought to convince skeptical readers of the "lofty satisfaction" afforded by disinterested inquiry into the nature of movement as such, Marey did so by championing the physiological efficiency of the natural world. "There is no doubt," he wrote, "that every advance in our knowledge of the movements of locomotion will bring out even more clearly the perfect harmony that exists between an organ and its function."[16] Scrutinizing the physiology of human locomotion, in other words, whatever its practical benefit, brings us closer to understanding the absolute efficiency—the perfect fit between organic form and function—that defines the natural world. Such is the kind of efficiency, Marey implies, to which we should aspire in each of the movements, motions, and gestures that define our everyday and our working lives.

It is no surprise, then, that when Marey began to investigate the gains of men and women with mobility impairments—movements marked by the perceived absence of "the perfect harmony that exists between an organ and its function"—he equated disability with inefficiency. Marey was not alone in using chronophotography to study "pathological locomotion" at the end of the nineteenth century. But unlike the experiments conducted by Albert Londe at Jean-Martin Charcot's Salpêtrière clinic or by Muybridge at the University of Pennsylvania, to name but two prominent figures in a wide field, Marey's studies did not conspicuously indulge in the spectacle of the disabled body in motion.[17] Rather, his method aimed to remove the disabled body from the visual representation of its movement. Marey's earliest studies of pathological locomotion date to 1886, when he brought his chronophotograph into a Parisian hospital to record the movements of patients with wooden prostheses, club feet, and wasting to their lower limbs.[18] Although Marey initially used standard chronophotography, he soon developed a specialized technique that took inspiration from Jacques-Louis Soret's use of geometric chronophotography in the arts. The Swiss physician placed incandescent bulbs on the joints of dancers and photographed their movements across the stage and through the air in a theater lit by a handful of red lanterns. As Marey observed, these images capture "some very curious trajectories, in which the curves obtained showed a beautiful and regular interlacement."[19] Marey brought Soret's modifications to his own method out of the theater and into the hospital by attaching small electric light bulbs to the joints of men and women with mobility disabilities. These bulbs were connected to a generator by a trolley that ran along two overhead wires. With a chronophotograph placed in the corner of the room, the subjects were then instructed to walk from one side to the other. Later adjustments were made by Marey's assistant Georges Demenÿ and surgeon Eduard Quénu, who took over for Marey and worked for a further two years in a specially outfitted laboratory in the Hôpital Beaujon (figures 3.6–3.8).[20]

True to Marey's broader taxonomic project, these studies of pathological locomotion were at first intended to show how each subject walked with a limp or claudication specific to their disorder.[21] The results, however, as Marta Braun and Elizabeth Whitcombe note, led Marey to conclude that the difference between pathological and normal locomotion is one of degree rather than of kind. As Marey wrote, "Certain disturbances in different claudications are probably only the exaggeration—greater or lesser—of movements that are hardly apparent but nonetheless exist in a normal state."[22] This finding seems to contradict popular ideas about the absolute difference of disability. But Marey's approach was in fact very much of its moment. As Georges Canguilhem observes, the "real identity of normal and pathological" phenomena became "scientifically guaranteed dogma" during the nineteenth century. Not qualitatively different, the pathological is a "quantitative variation" of the normal—marked semantically "not so much by *a* or *dys* as by *hyper* or *hypo*."[23] When we recall the didactic thrust of Marey's research, the likeness he discerns between the movements of ambulatory subjects with and without mobility impairments is striking for another reason as well. Not only do the movements of disabled subjects closely resemble those of nondisabled subjects, but they also bear the same relation to the norm as do inefficient or fatigued movements. Once the body is abstracted away from the chronophotographic image of its movement, in other words, it matters little whether that body is disabled, fatigued, inexperienced, or inefficient. In each of the permutations, the body bears the same relation to the ideal. And in each instance, the therapeutic, educative, or rehabilitative path ahead is plain to see.

Two images produced by Demenÿ and Quénu illustrate the kinds of reading practices fostered by these chronophotographic studies of pathological motion. In the first, taken with a rotating-plate chronophotograph of a subject walking from right to left in front of the lens, intermittent spots of light mark the paths traveled by the subject's shoulder, hip, knee, and ankle (figures 3.9–3.11). By themselves, these images reveal little about why we should classify this movement as pathological. As Braun and Whitcombe note, Marey read images like these deductively by proceeding "from the organization of movement to its disorder, comparing exaggerations made on the plate by the affected limbs curve by curve and line by line with their normal counterpart."[24] By recording variations of slope, angle, and symmetry, researchers could pair a particular disorder with a representative gait. Researchers could also imagine what successful rehabilitation would look like or even judge the promise of a given treatment by reading in the opposite direction, from the disorganization of movement to its therapeutic reorganization. Nor were these applications lost on medical professionals of the day. As early as 1899, Parisian physicians adopted Marey's electric light bulb method to determine the efficacy of various treatments for "chronic spinal diseases." One study printed in the *Therapeutic Gazette* asked readers to compare chronophotographic images of the "gait of the ataxic before treatment" with the "gait of the ataxic after suspension." That the lines representing the subject's movement more closely approximate the "normal gait" in the latter image, the authors conclude, is patent evidence of the subject's rehabilitation.[25]

Taken with a fixed-plate chronophotograph of a subject walking directly toward the lens, the second image of "pathological locomotion" by Demenÿ and Quénu represents movement not as a trail of dots but as

3.6 Demeny and Quenu, taking over an experiment from Marey, brought Soret's methods from the stage to the hospital floor. E.-J. Marey, *Movement* (1895).

a series of continuous lines that follow no evident pattern (figure 3.12). Knowing that the bulbs have been placed on the subject's joints allows us to intuit the outline of their body. But it is far more difficult to follow that body's movements through space. Indeed, if the image taken in profile clarifies the direction of the subject's motion and conveys the position of the five illuminated markers at regular intervals, this anterior image establishes each limb's range of movement but little else. To understand this as a picture of pathology, we read intuitively rather than deductively. Instead of comparing this image line by line and curve by curve with an image of normal locomotion, we note a set of attributes that distinguish the formal specificity of pathology: irregular spacing, sudden changes of direction, squiggly lines and indecipherable patterns, and, above all, repetitive, indirect, or unnecessarily drawn-out movements. By turns unruly and ornate, these patterns of light capture the visual traces of wasted effort and energy. Accordingly, these images are pedagogically useful not only because they allow us to picture successful rehabilitation, but because they establish a set of visual conventions with which we can recognize inefficiency at a glance.

Photochronographie au moyen de la lumière électrique.

Disposition pour l'étude de la locomotion pathologique.

3.7–3.8 Representation of the apparatus developed by Marey and used by Demenÿ and Quénu, ca. 1887. "Chronophotograph using electric light: provision for the study of pathological locomotion." Bibliothèque de l'Hôtel de Ville, Paris.

3.9–3.11 Marey, "Photochronographic test obtained by means of incandescent lamps and giving the various trajectories of the shoulder, hip, knee and ankle in a patient suffering from atrophy of the femoral triceps," ca. 1887. Bibliothèque de l'Hôtel de Ville, Paris.

Although the chronophotographic images of pathological locomotion produced by Marey, Demenÿ, and Quénu met with enthusiasm from scientists and piqued the interest of many lay readers, these studies were ultimately less than entirely successful.[26] Not only did Marey's technique demand more control over room lighting than was always possible, but the requisite system of cables and guide wires also proved prohibitively expensive. As a consequence, Marey and his collaborators returned to the dynamometer-driven systems of graphic inscription already widely in use.[27] But these experiments were hardly without influence, whether one looks to the "new kinaesthetic" of modernist visual art or to "interrupted light studies" foundational to the field of gait analysis and to more recent experiments in motion capture.[28] Alongside this history of technical innovation, however, the legacy of Marey's electric light bulb method is also to be found in the mode of visual literacy it created. As we will see, coiled lines and convoluted patterns would continue to signify pathology of one

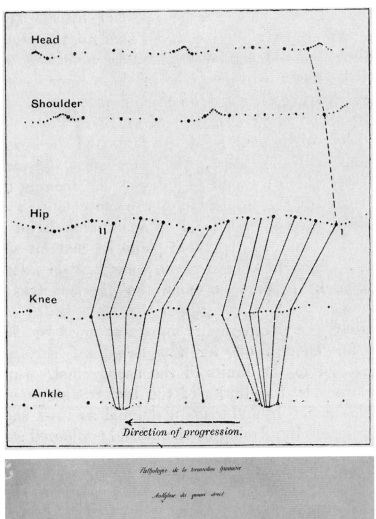

Head

Shoulder

Hip

II   I

Knee

Ankle

Direction of progression.

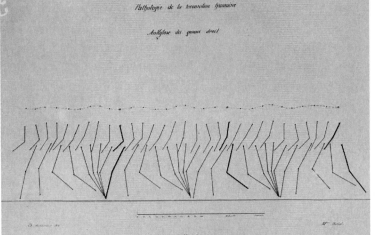

Pathologie de la locomotion humaine

Ankylose du genou droit

Marey (du genou)

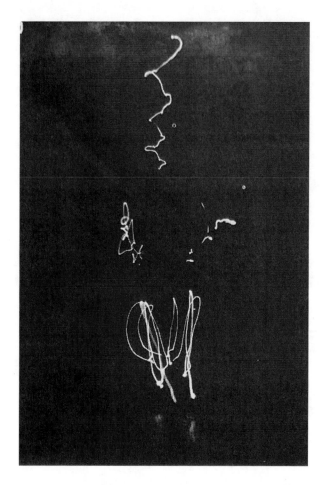

3.12 Demenÿ and Quénu (Marey's Laboratory), *Pathological Walk from in Front, Made Visible by Incandescent Bulbs Fixed to the Joints*, ca. 1889. Reprinted in Michel Frizot, *A New History of Photography* (1999).

kind or another to Marey's heirs in popular cinema and scientific management. Even more important, though, was the idea that by stripping away the particularities of embodiment and experience, one could visualize the truth of any movement and the very essence of work as such. For the labor consultants to whom we now turn, the promise of Marey's chronophotographic studies of pathological locomotion lay most immediately in its potential for improving management's bottom line. But when the same consultants ventured to use motion study with the residents of an epileptic colony, they not only returned Marey's technology to its origins in disability culture. They also sought to literalize the hermeneutic underwriting the broader print culture of social welfare, though ultimately without success.

Learning Curves

For many years, historians assumed the US labor consultants who popularized the use of motion study to maximize industrial efficiency had no more than a passing familiarity with Étienne-Jules Marey. The shop floors in Providence and Boston where the husband-and-wife team of Frank and Lillian Gilbreth made a name for themselves could seem no further removed from Marey's lavishly resourced Station Physiologique outside Paris.[29] Even today we most often find the Gilbreths and Marey as interlocutors in expansive illustrated histories of visual modernity, works that track a continuum of interest in the study of movement that runs from Aristotle and Galileo through the advent of photography and the rise of cinema. Ambitious in scope and synthetic in aim, these narratives are usually more concerned with intellectual kinship than with the particulars of transmission. As if modeling the kind of visual literacy that Marey and the Gilbreths helped to create, they superimpose one career arc on top of another in the hopes of backlighting a shared trajectory. The result is a picture of affinity and influence strongly suggestive of direction and momentum but ultimately somewhat fuzzy around the edges. Sigfried Giedion's magisterial *Mechanization Takes Command* (1948) is representative. "We have found no mention of Marey's work in Gilbreth's studies," Giedion observes. "But it matters little, for our purposes, whether Gilbreth had heard of it or not." More important than determining who knew whom is understanding the inchoate visual ethos of modernity to which we are all heir. "The fact that a similarity of methods can be arising unconsciously in such heterogeneous fields," Giedion writes, "is among the most hopeful symptoms of the period."[30]

More recent scholars have complicated Giedion's eloquent ambivalence, taking to the archives to show how much the Gilbreths did in fact know about Marey's work.[31] But though the Gilbreths made a career of repackaging slight modifications to Marey's apparatuses as technical game changers, their most important innovations may have been to the interpretative practices the French physiologist developed. Like Marey, the Gilbreths assumed that motion study, by abstracting the essence of movement from the contingency of the body, indexed a truth invisible to the naked eye. But if Marey thought this truth concerned the nature of movement as such, for the Gilbreths motion study captured the inherent meaning of work. This visual syntax made it possible not only to determine who was working efficiently and who wasn't but also to shore up the fantasy that all efficient workers were essentially interchangeable. The Gilbreths thus saw in industrial motion study the same universalizing logic of abstraction that guided Marey's studies of pathological locomotion. Motion study, they argued, reveals how work renders differences of ability, race, class, and gender entirely moot. In this regard, the arc of the Gilbreths' career was shaped not only by the "efficiency craze" of the early twentieth century or the entrenchment of the Fordist economy, as cultural historians commonly point out. Rather, the Gilbreths' brand of industrial motion study epitomized nothing so much as the labor ideology of social welfare provision. It should come as no surprise, then, that the Gilbreths would seize the opportunity to set up shop in an institution for people with epilepsy, short-lived and abortive though this collaboration would ultimately be.

Before specializing in filmic analysis, the Gilbreths approached motion study as a pen-and-paper affair. As outlined in *Bricklaying System* (1909), the Gilbreths' practice was initially grounded in painstaking observation and description. The first step was to identify the workers who performed a given task with the greatest efficiency. The next step involved studying such a worker's technique as closely as possible in order to break it down into its constitutive parts. The information gleaned would then be distilled into "a series of instructions to show each and every motion in proper sequence" that could be distributed to all employees. In this way, a new hire could bypass the usual learning curve and begin "to work intelligently from his first day, and to become a proficient workman in the shortest possible time."[32] When the Gilbreths turned to visual motion studies in 1912, they used the same method, though now with the help of a modern cinematograph. First implemented for the New England Butt Company of Providence, Rhode Island, the method of "micro-motion study" called for filming laborers "against a cross-sectioned, background, floor, and workbench." These films were then examined frame by frame through a magnifying glass or a viewing station that resembled a microfilm viewer (figure 3.13).[33] By comparing the position of the worker's body from one frame to the next, the Gilbreths could measure the length of each movement. Calculating the minimum distance that could be traveled while executing each of these steps made it possible to piece together a new and more streamlined choreography.[34] Micromotion study was thus a more accurate version of the older pen-and-paper method, drawing not only on the perceptions and intuitions of a skilled observer but also on the finer measurements derived from serial photography.

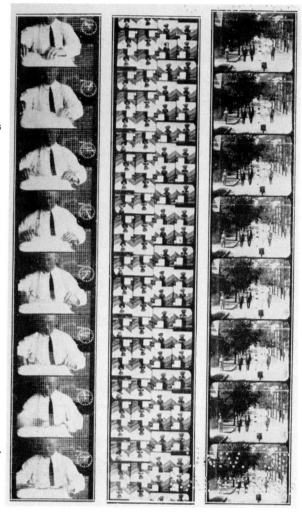

3.13 Images of micromotion studies in *Applied Motion Study* (1919). Left to right, the captions read: "Automatic Micromotion Study with vertical penetrating screen in the plane of the motions"; "Multiple use of film reducing cost and time and motion study while retaining accuracy and permanence of the detailed record"; "Autoteletime study for recording motions at a great distance and the position of the finger of the michronometer less than thirty feet away."

It was only when the Gilbreths turned to Marey's light bulb method that industrial motion study would begin to make work as such visible at a glance. What for Marey, Demenÿ, and Quénu had been a novel experiment without an especially long shelf life was to become a professional calling card for the Gilbreths. They named this new technology the *cyclegraph*, a term intended to highlight the modernity and hence also the originality of its design but also the repetitive and cyclical nature of industrial labor itself. Whereas Marey and his collaborators attached lamps to the joints and the heads of the disabled people whose gaits they studied, the

Gilbreths focused on scenes of work and on workers' movements. After mounting an electric light on a ring that was then slipped onto a laborer's finger, the Gilbreths used time-lapse photography to track the movement of light during the performance of a given task. In the images thus produced, the worker traces a continuous bright line that folds back on itself with each completed sequence. In some cases, depending on room lighting, the laborer's body is a faint blur in the background; in others it disappears altogether. And as with Marey's studies of pathological locomotion, a recognizable iconography of visual syntax soon resulted. Whether analyzing the movements of carpenters, typists, or surgeons, the Gilbreths read squiggly lines, irregular patterns, and eccentric circles as of inexperience, ineptitude, or laziness. Efficient labor, by contrast, was identifiable by straight rather than undulating lines; precise repetition with little deviation between cycles; and evenly segmented phrasing. Just as Marey understood pathology as an exaggeration of the norm rather than its aberration, moreover, the Gilbreths decoded the cyclegraphic traces left by inefficient laborers line by line and curve by curve against motion studies of more productive workers. Any deviation from the latter trajectory was evidence of inefficiency but no real cause for alarm. The pattern left behind by what the Gilbreths called "the one best way," after all, lit the pedagogical path forward.

Not everyone, however, seems to have found cyclegraphic motion study self-explanatory. Much of the Gilbreths' time in the years to come, in fact, would be spent teaching workers, managers, and the public to make sense of the revelatory images of labor they produced. An early sortie was an article that the Gilbreths placed in the *American Machinist* outlining the cyclegraphic method alongside a series of representative images (figure 3.14). The first set of images, paired as "before" and "after," records the motions of a worker picking up photographs from a stack. Neither the hand nor the body to which it belongs is visible; the laboring movement, readers are told, is more important than the laborer themself. "It will be noted in the first illustration how the hand passes through quite an arc in moving from one point to another," the article's author notes. The second image shows "how practice has cut out quite a portion of this distance if the hand can be trained to move in a horizontal path."[35] Even the simplest of movements can be simplified yet further, allowing for even greater conservation of energy and effort. The laborer whose body we cannot see, however, is not the only beneficiary of the Gilbreths' tutelage. The article's readers are also being taught—or being given the chance to "pick up"— the language of cyclegraphy. Just as laborers learn how to streamline their

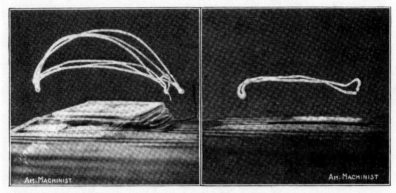

3.14 Illustrations of the Gilbreths' visual motion studies in *American Machinist* (1913).

movements, readers learn to distinguish between efficient and inefficient at a glance. Equally important, readers also learn that the latter can easily be remade in the image of the former with the expert assistance of a motion studies consultant.

This process of public pedagogy and brand making continued over the years as the Gilbreths presented slight modifications to the original cyclegraph as new technologies. While clearly an effort to remain relevant in the competitive field of industrial management, well-marketed updates were also a chance to further specify how the images produced by industrial motion study should be read. The first of these new devices was the so-called chronocyclegraph, which added an interrupter that cut electricity to the light bulb at regular intervals and thus replaced the solid lines of the cyclegraph with a series of dots or dashes. In addition to its trajectory, the Gilbreths declared, the timing of a movement could now also be determined at a glance.[36] By shaping these specks of light into pointed lines resembling arrows, a further twist on the chronocyclegraph made it possible to identify the direction of the original movement. The unwieldy name stereochronocyclegraph was given to yet another revision that used a specialized camera to produce two slightly offset images from a single exposure. When the images were examined through a stereoscopic viewer, the original movement now appeared to be three-dimensional. According to the Gilbreths, this method made it easier for workers to recognize why one technique was more efficient than another and to practice the new procedure for themselves. They also built wire models of these kinesthetic trajectories, approximating the distance between spots of light with dabs of dark paint, for much the same purpose.

These and other modifications to the Gilbreths' cyclegraph were intended to make the luminous curves produced by the original device more legible. But by incorporating more data and asking viewers to navigate label and scaling systems that were not intuitive, these innovations often confused matters. While valuable in theory, that is, in practice information about speed, direction, and timing could easily become "chart junk," a term that Edward R. Tufte uses to describe excessive detail that derails a graphic illustration's main communicative goal.[37] In the chronocyclegraphic study of "Two Hands Folding Cloth," for instance, the worker's lack of experience or skill is evident in the intricate and seemingly haphazard trajectories that their movements trace (figure 3.15). Rather than helping us discern what mistakes have been made and where, however, the pulses of light and segmented phrasing intensify a vague impression of disorganization. Nor is it easier to learn from images of patently efficient movements. Students encountering the stereochronocyclegraph of a "Man Hammering Nail into Board" would certainly have praised the subject's fluid movement (figure 3.16). But they would probably have had difficulty taking this example to heart and modifying their own technique accordingly.

The question of how to read cyclegraphic studies of industrial labor continued to occupy the Gilbreths in the years that followed. But where they had initially focused on worker technique—on identifying inefficient methods and teaching best practices—they soon turned their attention to worker physiology. In addition to inexperience and improper training, the Gilbreths now claimed that their cyclegraphic methods could register evidence of bodily fatigue. In supplementing motion study with "fatigue study," the Gilbreths clearly sought to align themselves with European physiologists against Taylor, who was increasingly accused of disregarding the physical limits of human exertion. This venture, however, was fraught from the beginning, motivated on the one hand by market necessity and on the other by the faint resemblance that the Gilbreths' cyclegraphic motion studies shared with the famous fatigue curves produced by European physiologists like Angelo Mosso.[38] For their part, the Gilbreths had little genuine interest in exploring the physiology of fatigue. Instead, they could only postulate its existence wherever a cyclegraphic trajectory diverged from the norm. And whereas Mosso and his collaborators limited their

3.15 Frank B. Gilbreth, "Chronocyclegraph of Two Hands Folding Cloth," ca. 1915. Frank B. Gilbreth Motion Study Photographs (1913–1917), the Kheel Center for Labor-Management Documentation and Archives, Cornell University.

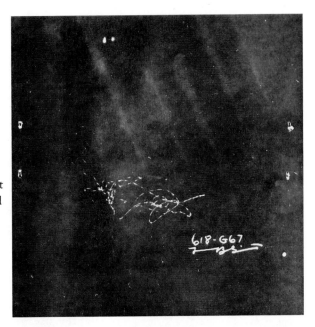

3.16 Frank B. Gilbreth, "Studies in Manual Training School (Carpentry)," ca. 1915. Frank B. Gilbreth Motion Study Photographs (1913–1917), the Kheel Center for Labor-Management Documentation and Archives, Cornell University.

analysis to a single motion, the Gilbreths examined complex sequences of movement in which a decline in performance could have any number of causes. A report filed in 1915 suggests that this point was hardly lost on the Gilbreths. Analyzing a chronocyclegraphic study of a group of fencers, an assistant conceded that it was impossible to tell which deviations from the standard curve were evidence of fatigue and which were due to "hesitation," "unsteadiness," or inexperience. The conclusions reached are aptly tentative: "Fatigue seems to be shown in the following cyclegraphs and chronocyclegraphs," but there would be no way of knowing for sure.[39]

By the time that the Gilbreths published *Fatigue Study* in 1916, they had all but abandoned these early efforts to read cyclegraphic trajectories as fatigue curves. Rather than coming to terms with the sizable body of experimental research on the subject, the Gilbreths instead made a bold about-face. Identifying the signs of fatigue, they now claimed, required neither specialized instrumentation nor scientific expertise. One needed only common sense and an understanding of the individual and social costs of unchecked fatigue. Industrial motion study, the Gilbreths were careful to stress, did remain the prerogative of experts like themselves. But anyone attuned to the everyday signs of fatigue—legible, for instance, when comparing "the appearance of the workers at various times of the day, and at the end of the day"—could carry out a fatigue study.[40] Indeed, the Gilbreths began their book on the subject with an unprecedented abdication of authority: "A crowd of workers come out of the factory after the day's work. Some rush home; others walk at a leisurely pace. Some move slowly with effort. Some have their heads back and a satisfied expression on their faces. Others have their heads bent forward, and look as though life were not worth while. What is the difference between the members of this group? Mainly a matter of fatigue. Fatigue is the after-effect of work."[41] In place of the hierarchical gaze of the efficiency expert scrutinizing the movements of workers on the shop floor, the Gilbreths now approached fatigue from the street-level vantage of workers and the communities to which they returned. Nor is the image with which *Fatigue Study* opens an abstract portrait of laboring bodies on the order of those produced with cyclegraphic methods. The picture painted here includes details that allow us to distinguish one laborer from another and to speculate about their off-the-clock lives. Such an individuating perspective was also key to the reformist agenda laid out in the rest of the book, which calls for adapting the workplace to the worker rather than the other way around. Eliminating fatigue, the Gilbreths argue, requires attending to the interaction of the individual with the environment and the demands of the job. Even small alterations can have considerable effects, whether installing footrests on a worker's stool, raising a worktop for a laborer who prefers to stand, or simply ensuring that tools are within easy reach.

Suggestions like these anticipate the insights of the fields of human factors and ergonomics.[42] The Gilbreths likewise aligned themselves with contemporary trends in industrial betterment, welfare work, and industrial psychology, the latter Lillian's field of expertise. As such, this turn to a pedestrian notion of fatigue also led the Gilbreths to rethink the ideal of "the one best way," long a mission statement and marketing mantra. Rather than establishing hard-and-fast rules for a particular task, in many cases the Gilbreths now sought to create guidelines for particular bodies. Efficiency remained the foremost goal. But in parting ways with a Taylorist model of maximizing productivity at any cost, the Gilbreths made common cause with a growing number of industrial managers who placed a premium on vocational placement. As Elspeth Brown notes, this school of thought presupposed that everyone was naturally suited to one occupation or another. The task facing management consultants was to find and facilitate the proper fit. To be avoided at all costs was "the tragedy of vocational waste," which "stemmed from the unintentional 'misfit' between a worker and his or her job" and caused unnecessary and often debilitating fatigue.[43] This new emphasis on vocational placement likewise changed how the Gilbreths understood the relation between cyclegraphic representation and fatigue. If the luminous trajectories produced by motion study did not allow fatigue to be measured directly, the data they encoded could nonetheless help trained professionals assess and adjust the fit between worker and workplace. And the proper fit in turn minimized fatigue, which would be evident to lay observers and to workers alike. The one best way, in other words, now meant using motion study to find the best fit between a specific working body and a specific working environment. As we will see, this interpretive shift prepared the way for a host of (nominally) new technologies. But it also brought the Gilbreths' project into the orbit of social welfare provision, which, as we have seen in this book's first two chapters, was likewise keenly concerned with finding a place for everyone—and for every body—in the work society. But in making this connection, the Gilbreths would also draw on and extend motion study's involvement with another "benevolent" endeavor—namely, that of empire.

Imperial Fatigue

Not long before the methods of analysis and interpretation developed by Marey and his colleagues were taken up by Taylorist engineers in the United States, motion study traveled to the edges of French colonialism. There chronophotography was part of a broader portfolio of visual technologies used to classify racial difference along an evolutionary axis of civilization. Images of the putatively anarchic and precivilized were used to justify colonial intervention as a benevolent undertaking, a mission carried out not only for the material enrichment of the colonizer but also for the cultural progress of the colonized. As historians have shown, anthropology played no small role in this project. Initially, though, the discipline relied on anthropometric methods of observation and measurement to determine the racial characteristics typical of particular categories of people.[44] Chronophotography offered a new and presumably more accurate means of determining much the same by focusing on motion. As Fatimah Tobing Rony notes, movement soon came to be understood as a unique index of racial essence that was "'in between' nature and culture, acting and being."[45] As a consequence, the visual record of French colonialism is rife with chronophotographic images of Indigenous non-European people in motion. Researchers also trained their cameras on "civilized" white Europeans, but generally only to establish a control group with which the "primitive" gaits of colonial subjects might be brought into sharper relief. French anthropology thus inherited from Marey not only a range of devices and techniques with which to capture infinitesimal nuances of movement but also an interpretative framework for assigning cultural meaning to "pathological locomotion." Divergences from the norm that might in other contexts be attributed to impairment or worker fatigue were now read as signs of racial difference.

A central figure in the history of ethnographic motion study is the anthropologist Félix-Louis Regnault, who began working at the Station Physiologique in the early 1890s. Building on Marey's and Demenÿ's pathbreaking chronophotographic and dynamometric studies of human locomotion, in the summer of 1895 Regnault used a chronophotograph to scrutinize the movements of West African and Malagasy performers at the Paris Colonial Exhibition. These films feature men, women, and children, usually alone and in profile, as they walk, run, jump, pound grain, make pottery, or carry various items.[46] Drawing on a cross-section of colonial subjects from Senegal, Mali, New Caledonia, and New Guinea, Regnault sought to determine the precise gait specific to each group. He also intended to demonstrate the value of chronophotography for scientific documentation more broadly. Regnault later used these images, in fact, to convince the Ethnological International Congress to adopt a resolution calling for chronophotographic archives to be established in "all museums of anthropology."[47] Beyond drawing ever finer distinctions among different colonized peoples, however, Regnault was equally invested in shoring up the boundary between "civilized" and "primitive" races. A chronophotographic series

Grimpeur soudanais. — Chronophotographie de M. Comte.

Grimpeur européen. — Chronophotographie.

Dr Félix REGNAULT.

3.17 Félix-Louis Regnault, "Le Grimpeur," *Revue encyclopédique* (1897).

of colonized people and white Europeans climbing trees on the Champs de Mars in Paris lays this motivation bare (figure 3.17). Although Regnault accounted in great detail for the variety of climbing techniques mobilized by a range of West Africans, he went on to collapse these distinctions by creating a composite colonial subject that could be more easily compared to an equally monolithic white European figure. As Peter Bloom argues, the resultant images, particularly as printed in the popular press, make clear that Regnault was interested not only in revealing what escaped the unaided eye but also in reaffirming the us/them distinction readers no doubt assumed to be evident at first glance.[48]

Elsewhere in Regnault's chronophotographic oeuvre, however, the relation between normal and pathological is drawn somewhat differently, reflecting a set of concerns bound up less immediately with colonial than with continental politics. In the wake of a decisive loss in the Franco-Prussian War (1870–71), French public discourse gradually arrived at a discomforting consensus: that civilization itself had had a degenerative effect on the physiological fitness of the national body politic.[49] In a sweeping debate that coalesced around the question of how soldiers should march, scientists, social hygienists, and anthropologists saw in chronophotography a means of remedying the physiological costs of modern life. As Marey wrote in a preface to Regnault's 1898 treatise on the subject, *Comment on marche*, or how to march: "Chronophotography becomes an educator of our movements, allowing us to recognize the ideal perfection to which we should aspire and to identify both our deficient movements and the progress we have made" in correcting them.[50] Regnault argued that French armed forces should adopt *la marche en flexion*, a more efficient gait in which the knees are deeply bent and the torso angled forward that was commonly seen as more natural than the standard upright European posture. Regnault based his findings on chronophotographic studies of both well-trained military officers and colonized people from West Africa and Madagascar. Because the latter embodied the very essence of Rousseau's "natural man," the thinking went, they were the best of all possible models for the overcivilized European. Such praise for the "primitive" *marche en flexion*, of course, or for the "savages" who knew no other way of moving through the world, did little to destabilize—much less invert—the hierarchical priority of the colonizer over the colonized. Rather, by choosing to walk closer to the ground, white Europeans could at once improve their locomotive efficiency and underscore their mastery over people whose movements were presumably guided by instinct alone.[51]

If motion study was crucial to visual anthropology's foundational encounter with racial difference at the end of the nineteenth century, not long thereafter motion study was also taken up by French physiologists, engineers, and hygienists to improve the efficiency of colonial laborers. In this context, the movements of Indigenous non-Europeans were scrutinized not only to situate them more accurately on the evolutionary ladder but also to slot them into physiologically appropriate positions in the colonial workforce. As such, motion study is part of a broader history of empirical experimentation that gives the lie to the universalism often ascribed to the European science of work. Anson Rabinbach, as we have seen, influentially argues that European physiologists approached the human organism as a thermodynamic machine governed by physiological laws that applied equally to all bodies. The "human motor," as a common locution of the period put it, was "a productive machine, stripped of all social and cultural relations."[52] As Elisa Camiscioli and Laura Frader have shown, however, the European science of work was used in colonial spaces to distinguish among different kinds of "human motors" and thus to ground the "social and cultural relations" of race in the truth of physiological mechanics. In most instances, the results were predictable: African and Asian bodies were "proven" to be incapable of keeping pace with European bodies "with regard to endurance, the speed of neuromuscular response, and energy expenditure."[53] The studies that Jules Amar conducted in North Africa from 1907 to 1909 are typical in this regard. Using motion study alongside a range of ergometric devices, Amar set out to settle the "question of the Arab's energy." The results he came to, however, inevitably shored up a racial typology of long standing. Of the three kinds of laborers tested in his study, Amar concluded that only the Kabyle—historically understood to be whiter and more amenable to assimilation than either Arabs or Berbers—were suited to industrial work, which required rapid movements punctuated with short, frequent stops.[54]

Amar and others associated with the European science of work thus took motion study to the colonial peripheries in order to classify colonial laborers according to their physiological capabilities. But in so doing, Amar also came to the same understanding of pathological locomotion at which the Gilbreths—with whose work Amar was familiar—ultimately arrived. Movement could be pathological because it deviated from an established norm, but also because it was out of place. Pathology, in other words, was for Amar a matter of improper fit between worker and working environment. In this regard, Amar's studies of colonial labor built on his efforts to taxonomize human physiology according to racial types. Just as one might divide the world into "digestive types" and "muscular types" of human physiology, each of which was suited to a particular kind of labor, so too could racial groups be properly pigeonholed in the global industrial economy. Such was ultimately the aim of Amar's experiments with what he called an ergometric cycle. "It is the duty of the European worker," Amar concluded, "to *direct* native labor, which is naturally adapted to fatiguing kinds of work, which will not tax the native's endurance as greatly as it would ours."[55] After World War I, Amar argued that the same approach could likewise be used to return disabled veterans to work (figures 3.18–3.19). Here as well it was a matter of putting "the right man in the right place." Indeed, the war cripple was but the latest entry in Amar's taxonomy of laboring types. As with other types, the goal was "to assist in the work of organizing labor according to rational laws; to assign to each man his true function in the social machine; to enable the hale man and the war-cripple to collaborate in the economic tasks of to-morrow; to formulate concisely the doctrine of the maximum utilization of the physical and psychical energies, without losing sight of the moral factors."[56] There was a crucial difference, however, between the rehabilitation of the wounded soldier and the physiological evaluation and industrial placement of the colonial laborer. Whereas for disabled veterans, finding one's place in the "social machine" also meant reclaiming one's status in the work society, the proper industrial fit held no such redemptive power for the colonial laborer.

If motion study was important to French colonialism's engagement with racial difference, this novel technology was also crucial to the cultural agenda of US imperialism. In this context, however, motion study was carried out not by anthropologists or industrial physiologists but rather by popular cinema. As Charles Musser has argued, popular cinema may not have played as great a role as yellow journalism and the jingoistic press of Hearst and Pulitzer in starting the Spanish-American War, but its contribution was not insignificant. "It would be a gross exaggeration to say that cinema launched a new era of American imperialism," Musser concedes. "But cinema found a role beyond narrow amusement, and this sudden prominence coincided with a new era of overseas expansion and military invention. Who can say what fantasies of power audiences experienced in those darkened halls, and how these emotions continued to resonate outside the theater?"[57] Musser's canonical account explores how the Spanish-American War provided a rich store of wildly popular material and sparked unprecedented commercial competition among leading production outfits. More recently, scholars such as Kristen Whissel and Amy Kaplan have shown that early cinema's representation of the Spanish-American War was also a response to a host of perceived threats to white masculinity, from overcivilization to the New Woman and the closing of the frontier. Filmic representations of masculine empire building offered an antidote to the "all-too-familiar image of an enervated male body exhausted and effeminized by the demands of industrial capitalism and technological modernity that circulated through popular American culture."[58]

Popular cinematic representations of the Spanish-American War might also be read as motion studies. Indeed, as Martha Banta and others have argued, these films invited audiences to inspect new military ma-

3.18 Kabyle laborer on Amar's ergometric cycle. Jules Amar, *Le rendement de la machine humaine* (1909).

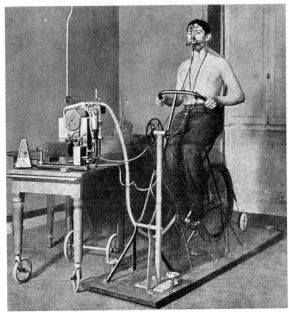

3.19 Disabled veteran on Amar's ergometric cycle. Jules Amar, *The Physiology of Industrial Organisation and the Re-employment of the Disabled* (1919).

chinery and to observe soldiers drilling for battle. The gaze established in the process is at base one of managerial scrutiny. As such, the visual pleasure afforded by the cinema of US imperialism ultimately has less to do with breathtaking spectacles of battle than with well-coordinated movements of men, ships, and trains.[59] Whether taken of soldiers marching in formation or of battleships cruising through the Caribbean, the films shot by Biograph cameraman Billy Bitzer and by William Paley, his counterpart at Edison, gave audiences the opportunity to see mobile, dynamic, and disciplined bodies working to extend the global reach of the US military and of US industry.[60] Equally important to this visual project was the scrutiny of bodies that did not move smoothly across the prelaid trajectories of military—but also racial—discipline. Indeed, Cuban refugees and African American soldiers frequently enter the visual field in order to be evaluated. For their part, Cuban refugees are typically presented as feminized figures awaiting the US military's muscular embrace. Marked as fundamentally different from the norm established by white US soldiers, their movements serve to justify the benevolence of US imperialism writ large. The movements of African American soldiers pose much the same questions: Can these pathological subjects be recuperated by and incorporated into the broader body politic? Can they successfully take up the work of empire themselves?

The formal similarity between chronophotographic studies of pathological locomotion and early cinematic representations of the Spanish-American War are most pronounced in the genre of the war actuality. A term used to describe a range of documentary films produced before World War I, the actuality of the 1890s was generally restricted to a single shot and edited with concern above all for "clarity and logic in the presentation of information."[61] Unlike staged reenactments, the war actuality was filmed on location and composed of footage taken of real events. As described in a special Edison catalog printed in May 1898 titled "War Extra," "They are sure to satisfy the craving of the general public for absolutely true and accurate details regarding the movements of the United States Army getting ready for the invasion of Cuba."[62] As such, the war actuality is marked by a persistent emphasis on movement and on short bursts of action, from soldiers marching in formation to supply trains being unloaded and navy vessels refueled. Indeed, movement often becomes as central an object of representation as the military activities that provide the genre's ostensible subject matter. The war actuality can thus itself be understood as a mode of motion study. Audiences were invited to gaze on the movements of empire but also to judge how well particular workers were fitted for the jobs to which they were assigned and how well their movements could be incorporated into the rhythms of industrial modernity.

That these films would have been understood as motion studies is suggested, at least in the case of Edison's war actualities, by the catalogs produced for sales and promotion. As Musser points out, catalogs advertised the newest offerings to would-be buyers. But they also included suggestions for how exhibitors might incorporate their purchases into longer programs, which commonly included a range of films, slide photography, and oral commentary. Today, scholars are drawn to these catalogs for the information they provide about films that do not survive. Although usually not more than a few sentences long, these vignettes convey a rough sense of what a given film was about and how it was shot. As such, the catalog description might itself be thought of as an exercise in motion study, a textual transcription of the events represented on the screen. As is clear when we read these entries alongside the films that do survive, though, catalog descriptions do not always aim for a one-to-one translation. Indeed, these textual practices of motion study by turns complement, complicate, and even refute the visual representation of movement in the film being described. They draw readers' attention to motions that are easy to overlook (or that require some amount of wishful or jingoistic thinking to discern). Just as often, these catalog descriptions encourage viewers to distinguish between what in the earlier idiom of scientific cinema was called normal and pathological locomotion—and to conjecture on whether and how the latter might be remade in the image of the former.

The "War Extra Catalogue" published in May 1898 by the Edison Manufacturing Company is a case in point, a compendium of prose synopses that reframe the films they purport merely to describe. Many of these actualities are scenes of military preparation that feature soldiers en route to Cuba. At once orderly and idyllic, the films encourage viewers to imagine that the looming conflict will be as well-organized and capably run as any US base during peacetime.[63] In *Military Camp at Tampa, Taken from the Train*, for instance, the transformation of the camp into a bureaucratically managed battlefield is effected by juxtaposition, as the movements of individual soldiers are compared with the momentum of the "rapidly moving train" on which the camera rests (figures 3.20–3.23). The film opens with a panoramic view of the camp that captures a bustle of activity: "A wide plain, dotted with tents, gleaming white in the bright sunshine. Soldiers moving about everywhere, at all sorts of duties."[64] As the train passes along the camp's edge—the track now running parallel to a dirt path that the soldiers traverse, singly and in groups—confusion gives way to orderliness. Regularly spaced telephone poles mark the incremental passing of time like ticks on a graduated x-axis, as if translating the visual abstraction of chronophotography into the cinematic syntax of landscape and setting. Measured against the train's progress, the movements of these soldiers appear optimally efficient. The same cannot be said of a group of men whom the train next passes. These latter remain more or less stationary and, with bodies turned away from the path leading to the camp, face the train itself. Ultimately, though, stragglers register less as a threat to the smooth operations of the war machine than as a sign that the work of mustering-in remains ongoing. Like others before them, these new recruits will soon fall in line.

Descriptions of other films in the "War Extra" iron out the promiscuous itineraries of individual inclination less by means of misdirection than by outright misrepresentation. *U.S. Cavalry Supplies Unloading at Tampa, Florida*, for instance, likewise takes place next to the railroad tracks: "Here is a freight train of thirty cars loaded with baggage and ambulance supplies for the 9th U.S. Cavalry. In the foreground a score of troopers are pulling, lifting and hauling an ambulance from a flat car. It slides down the inclined planks with a sudden rush that makes the men 'hustle' to keep it from falling off. Drill engine on the next track darts past with sharp quick puffs of smoke. A very brisk scene."[65] The film itself presents a rather different picture of the action described here. The soldiers do "hustle" once the cart being pulled off the train begins to slide down the inclined planks and threatens to run over the men positioned to receive it. And this successful recovery does transform what could easily have become a horrific industrial accident into a scene of military camaraderie. With this crisis averted, however, the "score of troopers" gathered at the tracks is confronted with a situation less calamitous than intractable: the cart becomes stuck in between the railroad ties beneath the track. A handful of soldiers push and pull, though to little effect, while others circle the cart and half-heartedly assess the situation. Only briefly then is this film "very brisk," as the catalog notes; the scene is rather one of abrupt, inefficient movements that lead only haphazardly to a resolution of the conflict at hand. The fluid phrasing of the catalog description thus corrects for the haphazard movements captured in the film, performing a sleight of hand by which this chaotic response to a potentially dangerous mishap comes to resemble the routine choreography of industrial process. As in *Military Camp at Tampa, Taken from the Train*, this catalog description goes on to draw a parallel between the soldiers gathered around the stranded cart and the "drill engine on the next track [that] darts past with sharp quick puffs of smoke."[66] Though the camera is stationary, the catalog description's focus follows the train out of the scene in order to picture the efficiency of movement that the labor of the soldiers so evidently lacks.

Unlike the movements of white soldiers, which the catalog frames as absolutely efficient, the movement of people of color in these films is presented as inefficient and in need of attention. Typical are the contrasts drawn in *10th U.S. Infantry, 2nd Battalion, Leaving Cars*. Here we see a column of white soldiers as it "marches in fours and passes through the front of the picture."[67] The movement is grandiose and momentous, calculated to inspire enthusiasm and awe as so many bodies move in unison. But this spectacle of bodies as machines in motion is offset by the figure of a Black onlooker who walks with a "sun-umbrella" and "strolls languidly in the foreground." The juxtaposition is clear. This "comical looking … 'dude'" serves to foreground how this martial spectacle of efficient white locomotion has the power to keep misfits in line and to create a docile body politic in awe of the state. We should also recall in this context the origin of blackface minstrelsy in the efforts of vaudeville performer T. D. Rice to mimic the movements of a physically disabled slave named Jim Crow. To "Jump Jim Crow," as the refrain from Rice's influential song put it, was thus to re-create a choreography that in the chronophotographic tradition from which popular cinema was born would have been described as pathological locomotion. But while Edison's "War Extra" presents this scene as minstrel satire, the film also parodies the fantasy of mustering-in that shaped how African American advocates of the war imagined the domestic benefit of Black participation in US imperialism. If many Black Americans hoped that they would gain some semblance of respect by fighting in the war, this was not to be the case.

Whereas *10th U.S. Infantry, 2nd Battalion, Leaving Cars* uses the tropes of minstrel performance to set the locomotive efficiency of white soldiers into relief, an actuality titled *Colored Troops Disembarking* is explicitly framed as a motion study of Black soldiers (figures 3.24–3.25). As the ship *Mascotte* docks, the stage is set for a controlled environment. The camera seems to capture a perspective that blends scientific objectivity with the voyeurism of seeing "real life" minstrel performance unawares, or the same

3.20–3.23 Still images from *Military Camp at Tampa, Taken from the Train* (1898), Thomas A. Edison, Inc. Library of Congress Paper Print Collection.

fantasy of T. D. Rice in the origin story of minstrelsy: viewers are now in the position of Rice watching the "pathological" movements of Black individuals. One by one, the soldiers make their way down a gangplank that has been placed at an "extra steep" angle because of the unusually high tide. The scene is accordingly set with terse statements of fact: "The steamer 'Mascotte' has reached her dock at Port Tampa, and the 2d Battalion of Colored Infantry is going ashore. Tide is very high, and the gang plank is extra steep; and it is laughable to see the extreme caution displayed by the soldiers clambering down. The commanding officer struts on the wharf, urging them to hurry. Two boat stewards in glistening white duck coats, are interested watchers—looking for 'tips' perhaps. The picture is full of fine light and shadow effects."[68] Whereas the white commanding officer "struts on the wharf," a turn of phrase that suggests self-confidence and poise while also conjuring machine-like movement, the Black soldiers exiting the ship are made to appear ludicrous. Their descent is lumbering and irregularly paced; the awesome spectacle of uniform locomotion featured in *10th U.S. Infantry, 2nd Battalion, Leaving Cars* is replaced by a ritual debasement of African Americans that harnesses familiar minstrel conventions to the putatively objective discourse of film. The result is a portrait of pathological locomotion rendered transparently indexical of racial difference. But insofar as this is also a scene of pedagogy, as indicated by the shouting officer below, *Colored Troops Disembarking* recuperates the rehabilitative dimension of the imperial project for African Americans. The promise exists nonetheless, in other words, that the soldiers whose movements are scrutinized here only to be mocked might yet be brought into the national fold, were they to heed the instructions of the white officer who seeks to direct their movements from the shore.

The "War Extra" is likewise filled with films that scrutinize the locomotion of Cuban people. But whereas the movements of Black soldiers—alternatively lethargic and excessively lively—are contrasted with the efficiency of white soldiers, the presence of Cuban refugees serves to remind viewers that US imperialism is at root a benevolent enterprise. *Cuban Refugees Waiting for Rations*, for instance, opens on a small group of *reconcentrados* in front of a Red Cross relief station (figures 3.26–3.27). The scene is purposefully pitiful: "They stand in line waiting, each man with his tin dish and cup. One expects to see just such men as these, after centuries of Spanish oppression and tyranny."[69] These men, the catalog suggests, have been reduced to begging by the injurious nature of European colonialism; incapable of self-reliance and bereft of manhood, they

3.24–3.25 Still images from *Colored Troops Disembarking* (1898), Thomas A. Edison, Inc. Library of Congress Paper Print Collection.

are entirely dependent on American benevolence. The clearest sign of the refugees' abasement is to be read in their gait. "As they come forward, their walk, even, is listless and lifeless." The conclusions we are to draw from this motion study, moreover, presuppose that human locomotion is indexical of racial essence: "The picture affords an exceedingly interesting racial character study."[70] In contrast to the halting and tentative movements of the Cuban refugees, the strides of the white US officer who enters the frame from the bottom left bespeak a sense of masculine purpose and efficiency. The officer's first task, however, is not to minister to the refugees but to attend to a nearby group of white women. Placing himself between these women and the Cuban men, the officer becomes a bulwark of sorts, as if to ensure that charged sympathies do not beget more compromising forms of intimacy. The anxiety legible in the choreography or blocking of this film is even more evident in the catalog description. The women volunteering with the Red Cross are described there as "seeing the sights," a phrase that obscures their humanitarian efforts while also making clear that their ultimate role in the film—like the Cuban refugees—is to provide white officers an opportunity to model the masculine virtue of US imperial intervention.

We find a similar emphasis in an actuality titled *Cuban Volunteers Marching for Rations*, though with a rehabilitative twist. Like *Cuban Refugees Waiting for Rations*, this film transforms the charitable encounter into a potent display of martial masculinity. But rather than underscoring the fundamental difference between Cubans and American soldiers, *Cuban Volunteers Marching for Rations* suggests that US imperialism has the potential to make the former more like the latter. Indeed, though each of the Cuban soldiers carries a "tin cup and dish" that serves as a reference to *Cuban Refugees Waiting for Rations*, relief in *Cuban Volunteers Marching for Rations* is earned rather than doled out. As we read in the catalog description of the latter film, the "command is given 'forward march' and the column approaches the audience. A fine looking body of men, worthy of a people battling for freedom."[71] The benevolent impact of imperial intervention is thus staged as a restoration of efficient movement that is in turn underscored—as the "tin cup and dish" give way to military accoutrements—by a change of theatrical props. The effect is ultimately to underscore the fantasy of labor that unites the European science of work, colonial anthropology, and the cinema of US imperialism with the print culture of social welfare: the fantasy that human bodies at work are interchangeable.

3.26–3.27 Still images from *Cuban Refugees Waiting for Rations* (1898), Thomas A. Edison, Inc. Library of Congress Paper Print Collection.

The Movement of Analogy

The Gilbreths' ultimately ill-fated attempt to bring industrial motion study to social welfare provision was motivated by much the same fantasy. If workers could be taught not only the most efficient way to perform a given task but also to find their proper place in the world of work, might not the same methods be used with members of the "dependent classes" targeted by social welfare institutions of all stripes? Never ones to shy away from a challenge, much less a promising new market, the Gilbreths set out to bring industrial motion study to the provision of social welfare, beginning with a series of plainly opportunistic efforts to address the "crippled soldier problem" that emerged in the wake of World War I. Introduced in 1915, the so-called simultaneous motion chart or simply "simo chart" was a first step down this path (figure 3.28).

At base, the simo chart codified the Gilbreths' earlier efforts to read cyclegraphic images for the proper fit between worker and workplace. This two-dimensional graph translated visual representations of the laboring body into the schematic idiom of the workflow chart. The horizontal axis listed those parts of the body required for the execution of a given task, and the vertical axis marked elapsed time. Transposing data from cyclegraphic and micromotion studies, the Gilbreths plotted the position and activity of hands, arms, legs, and head at regular intervals. In some instances, this diagrammatic portrait of the body at labor was used to reconfigure a job so that each part of the laborer's anatomy could be effectively utilized at all times. But the simo chart could also be used to adapt labor processes to the skills and capacities of individual workers. In the case of a worker who could perform all but the last step in a sequence of tasks with speed and accuracy, for example, a job might be redesigned to allow a moment in which all limbs are at rest before the final step. For an amputee worker, the simo chart could be used in similar fashion to reassign any task that would otherwise have been performed by the absent limb. With this in mind, the Gilbreths soon promoted the simo chart as an instrument of vocational rehabilitation for disabled veterans. The task at hand seemed but a logical extension of industrial fatigue elimination: "adapt the method [of analysis] to the worker"; "assign the worker an appropriate type of work, if he has no strong preference or aptitude for any particular kind of work"; "suggest inventions or changes that will make work and worker a better fit."[72]

In many ways, the Gilbreths' translation from cyclegraph to simo chart would seem to return industrial motion study to its material roots in the

3.28 Frank B. Gilbreth, "Simultaneous Motion Cycle Chart of Transferring Organisms." Chart shows motion data from right and left arms and hands in the process of transferring organisms to inoculating tubes, March 10, 1917. Frank B. Gilbreth Motion Study Photographs (1913–1917), the Kheel Center for Labor-Management Documentation and Archives, Cornell University.

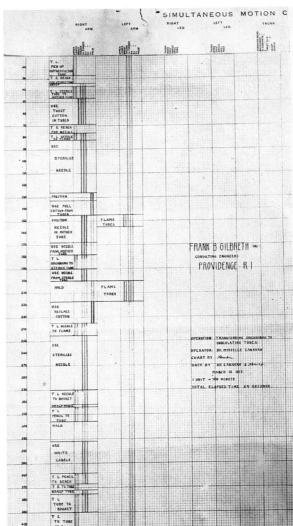

scrutiny of mobility disability. But their subsequent embrace of "motion study for the handicapped" is most notable for how it extends the formal logic of pathological locomotion to its breaking point. By insisting that all working bodies are or can be made the same, the Gilbreths ultimately succeed in capturing not the visual essence of work as such but rather the analogy at the heart of motion studies. We see this project's central fantasy begin to unravel in the paternalistic and patently unrealistic forays the Gilbreths made into disability rehabilitation. Not only do marketing concerns dominate their letters during this period, but the Gilbreths' work in the field makes clear that they viewed disability less as a matter of lived experience than of experimental design. A Gilbreth study intended to show dental schools how they could accommodate disabled trainees, for instance, featured a test subject with one arm tucked underneath his lab coat. Similar experiments with "blind" workers regularly feature sighted volunteers outfitted with opaque glasses. Though these kinds of studies may strike us as insipid or insulting, they found a receptive audience among the Gilbreths' peers. In 1918, discussion of the Gilbreths' methods at the American Mechanical Engineers Association yielded a wealth of platitudes about the nation's debt to wounded veterans, but also a stunningly naive brainstorming session about returning the latter to productivity. As one participant wondered, might not a disabled worker "with a spasmodic jerk" simply be given a hammer and placed in an industry where this motion, repetitively executed, could be put to good use?[73]

On paper and among like-minded industrial consultants, the Gilbreths might well have been able to convince themselves and others that motion study captured the essence of work and could thus be used to slot everyone (and every body) into the industrial economy. When given the opportunity to put this theory into practice at the Craig Colony in upstate New York, the Gilbreths—and Frank in particular—soon began to suspect that, at least with regard to the "pathological" movements of people with disabilities, a squiggly line might be just a squiggly line. The project began optimistically enough. In January 1919, after a brief trip to the Craig Colony, Frank wrote to Lillian, "It is the largest Epleptic [*sic*] Hospital in the world" and had "'plenty of money' for research left by Craig."[74] The administrators had already begun filming patients having epileptic episodes but evidently felt that the Gilbreths' methods might nevertheless yield beneficial results. Indeed, it is easy to speculate, given the pride of place historically given to labor in social institutions modeled on the colony plan, that Craig administrators hoped that motion study would help train people with epilepsy to work more efficiently and thus also to harness the rehabilitative promise of work as such. For their part, the Gilbreths saw this collaboration with the Craig Colony as "the greatest chance [they had] ever had."[75] Even early on, though, there seem to have been misgivings on either side that went to the core of what the Gilbreths promised their clients. When Frank "explained some Mo. Cycle Charts," for instance, "they made no direct hit. Their attitude was, 'Well, what of it[?]'"[76] In letters to Lillian, Frank initially brushed off concerns like these. But before long the question of exactly how motion studies help rehabilitate people with epilepsy began to loom large.

The films that Frank took at the Craig Colony later that year bear out this wavering of purpose. Whether micromotion studies of men and women with epilepsy walking the institution grounds or cyclegraphic studies of patients lifting blocks at a workbench, these images reveal little about the nature of epilepsy or about "the one best way to work" for epileptic laborers. Frank's notations alternate between flat and schematic observations, the latter as if to offer methodological clarity in place of conclusive results. If the prose descriptions in Edison's "War Extra" catalog by turns flesh out, reframe, and contradict the films they gloss, Frank's observations seem little more than placeholders—showing a wishful thinking, perhaps, that there would be more to say later. "Group of epileptics. Note different positions," one typical caption reads (figures 3.29–3.33). Gone is any sense that the Gilbreths' work at the Craig Colony was the "greatest chance" they ever had, replaced perhaps by an awareness that this opportunity muddied their focus on industrial efficiency. Rather than distilling the quintessence of work by abstracting away the particulars of embodiment, these images convey little more than a vague sense of daily life at the Craig Colony (figures 3.34–3.35). The exercise and activities that the Gilbreths asked institutionalized people to perform before their camera were no doubt novel in their own right but similar enough to the make-work they were asked to do on any other given day.

That work had dropped out of the picture, so to speak, more or less entirely in the Gilbreths' research at Craig Colony is evident in an article they wrote but never published called "Motion Study of Epilepsy and Its Relation to Industry." The authors begin confidently enough, stating in no uncertain terms "that Motion Study is applicable to all activity." They note further that "a broad study of the handicapped in industry, including the problems of their health, placement, training, prosperity, and economic efficient use, enables us to state that much of that which is ordinarily considered a handicap can be overcome, with proper study and education of both managers and the handicapped."[77] But when the Gilbreths broach the subject of epilepsy, the certainty of experience gives way to cautious optimism. Previous success in the work of rehabilitation, they venture, "leads us to have faith that the problem of using the epileptic in industry will also be solved."[78] What follows is less an explanation of conclusions reached than further elaboration on the investigators' tightly

3.29–3.33 Still photographs from Frank Gilbreth's work at the Craig Colony in Sonyea, New York, in 1920. Caption on reverse of 3.33: "Group of epileptics. Note different positions." Box 120, folder 6, Gilbreth Library of Management Papers Msp8, Purdue University Libraries.

3.34–3.35 Still photographs from Frank Gilbreth's work at the Craig Colony in Sonyea, New York, in 1920. Caption on reverse of 3.34: "Epileptic putting blocks in place. Note rubbing his head while thinking what to do next." Caption on reverse of 3.35: "Epileptic putting blocks in place. Note how high the hand is raised from the blocks." Box 120, folder 6, Gilbreth Library of Management Papers Msp8, Purdue University Libraries.

held faith in their methods. Indeed, the Gilbreths continually return to the idea of "LIKENESS" in their subsequent analysis, as if anxiously underscoring that the conceptual reciprocity between inefficiency and disability will yield new insights. The Gilbreths emphasize, for example, that the "hesitation and indecision" that mark the performance of nondisabled workers bears "a surprising LIKENESS" to the "behavior of epileptics, as shown by [their] micro-motion study records" (figures 3.36–3.37). And though such hesitation is prevalent among workers of all stripes, the Gilbreths further observe, "We have found that a surprising amount of it can be overcome merely by showing and explaining the peculiarities of the cyclegraph to the worker who made the motions that it portrays," whether that worker has epilepsy or not.[79] Ultimately, however, the essay ends on a diffident note, tacitly acknowledging that the subject has indeed gotten away from its authors. "We do not know what therapeutic effect such teaching would have upon epileptics," they conclude, "but we *believe* the effect would be good, because it has proved so with ALL TYPES, everywhere, handicapped as well as unhandicapped, in the industries wherever it has been done."[80]

We can only speculate about why this essay remained unpublished, particularly given that "Motion Study of Epilepsy and Its Relation to Industry" could presumably have been included in the Gilbreths' *Motion Study for the Handicapped*, a volume filled with essays that are equally speculative. But Frank's letters to Lillian do give us some indication why they may have concluded that the lessons learned at the Craig Colony were best left in upstate New York. Writing of the "Epeleptic [*sic*] paper," Frank compared it to another failed effort to expand the Gilbreth brand: "I finally decided that I didn't know what we were trying to do with it. I think we should put more ado for our regular business in it, because it is like waterproof cellars over again. We must be careful not to get people to think we have changed our business. I wish you could slip in something that would show that our regular business is Motion Study and the best way to do the work."[81] Their ardent insistence on the LIKENESS captured at the Craig Colony notwithstanding, even the Gilbreths were left unpersuaded by their best efforts to prove how motion study captured the rehabilitative power of work as such. If the Gilbreths' efforts at the Craig Colony could be said to have proved anything, it was the importance of finding the proper industrial fit, though not in the conceptual sense that motivated their work more generally. Indeed, rather than transforming the residents of the Craig Colony into ideally efficient workers ready to be placed in an increasingly specialized industrial economy, the Gilbreths could

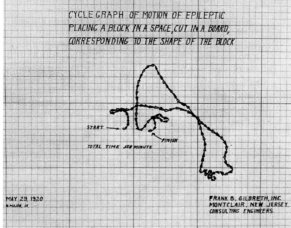

3.36–3.37 Drawing from a cyclegraph taken at Craig Colony. Caption on reverse of 3.36: "The motion shown on this print shows the path followed by the nail of the first finger." Box 120, folder 6, Gilbreth Library of Management Papers Msp8, Purdue University Libraries.

only affirm what they—and the Craig Colony administrators—probably already believed: that these people were already where they belonged, institutionalized and cast out of industrial modernity.

It is perhaps fitting that the long history of adjacency, potential, and near misses linking motion study to the print culture of social welfare faltered on the question of analogy, given how promiscuously this novel visual technology circulated in social contexts marked by the vicissitudes of race, disability, and class. Among contemporary scholars, of course, analogy is a notoriously "vexed issue."[82] Analogies between different social identities, while at times crucial and politically advantageous, risk a range of distortions and elisions. A great deal is lost in translation—or in transit—as we shuttle from what we think we know about one term in the pairing to what we think we know about the second. Indeed, insofar as the term describes the movement of knowledge from one context to another, analogy itself might be framed as a kind of motion study. As Celeste Langan argues, this movement is a "perpetual negotiation" between two ideas, phenomena, or concepts that encourages us to see it for what it is not—a relation of absolute equivalence.[83] As an instrument of analogy, motion study purports to capture and make legible the absolute equivalence of all labor, once the particularities of embodiment have been stripped away. Its failure to do so not only reveals the shortcomings of this particular technology; it also points up a contradiction at the heart of the print culture of social welfare more broadly, which, like the Gilbreths, endeavors to will likeness into identity.

4
INSTITUTIONAL RHYTHMS

In the first few decades of cinematic production after the Spanish-American War, people on the social and imperial margins continued to be seen rather than heard. Only gradually, in fact, did sound become part of the picture, so to speak, for films on any subject. While early cinematic exhibitions often used musical accompaniment, it was not until the 1920s that recorded dialogue was integrated into the narrative action. Famously, the first full-length "talkie" was *The Jazz Singer* (1927). Starring Al Jolson in blackface, this technological wonder featured a modern "Black" voice that echoed the racial fantasies of antebellum minstrelsy. Needless to say, Jolson's smash hit did not have an activist agenda. But in the decades preceding its release, Black song did play an unlikely part in the print culture of social welfare. In kinship less with the demeaning melodrama of blackface cinema than with the managerial gaze of the war actuality, a small group of charity workers and reformers began collecting and transcribing African American work songs. It was a partnership as improbable as it was one-sided. The songs created by enslaved people and their descendants, often under the most brutal of conditions, were pressed into service by reformers struggling to justify the coercive practices of social welfare provision. Was the work demanded in the almshouse, the insane asylum, or the industrial school truly meaningful? The work song offered an answer at once eloquent and equivocal.

The musical transcriptions that found their way into the late nineteenth-century print culture of social welfare are part of a broader history of popular and scholarly interest in the work song. And the genre itself is likewise of much older provenance. If we follow Bruce Jackson's influential lead, it seems probable that work songs have always existed and have flourished everywhere. For Jackson, any song used to pace—rather than accompany—physical labor counts as a work song.[1] The melodies employed to stamp barley in ancient Greece, to weave tweed in the Scottish Hebrides, and to navigate the waters of the Caribbean belong to a transhistorical genre defined less by a particular set of formal attributes than by its capacity to choreograph human movement.[2] At its most elemental, the work song coordinates the efforts of a group of people who need to perform certain tasks at the same time, at the same speed, or in interlocking rhythms.[3] This coordination might allow workers to apply maximum force at just the right moment or to maintain their safety over the course of the day. When the work in question is coerced or strictly policed, work songs can also make it difficult for overseers to single out individual workers for punishment. In these situations, moreover, or whenever the obligation to work is externally imposed—whether by economic necessity or state violence—work songs can offer an emotional outlet and even some degree of control. As Jackson observes, the genre changes "the nature of the work by putting the work into the worker's framework."[4]

In the United States, the extensive literature on the genre of the work song amassed by folklorists and musicians dates to the 1930s. This body of writing and recording focuses on the work songs created by Black Americans under successive regimes of racial discipline, from chattel slavery to the convict lease and the Southern penitentiary. While his efforts were not entirely unprecedented, John Lomax is often credited with "salvaging" the genre for academic and lay audiences alike. Indeed, stories of how John Lomax and his son Alan dragged their hulking recording equipment into prisons across the South to capture a "great panoply of original songs" are now themselves the stuff of folklore.[5] Later collectors looked to Southern prisons for the same reasons that brought the Lomaxes there. As Bruce Jackson writes of his own field research, "The last place in North America where work songs survived as a viable tradition was in southern agricultural prisons because many of those institutions maintained, until the 1960s and 1970s, the racially segregated and physically brutal culture of the nineteenth-century plantation."[6] Signposted by names like Lomax and Jackson but fleshed out by the efforts of countless others, professional and amateur alike, the expansive tradition of twentieth-century folklore has produced a wealth of audio recordings, as well as a rich body of written transcriptions and ethnographies. This latter archive includes scholarly monographs, trade books, anthologies, and liner notes. Whatever their preferred medium, method, or genre, twentieth-century collectors of African American work songs generally approached their task with a shared sense of urgency. As the poet and scholar Sterling Brown described his own motivation, a "new-fangled machine killed John Henry"; its "numerous offspring would soon kill the work song of his buddies."[7]

To say that the social welfare reformers of the late nineteenth century paved the way for this celebrated tradition of folklore and audio ethnography is to give them at once too much and too little credit. For though these earlier researchers and aficionados preceded Lomax and his contemporaries by several decades, their transcriptions and ethnographies were scattered and sparse, never amounting to anything that could be described as a tradition, much less a movement. And though turn-of-the-century reformers argued that work songs were threatened by the encroaching forces of industrial modernity, they were ultimately less concerned with safeguarding these cultural artifacts for their own sake than with analyzing the social truths they were thought to contain. For some reformers, the data mined from African American work songs could be used to bolster familiar racial typologies. For others, work songs offered crucial insight into the noneconomic, even spiritual value of work as such. The conviction that work is morally valuable in and of itself, of course, has long been a touchstone for social welfare practice, as for the work society writ large. But in the latter few decades of the nineteenth century, in the face of mounting concerns about the coerced labor performed in a range of custodial institutions, shoring up faith in this truism became especially pressing. Nowhere was the use of inmate labor more conspicuous than in the rise of large-scale, highly rationalized, and monopolistic prison industries in the North and the convict lease system in the South.[8] Similar practices were employed in specialized institutions for people with disabilities and African Americans, among others, which combined penal-style discipline with medical and racial paternalism to promote coerced labor as both therapeutic and cost-effective.[9] Across the board, the ballooning profitability of inmate labor—and belief in its deterrent value—outstripped reformers' abilities to justify these increasingly violent practices in anything but economic terms.

In the midst of this crisis of institutional labor, reformers banded together under the banner of charities and correction to reimagine social welfare provision from the ground up. Central to this project was rethinking how institutional labor could be made truly meaningful for all parties concerned, for professionalizing social welfare workers as well as for inmates, residents, and patients. In this regard, charities and correction were part of the wider embrace of "scientific charity" at the turn of the twentieth century. As such, the ideals of institutional reform went hand in hand with the ideals of bureaucratic rationality that, as we saw in previous chapters, also guided the operations of the Pension Bureau and charity organization societies. When African American work songs were conscripted into the agenda of charity and corrections, they thus took their place alongside relatively novel industrial print forms such as the report, the memo, and the conference proceedings. The obvious differences between and among these various genres notwithstanding, each was used to ascertain the circumstances under which institutional labor could be said to possess noneconomic value—and to define the nature of that value. Given the genre's familiar associations with self-directed and purposeful labor, the allure of the work song would seem clear. But the reformers also speculate that the work song might ultimately be used not only to redeem the worst abuses of institutional labor but also in a rather more directly diagnostic capacity to determine whose work ethic was sound and whose wasn't.

In accounting for how the African American work song entered the print culture of social welfare at the turn of the twentieth century, the story told here reverses the pattern followed in previous chapters. Rather than exploring how a bureaucratic genre of social welfare provision found traction in public culture at large, this chapter asks how a vernacular cultural form was taken up by a reformist community in the throes of professionalization. One print form among many in the orbit of charities and correction, the work song consolidated two evidently irreconcilable impulses driving the ongoing work of institution (re)building. On the one hand, these songs suggested that labor is meaningful only when directed by the physiological rhythms of the laboring body. To some reformers, this universal "truth" aligned the work of charities and correction professionals with what today would be called romantic anticapitalism—a nagging suspicion that capitalist labor can never be as fulfilling, spiritually or otherwise, as bygone modes of work. On the other hand, though, the work song's synchronicity of inclination and production also provided a model of capitalist discipline, a tool with which to force workers into the rhythms of industrial profit making. Ultimately, this tension allowed the work song to become a sounding board for a profession in transition, a tradition caught between the religious surety of antebellum volunteerism and the rational optimism of social science.

To tell the forgotten story about how the work song came to mediate the turn-of-the-century crisis of institutional labor thus means looking not forward to the Lomaxes, but back to the roots of charities and correction in earlier reformist traditions. These traditions were preoccupied not with the work song but with the African American spiritual. After exploring the perhaps unlikely afterlives of the Civil War–era Port Royal Experiment in the professionalization of charities and corrections, the chapter offers two case studies. The first, a comparative study of global vernacular work song traditions by the German economist Karl Bücher, illuminates how ethnographic transcriptions in the field and stenographic transcriptions in the settings of white-collar professionalization were tasked with the same cultural work. Turning then from Leipzig and Chicago to Chapel Hill, the chapter then explores how the sociologist Howard Odum launched the Institute for Social Research at the University of North Carolina (UNC) with a series of folk music anthologies. Although Odum and his colleagues at UNC were wary of the baggage that charities and correction began to carry by the 1920s, in emphasizing the redemptive rhythms of institutional labor UNC researchers trod a well-worn path. As in Bücher's *Arbeit und Rhythmus*, the work song for Odum encapsulated at once a reformist optimism about the power of productive labor to return anyone to the social fold and a deep-seated ambivalence about what that premise—and such a return—actually entailed in practice.

From Spirituals to Work Songs

Reformist efforts to transcribe the songs of enslaved people were conducted sporadically across the nineteenth century, but the locus classicus for this ethnographic project is the Port Royal Experiment.[10] A Civil War–era "rehearsal for Reconstruction," the Port Royal Experiment was launched in 1861 by Northern forces on the Sea Islands of South Carolina and Georgia. After the area fell to the Union navy, Treasury agents, entrepreneurs, and missionaries arrived from the North to help guide the transition to freedom. From the outset, there was broad enthusiasm about the prospects for success. Federal officials and private investors embraced the Sea Islands as a chain of perfectly enclosed social laboratories in which to plan the economic rebuilding of the South. Known collectively as Gideon's Band, the reformers, abolitionists, and educators who traveled to Port Royal thought conditions equally favorable for redressing the moral blight of slavery. In the spirit of antebellum volunteerism, Gideon's Band was motivated by a sentimental, often paternalistic, desire to welcome enslaved people into the human community. Widespread confidence about the mission at hand, however, soon gave way to intense disagreements among the various Northern interests represented on the Sea Islands. White Northerners also clashed with the people they claimed to help, the so-called contraband slaves—a military neologism marking the uncertain legal status of men and women no longer enslaved but not yet free. At stake in these debates was ultimately what economic life would look like and mean on the Sea Islands and across a reconstructed South after the war. Would the system devised at Port Royal subordinate freed people to the demands of Northern capital or would it be guided by the Indigenous practices of Sea Island communities and be alive to the economic autonomy so fiercely asserted by formerly enslaved people?[11]

In the end, what emerged from the Sea Islands was not the radical vision of land redistribution that contraband slaves demanded and progressive reformers supported. Instead, formerly enslaved people were dispossessed of their subsistence plots and forced by vagrancy legislation and debt peonage into the capitalist market. While devastating by any measure, the collapse of the Port Royal Experiment is eclipsed in popular memory by the failure of Reconstruction a decade later. Today, in fact, the Port Royal Experiment is best known not for the social experiment in free labor conducted on the Sea Islands but for the slave spirituals collected there. Enthralled by the religious music they chanced to overhear at Port Royal, many white Northerners set out to commit these songs to the page. The same insular boundedness that made the Sea Islands perfectly suited for a social experiment in free labor, many reformers believed, also made them perfectly preserved enclaves of slave culture. From Lucy McKim's pioneering articles in *Dwight's Music Journal* to Thomas Wentworth Higginson's *Army Life in a Black Regiment* (1869) and countless private letters and memoirs, the Port Royal Experiment yielded a wealth of writing about and transcriptions of slave spirituals.[12] These accounts thrilled supporters in the North, who were eager not only for news of the war but also for portraits of "authentic" slave life that conveyed the humanitarian urgency of the Union cause. As the editors of the landmark anthology *Slave Songs of the United States* (1867) noted, "The wild, sad strains tell, as the sufferers themselves could not, of crushed hopes, keen sorrow, and a dull, daily misery, which covered them as hopelessly as the fog from the rice swamps."[13]

Transcriptions of the spirituals made at Port Royal set the terms on which the genre gradually came to be embraced across US public culture after the war, whether in popular magazines, middle-class parlors, or urban concert halls. As a distinguished body of scholarship has shown, this peculiar reception history was shaped by two broadly overlapping sets of preoccupations. First, the ethnographic accounts that emerged from the Sea Islands were skeptical about whether Western musical notation could capture the "exotic" melodies or idiosyncratic performance of religious slave music. As Ronald Radano observes, these kinds of concerns date back as far as the 1700s in the annals of Anglo-European musicology. But the writing produced at Port Royal gave popular purchase as never before to the idea that Black musical performance "exceeds notation."[14] Second, public interest in the spiritual was also stoked by the narrow mode of interpretation inaugurated at Port Royal. As the sociologist Jon Cruz has demonstrated, songs that originally filled a disparate range of social, religious, and political functions came in the accounts that emerged from the Sea Islands to represent the absolute truth of slave experience. Cruz coins the term "ethnosympathy" to describe how the spiritual was conscripted into a "new humanitarian pursuit of the inner world of distinctive and collectively classifiably subjects." This "pathos-oriented mode of hearing" allowed reformers and then the public at large to approach the spirituals as "windows into the lives" of enslaved people and into the experience of slavery itself.[15] More recently, Daphne Brooks has emphasized how this cultural hermeneutics ultimately had less to do with slave experience than with white catharsis. Where the spirituals and the formerly enslaved people who performed in concert halls across the United States and internationally were taken to embody "the physical and aural manifestation of slavery's traumas," intensely empathetic white audiences "expressed a simultaneous affirmation and disavowal of their own complicity with the narrative of slavery."[16]

Important though scholarly attention to the depoliticization of slave music on the Sea Islands has been, the prominence of the spirituals in cultural histories of Port Royal has obscured another important legacy of that failed rehearsal for Reconstruction—its role as a turning point in US social welfare provision. If the first white reformers to arrive on the Sea Islands set out to help freed people to assert their full humanity, such radically emancipatory ambitions soon gave way to the morality of the market. Freedom came to mean only the freedom to contract one's labor, even if under coercion or the threat of imprisonment. By the same token, the sentimental humanitarianism that brought Northern reformers to the Sea Islands and shaped popular reception of the spirituals was gradually replaced by a more plainly disciplinary emphasis on the social value of work in and of itself. Illuminating in this regard is the career of Edward L.

Pierce, the New England lawyer who first called the Union's attention to the needs of contraband slaves on the Sea Islands and recruited Gideon's Band.[17] While he shared the feelings of compassion and outrage that drew other white Northerners to the region, Pierce soon came to believe that preparing formerly enslaved people for freedom had less to do with recognizing their right to self-sovereignty than with shunting them into the labor market. As Amy Dru Stanley notes, Pierce told contraband slaves that "if they were to be free, they would have to work, and would be shut up or deprived of privileges if they did not."[18] In an effort to make good on this threat, Pierce devised a system of workhouses and prisons for contraband slaves on the Sea Islands. The end of the Port Royal Experiment did little to temper Pierce's commitment to work-based welfare provision. Indeed, he drew on the lessons learned on the Sea Islands in his new position as secretary of the Massachusetts Board of State Charities. In that capacity, Pierce proposed that local overseers of the poor should be allowed to extract labor from alms seekers—whether "chopping wood [or] picking stone"—as payment for food or a night's lodging. As a member of the legislature three years later, Pierce introduced a similar measure subjecting "beggars who refused to work to conviction as vagrants and forced labor."[19]

Pierce's postwar career trajectory was not anomalous. Many alumni of the Port Royal Experiment gradually set aside the Christian humanitarianism of antebellum volunteerism in favor of more explicitly punitive practices of social welfare. Indeed, prisons, asylums, and reformatories came to mirror the Sea Islands—self-enclosed spaces of coerced labor that were celebrated as rehabilitative. Reformers soon gave the name *charity and corrections* to this expansive project, which sought at base to rationalize the provision of social welfare and double down on the social value of work for its own sake. The transition to charity and corrections, of course, did not happen overnight. The years and decades after the Civil War instead marked a period of uneasy transition and recalibration across the fields of institutional work. And the project of charity and corrections coexisted awkwardly at times with the belief that social welfare remained at base a humanitarian, if not explicitly spiritual, undertaking. The transitional quality of charity and corrections is marked by a residual belief in the religious necessity of helping those in need with an equally zealous faith in bureaucratic rationalism and industrial print culture. But there was a nagging question throughout: as reformers were struggling to define what they did as professional work, they still had to show that the work they demanded of people in institutional contexts had noneconomic value. And so when they turned to Black song, they turned not to the spiritual but to the work song.

The work of wrangling the competing and seemingly contradictory priorities of the moment into a more or less cohesive agenda was spearheaded by the National Conference of Charities and Correction (NCCC), an annual gathering first held in 1874. Initially, the NCCC meetings took place as a breakout group of sorts at the American Social Science Association (ASSA), which had been created in 1865 with a mandate to "guide the public mind to the best practical means of promoting the Amendment of laws, the Advancement of Education, the Prevention and Repression of Crime, the Reformation of Criminals, and the Progress of Public Morality."[20] The two groups' aims were considered compatible, if not ultimately interchangeable, in the first few years of the NCCC's existence. Before long, however, NCCC members began to feel that the ASSA's theoretical approach to social science was at odds with their own rather more pragmatic focus on reform. A movement was thus begun to establish the NCCC as an independent organization. And while the issues addressed by both groups continued to overlap for several years, as did their membership rosters, a formal separation took place in 1879. Each organization set out to develop its niche, with the ASSA concentrating on research and the NCCC on reform. These two categories, of course, were never mutually exclusive. But the division of intellectual labor between research and reform set the terms on which sociology and social work emerged as distinct academic disciplines later in the twentieth century. Looking back on this split years later, NCCC members saw no reason for regret. As one writer declared in the *Proceedings of the National Conference of Charities and Correction* in 1893, the organization's history of achievement spoke for itself: "You will find the ideas which have been formulated in the Conference built into the walls of prisons and hospitals for the insane" and incorporated into the spiritual bedrock of society.[21]

To be sure, the suggestion that NCCC ideas provided a cornerstone for brick-and-mortar institutions is rhetorically powerful. But as reprinted in a collection of papers originally presented at an NCCC convention, this flourish of self-congratulation also underscores how the professionalization of charities and correction relied on print culture in general and on the genre of the conference proceeding in particular.[22] Before ideas could become bricks, they had to become pages. And these pages were in turn annually collated into bound volumes that not only bore witness to a history of specific debates and local interventions but also sought to champion the cumulative—even utopian—ambition of engaged social science (figure 4.1). The *Proceedings of the National Conference of Charities and Correction* thus served a dual function. They established a specialized rhetorical community, long a hallmark of professionalization, while also embodying the spiritual impact that the NCCC sought to have in the world.[23] Practically speaking, this balancing act was not the cut-and-dried exercise in transcription we might expect. The bulk of each volume of the *Proceedings* consists of reprinted versions of papers that conference members read aloud and later submitted in hard copy, generally after more or less extensive revision.[24] Neither were printed accounts of discussions word-for-word transcriptions. Not only did scheduling snags prevent stenographers from attending every session, but the editors evidently had so little faith in transcriptions produced on the spot that they began asking attendees for "abstracts" of their contributions to discussion.[25] Unsurprisingly, these documents are conspicuously eloquent and concise; some are even footnoted. All appearances to the contrary, it is thus clear that the *Proceedings* of the NCCC are not unmediated transcripts of everything said at a given meeting. Rather, these volumes are collages of multiply authored texts, each of which bears a unique relation to the event at hand while also sharing in a tacitly acknowledged commitment to the spiritual project of charity and corrections.[26] In the *Proceedings*, we might thus suggest, transcription aspires to something like musical notation. It aims not only to account for what happened when but also to allow readers to re-create the fullness of the original conference. That such a promise was never realized did not make it any less worth pursuing. Indeed, what one participant noted of the music played between sessions might have appeared on the masthead of the *Proceedings*: "It is impossible to report in words the good spirit that prevailed among the members, the warm hospitality of the people, and the charm of the music."[27]

The formal effort that went into translating the spiritual work of social welfare onto the page dovetails with the contents of the *Proceedings*, which cover a disparate range of topics but continually circle back to the material labor demanded of relief seekers. Was this labor meaningful in any higher sense—beyond, that is, the economic gain accrued by institutions and municipalities? The professional status of welfare workers was thus dependent not only on their bureaucratic abilities but also on the meaning that could be ascribed to the work they required of others. Even the most rational professions, it seems, could not claim the mantle of social science if their practitioners did nothing more than force poor people into pointless

PROCEEDINGS

OF THE

NATIONAL CONFERENCE

OF

CHARITIES AND CORRECTION

AT THE

TWENTY-SIXTH ANNUAL SESSION HELD IN THE CITY OF
CINCINNATI, OHIO, MAY 17–23, 1899

EDITED BY

ISABEL C. BARROWS

BOSTON, MASS.: GEORGE H. ELLIS, 272 CONGRESS STREET

LONDON

P. S. KING & SON, 2 AND 4 GREAT SMITH STREET, WESTMINSTER, S.W.

1900

4.1 Title page of the *Proceedings of the National Conference of Charities and Correction* (1888).

toil. The NCCC's efforts to answer this question in the affirmative were commonly grounded in an optimistic faith in its members' organizational abilities. As one speaker argued, administrators needed only "ingenuity, energy, and patience in order to arrange the work so that every inmate who can work, more or less, shall do so, and at the same time so that the needful work of the institution be kept up."[28] Confidence of this sort relies on a technocratic tautology: because all work is inherently "needful"—for institution and inmate alike—reform is only a matter of finding an arrangement that would allow everyone to join.

In more substantive arguments, institutional labor was commonly celebrated for its educational value. What counted as educational, of course, varied from one paper to the next. To many NCCC members, institutional labor possessed pedagogical value only when it was insulated from the market. The director of the Kentucky Institution for Feeble-Minded Children, for instance, found wide agreement among his colleagues when he argued in 1877 that inmate labor should be regarded not simply as the expeditious means of meeting overhead costs that it clearly was but rather "as *educational*, in the highest sense of the word."[29] The audience was no less receptive, however, when the same speaker went on to boast that nearly 75 percent of his residents were self-supporting, effectively collapsing any real distinction between educational and economic value. Another common justification for institutional labor in the *Proceedings* took the opposite tack, arguing that institutional labor was educational only when genuinely profitable. Prison reform was a touchstone for NCCC members in this camp. Even as fierce a critic of the convict lease system as the novelist George Washington Cable reasoned that inmate labor should not be abandoned. Coerced labor could indeed have educational value, he argued, when prisoners were forced to earn their keep like anyone else. In an 1884 conference paper that would later be republished as "The Freedman's Case in Equity," Cable laid out his vision of "the model prison" before inviting audience members to eavesdrop on an imagined conversation between the warden and an incredulous visitor: "Trying to live without competing in the fields of productive labor is just the essence of the crimes for which they were sent here. We make small work of that."[30]

Beyond reformatories and penitentiaries, NCCC members also looked to Black industrial schools to champion the noneconomic value of institutional labor. In doing so, they linked the professional aims of charities and correction not to the abolitionist energy that fueled the Port Royal Experiment but to the post-Reconstruction project of subordinating Black labor to the demands of racial capitalism. In 1887, for instance, the conference featured a panel called "African and Indian Races" with presentations by NCCC luminary F. B. Sanborn and Samuel Chapman Armstrong, the founder of Hampton Institute. Whereas Sanborn delivered an apologist history of Atlantic slavery and Native American genocide, Armstrong focused on the conference's work with Black Americans at present.[31] The task at hand, he argued, was to build on the progress made during slavery. If slavery "kept millions from rising to a higher plane," it nonetheless "held multitudes up from lower depths, and trained them in the elementary civilization of language, labor, habits, and religion."[32] For Armstrong, the conference could best foster this ongoing project by supporting Black industrial schools, the very embodiment of labor's educational value. Armstrong's perspective was the consensus opinion at the NCCC for years to come, but Black voices did occasionally find their way into the print record. In 1904, for instance, the title of the presentation that William E. Benson of the Kowaliga School was scheduled to give was probably meant to appeal to the NCCC's largely white membership: "The Prevention of Crime among Colored Children. Manual Training as a Preventive of Delinquency." But no sooner had he taken the podium than Benson revealed his bait and switch. "The crime record of the Negro is more apparent than real," he declared, ginned up by the biases of police officers and judges. Nor had the helping hand of charities and correction yet reached rural Black communities.[33] His and other schools were left to carve out their own understanding of "the dignity and success of labor." And in so doing they drew not only on the rational precedent of charities and correction but also on the fugitive practices of economic autonomy developed by freed people like Benson's grandfather.[34]

From educational value to civilizationist backstop, the difficulty of accounting for the noneconomic value of institutional labor led NCCC members to cycle through a host of explanatory rubrics. But each of these various cognates was ultimately a placeholder for the spiritual meaning that reformers continued to attribute to work—by turns implicitly, by turns explicitly—in this transitional moment in the history of US social welfare provision. No single figure better represented the residual spirituality of charity and corrections than Charles Richmond Henderson, who in 1899 became the only sociologist elected president of the NCCC. Trained as a Baptist minister, Henderson joined the faculty of the newly created University of Chicago in 1892. In 1895 and 1901 Henderson left Chicago to study in Germany, where he earned a doctorate in economics and statistics from the University of Leipzig.[35] Over the course of an academic career that colleagues praised for touching "upon practically the whole of applied sociology, much of this work being of a pioneer nature," Henderson published books on subjects ranging from prison reform to social welfare provision and eugenics.[36] Among the most prominent titles were *An Introduction to the Study of the Dependent, Defective, and Delinquent Classes* (1893), *The Social Spirit in America* (1897), *Modern Methods of Charity* (1904), and *Citizens in Industry* (1915). Whatever the topic, Henderson's writing often circled back to the transformative social value of work. When writing about prisons, for instance, Henderson argued that institutional labor should be seen not as "a means of punishment for past vice, nor primarily for income," but "a necessary condition of health, morality, and happiness."[37] Other institutions of social welfare faced much the same question: not whether inmates should work, but "what shall that employment be? No more serious problem can be proposed for thoughtful and reasonable people of any commonwealth."[38]

In the speech he gave at the NCCC after being elected president in 1899, Henderson made clear that the "serious problem" at hand was ensuring that institutional work had noneconomic value. Henderson's speech, as reprinted in the *Proceedings*, begins by distinguishing the "employable" from the "unemployable" but goes on to suggest that such distinctions are moot: everyone should work. This imperative holds equally for "a certain refractory element which never in this world can be fitted into competitive society."[39] These "unhappy children," Henderson argued, were to be given "the rational pleasure and education of regular productive industry and instruction and social fellowship" in institutional settings.[40] This work would have all the hallmarks of productive labor, but it was in reality useful only in marking time before the supreme benevolence—for Henderson the true basis of charities and correction—could take over. Work performed in this way, Henderson assured listeners, remains educational. "This does not imply that we exclude [industrial] education from the care of those who are too feeble or deformed for the normal struggle of life. The home of the feeble-minded, even the asylum for lifelong State custody of irresponsible women, is still a school; and the educational process continues to that point where the dim lamps flicker and the angels on the luminous side have their brighter lights ready to guide the little pilgrim to the unseen."[41] For Henderson and others in the transitional orbit of charities and correction, all work thus becomes spiritually meaningful with time. From this vantage, the bureaucratic protocols and documentary regimes mobilized by charities and correction fostered what might be called messianic busywork—a textual undertaking in which making the noneconomic value of institutional labor legible requires both professionalism and patience.

Work and Rhythm

Henderson is well known to historians of the early twentieth century, given how often he weighed in on the social issues of the day. Henderson's name signposts many of the era's most significant—and most objectionable—intellectual developments. Less well-known is Henderson's contribution to the comparative study of work songs published by his doctorial adviser, the Leipzig economist Karl Bücher. Starting with the 1902 edition, Bücher's *Arbeit und Rhythmus* (Work and Rhythm) included an appendix of African American work songs compiled and annotated by Henderson's students at the University of Chicago and by colleagues at the NCCC. *Arbeit und Rhythmus* might seem something of an outlier in Henderson's oeuvre, a favor for a friend rather than a service to the profession. But the book does address many of the same concerns that shaped the agenda of charities and correction in the United States. Perhaps most prominently, Bücher's romantic anticapitalism—his eagerness to find a more "authentic" relation to human labor in the music of "pre-industrial societies"—resonates with US reformers' belief that all work is inherently meaningful. And just as US reformers sought to have it both ways, arguing that even the most abusive labor possesses moral value in and of itself, Bücher saw in "primitive" work songs a means of reenchanting the capitalist world. Not the anomaly they might seem, in other words, the transcriptions and commentaries that Henderson and his reformist colleagues contributed to *Arbeit und Rhythmus* take up the ideological project at the heart of the NCCC *Proceedings*. African American work songs are presented here not only as cultural artifacts in need of preservation but also as a means of accounting for the noneconomic value of work as such.

Originally published in 1896, *Arbeit und Rhythmus* was surprisingly popular in its day and went through six editions before 1925. Reviewers praised both Bücher's accessible style and his ethnographic approach.[42] While he never went into the field himself, Bücher drew together a prodigious bibliography of travelogues, ethnological reports, and imperial records, works that describe in enthusiastic detail a range of labor practices in Asia, Africa, and Australia, among other exotic locales. German- and later Russian-speaking readers were delighted by these portraits of working life on the other side of the globe. Many also found themselves in agreement with what *Arbeit und Rhythmus* had to say about their own experiences at work. In a narrative of evolutionary decline, Bücher pitted the preindustrial *Naturmensch* against the *Kulturmensch* of his own milieu. The latter, he lamented, had suffered considerably under the all-consuming rationality of industrial modernity. For the *Naturmensch*, on the other hand, work, art, and play were not distinct categories of human endeavor. Each of these interweaving domains was governed instead by the physiological rhythms of the body, and all were as such intrinsically pleasurable. The work song was for Bücher the epitome of this unity of purpose and expression, of labor and leisure. It captured at once the joy of industriousness and the dignity inherent in "the possession and use of the products of one's own labor."[43] Where the whirring of the machine rather than the song of the body set the pace of human endeavor, Bücher concluded, labor lost any such meaningfulness.

If *Arbeit und Rhythmus* spoke to armchair ethnographers, the book also addressed Bücher's colleagues in the field of economics. Beginning with *Die Entstehung der Volkswirtschaft*, published in 1893 and translated as *Industrial Evolution* in 1899, Bücher devoted much of his academic career to questioning the hegemony of classical economics. Because classical economics could not account for nonmarket kinds of exchange, he argued, the portrait of economic activity it delivered was reductive at best. Bücher instead studied a variety of exchanges he thought were hiding in plain sight: the giving of gifts, the borrowing of goods, and labor provided in return for future help, or *Bittarbeit*.[44] Nonmarket exchanges of this sort, Bücher maintained, were especially prevalent among the "primitive" cultures that classical economists assumed to be disorderly, inefficient, and indolent. Taking issue with conventional images like these, Bücher sought to lay bare the rules governing a set of labor practices that, with regard to the meaningfulness of individual experience, far surpassed Western industrialism. Work of this sort, Bücher argued, "assured to primitive man a measure of enjoyment in life and a perpetual cheerfulness which the European, worried with work and oppressed with care, must envy him."[45] Bücher did not, however, advocate returning to an earlier stage of economic evolution.[46] *Arbeit und Rhythmus* instead imagines a future in which the forces of industrial production could be reconfigured to produce a yet "higher rhythmic unity." Such a unity was ultimately the best of both worlds, giving "the spirit back that joyous cheer, and the body that harmonious development, which characterizes the best of the primitive people."[47]

In theory, the evolutionary distinctions that Bücher draws allow him to imagine a mode of labor driven not by the demands of the market but by the rhythms of the body and the reciprocal ties of community. As illustrated in Bücher's materials, however, these distinctions are hardly absolute. Many of the vignettes that make up *Arbeit und Rhythmus*, in fact, confuse the primitive and the modern in ways that lend Bücher's descriptive foray a prescriptive feel. The *Naturmensch*, we are meant to understand, has much to teach the *Kulturmensch*. It is not always clear, however, what lesson readers should draw from these provocative comparisons. Bücher's enthusiasm for the rhythms of preindustrial labor can at times seem disingenuous, a willful misreading that finds in the *Naturmensch* merely an idealized image of the *Kulturmensch*. Consider, for instance, Bücher's discussion of work songs used by "larger groups of people." He begins by matter-of-factly likening industrial to preindustrial labor, observing among other similarities that the modern military march—a source of intrigue for Marey and Regnault as well, as we saw in chapter 3—finds a corollary in the rhythmic walking and singing of primitive peoples. Before long, however, the intimacy between modern and primitive seems to all but dissipate. Indeed, as Bücher goes on to quote from *The Basutos: Or, Twenty-Three Years in South Africa* (1861) by French missionary Eugene Casalis, preindustrial modes of labor and the musical forms they produce are described as unrelentingly strange (figure 4.2).

Bücher focuses in particular on Casalis's description of how the Basuto prepare an oxen skin, a process that strikes Casalis as both comic and horrific: "A dozen men, in squatting position, seize it by turns, rub it between their hands, twist it, and toss it about with such rapidity, and in such a ridiculous manner, that it really seems as if their treatment had put life into it."[48] Presenting these observations with little commentary, Bücher would seem to endorse the disdain Casalis shows for the Basuto workers. But Bücher is also at pains to underscore that music is the animating force by which this idolatrous labor is accomplished: "It is a mixture of nasal grunts, clucking, and shrill cries, which, though, most discordant, are in perfect time. One would imagine it to be a chorus of bears, boars, and baboons." Unsurprisingly, to French missionary and German annotator alike, these laborers soon begin to resemble in action the animals whose sounds they echo in song. "Beside themselves with the noise and the madness of their song," some of the workers "imitate the graceful movements of the gazelle; others spring up on their prey with the fury of the lion; others, again, without discontinuing their work, amuse themselves with the corners of the skin, as a cat would with a mouse."[49]

With this anecdote, Bücher would seem to distinguish more or less absolutely between primitive labor and the disenchanted world of industrial modernity. But the episode to which he next turns suggests by contrast that "hellish noises" of this sort might well be recuperated for the modern colonial enterprise. Recalling the reportage of a Parisian illustrated magazine, Bücher describes how the French colonial authorities used Indigenous work songs in the construction of a railroad connecting Senegal with Nigeria. Local musicians hired to "entertain the black natives employed for the excavation project" whipped the workers into a frenzy. These

4.2 "Railway construction work with musical accompaniment in French Sudan. Based on a drawing in 'Illustration,' 1899." Karl Bücher, *Arbeit und Rhythmus* (1909).

latter then "marveled at the locomotive and the railway with the same fiery imagination with which they had once praised the robberies and bloody deeds of their prince Samory."[50] In Bücher's telling, the railroad is the epitome of Western technological modernity, but its sheer force also recalls the fierce resistance to French colonial rule in West Africa led by Samori Toure.[51] But insofar as the Indigenous musicians hasten the building of imperial infrastructure, their songs are hardly opposed to colonial modernity—nor, for that matter, do they become a redemptive bulwark against the stultifying rhythms of the same. These songs, it would seem, are not work songs in the strict sense of the genre that Bücher develops at the outset of *Arbeit und Rhythmus*. More musical accompaniment than an intrinsic expression of the physiology of human labor, they become a tool of industrial management akin to music pumped into a locked factory.[52]

This same ambivalence about whether "primitive" work songs are most valuable for encoding an authentic relation to work and to the body or for enforcing the rational discipline of industrial production likewise shapes how *Arbeit und Rhythmus* frames African American contributions to the genre. The appendix "Arbeitsgesänge der Neger in den Vereinigten Staaten von Noradamerika" presents this material in typically erudite fashion.

After a brief review of the relevant literature, Bücher begins by reprinting a handful of songs from popular US collections like *Cabin and Plantation Songs as Sung by Hampton Students* (1876) and *Plantation Songs for My Lady's Banjo, and Other Negro Lyrics and Monologues* (1902). For the most part, Bücher's commentary reproduces the prejudices of his sources. He begins by noting that these songs would be familiar to readers versed in the history of US slavery. The spirituals in particular needed no introduction, thanks to the global vogue that began with *Uncle Tom's Cabin* (1852) and coalesced after the Port Royal Experiment and the international tours of the Fisk University Jubilee Singers.[53] In the postbellum era, though, even the most familiar of religious melodies could take on new life. As Bücher argues, many of the songs that had once voiced the fierce resilience of the enslaved—what the African American writer James Weldon Johnson called the "fiery spirit of the seer"—now coordinated Black labor "on the basis of free competition."[54] For Bücher, this development is far from objectionable. While the free Black laborer is industrious, Bücher concludes rather offhandedly, "he has not endurance, and we are given to believe those who assure us that he accomplishes less today as a free man than previously under slavery." These kinds of racist commonplaces make clear that Bücher did not read his source material critically. But they also point up how much *Arbeit und Rhythmus*, in its desire to identify a mode of labor guided by the physiology of the body and perfectly synchronized with the demands of the market, shares with the agenda of charity and corrections.

The original transcriptions of previously unpublished work songs that Bücher commissioned from Henderson thus mark the convergence of two only ostensibly different approaches to (the cultural expression of) work. Though the German economist looked to the labor practices of so-called primitive people in the interest of reenchanting industrial modernity, his approach to the performance traditions documented in *Arbeit und Rhythmus* often highlights how this material could be used to reinforce the hegemony of capitalist rationality. By the same token, Henderson and his colleagues maintained that industrial labor was the only effective means of "readjusting" members of the "dependent, defective, and delinquent classes," among whom they counted African Americans. But the US scholars and reformers who contributed to *Arbeit und Rhythmus* nonetheless held out hope that even institutional and other forms of coerced labor could be redeemed. In the book's appendix, "Arbeitsgesänge der Neger in den Vereinigten Staaten von Nordamerika," this ambivalence plays out in the commentaries produced by Henderson's students and colleagues to accompany the transcriptions they made in the field. Adopting an expository style that meshes with Bücher's own and represents a departure from the conventions of reformist debate, these commentaries argue by description rather than by proposition. But in their efforts to construct an ideological scaffolding around the transcriptions they supplement and surround, these commentaries inevitably foreclose the ambivalence they work so hard to maintain.

Typical in this regard are the songs transcribed and annotated by the Reverend Robert Lord Cave. Describing a song he overheard on a building site in Nashville, Cave delights in the harmony of movements that accompany each turn of the melody (figure 4.3). Whether mixing mortar or carrying bricks, the laborers sang and moved in unison, their voices summoning a commonality of purpose. The lead was provided by a foreman named Cotton who sang out each line in a voice loud enough for each of the widely scattered workers to hear. "They kept exact time," Cave observes, "rocked their upper bodies back and forth, and sought to coordinate their movements so they brought down their hoes, let the bricks fall, and so on in time with the chorus's song."[55] In all of this, as Cave learns from the overseer, Cotton was invaluable "because he encouraged the others to work through his song." Cave pays no attention, however, to the words of Cotton's song, even as he dutifully transcribes them. Indeed, in focusing exclusively on the collaborative momentum of the song, Cave misses its very meaning. The chorus—"Oh give me a hammer, / Oh, give me a hatchet, / Oh give me a hammer/ For to knock out my brains"—suggests a force of repetition building not to the completion of the house but to a violent end or, in a more figurative vein, to a collective articulation of grievance.[56] It remains an open question, moreover, whether the lamentation in the chorus is imagined to be Judas's or whether it belongs to the chorus of workers themselves. These and other questions are lost on Cave's commentary, which ultimately shores up the orthodox economics of labor that Bücher sought to overturn. The song was most valuable, that is, insofar as it compelled workers to labor more efficiently.[57] In so doing, however, Cave's observations may also lay bare a fundamental contradiction within Bücher's romantic anticapitalism. An emphasis on the work song's rootedness in the physiological rhythms of the laboring body, it would seem, cannot help but reduce the semantic meaning of a given vocal performance to a series of embodied utterances. There can be little doubt that the words of many work songs serve as time-keeping vocalizations first and as bearers of semantic meaning only second, if at all. But here the desire to locate the

I. Beim Laden von Frachtgütern.

Nr. 196.

I'm but a pŏh [1]) ol' [2]) culled [3]) man,
I does de bes' [4]) I can.
I's bawn [5]) in Souf Ca'lina [6]) 'fo de wah. [7])
I takes my glass of Holland gin,
I tinks [8]) it taint no sin,
I drinks my sweetened toddy ebry mawn. [9])

Der Beobachter, Herr R. L. Care, bemerkt dazu: „Der Neger, den ich dieses Stück singen hörte, war damit beschäftigt, große Transport= wagen mit schweren Warenkisten zur Verschiffung zu beladen. Das Heben und Zurechtlegen derselben ging notwendig langsam von Statten, und der leise Gesang dazu klang wie eine Entschuldigung für die Un= fähigkeit des Arbeiters, die Kisten rascher zu bewegen. Er stimmte eine Zeile an, während er eine Kiste am einen Ende anfaßte, um sie umzuwenden, und beendete die Zeile mit der Vollendung dieser Aufgabe."

K. Bei der Bauarbeit.

Nr. 197.

Joshua was the son of Nun,
The Lord was with him till the work was done;
Judas was a deceitful man,
He betrayed the innocent Lamb.

Chor: I'm feeling so bad,
I'm feeling so sad,
I feel like I want to go home.
Oh, give me a hammer,
Oh, give me a hatchet,
Oh, give me a hammer
For to knock out my brains.

Der Beobachter, Rev. Robert Lord Cave in Rom, Georgia, „hörte diesen Gesang zum erstenmale von einer Anzahl Neger, welche den Maurern beim Bau eines Hauses zu Nashville in Tennessee als Hand=

1) poor.   2) old.   3) colored, i. e. black.   4) best.
5) born.   6) South Carolina.   7) before the war (vor 1860).
8) think.   9) every morning.

4.3 Two African American work songs transcribed by Reverend Robert Lord Cave and reproduced in Bücher's *Arbeit und Rhythmus* (1909).

meaning of the song in the bodies of its performers obscures the critique of profit-driven labor that those singers seek to articulate.

If his commentary on the song of the construction workers in Nashville emphasizes form to the detriment of content, in other contributions to *Arbeit und Rhythmus* Cave endeavors to balance one with the other. Rather than achieving the fullness of inherently meaningful work prized by Bücher and US social reformers, however, these transcriptions transform vernacular work songs into diagnostic instruments. Consider, for instance, how Cave describes the song of a Black laborer loading a wagon with heavy crates. "The lifting and arranging of the boxes was necessarily slow," he notes, "and the quiet song sounded like an apology for the worker's inability to move the crates more quickly."[58] To understand this song as an apology is certainly to misread the occasion of its enunciation. Because the singer had little idea he was being observed, he would not have addressed his lament to anyone but himself. Beyond the words of this self-consciously piteous refrain, however, Cave also reads the caesura in the middle of each line as an interruption that contributes to the worker's slow pace: "He began a line while taking hold of one side of the crate to turn it around, and then finished this line once the movement was complete."[59] Far more likely, of course, is that the caesura marks a pause for the taking of a breath, hardly a physiological expression of apology.

The same disjointed rhythm that for Cave signifies incompetence is also underscored by Bücher's annotative apparatus. The footnote markers that interrupt each line with translations of words printed in nonstandard English compound the sense of hesitation to which Cave's commentary points. To understand this song as an apology thus means hearing in the singer's rhythm not the unity of body and labor but the sound of the latter outstripping the former. As such, the relation between the physiological performance of labor and the musical performance of song in this work song does not index the universal moral truth of all labor, but rather the quantifiable truth of this particular body performing this particular task. The body thus becomes evidence that can be used against the laborer, the song a document proving that his work is neither efficient nor meaningful in and of itself. It would thus appear that the African American work songs annotated in *Arbeit und Rhythmus* do not bear out the ambivalent relationship between preindustrial and industrial labor that for Bücher lay at the heart of the genre. Instead of embodying the perfect synchronization of human physiology and market demand, these songs are primarily useful as diagnostic and disciplinary instruments. The fantasy that the work song might capture the inherent meaningfulness of all work, in other words, gives way to the necessity of ensuring that laboring bodies—and laboring bodies of color in particular—produce as efficiently and profitably as possible.

The contribution that Annie Marion MacLean made to *Arbeit und Rhythmus* is a striking exception to this pattern. A disabled PhD sociologist who had studied under Henderson, MacLean is an unsung forerunner of Chicago School sociology. Her obscurity today is due to the lack of opportunities for women in the academy in the early twentieth century, but also to the many leaves of absence she took for her often debilitating rheumatoid arthritis.[60] The transcriptions of and commentaries on African American work songs that she made for *Arbeit und Rhythmus* stand at the beginning of a wide-ranging scholarly agenda that aimed to rethink the (disabled, raced, and gendered) body's relation to institutional spaces of work, from fields to factories and universities. MacLean's groundbreaking studies of working women in the early twentieth century, for instance, abandoned the sentimental cast of existing scholarship by focusing on the strict division between work and leisure routinized by industrial labor practices.[61] The ethnography "A Town in Florida" that MacLean published in a volume called *The Negro Church* (1903) edited by W. E. B. Du Bois, by contrast, explores how Southern Black migrants to the North sought to reclaim the pace and variety of their working day.[62] Perhaps most trenchantly of all, MacLean's contributions to *Arbeit und Rhythmus* provided a blueprint with which to recalibrate the rhythms of academic institutions to the rhythms of the disabled laboring body.

MacLean gathered African American work songs for *Arbeit und Rhythmus* while teaching at Florida's Stetson University. While she was alone in focusing on matters of gender or transcribing the songs of Black women, in the main MacLean's methods were similar to those of the other contributors. When describing the songs that accompanied the hoeing of cotton fields, for instance, she recounts how the workers spread themselves across the field in a diagonal line, with the lead hoe and the lead singer in front. The lead hoe, MacLean observes, "must be so competent and composed a worker that he can set the tempo of forward movement for the entire group of workers."[63] The lead singer is rarely also the lead hoe, a position that leaves one with no breath to spare. But if the lead singer translates the pace set by the lead hoe into song, the lead hoe contributes what voice he can, echoing in the anonymity of the chorus the rhythm his own labor creates. In other transcriptions, MacLean's own research informs how she represents the rhythmic relation between labor and song even more clearly. In her commentary on the "Songs of the Washerwomen," for instance, MacLean describes how the women rubbed their garments on the side of their tubs to establish a regular pace that saw them through the rest of their load. But rather than converging on a shared rhythm, each woman worked at her own tempo. The women did sing together, however, and the chorus of their voices created a unity of "contentment" by which the competing rhythms of eight washboards were transformed into an ambient hum. It was a collaborative process of competition and resolution that "ceased immediately once a stranger appeared."[64]

MacLean leaves it unclear whether the washerwomen left off when she entered the room or not. But whether she watched from afar or was invited to join, MacLean's remarks about the community created by these Black women speak to many of the same concerns that guided her later efforts to make academic institutions responsive to the rhythms of her body, and not the other way around.[65] After being passed over for several on-campus positions, MacLean joined the University of Chicago's Home Study Department and taught sociology courses by correspondence for nearly twenty years. Her pedagogy involved sending lectures and individualized notes to students and corresponding with them about their writing and research projects. The flexibility was a boon for both students and teacher. "While students have a year in which to complete a course," MacLean observed, "with a possibility of reinstatement, many do the work in a much shorter time, and their lessons come in with clock-like regularity. Others work irregularly.... Mail days can never be entirely dull to one who has lessons in Sociology coming in."[66] Gone was "the drudgery of mere book keeping," replaced instead by "a pleasant association of congenial spirits."[67] But what MacLean valued most was how correspondence courses allowed teacher and student to encounter one another in mutual recognition of "the frailties of other human beings," thus ensuring that intellectual labor was guided not by the unceasing demands of institutional life but by the rhythms of the individual body.[68]

In a brief essay titled "This Way Happiness Lies," MacLean extrapolates from these insights to contemplate how all work might be remade in the image of correspondence teaching. She begins by acknowledging that her path might strike readers as unconventional, given that a "few years ago all the seemingly desirable things in the world were wrested from [her] by disease."[69] Addressing a dismissive interlocutor, MacLean explains how her idea of happiness has changed. "Since life for me henceforth must be confined within infinitesimal physical limits, I sought re-adjustment. I who had gone through the world with winged feet must henceforth be only an onlooker with a narrow field of vision."[70] With fieldwork impossible, MacLean realized that her interest in academic work all along had less to do with "the enchantment of distance" than with "garnering glory from the commonplace." Retooling the relation between work and happiness thus means engaging the world through networks of exchange.[71] The "mere business of Life" in this way becomes altogether less businesslike; it is instead a process of "cultivating" community and creating "new patterns" and "combinations" that continually reconstitute the rhythms of working life. In this regard, MacLean brings to her own labor the same appreciation of the body's role in determining the pace and the substance of one's work that she underscored in her contributions to *Arbeit und Rhythmus*. Unlike her mentor Henderson, for whom the noneconomic value of African American work songs was inseparable from their utility in enforcing penal discipline and industrial competition, MacLean finds in Black song a model for rethinking the disabled body's relation to the labor it produces.

Ultimately, the history of how African American work songs came to be included in *Arbeit und Rhythmus* is a story less about interdisciplinary collaboration than about disciplinary overlap. In an era when the social sciences were still in formation and the line between research and reform more a matter of rhetorical preference than institutional organization, the task of capturing the noneconomic value of work as such knew no bounds and welcomed all comers. It is no surprise then that the romantic anticapitalism of a heterodox German economist would resonate with the coercive discipline of charity and corrections (and vice versa) or that the written record of an annual professional conference would share a set of goals—if not also methods—with erudite transcriptions of vernacular musical performance. But if this muddle of disciplinary and professional interests created space for the dissident solidarities voiced by MacLean and others on the margins of *Arbeit und Rhythmus*, for the heirs of charity and corrections the genre of the work song pointed to a more methodologically uniform future that was at the same time a return to Port Royal.

Institution Building

Published in 1925 in collaboration with Guy Benton Johnson, *The Negro and His Songs* was based on materials that Odum collected in Georgia and Mississippi from 1907 to 1909 and first wrote up in a smattering of academic articles. The book begins with an odd anecdote. Listening to the singing of a road gang outside his Chapel Hill home, Odum contemplates the relation between the intellectual labor of institution building and the physical work of building universities. "This dean accordingly sat himself down on his rock wall to see if perchance he might not take down some of the songs which he heard, the singing of which he so much enjoyed. He was thinking how oblivious the workers were to his presence and to all things else save their work. He marveled that [*sic*] the words of the song he could not gather; nevertheless he would be persistent, he would get them. And so he did, with the somewhat startling effect, approximately versed to meet the workman's technique."[72] Describing himself at work watching others at work, Odum cannot help but draw comparisons. Rather than likening transcription to the laying of pavement, though, he seeks to capture the spiritual affinity his academic work shares with the labor extracted from the leased prisoners in front of his house. These latter find as much engrossing pleasure in their task, Odum believes, as he does in his. And just as road laborers match the pacing of their song to the rhythms of their bodies, Odum patterns his prose on the halting lilt of his comprehension: "Nevertheless he would be persistent, he would get them. And so he did, with the somewhat startling effect, approximately versed to meet the workman's technique." Odum is soon woken from this bookish reverie, however, by the very voice that first set him adrift. As if anticipating the narcissistic bent of Odum's musings, the leader of the gang turns the ethnographic gaze back on the dean and on scholarly labor as such:

> White man settin' on wall,
> White man settin' on wall,
> White man settin' on wall all day long,
> Wastin' his time, wastin' his time.

The singer's improvised parody demonstrates how sharply his perspective differs from Odum's: forced labor on the university grounds shares nothing with the leisurely intellectualism indulged in there. It is ultimately unclear, though, who has the last laugh. While the singer literarily dictates the terms of his disidentification with the academy, for Odum this sneering performance nonetheless remains a work song. And as such, like each of the other entries in Odum's anthology, it also embodies the inherent meaningfulness of all work.

The tension between cultural performance and scholarly gloss that Odum unwittingly stages in this anecdote is evident throughout *The Negro and His Songs* and probably contributed to the book's falling out of favor among folklorists and musicologists. As Bruce Jackson has written, both *The Negro and His Songs* and its companion volume, *Negro Workaday Songs* (1926), are best understood as period pieces. Odum and Johnson "were so interested in sociology and causes and conditions that they failed to include the kind of information that might have made their texts of more general use."[73] For his part, Odum might not have disagreed with this appraisal, at least not entirely. It was no secret that Odum's purpose in *The Negro and His Songs* was shaped less by recent trends in folklore and musicology than by a desire to bring the methods of social science to bear on "race relations" in the South. Indeed, the book was the first volume to appear in UNC Press's Social Study Series, a collaborative venture with Odum's Institute for Social Research that was meant to establish Chapel Hill as a Southern outpost of modern sociological thought to rival New York and Chicago. Subsequent titles included *An Approach to Public Welfare and Social Work* (1926), *Public Poor Relief in North Carolina* (1928), and *The North Carolina Chain Gang: A Study of County Convict Road Work* (1927).

This wide-ranging research agenda was to signal a decisive break with both the provincial chauvinism that had long characterized the Southern academy and the paradigm of charity and corrections. To Odum and his colleagues, this latter tradition was begun with the best of intentions but lost its way before long. Instead of providing the "treatment and restitution" that would allow the socially disadvantaged to become self-supporting, reformers grew content merely to warehouse them in increasingly abusive institutions of "permanent care or custody."[74] The shift from charity and corrections to "social welfare" and "social work"—officially codified in 1917 when the NCCC was renamed the National Conference of Social Work—was thus at once a departure and a return. For UNC researchers, it announced an embrace of modern sociological research methods and a recommitment to the transformative power of labor that had long guided the efforts of social reformers.[75] As Odum concluded, it fell to professional social workers to determine how best to return "the poor, ill, defective, perverse, or otherwise handicapped" to work.[76] Echoing the sentiments ventured a generation earlier by Henderson, UNC researchers held that "self-respect, earning capacity, rebuilding of character and fortune are the normal and logical expectation of society's unfortunates."[77] Such was at base the reformist agenda behind the Social Study Series.

For Odum, making the work song emblematic of this new ideal of social welfare provision also required updating his earlier approach to African American folk music. A decade or so before arriving at Chapel Hill, Odum took an interest in Black religious song and conducted ethnographic research in "fifty Negro communities in the South." His aim was to prove that what passed for authentic Black folk expression in US popular culture was anything but. To be sure, Odum was not alone in this venture in the early twentieth century. Many Black writers and artists were engaged in similar endeavors, as were white folklorists, both amateur and professional. Unlike many other researchers, however, Odum was not interested in preserving Black religious music for its own sake. Instead, he argued that these songs contained valuable data for "students of race traits and tendencies." Odum's first publication in this vein was a 1909 article that drew methodologically on his dissertation in psychology at Clark University. There Odum argued that the "insight into negro character gained from their folk-songs and poetry accompanied by careful and exhaustive concrete social studies may be accepted as impartial testimony."[78] To his peers in psychology, Black religious song was thus a neglected trove of objective social truths with which to flesh out the typology of racial "character." Odum's tone and occasional cultural allusions also suggest, however, that he had a white Southern lay audience in mind. For these readers, Odum hints, Black religious music promised to reveal "what the Negro thinks" and "what the Negro wants." In either case, Odum's exegetical authority is clearly grounded in racist paternalism. Where Black religious music encoded the "truest expression of the folk-mind and feeling," neither white sociologists nor lay Southerners needed to engage directly with African Americans themselves.[79] Just as crucially, Odum's interpretative project also defined social welfare as a psychological endeavor. Improving the situation of those on the social margins, in other words, whether as a social welfare professional or an "interested" community member, required only knowing "the inner consciousness of a race."

Anticipating his later embrace of the pragmatic agenda of social work, Odum's next series of Black folk expressions swapped the work song for the spiritual and tempered his earlier focus on "race traits and tendencies" with qualitative social analysis. This shift, Odum explained, had as much to do with the musical practices he observed in the field as with his own disciplinary preoccupations, which now bore the influence of a second doctoral degree, completed in sociology at Columbia. Not only had religious music already been given its due, Odum claimed, but "social songs," among which work songs were the most numerous, were of far greater relevance for Black life and postbellum racial politics more broadly. As Odum asserted, "The diminishing importance of the older religious themes" clearly indicated "that the Negro has finally outgrown the former disposition to sing himself *away from* a world of sorrow and trouble and is coming more and more to sing himself and his troubles *through* that world."[80] Whereas the spiritual captured the ethereal aspirations occasioned by the experience of slavery and gestured to a world beyond or other than that which presently existed, the work song announced a material commitment to the world as it was. This notion of materiality in turn demanded a new mode of interpretation. Rather than parsing work songs for evidence of the interior lives of formerly enslaved people, sociologists could use them to assess and promote the economic integration of Black Americans on terms that did not challenge the social status quo. For Odum, singing through the world was thus a process of economic accommodation in which African Americans could find their place in a workforce stratified by hierarchies of race, ethnicity, gender, ability, and class. Crucially, this process was not a Spencerian survival of the fittest. Instead, the physiological harmony of the laboring body and its task captured in the work song prefigures a social harmony of individual desires and collective obligations. From this vantage, in fact, the materiality of the work song was itself rather aspirational, if not outright immaterial. Just as these songs could be used to scrutinize particular labor practices and formations, in other words, they also embodied—materially or otherwise—the transformative power of all labor.

In this regard, Odum's understanding of the work song as a genre should strike us as familiar. Like Bücher, Odum argued that the work song was defined above all by the organic unity it established between the rhythms of the body and the rhythms of work. And like Bücher, Odum's preferred idiom is tautology: "As motion and music with the negro go hand in hand, so the motion of work calls forth the song; while the song, in turn strengthens the movements of the workers."[81] But if Bücher's evolutionary approach distinguishes more or less absolutely between the "primitive" past and the "modern" present, Odum recasts the rhythms of the work song as a synchronicity of antebellum and postbellum racial regimes. Consider, for instance, the eagerness with which Odum assures readers that Black work songs are no less prevalent at the turn of the twentieth century than they had been under slavery. The white Southerners "who have ample opportunity for continued observation," he acknowledges, "maintain that the negro is fast losing his cheerfulness and gayety, his love of song and practice of singing."[82] Although sympathetic to these kinds of concerns, Odum nonetheless offers his "objective" research as evidence to the contrary: "The negro still retains much of his disposition to sing while at work. Whoever has seen in the spring-time a score of negroes with hoes, chopping in the fields to a chant, making rhythm, motion, and clink of hoe harmonize; whoever has heard in the autumn a company of cotton-pickers singing the morning challenge to the day, and uniting in song at the setting of the sun and 'weighing-time'—will not soon forget the scene. The negroes still work and sing."[83]

Odum's depiction of Black laborers clearly tempers the "rigor" of sociological description with apologist nostalgia. As gauzy recollections blur into ethnographic observation, the physiological harmony of body and labor affirms the continuity of Black Americans' economic and social subservience before and after the Civil War. This copresence of past and present in turn becomes a template for the future: "Song is conducive to good humor," Odum observes, "and good humor brings better work." As such, "both the direct and indirect effect of singing upon the worker make it advisable that his song continue as long as he works."[84] The advisability of the work song also lay in its utility for industrial discipline. Indeed, in a plainly instrumental turn Odum suggests that the genre's fugue-like structure illuminates not only the physiological harmony between the laboring body and the task at hand but also how erstwhile agrarian workers might subordinate themselves to the demands of industrial production. As Odum writes of a subgenre he calls the "heave-a-hora": "While they pull or work, the leader cries out 'Come on menses!' And while the 'menses' come, they work as a machine."[85] Far from achieving any sense of fully realized humanity, the workers here become interchangeable parts.

Odum's Fordist recasting of agrarian labor finds a formal correlative in his own efforts to bring these performances to the page. All work songs, Odum argues, consist of a single phrase repeated as long as necessary and amended at will. This process of composition would seem entirely organic, much like the collaborative enterprise of collective labor itself. As Odum observes, "The harmony of the group of negroes working on the bridge, the house, the railroad, or at the warehouse and in the mind is typified by the union of the many work-song phrases."[86] Over time, "these exclamations become connected" and then form couplets and "distinct songs." When Odum endeavors to reproduce this process by means of transcription, however, he ultimately streamlines the organic give-and-take of communal creation into a mechanically replicable template. The fifty-seven-line work song that Odum constructs from as many discrete phrases is a case in point (figure 4.4). Removed from the original context of its enunciation and divorced from the scene of labor that initially gave it shape, each line is placed in arbitrary sequence that becomes a discrete song only by virtue of having an identifiable beginning and conclusion. Not the product of an idealized mode of labor directed by the physiological rhythms of the body, Odum's poetic mélange is a picture of rationalization. By means of citation and recombination, it orchestrates an act of generic retooling that underscores the malleability of the genre. A machine built to spec, the work song here reveals how the coherence of purpose created by a group of individual worker-musicians can be put in the service not of self-realization but of profit maximization.

corresponds to a high note, and the short foot to a lower one.   While
they pull or work, the leader cries out —

"Come on, menses!"

And while the "menses" come, they work as a machine.   The leader
repeats this as often as he works, or until he likes another phrase
better.   As a rule, the leader will use a single phrase an average of
ten or fifteen times before passing to another.   The examples that
follow will indicate the free range which they cover, and the ease
with which the negro composes them.   It will be seen that there are
no strict essentials which must belong to the song: the fitting words
may be the invention of the moment.   The harmony of the group
of negroes working on the bridge, the house, the railroad, or at the
warehouse and in the mine, is typified by the union of the many simple
work-song phrases.   They may be studied for themselves.   Each line
constitutes an entire work-song phrase, complete in itself.

Hey — slip — slide him — a — slip-slide him.
Ev'ybody bow down an' put yo' han's to it.
Come an' go wid me — come an' go wid me.
Heavy — heavy — heavy — heavy — hank — back.
All right — all right.
Draw — back — adraw — back.
Tear 'em up-a-tear 'em up.
Come hard ag'in it-a.
Work hard again it so.
Break it, boys, break it.
Hike, hike, kike-back.
Come on here.
What's a matter? white-eyed.
What's a matter — fagged out?
What's a matter — monkey got you?
Haul it — haul it back.
Here — yeah — here, you.
Turn — turn it — turn her on.
Let's turn 'em over.
Turn it one mo' time.
How 'bout it?
Knock down on it.
Up high wid it, men.
Get up — get it up any way to git it up.
Yonder she go.
Put yo' nugs on it.
Lay yo' hands on it.
Put 'im up on it.
Get up, Mary, Janie, etc.
Hello — hello — hello!
Yang 'em — Yang 'em.   (Go 'round an' pick 'em up.)

4.4 Odum's
compilation of
one-line work-
song phrases,
which contin-
ues for another
twenty-six lines
on the following
page. Howard W.
Odum, "Folk-
Song and Folk-
Poetry as Found
in the Secular
Songs of the
Southern Negroes
(Concluded)"
(1911).

In *The Negro and His Songs* and his earlier research articles, Odum thus
outlines two seemingly distinct roles for the work song in the print culture
of social welfare. By synchronizing the rhythms of the body with those of
economic production, the genre embodied the transformative potential
of labor as such. But these same songs could likewise be used to assess
specific performances of labor and to coerce individual bodies into industrial rhythms they had no part in shaping. This divergence of approach is
borne out even more clearly in the "phonophotographic" studies of African American work songs reprinted in the follow-up to *The Negro and
His Songs*, Odum and Johnson's *Negro Workaday Songs*. Conducted by the

psychologist Milton Metfessel in partnership with the Institute for Social Research, these studies translated musical performances into visual representations. As Metfessel described the phonophotographic technique he developed with Carl Seashore at the University of Iowa: "The sound wave photograph is made on the moving picture film by three light points. The diaphragms pick up the vibrations of sound, and the mirrors translate the vibrations into an up and down flashing of the light. The light flashes at the same rate at which the vocal cords are sounding."[87] The movements of light are then traced onto a two-dimensional graphic field, the x-axis marking time elapsed and the y-axis, pitch (figure 4.5). Initially, Metfessel's aims were aligned with the tradition of late nineteenth-century audio ethnography. Like Benjamin Ives Gilman and Jesse Walter Fewkes, Metfessel hoped that musical transcriptions made with the help of "mechanically neutral" recording technologies would succeed in capturing sounds that otherwise "resisted" written notation.[88] Also citing the earlier writings of J. W. Work, Natalie Curtis-Burlin, H. E. Kriebel, and James Weldon Johnson, Metfessel strove to map out what Johnson called "the curious turns and twists and quavers and the intentional striking of certain notes just a shade off key, with which the Negro loves to embellish his songs."[89]

When Metfessel turned to work songs in particular, however, he and his collaborators at the Institute for Social Research imagined that phonophotography might produce not only more accurate representations of Black musical performance but also new insights into Black labor. For these studies, Guy Benton Johnson accompanied Metfessel and Seashore to Hampton Institute, where they recorded student performances. The team also made arrangements with a number of colleges and high schools in Chapel Hill and Raleigh to meet with students locally. In each of these settings, test subjects were asked to sing, solo and in groups, in front of two cameras. The first of these was a motion picture camera, the other a phonophotographic device. When Odum and Johnson recalled these phonophotographic studies in *Negro Workaday Songs*, they conjured Odum's earlier typological interest in "race traits and tendencies." Many of these songs, they wrote, were sung "by typical laborers, working with pick and shovel. There was the lonely singer, with his morning yodel or 'holler.' There were the skilled workers with voices more or less trained by practice and formal singing. There was the more nearly primitive type, swaying body and limb, with singing."[90] The conclusions that Odum and Johnson draw from Metfessel's phonophotographic studies of these various performers are similarly descriptive, seeming to underscore the potential of a method

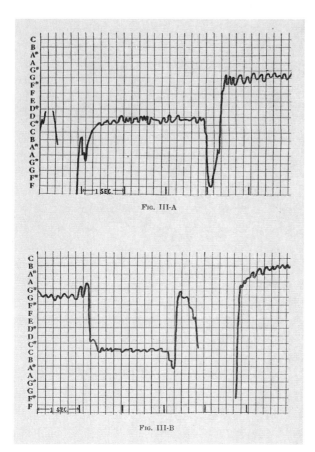

FIG. III-A

FIG. III-B

4.5 Graphic tracing of a phonophotographic study of an unspecified "yodel or 'holler'" performed by Cleve Atwater. Howard W. Odum and Guy B. Johnson, *Negro Workaday Songs* (1926).

still in its infancy while also conceding their own inability to read the images of work produced in this manner. Typical of their tentative analysis is Odum and Johnson's gloss of a holler or yodel performed by a man named Cleve Atwater. "The most remarkable thing about this record," Odum and Johnson claim, "is the sudden changes of pitch which it portrays."[91] The "rapid rises and falls" in the singer's voice lost to the human ear are made legible to the eye in the sloping lines of Metfessel's graph. But although clearly amazed at being able to see what they cannot hear, Odum and Johnson can only speculate about what this "remarkable" change in pitch means for the work of social welfare.

The sociological promise of the new technology would be realized two years later, with the publication of Metfessel's *Phonophotography in Folk*

Music, also part of the UNC Social Study Series. *Phonophotography in Folk Music* supplements Metfessel's interest in charting the physiological rhythms of labor with attention to the putatively scientific measurement of emotion and innate musical ability.[92] With regard to social welfare work, the central breakthrough of Metfessel's book is how it juxtaposes phono-photographic renderings of a given vocal performance with still images from the cinematic film made of the movements of the vocalist's body at work. Absent from *Negro Workaday Songs*, these stills seem to bear a straightforward relation to the abstract images they accompany, as if providing an explanatory key. Viewers are indeed encouraged to map the sequence of still images onto the x-axis of the phonophotographic image, such that we might see in the flexing of an arm or the curling of a lip the physiological provenance of a given dip in the curve. Just as often, though, the phonophotographic and filmic images in Metfessel's volume seem to be at cross-purposes. The result is a sense of interpretative confusion that is also a contest over the materiality of the work song. On the one hand, the still images suggest that the meaning of the work song derives from the embodied performance of work. The accompanying phonophotographic images, on the other hand, locate the meaning of these songs not in the materiality of the labor they facilitate but in the materiality of writing and by extension the materiality of the device that makes this writing possible. Ultimately, competing ideas about the materiality of the work song point up larger questions about the genre's role in the print culture of social welfare. How one identifies the materiality of the work song, in other words, depends on whether the genre is taken to embody the transformative power of all labor or whether work songs are used as diagnostic tools with which (materially) to enforce the mandate of the work society.

This conflict over the work song's materiality—whether rooted in the physiology of labor or the technology of writing—is exemplified by the phonophotographic rendering of a song titled "You Ketch Dis Train" (figure 4.6). Performed by an unnamed laborer while clearing ground, this recording is of greatest interest to Metfessel for the tonal variation brought about by each iteration of the vocable *huh* but also for the subtle shifts in pitch with which the singer elaborates the melody. With regard to the latter, Metfessel offers this gloss: "*You*, graph 1, sec. 1, is mostly a rising intonation, as is *dis*. Farther on in the song, *train*, is falling, *I'll* a long rise, *ketch* a short fall, *it* a short rise, and *too* a relatively slow rise."[93] This narrative translation would seem to read the phonophotographic rendering of "You Ketch Dis Train" as a portrait of virtuosity. The laborer would appear to move from note to note with both grace and control, modulating the degree of rise or fall precisely and deliberately—and with variations of pitch so slight as to be "audible" only to the phonophotographic apparatus. But when this phonophotographic rendering is read against still images of the singer at work, the reciprocity that Metfessel's prose suggests between the rhythms of work and those of song is interrupted by a cinematic gaze that reduces the work song to a spectacular moment of impact: "the *Huh!* as the pick strikes the ground." This visual reduction of the singer's rhythmic and melodic virtuosity to the materiality of a single moment in the labor he performs has the effect ultimately of shifting how we read these images together. No longer listening to the song or seeing how the phonophotographic representation of that song bears witness to the synchronicity of physiology and economy, we are rather placed in a position of managerial oversight. Our task is thus not to take an example from the labor being performed here, but rather to evaluate it.

This conflict, which in the context of the Social Study Series might be described as that between Black labor and white (scholarly) management, plays out even more dramatically in Metfessel's reading of the photographic record of "I Got a Muly," also performed by a series of unnamed singers (figures 4.7–4.9). The session would seem to begin well, and Metfessel praises the first singer's first rendition of the song as a compelling exemplar of the "wide variability of the Negro vibrato."[94] The second version is likewise valuable, demonstrating "successively wider" shifts in pitch and tone and also exemplifying "a typical Negro attack." Trouble begins, however, with the third version, which was evidently "sung under protest." After Metfessel and his collaborators "pressed him to the task," this third singer only "half-heartedly complied. The frown seen in the moving pictures and the queer sequence of notes and intonations in the song are expressive of the irritation he felt."[95] Metfessel would have readers believe that this last performance of "I Got a Muly" was ultimately unsuccessful, providing little useful information about the characteristics of Black song or the rhythmic intertwining of human physiology and human labor. Indeed, Metfessel's description of the singer's irritated "frown" and his "queer" performance—one marked by "clipping," "distortion," and "slipshod" falsetto—would seem to frame this as a study rather of idleness and shirking. What Metfessel fails to see, however, is the effort that the singer puts into making his song illegible as work according to the standards of white sociology. Like the gang leader whom Odum encounters on his front lawn, the singer who refuses to sing "I Got a Muly" is concerned

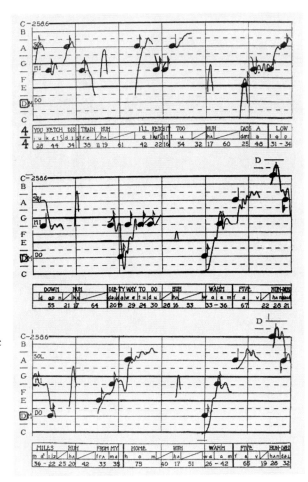

4.6 Graphic tracing of a phonophotographic study of a man singing "You Ketch Dis Train" while clearing ground with a pick. Milton Metfessel, *Phonophotography in Folk Music* (1928).

to differentiate his endeavors from the labor of white social work and to show that the latter is not in fact inherently meaningful, much less socially transformative. White social work instead requires and projects a mode of repetition that can only tediously affirm what it claims to know in advance. Social work is drudgery. Not a failure of performance with regard to either vocal delivery or industrious output, in other words, "I Got a Muly" speaks across the various approaches and subject matters collated in the Social Study Series to the leased prisoner working outside Odum's house. Theirs is ultimately a work song that refuses work in precisely the same terms that the UNC researchers praise it.

4.7 "I Got a Muly (First Version). The [*ah*] sound at the beginning." Milton Metfessel, *Phonophotography in Folk Music* (1928).

4.8 "Third Version of 'I Got a Muly' by a reluctant workman. The [*o*] sound in *wohn-uh* (want to)." Milton Metfessel, *Phonophotography in Folk Music* (1928).

In the years to come, authors affiliated with Odum's Institute for Social Research would continue to draw self-reflexive parallels between the modes of labor they studied and the work of sociology. Subsequent books in UNC Press's Social Study Series also returned to the African American work song, though not by means of phonophotography. Rather, the next institute publications to explore the rehabilitative potential of Black folk music were part of a 1930 study of the economy and culture of the Gullah community on the South Carolina Sea Islands that was in effect an effort to assess the legacy of the Civil War–era Port Royal Experiment. As with Odum's decision to launch the Social Study Series with *The Negro and His*

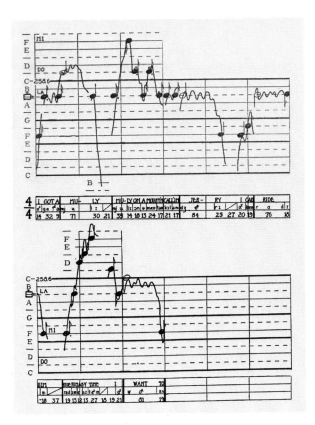

4.9 "I Got a Muly (Third Version)." Milton Metfessel, *Phono-photography in Folk Music* (1928).

Songs, the question of why the institute turned to the Sea Islands in 1930 can be answered matter-of-factly. A researcher named Thomas J. Woofter had recently been arrested for driving under the influence in Chapel Hill, an incident that caused considerable friction between the university and locals. In an effort to appease the angry community, Odum sent Woofter to the Sea Islands, trusting that a long-term project would keep him out of sight and out of mind long enough for the controversy to pass.[96]

The necessity of temporarily banishing Woofter from campus was also an opportunity, of course. A growing number of academic researchers, both at UNC and elsewhere, had begun to worry that the distinctiveness of Gullah life on the Sea Islands was threatened by modernization on the mainland. And so the idea of launching an extensive study of the region—under whatever circumstances—was met with genuine enthusiasm. As Woofter himself noted in the book he wrote in exile, *Black Yeomanry:*

Life on St. Helena Island (1930), a bridge being constructed across the Beaufort River would remove "the last barrier of isolation." Any effort to preserve "the unique culture of this place ... must be done quickly."[97] Not just a convenient means of closing ranks around an embattled colleague, in other words, the institute's work on the Sea Islands was part of the social agenda that Odum had laid out in *The Negro and His Songs* and *An Approach to Public Welfare and Social Work* and that was fundamental as well to the earlier efforts of reformers in the National Conference of Charities and Correction. The three books that resulted from this collaborative undertaking—Woofter's *Black Yeomanry* and two more by husband and wife Guy Benton Johnson and Guion Griffis Johnson—addressed not only the cultural heritage of the Sea Islands but also the economic patterns that had produced that heritage. But if the questions that drew UNC researchers to the Sea Islands were much the same that first motivated the architects of the Port Royal Experiment, Odum's colleagues found little reason for optimism. The reformative power of labor, they argued, had not yet had a chance to set in. The work of rehabilitation still lay ahead.

The books written by Woofter and Guy Johnson are detailed but often rather impressionistic accounts of life on St. Helena Island. In *Black Yeomanry*, Woofter dedicates a chapter each to "The People," "Health," "Breadwinning," "Education," and "Religion," among other topics. His method combines ethnography, quantitative analysis, and institutional history, with a primary focus on the ongoing work of the Penn School, which was established on St. Helena by abolitionists during the Port Royal Experiment. Woofter touches only briefly on the role of folk music and culture, a task taken on instead by Guy Benton Johnson, Odum's collaborator on *The Negro and His Songs* and *Negro Workaday Songs*. In *Folk Culture on St. Helena Island, South Carolina* (1930), Johnson added his voice to an increasingly heated debate about the origins of African American spirituals. Parting ways with the amateur musicologists and folklorists who, some sixty years prior, described to rapt readers in the North the captivating songs they had overheard on the same soil, Johnson argued that the musical forms preserved on the Sea Islands were Anglo-American rather than African in origin. He also claimed that the Gullah language was derivative of the English dialect spoken by the earliest colonists and not an African dialect. But while their approaches differed in method and subject, both Woofter and Johnson were ultimately concerned with judging the outcome of the social experiment in free labor that the federal government conducted during the Civil War. As Woofter wrote in a concluding chapter on the fate of the Port Royal Experiment and its subsequent "world-wide significance in dealing with backward races": "Two generations have been reared and the third is coming up since [Edward] Pierce wrote to President Lincoln that the people of the Sea Islands had in them great possibilities of improvement provided wise measures were adopted to 'elevate them and prepare them to be self-supporting citizens.' Enough time has elapsed to begin to see the results of the forces which have operated."[98] Although they posed the question with clarity and force, neither Woofter nor Guy Johnson ventured an answer as such. For his part, Woofter found evidence to support both sides of what he now saw as an either/or proposition: "In balancing the books on this experiment, a review of the preceding pages indicates many facts creditable to the community as a going concern and a few phases of life in which the Islanders have not adapted themselves to the American standards."[99] It would be left to Guion Griffis Johnson to bring the institute's work on the Sea Islands to a meaningful conclusion, evaluating just what the rehabilitative effects of free labor had been.

Guion Griffis Johnson opens her discussion of the Port Royal Experiment with a stirring portrait of the naval maneuvering by which the Sea Islands came into Union possession. Passing by the two forts guarding the entrance to Port Royal Sound, the advancing fleet "turned and delivered, in their changing rounds, a terrific shower of shot in flank and front."[100] By day's end, federal troops had taken possession of the area in its entirety, soon discovering that the planters had fled: "Not a white person of Confederate sympathies could be found in Beaufort or on the plantations." As described by General William T. Sherman, in charge of the expeditionary corps that soon landed at Port Royal, "The wealthy islands of Saint Helena, Ladies, and most of Port Royal are abandoned by the whites, and the beautiful estates of the planters, with all their immense property, left to the pillage of hordes of apparently disaffected blacks."[101] This scene of chaos and disarray is for Johnson ground zero for Port Royal's "rehearsal for Reconstruction." In the pages that follow, she details the competing efforts of abolitionists, missionaries, federal agents, and contraband slaves themselves to structure the organization of free labor on the Sea Islands. In the end, Johnson concludes that this social experiment in free labor was every bit as much a failure as Reconstruction would itself be. The "character of the Negro as a hired laborer," she observes, "had been injured by the inflated prices which the soldiers paid them for their wares and by the injudicious policy of their well-meaning friends of the North."[102] Nor did the mandate of the Freedmen's Bureau to protect formerly enslaved men and women from planters have any positive effect. Rather, such efforts to insulate the freed men and women from the market changed the nature of the work they could accomplish. Theirs was not free labor and, as a result, neither was it rehabilitative. In the words of a missionary enthusiastically cited by Johnson: "Their freedom had come too easy for them."[103]

Du Bois came to a markedly different conclusion when describing the failure of the Port Royal Experiment in *The Souls of Black Folk* some thirty years earlier. Black labor, he suggested, was never given a chance to be free, at least not in the way that the formerly enslaved men and women on the Sea Islands understood that term. The latter organized themselves against the demands made by returning planters and then by their erstwhile advocates in the Freedmen's Bureau, but ultimately to little avail. For Du Bois, the scene that came to exemplify the devastating betrayal that brought the rehearsal for Reconstruction to a close took place on Edisto Island in 1864. General Oliver Otis Howard, soon to be commissioner of the Freedmen's Bureau, had come to tell the freed men and women that the confiscated lands they had been promised would be returned instead to pardoned Confederates. In *The Souls of Black Folk*, this event provides the dramatic backdrop for Du Bois's most harrowing gloss of the sorrow songs. "Ten master songs, more or less, one may pluck from this forest of melody," he writes. "One of these I have just mentioned. Another whose strains begin this book is 'Nobody knows the trouble I've seen.' When, struck with a sudden poverty, the United States refused to fulfill its promises of land to the freedmen, a brigadier-general went down to the Sea Islands to carry the news. An old woman on the outskirts of the throng began singing this song; all the mass joined with her, swaying. And the soldier wept."[104]

Du Bois's description of this devastating scene—the spiritual become an expression of solidarity in the face of an unprecedented loss that would, in time, be repeated over and again—is justly famous. But it is not the last word. Indeed, the historical record on which Du Bois draws presents a slightly different picture. Many of the freed people on Edisto Island, particularly those who had taken up arms in anticipation of Howard's visit, seem to have felt far more anger than sadness at the scene they knew was about to unfold. And nor was their song spontaneous. As a missionary present recalled, "A committee of black men goes out to consult. Meanwhile, what shall be done with the silent assembly, whose fierceness flashes from their eyes like that of a tiger in the jungle? Judge Whaley talks. The general proposes they sing. No response. 'How *shall* we sing the Lord's song in a strange land!'"[105] The freed men and women do eventually give in to Howard's wishes and begin singing. But if their song illustrates for Du Bois the origins and power of the slave spiritual, it is worth remembering that this command performance is requested by a general eager to cajole the singers to accept their economic disenfranchisement. The song they sing, in other words, is no longer an exemplar of the genre of the spiritual as the general and others on the Sea Islands had come to appreciate it.[106] It is also and more immediately a work song. Crucially, though, this command performance manifests not the meaningfulness of all work but the freed people's desire to reclaim the varieties of endeavor written off as idleness. "Nobody Knows the Trouble I've Seen" thus sounds a forceful note of dissent against the work society being reconsolidated on the Sea Islands and beyond.

CODA
REMAKING RECIPROCITY

Work Requirements does not aim to present a comprehensive account of US social welfare provision in the decades before the formal creation of the welfare state during the New Deal. Rather, the book turns to the patchwork of public and private initiatives that took root across the late nineteenth and early twentieth centuries to explore how people on the social margins have historically been conscripted into the unacknowledged representational project at the heart of the work society as such. The print culture of social welfare, in other words, helps us understand the effort that went into making work seem naturally meaningful. This effort is no less pressing today, of course, even after the passage of the Personal Responsibility and Work Opportunity Act in 1996 sought to "end welfare as we know it." Indeed, the task of shoring up the noneconomic value of even the most arduous and least profitable kinds of work in the context of social welfare provision is now mediated by an ever-widening circle of actors—from government agencies to public bureaucracies, nongovernmental organizations, nonprofit firms, and mixed private-public ventures. In theorizing how work-based welfare policies are administered on the ground, a rich body of empirical literature has followed Michael Lipsky in emphasizing the authority exercised by "street-level bureaucrats" who operate on the front line of policy delivery.[1] As Bernado Zacka has written, it would be easy enough to imagine these agents as rigid automata bound by the letter of the law. But "they are in fact vested with a considerable margin of discretion."[2] Not mere "implementation functionaries," these bureaucrats play a decisive role in shaping workfare policy and "redrawing the boundaries between work and the welfare state."[3]

The story told in this book underscores the value of approaching these bureaucratic acts of mediation as part of a much older hermeneutic project, an ongoing but rarely acknowledged effort to secure the seeming self-evidence of work's noneconomic value. As the print culture of social welfare makes clear, this project has not gone uncontested. Indeed, recognizing that work requirements are necessarily formal requirements allowed people caught in the clerical networks of turn-of-the-century social welfare to contest the logic of the market. Questions about whether this or that activity should qualify as work went hand in hand with questions about why a refusal to work on the terms given should be disqualifying— or why work should matter so much in the first place. In this regard, the formal genealogies traced in *Work Requirements* run adjacent to and at times traverse adjacent histories of mutual aid, self-help, and communal care that do not, like the print culture of social welfare, take their bearings from elite institutions or the state. By the same token, the counterfactual histories and impossible futures glimpsed in this book also anticipate more recent and more programmatic interest in universal basic income (UBI). Over the last few decades, writers and activists of all stripes have supported policies that would ensure every citizen a minimum income. For some commentators, such a universal provision would do away with the necessity of the welfare state's targeted programs (a proposition that, particularly in libertarian elaborations, often loses sight of social and access needs that exceed the "basic").

For others, UBI would mark a crucial first step toward social justice for historically marginalized people. As Martin Luther King Jr. wrote, "Those at the lowest economic level, the poor white and Negro, the aged and chronically ill, are traditionally unorganized and therefore have little ability to force the necessary growth in their income."[4] Echoing calls by the Black Panther Party and the National Welfare Rights Organization, King identified a UBI as one possible solution to this intersectional crisis. More recent commentators also argue that the shift from an industrial to a "social knowledge" economy should prompt us to rethink our "over-reliance on the labor market" in addressing poverty, inequality, and social marginalization. Ours should be not a work society but a "real sharing economy."[5]

To be sure, no concrete proposals emerged from the turn-of-the-century print culture of social welfare. But this archive's focus on the textual genres developed to mediate between individuals and institutions—and that were used by turns to bolster and interrogate the inherent noneconomic value of all labor—can help answer one of the most common arguments made against UBI proposals. As the feminist political theorist Carole Pateman has suggested, the criticism provoked in recent years by the unconditional character of basic income centers on questions of reciprocity. Opponents argue that UBI breaches "the principle of doing 'one's fair share [in] a cooperative scheme from which one expects to benefit'—because recipients get something from nothing."[6] These arguments, Pateman notes, rely on a "narrow, economistic sense of reciprocity." The guiding assumption is that receiving any social benefit obligates the beneficiary to make a specific and equitable contribution in return. Dispensing with the morality of the market, Pateman proposes a wider understanding of reciprocity that acknowledges social life "as a web of mutual aid and forbearance, a dense network of interdependence." From this vantage, social benefits and social contributions "have no strict correlation with one another."[7] The reciprocity that defines citizenship or social belonging more generally is here not a zero-sum game. Instead, Pateman imagines reciprocity as an interweaving of social interdependencies—obligations, responsibilities, and support irreducible to immediate recompense. Reciprocity is thus not something to be acknowledged and made good on, but rather something to be made and remade.

This notion of reciprocity as the making and remaking of social obligations might also describe the turn-of-the-century print culture of social welfare. As we have seen, the same modes of writing and representation used to bolster the noneconomic value of labor in and of itself—and thus to make good on one's duty to the work society—could also be used to articulate modes of connection and interdependence not grounded in the market. In this regard, the print culture of social welfare shares a striking affinity with the contemporary work of the interdisciplinary artist and weaver Raisa Kabir. Against the backdrop of global capitalism's eugenic devaluing of laborers deemed neither "useful" nor "functioning," Kabir's textile productions explore how "marginalized communities rely—and have always relied—on support networks of care and structures of mutual aid to survive that are separate to the state."[8] In one such exploration, a film titled *House Made of Tin (A Socially Distanced Weaving Performance)*, Kabir asks audiences to reconsider the relations among labor, care, and reciprocity (figures C.1–C.3). The performance was created between pandemic lockdowns in October 2020, when Kabir announced an open call for BIPOC, disabled, and queer participants to collaborate on a geometric textile sculpture. Eight weavers gathered in East London's Springfield

Park, masked and socially distanced, and—after a shared meal—took their places on the grid that Kabir and their collaborators had set up on the field. Each participant was outfitted with a backstrap loom, created by tying the threads around the body of the weaver. Still used by many of the Indigenous communities with whom Kabir has studied, backstrap looms are usually tied to a tree or post. But in *House Made of Tin (A Socially Distanced Weaving Performance)*, the ends were connected to other weavers, the scaffolding of the performance ultimately underscoring Kabir's contention that the process of (and preparation for) the weaving mattered far more than did the tapestry produced.

The warp, or the vertical threads, consisted of a variety of bright colors—mints, greens, pinks. The weft, or the horizontal threads woven under and over the warp, was made of wool, leather, and other dense materials. Meeting at multiple points, the warp and weft together created sharp right angles and the overall appearance of a tic-tac-toe game. Some of the strands were tight and thick, but others were loose, knotted, or beautifully messy. A film made of the performance, later exhibited at the Ford Foundation Gallery in New York, captures the same textured multiplicity of perspective, aim, and execution. At times, images are overlaid one on another to show several actions at once; at others, the screen itself becomes a grid, divided into four quadrants, each of which documents a particular moment of performance. Sounds also overlap and echo beyond their diegetic origins. We hear laughter, instructions, and even confusion—but also snippets of jokes, stories of grief, and crip pandemic coping strategies. These and other sounds from the performance itself are mixed together with Kabir's voice-over, which serves as both an audio description of everything that happens on the screen and an explanation of the weaving process that empowers viewers to imagine themselves as collaborators. We also hear voice memos that participants left for Kabir reflecting retrospectively on their experience of the day.

Ultimately, these various ways of accounting for the collaborative work at the center of *House Made of Tin (A Socially Distanced Weaving Performance)* converge on the recognition that its reward is neither monetary nor moral—the satisfaction or fulfillment that we are taught to expect from an "honest day's work." Instead, the performance fostered what one participant called a "slowness and holding space for each other outside the space of capitalism." The weave of reciprocities simultaneously acknowledged in and created by *House Made of Tin (A Socially Distanced Weaving*

C.1 Raisa Kabir, *House Made of Tin (A Socially Distanced Weaving Performance)* (2020). Original caption reads: "Our weaving slowly takes shape." Still image © Raisa Kabir, courtesy of the artist.

C.2 Raisa Kabir, *House Made of Tin (A Socially Distanced Weaving Performance)* (2020). Original caption reads: "The loom became a physical support network." Still image © Raisa Kabir, courtesy of the artist.

the structure, collectively woven, connecting us all.

C.3   Raisa Kabir, *House Made of Tin (A Socially Distanced Weaving Performance)* (2020). Original caption reads: "The structure, collectively woven, connecting us all." Still image © Raisa Kabir, courtesy of the artist.

Performance) are thus irreducible to purely economistic exchange. Indeed, the performance itself—and not the tapestry it produces—amounts to a sign that can only be read in the making. It endeavors, strand by strand, to make legible not the meaning of work in and of itself, but the meaning of being with and for others.

ACKNOWLEDGMENTS

This book is about why we assume all work is inherently meaningful and about how people on the social margins have been made to ensure us that it is. But it began—long ago—as the book about poetry I always thought I'd write. From my earliest years as a reader and writer and later as a graduate student, I was drawn to the forceful economy of poetic expression. I relished the finely tuned attention and methodical sense making that poetry demands of us, not least of all because of the difficulty my eyes have holding printed text in focus. Scanning and skimming have never come easily to me, which has proven both a virtue and a hardship. In the intervening years, my interest in poetic form and literary history gave way to broader questions about how writing and representation mediate between individuals and institutions. The stakes came to feel different, to be sure, the further I moved away from the strictly literary. But the habits of focused close reading that poetry taught me and the care with which I learned to interrogate the relation between part and whole and to trace the circulation of cultural forms across disparate contexts—all this profoundly shaped the book that eventually became *Work Requirements*. And so while they might not recognize their influence in this peculiarly interdisciplinary undertaking, my first thanks are due to those from whom I learned to read poetry, above all Marjorie Levinson and Bob Perelman.

I am also grateful to the many friends, peers, and colleagues who have helped me find my bearings as an increasingly scattered set of interests led me from one genre to another and one field to the next. And although they too might have difficulty seeing themselves in this book, I owe thanks to Rachel Adams, Lindsey Andrews, Erin Aoyama, GerShun Avilez, Nancy Bentley, Bernd Blaschke, Julia Bloch, John Connor, Adrian Daub, Sarah Dowling, Scott Enderle (dearly missed), Jed Esty, Travis Foster, Nicholas Gaskill, Katherine Hunt, Tsitsi Jaji, Jane Malcolm, Annie McClanahan, Melanie Micir, Mara Mills, Christen Mucher, Clare Mullaney, Philip Nell,

Rachael Nichols, Emily Ogden, Cristina Pangilinan, Vincent Platini, Lloyd Pratt, Lindsay Reckson, Paul Saint-Amour, Ben Singer, Michael Snediker, and Johanna Winant. Heather Love—an invaluable sounding board, incomparable model, and crucial supporter of this project in all of its waywardness—has an especially important place in this or any list.

The interdisciplinary, genre-spanning drift of my writing has been mirrored by a career trajectory every bit as peripatetic, though often less exciting than exhausting. I began work in earnest on this book in the wake of a "great" recession and finished the manuscript in the midst of a horrific pandemic. The years in between have brought about extraordinary social changes—rarely for the better, it too often seems. And academia is of course no exception. But during an unprecedented decline in the academic job market, I was fortunate to receive a number of fellowships that allowed me to collaborate with colleagues across the disciplines and—something we don't often mention—to pay the bills. The first stop on this sojourn was Harvard's W. E. B. Du Bois Research Center, where I joined a cohort of fellows that included David Bindman, Adrienne L. Childs, Meghan Healy-Clancy, Theodore Miller, Jonathan Munby, Sophie Oldfield, Ronald K. Richardson, Mark Solomon, Nirvana Tanoukhi, Lisa Thompson, Emily Thornbury, Omar Wasow, and Louis Wilson. In the English Department at UC Berkeley, where I was an ACLS New Faculty Fellow, I had the good fortune to share ideas and work with Elizabeth Abel, Kathleen Donegan, Nadia Ellis, Eric Falci, Catherine Flynn, Mark Goble, Abdul JanMohamed, Georgina Kleege, David Landreth, Celeste Langan, Steven Lee, Colleen Lye, David Marno, Samuel Otter, Scott Saul, Elisa Tamarkin, and Bryan Wagner. Sue Schweik has been a guiding force in this book's development since my days at Berkeley. She has my deepest thanks, as does Leroy F. Moore Jr., whom I also met in the East Bay and whose conversation and collaboration over the years have challenged me to think in new ways about the relation between disability history and disability justice.

I also owe a debt of gratitude to the members of the Medical Humanities seminar in the Center for Cultural Analysis at Rutgers University, which taught me both the challenges and rewards of genuinely interdisciplinary thought: Nick Allred, Hilary Buxton, Carla Cevasco, Jorie Hofstra, Ann Jurecic, Joanna Kempner, Catherine Lee, Lisa Mikesell, Kathleen Pierce, Jeanette Samyn, Susan Sidlauskas, Louis Sass, and Louise Tam. Thanks as well to Henry Turner, Meredith McGill, and Brad Evans, and in particular to Amy Zanoni, who patiently helped me teach myself the historiography of the welfare state. An earlier fellowship at the First Book

Institute hosted by Penn State's Center for American Literary Studies gave me the opportunity to reimagine both the stakes and the scope of this project. For generous feedback and camaraderie, I thank Adrienne Brown, Sean Goudie, Sarah Juliet Lauro, J. Samaine Lockwood, Ted Martin, Danielle Heard Mollel, Christen Mucher, and Sonya Posmentier. Special thanks to Priscilla Wald, who since the First Book Institute has been an outspoken champion for this book (and for my family). A fellowship from the Andrew W. Mellon and Volkswagen Foundations at the Freiburg Institute for Advanced Studies provided an idyllic but rigorous space in which to complete a first draft of *Work Requirements*. Many thanks to Laura Bieger, Dustin Breitenwischer, Carsten Dose, Petra Fischer, Winfried Fluck, Bernd Kortmann, Britta Küst, Barbara Mennel, and Roland Muntschick.

An NEH Fellowship brought me to the Newberry Library in Chicago, an ideal place to complete the manuscript. Members of the fellows' seminar were the first readers of what would become the book's introduction, which has benefited tremendously from their incisive feedback. Thanks to Nicholas Abbott, Heather Allen, Tom Arnold-Forster, Karen-Edis Barzman, Keelin Burke, Federica Caneparo, Deborah Cohen, Madeline Crispell, Laura Edwards, Elisa Garcia, Mary Hale, Kim Hedlin, D. Bradford Hunt, Thomas Kernan, and Liesl Olson. Many thanks as well to colleagues in the Literature and Creative Writing Department at Hamilton College, the Bates College English Department (especially Eden Osucha), and Harvard's History and Literature program. And for several happy and productive years at the Freie Universität Berlin, I thank the Languages of Emotion *Exzellenzcluster* and the JFK Institute for North American Studies. At Duke University Press, it has been a pleasure to work with Courtney Berger, Sandra Korn, Liz Smith, and the rest of the editorial and production staff. Many thanks as well to the anonymous readers, at both Duke and the University of Minnesota Press, for providing helpful suggestions and provocations for finalizing the manuscript.

Archival research for *Work Requirements* was made possible by a number of generous research grants. The Norton Strange Townshend Fellowship on American History brought me to the Clements Library at the University of Michigan and a Countway Fellowship in the History of Medicine to the Boston Medical Library. I was able to visit several other archives with the support of a Franklin Grant from the American Philosophical Society and two awards from Harvard's Anne and Jim Rothenberg Fund for Humanities Research. I am also grateful for a Mellon Foundation Fellowship from the Library Company of Philadelphia and for grants from the German Academic Exchange Service and the Rockefeller Archive Center.

The fellowships and funding that supported the writing of this book have been immensely helpful. I am grateful, to say the least, to have had the opportunity to dig into new archives and tell long-forgotten stories. But the peculiar and often wearisome work of grant capture has also influenced the shape of this book—creating a strange convergence between the object and circumstances of my scholarly labor. As a scholar without the privileges and protections of stable employment, writing a book about how work became the truest sign of social deservingness has required the near constant production of applications, proposals, and cover letters. Much of the material that eventually became *Work Requirements*, that is, was first put on paper not in order to advance the scholarly conversation but to ask for money or to assure potential employers of my (intellectual) work ethic. The unlikely role that these bureaucratic information genres have played in the writing of this book would seem to suggest just how far the process has taken me from the questions about poetry with which I began. But it likewise underscores the folly of pretending that the profession is not part of the work society or that we are all talking about the same thing when we talk about "our work."

As the Marxist feminists to whom this book is indebted remind us, we cannot hope to understand how work societies operate—whether on campus or in the world at large—without attending to the work of social reproduction. I have much to be thankful for here as well, both for the family and friends who have created space and time for writing and for ample opportunity to reciprocate. Our upstate family—Vesna and Kir Kuiken, Wendy and Jesse Roberts, Kendra Sena and Tim Wientzen—is a care network and a lifeline. From my parents and siblings I received unwavering support and steadfast optimism that often felt misplaced but was nonetheless deeply appreciated. To the Goldsteins and Fretwells, I owe thanks for childcare and material support of all kinds. I had the thrill of watching Noam come into (two) language(s) while ironing out unruly prose and struggling to get my point across. I'm still rarely sure who is teaching whom. My biggest debt is to Erica, to whom this book is dedicated and whose support and love—no matter how heavy the lift or Sisyphean the task—always looks effortless. Her care is a genre unto itself.

Introduction

1 McCoy, "Disabled and Disdained."

2 Ritchie, "Local Incident Goes Viral."

3 In this book, particularly in chapter 2, I use the word *begging* to describe a mode of solicitation in which practitioners self-consciously manipulate the pejorative connotations of that word and of the epithet *beggar*.

4 Ritchie, "Local Incident Goes Viral."

5 Menafee, "A School Treasurer's Story," 152.

6 On ableist tropes of "overcoming," see Shapiro, *No Pity*; Mitchell and Snyder, *Narrative Prosthesis*; Schalk, "Reevaluating the Supercrip"; Kafer, *Feminist, Queer, Crip*. On Helen Keller's relation to this trope, see Kleege, *Blind Rage*. Menafee's personal narrative might seem but a pat celebration of self-help in much the same vein. But his concern with what today would be called workplace accommodation gives pause. Consider, for instance, how Menafee credits a donated typewriter with his improved prospects. "My success in life," he writes, "depended largely upon my securing it." Just as the typewriter was originally invented for blind people, neither was stenography an arbitrary career choice. It was one of the few fields open to disabled workers at the time and a job that reformers routinely pointed to in arguing that anyone—and any body—could find a place in the workforce. What begins as an intensely personal story of injury thus by the end becomes a representative tale of economic success. Menafee, "A School Treasurer's Story," 156.

7 In colloquial usage, *welfare* today usually refers (pejoratively) to federal programs that provide cash aid to poor single mothers and their children, namely Aid to Families with Dependent Children before 1996 and Temporary Aid to Needy Families (TANF) afterward. Scholars of the welfare state, however, understand welfare far more broadly to include any number of government assistance programs. As Premilla Nadasen, Jennifer Mittelstadt, and Marisa Chappel suggest, this list might include "Old Age Assistance, Aid to the Disabled, Supplemental Security Income, Social Security, Medicaid

and Medicare, unemployment insurance, public housing, legal services, student grant programs, corporate bailouts, corporate subsidies, and food stamps. Some of these are programs targeted to the poor, but the nation's most generous social welfare measures—such as Social Security, Medicare, and veterans' benefits—are available to people regardless of income status." Nadasen, Mittelstadt, and Chappell, *Welfare in the United States*, 1.

8 As Judith N. Shklar writes, "Workfare [inaugurated by TANF] has nothing to do with economics. It is about citizenship, and whether able-bodied adults who do not earn anything actively can be regarded as full citizens." Shklar, *American Citizenship*, 98.

9 Stone, "Welfare Policy and the Transformation of Care," 183–84. As Noah Zatz writes, "Some state TANF programs focus exclusively on immediate paid private employment or on unpaid 'work experience' providing public services like cleaning parks (also known as 'workfare'). Others emphasize a variety of professional services designed to improve future employability, including job training; education; and rehabilitative services addressing disability, substance abuse, or domestic violence. Still others allow similar activities under the rubric of 'community service' and also include unpaid care for sick or disabled family members, grandchildren, or foster children. Notwithstanding these varied approaches to unpaid work, TANF programs collectively differ from EITC [Earned Income Tax Credit], which includes only paid activities as work." Zatz, "What Welfare Requires from Work," 376.

10 In this book, I do not differentiate among terms like *work*, *labor*, or *productivity* in any hard-and-fast sense. To be sure, such distinctions are often crucial to the arguments that philosophers and activists make about the vagaries of human endeavor. This rich body of writing—glossed briefly later in this introduction—spans centuries, if not millennia, and certainly informs my thinking here. My goal, however, is not to develop a cohesive social theory or to document a particular set of historical practices. Rather, this book explores how and why definitional boundaries are drawn as they are in a given time and place and how these decisions give rise to formal conventions that traverse a range of cultural genres and media.

11 Gorz, *Farewell to the Working Class*, 126.

12 Chamberlain, *Undoing Work, Rethinking Community*, 2. On automation, see Smith, *Smart Machines and Service Work*.

13 Weeks, *The Problem with Work*, 8.

14 For this reason, as legal historians have observed, people who enroll in social welfare programs that provide cash aid—even popular programs such as Social Security Disability Insurance—may face stigma for doing so. Claiming the social rights guaranteed by the welfare state may actually jeopardize

one's social citizenship in the broader work society. See Bagenstos, "Disability, Universalism, Social Rights, and Citizenship." Bagenstos draws on the distinction between social rights and social citizenship that T. H. Marshall lays out in *Citizenship and Social Class, and Other Essays*.

15 Glenn, *Unequal Freedom*, 2.

16 Mitchell and Snyder, *The Biopolitics of Disability*; Taylor, "The Right Not to Work"; Puar, *The Right to Maim*. On the relations between and among disability, work, and citizenship, see also Garland-Thomson, *Extraordinary Bodies*; Oliver, *The Politics of Disablement*; Hirschmann and Linker, "Disability, Citizenship, and Belonging"; Belt, "Contemporary Voting Rights Controversies"; Hanass-Hancock and Mitra, "Livelihoods and Disability"; Bruyère, *Disability and Employer Practices*; Beckwith, *Disability Servitude*; and Longmore, *Why I Burned My Book*. As Michael Rembis notes, work is central to disability culture and experience, though its impact is diffuse: "One must consider the work of charity, and of begging, 'sheltered' work, activist work, the desire not to work, the inability to work, the active exclusion from work, and the ways in which gender, race, and class influence experiences within various types of 'work.'" Rembis, "Disability Studies," 229.

17 Glenn, *Unequal Freedom*, 68–69. See also Day, *Alien Capital*; Lowe, *Immigrant Acts*; Lye, *America's Asia*; Wong, *Racial Reconstruction*.

18 Kerber, *No Constitutional Right to Be Ladies*, 73.

19 Robinson, *Black Marxism*, xxix.

20 Wilderson, "Gramsci's Black Marx," 238. Wilderson's provocation is part of a broader agenda often described as an Afro-pessimist critique of racial capitalism. Approaching slavery as an ontological condition rather than a system of economic exploitation, Wilderson and other writers emphasize how notions of Black fungibility (rather than Black labor) define and organize Black value within ongoing relations of conquest. See King, *The Black Shoals*, 23. As Jackie Wang summarizes, "analyses that focus on how racism is incentivized by capitalism and instrumentalized for monetary gain can sidestep the intractable psychological dimension of racism." Wang, *Carceral Capitalism*, 89. Dylan Rodríguez writes along similar lines: "Unlike the historical capitalist substructure, the schematic logics of white supremacy are not accumulation, surplus value, and labor exploitation, but are *civilization* (read in verb, not noun form), *genocide*, and *incarceration*." Rodríguez, "Multiculturalist White Supremacy," 41. Du Bois's *Black Reconstruction* offers a compelling retort to Afro-pessimist criticism of racial capitalism. Du Bois titles his chapter on slavery "The Black Worker," leaving little doubt about his understanding of slavery and its relation to capitalism. See Du Bois, *Black Reconstruction in America*. As Walter Johnson clarifies, for Du Bois the slave is "a subject, at once, of capital and of white supremacy." Johnson, "To Remake the World."

21 Gordon, *Pitied but Not Entitled*; Nelson, "The Origins of the Two-Channel Welfare State"; Kessler-Harris, *In Pursuit of Equity*; Mittelstadt, *From Welfare to Workfare.*

22 Svendsen, *Work*, 19. There is good reason to suspect that Greek craftsmen did not share this antipathy toward work, but the philosophical tradition was ultimately to prove more influential. A tradition of Homeric hymns to Hephaestus suggests that craft and community were in fact inseparable for many Greeks: "With bright-eyed Athena he taught men glorious crafts throughout the world—men who before had used to dwell in caves in the mountains like wild beasts." Quoted in Sennett, *The Craftsman*, 21. As Judith N. Shklar writes in *American Citizenship*:

> The sheer novelty of the notion of the dignity of labor in general, and as an essential element of citizenship, can scarcely be exaggerated. It was one of the many contributions of the Enlightenment to American public culture that flourished here far more than it ever could in Europe. In the past it had been almost universally believed that physical work defiles us, that those who labor are impure. Certainly the philosophers of antiquity regarded productive and commercial work as so deeply degrading that it made a man unfit for citizenship. Nor did these attitudes disappear with slavery. European society was for centuries separated into three orders: those who pray, those who fight, and those who labor. The last were the despised peasantry, hardly to be distinguished from the beasts. (68–69)

23 Even Benedictine monks, among the most skilled farmers, craftsmen, and engineers of the era, were looked down upon by the Church hierarchy because they labored. Ciulla, *The Working Life*, 42–43.

24 McClanahan, "Introduction." As a result, the peculiarly unsatisfying experience of living to work rather than working to live came to be experienced as psychologically fulfilling.

25 Weber, *The Protestant Ethic and the Spirit of Capitalism*, 25, 123.

26 Rodgers, *The Work Ethic in Industrial America*, xiii. Even where dissatisfaction with industrial labor did find an outlet, moreover, the broader culture responded not by questioning the universality of the work ethic but by cultivating other activities in which it might be expressed more fully, from competitive sports to craft arts. See Gilbert, *Work without Salvation*.

27 McClanahan, "Introduction."

28 Weeks, *The Problem with Work*, 68.

29 Although management ideologues proudly underscore that this model could be no further from the drudgery endured by previous generations, members of the so-called creative classes embody the Weberian work ethic every bit as clearly as nineteenth-century factory workers. See Florida, *The Rise of the Creative Class*. As Sarah Brouillette writes, the artist has become

"the premier model of ideally flexible worker." Sanitized representations of the artist at work are taken to be "evidence that insecure employment in temporary networks is the key to groundbreaking innovation." Brouillette, "Academic Labor, the Aesthetics of Management." See also Jaffe, *Work Won't Love You Back.*

30 Smith, *An Inquiry into the Nature and Causes of the Wealth of Nations*, 1:47–48. As Ronald Meek clarifies, classical economists like Smith distinguished themselves from the mercantilists and physiocrats who preceded them by claiming that labor constitutes the unique essence of wealth, "thus doing away with the old idea that wealth, or private property, is something as it were *exterior* to man, and insisting instead that it is really something of which man is the very substance." Meek, *Studies in the Labor Theory of Value*, 136.

31 Marx, *Karl Marx*, 110.

32 Fromm, *Marx's Concept of Man*, 42–43.

33 Jameson, *Representing "Capital,"* 17.

34 See, among others, Weeks, *The Problem with Work*; Gorz, *Farewell to the Working Class*; Berardi, *The Soul at Work*; Larsen et al., *Marxism and the Critique of Value.*

35 Marx, *Capital*, 3:954.

36 Weeks, *The Problem with Work.*

37 Marx, *Capital*, 1:290–91.

38 Spratling, "Industrial Education for Epileptics," 75.

39 Russell, *Capitalism and Disability*, 13.

40 Du Bois, "Worlds of Color," 423.

41 Linda Kerber's description of vagrancy as a status offense—"The crime is not what a person has done but what the person *appears* to be"—is relevant here. Black women, Kerber argues further, "have been caught in the internal contradictions of a gendered ideology of an obligation to work that succeeded slavery. The ideology was deeply rooted in antique concepts that stressed the obligation of the poor not only to be self-supporting but also to be at work that is measurable and visible, and that envisioned Black women as appropriately engaged in physical labor from which their white counterparts were more likely to be protected." Kerber, *No Constitutional Right to Be Ladies*, 54, 80.

42 Beech, *Art and Value*; Brouillette, *Literature and the Creative Economy*; Bernes, *The Work of Art in the Age of Deindustrialization.*

43 Burden, *Chris Burden*, 162–63.

44 Molesworth, *Work Ethic*, 18–19.

45 Jakobsen, "Queers Are Like Jews, Aren't They?"; see also Grillo and Wildman, "Obscuring the Importance of Race."

46 My thinking about the representational effort that sustains the work society and bleeds into conventional notions of the aesthetic has been informed by Leigh Claire La Berge's work on "decommodified labor." La Berge uses that term to describe how contemporary art is powerfully shaped by capitalist modes of production even though it may not be exchanged like other commodities. La Berge, *Wages against Artwork*.

47 Handler, *The Poverty of Welfare Reform*, 9.

48 "Despite the practical and theoretical importance of clarifying what work means," the legal historian Noah Zatz writes, "the scholarly literature on work-based welfare reform largely neglects this question. Instead, the literature generally starts from the premise that work means paid employment, and it proceeds from there to debate the morality, effectiveness, and need for work-based policies." Zatz, "What Welfare Requires from Work," 375–76. See also Zatz, "Welfare to What."

49 Lipsky, *Street-Level Bureaucracy*; Brodkin, "Work and the Welfare State"; Zacka, *When the State Meets the Street*.

50 Nadasen, Mittelstadt, and Chappell, *Welfare in the United States*.

51 Rockman, *Welfare Reform in the Early Republic*, 5.

52 As John Guillory notes, documents or written records of transactions, exchanges, and events have of course always existed. But "the dominion of the document is a feature of modernity," brought about in large measure by the industrial print revolution of the late nineteenth century. Guillory, "The Memo and Modernity," 113.

53 Brodhead, "The American Literary Field," 27.

54 In recent years, disability has emerged as a central concern for scholars across the disciplines. This development reflects the institutionalization of disability studies, a field that coalesced in the 1980s around the efforts of scholars and activists to conceptualize disability as a social construction and disabled people as a political minority. *Work Requirements* takes part in a second—or perhaps even a third—wave of disability studies. The intellectual project of disability studies now moves beyond the inaugural critique of normativity by attending, in Rosemarie Garland-Thomson's phrase, to "what disability makes in the world." Garland-Thomson, "Disability Studies," 918. *Work Requirements* shares this commitment to the nimble study of disability history with books as different in method and approach as Samuels, *Fantasies of Identification*; Chen, *Animacies*; and Piepzna-Samarasinha, *Care Work*. This brief list illustrates the breadth of contemporary disability studies but also the field's guiding interest in how disability intersects with other social identities and histories.

55 Stone, *The Disabled State.*

56 See Rose, *No Right to Be Idle.*

57 Glenn, *Unequal Freedom,* 3.

58 Second Thessalonians 3:10.

59 Handler, *The Poverty of Welfare Reform,* 12.

60 Rothman, *The Discovery of the Asylum,* xxv. Even when the nakedly exploit-ative dimension of institutional labor grew difficult to ignore, reformers still argued that its primary value was noneconomic. As a social deterrent, inmate labor powerfully signified the misery of life outside the market. Such was the picture of institutional labor a New York journalist took away from a visit to a Rhode Island almshouse in 1853: "I saw a party of men carrying wood from one corner of the yard to another and piling it there, when it was all removed it was brought back again and piled in the old place." New York evidently had yet to learn the virtue of such arrangements, the "rigid adher-ence" to which "relieves Providence of all lazy drones, such as invest our poor houses to a great degree." "Letters to the Secretary of State on the Subject of Pauperism," *Columbia Republican* (1853); quoted in Katz, *In the Shadow of the Poorhouse,* 32.

61 White, "Labor Tests and Relief in Work," 96.

62 Hatton, *Coerced,* 5; Beckett and Western, "Governing Social Marginality," 44.

63 Initially, practitioners of scientific charity were not concerned with people of color. Such disregard—and often outright hostility—was well-established practice. From colonial outdoor relief to the Jacksonian almshouse, social provision was usually reserved for recognized members of the community. Just as settlement ordinances barred entry to outsiders "likely to become public charges," Indigenous people and free people of African descent were ineligible for the resources available to white people—by custom if not by the letter of the law. These relationships were "structured by the benign solicitude of the great white father for his wards," rather than by material generosity. Leiby, *A History of Social Welfare and Social Work,* 11. There were exceptions to this rule. The work of white missionaries in communities of color in the United States and abroad, for instance, was commonly framed as an exercise in social welfare, as was the abolitionist movement and even the Freedmen's Bureau. Indeed, historians have suggested that the latter failed in large measure because its mission was approached as a charitable under-taking rather than a question of civil rights. Where federal officials did not recognize freed people as rights-bearing citizens, that is, their demands could be dismissed as those of undeserving beggars best served by being returned to the labor market, if necessary by force. Goldberg, *Citizens and Paupers,* 76–79. And while they faced discrimination at every step in the application process, African American veterans and their dependents were eligible for

(and often received) Civil War invalid pensions, the provision of which—as we will see in chapter 1—played a crucial role in the evolution of the modern US welfare state. Nor were segregated charitable institutions unheard of, from New York's Colored Orphan Asylum to Philadelphia's Colored House of Refuge, though the benevolent and mutual aid societies founded by African Americans probably had far greater impact. But if Black Americans were not entirely excluded from the mélange of social welfare practices established across the eighteenth and nineteenth centuries, they were much more likely to be sorted into work-based than into need-based systems of economic distribution. At the same moment, moreover, when social welfare institutions began to embrace bureaucratic protocols of scientific charity, the US workforce system was dramatically reshaped by postbellum regimes of racial discipline. The hegemony of the market and Black Americans' subservient place within it were enforced by debt peonage, vagrancy legislation, and lynch law.

64 In James Beniger's account, this latter "control revolution" was shaped most powerfully by the need to develop information-processing systems that could keep up with the ever-accelerating pace of capitalist production. Beniger, *The Control Revolution*, 7. Robert H. Wiebe also influentially describes this period as marked by a profound "search for order" aroused by widespread feelings of "dislocation and bewilderment." Wiebe, *The Search for Order*, 12.

65 Kaestle and Radway, "A Framework for the History of Publishing and Reading," 15–16. See Yates, *Control through Communication*; Frankel, *States of Inquiry*.

66 Job printing originally encompassed any work that made less than the full-sized sheet produced by large-scale presses. But today the phrase usually refers to anything not considered a book, periodical, newspaper, or specialist productions like packages. Before 1830, letterpress job work was relatively limited, hence most consumers instead opting for handwritten or engraved materials. But as demand grew for billheads, business cards, and handbills, small printers looked to advances in the jobbing platen press to keep up. Whether small, hand-operated presses or the power-driven machines used by large-volume professionals, the jobbing platen vastly accelerated the production of the small and ephemeral items used by industry, commerce, and government—while also dramatically reducing costs. Moran, *Printing Presses*, 143.

67 Gitelman, *Paper Knowledge*, 12.

68 Nancy Bentley makes a similar point with regard to "the diversity of newspaper, magazine, and book markets" and the "array of new visual, aural, and filmic technologies" created by the turn-of-the-century explosion in industrial print culture. Bentley, "Mass Media and Literary Culture," 191.

69 Gitelman, *Paper Knowledge*, 10.

70 On the history of mendicant literature, see Schweik, *The Ugly Laws*; Fabian, *The Unvarnished Truth*. Mendicant literature is also central to this book's second chapter.

71 Cohen, *The Fabrication of American Literature*.

72 As Marc Shell notes, the Greeks were among the first to wonder whether writing is productive or unproductive. For his part, Aristotle was unsure whether writing resembled the natural generativity of plants and animals or the unnatural generation of money. In usury, money proliferates by means of circulation and does not produce anything of actual substance. Shell, *The Economy of Literature*, 94. In the nineteenth century, these concerns took on renewed urgency amid the upheavals of industrialization and the market revolution. From Thomas Carlyle to Frederick Douglass, writers on both sides of the Atlantic watched the shifting economic landscape with apprehension but also excitement. See Gilmore, *American Romanticism and the Marketplace*. As Nicholas Bromell observes, politics and aesthetics converged in two interlocking questions: what is the nature of one's work as a writer, and how does it relate to the work performed by others? Bromell, *By the Sweat of the Brow*, 15. Put otherwise, could and should literary labor be reconciled to the market? In deliberating on the matter, many literary writers turned to the beggar, a cultural icon usually figured as disabled and assumed to exist outside of capitalist exchange. In the wake of Romantic efforts to define art in opposition to the market, allying the writer with the beggar was a powerful means of asserting literature's moral authority. But the stigma of idleness made doing so risky. For this reason, as Daniel Hack concludes, most nineteenth-century writers ultimately abandoned their (hypothetical) mendicant brethren, resolving instead to rebrand themselves as professional writers and productive laborers. Hack, *The Material Interests of the Victorian Novel*, 71. See also Langan, *Romantic Vagrancy*.

73 TenBroek, "The Right to Live in the World"; Taylor, "The Right Not to Work."

74 As David Mitchell and Sharon Snyder have influentially argued, such metaphorical and allegorical usages of disability function primarily as "narrative prostheses" and have little, if anything, to do with the lives of people with disabilities or with the history of disability. See Mitchell and Snyder, *Narrative Prosthesis*. See also Garland-Thomson, *Extraordinary Bodies*.

75 Kafka, "Paperwork," 341. Rather than treating bureaucracy as ideal type, Kafka elaborates, scholars in the field of paperwork studies have set out to investigate "the pens, papers, and other raw materials of power. In their focus on technologies of writing and the materiality of communication, many of these studies show a strong affinity for book history, despite our field's tendency to privilege texts that have been printed and bound" (341).

76 Brown, "Document," 643–44.

77 Gitelman, *Paper Knowledge*, 1.

78 Guillory, "The Memo and Modernity," 111, 130. See also Riles, "Introduction"; Vismann, *Files*; Kafka, "Paperwork."

79 Gitelman, *Paper Knowledge*, 30. More recently Matthew P. Brown has faulted paperwork studies for ignoring the readerly subjectivities elicited by documents. A representative case is Peter Stallybrass, who notes that job printing "transformed the texture of daily life" but did not necessarily have anything to do with reading. In suggesting that we use rather than read documents like preprinted blanks, Gitelman makes an even more direct connection to literature: "Whatever reading is entailed by genres like bills of lading and stock transfers," she writes, it does not have "much to do with the readerly subjectivities of literature." Gitelman, *Paper Knowledge*, 30–31. These kinds of approaches, Brown suggests, seem to rely on a somewhat reductive notion of reading. Who is to say, after all, that literary texts cannot be read instrumentally or distractedly? The reverse is also true: we can read bills of lading and stock transfers with the same attention we bring to works of literature. Such is the wager that literary critics have begun to make, pushing for histories of reading attuned to the surprising subjectivities fostered by informational genres. The payoff, we may conclude with Brown, is an ultimately fuller sense of what reading meant in earlier eras. Brown, "Blanks." My own sense is that the circulation of the ephemeral materials in the print culture of social welfare enacted a history of rereading that is also a history of reusing. When later writers, whether writing on behalf of institutions or as individuals, took up established forms, they used them by rereading them. They read into them, we might even say, the possibilities for thinking otherwise.

80 Caroline Levine and other literary scholars have imported the concept of affordance from the discipline of psychology to describe the usefulness of form along similar lines. See Levine, *Forms*. *Affordance* was first coined by James J. Gibson to explain how animals interact with their environment, such that certain elements of the environment offer or afford the animal the possibility of a certain action. A chair, for instance, "is for" or affords support. Importantly, for Gibson an affordance "is neither an objective property nor a subjective property; or it is both if you like. An affordance cuts across the dichotomy of subjective-objective and helps us understand its inadequacy. It is equally a fact of the environment and a fact of behavior. It is both physical and psychical, yet neither. An affordance points both ways, to the environment and to the observer." Gibson, "The Theory of Affordances," 129. When taken up as a theory of literary interpretation, the idea of affordances returns questions of readerly experience—often eclipsed by the imperative of critique—to the center of literary studies. As C. Namwali Serpell has argued, just as Gibson's chair "is for" support, so too do works of literature have properties that afford certain uses and options for moving through them.

And though literary affordances may vary more widely than environmental affordances, the possibilities for action are nonetheless finite, bound as they are to the particular formal qualities of the individual text at hand. Serpell, *Seven Modes of Uncertainty*, 9.

81 Best, *The Fugitive's Properties*, 25.

82 My sense of literariness at the heart of the print culture of social welfare—and of the formal relays connecting documents and works of literature more broadly at the turn of the century—thus parts ways with other accounts of the culture of social reform during this period. This scholarship often focuses on the rhetorical arguments leveraged for and against particular agendas or on broader efforts to delineate the philosophical meaning of benevolence and reform as such. Comprising "various persuasive texts and performances," the archive at the center of these debates is frequently called the "literature of reform." Ryan, "Reform," 197. Other scholars working in this vein explore how the institution of "Literature" was itself conscripted into reformist projects, whether by activists who championed the uplifting influence of the canon or by those who promoted the educative value of self-expression and what today is called "creative writing." Laura Fisher, for instance, has suggested that Progressive Era reformers were "guided by the belief that access to literary culture would transform the 'culturally impoverished' and bring about wide-ranging social change." Fisher, *Reading for Reform*, 2. Although this scholarship has been useful in framing the story I tell here, *Work Requirements* is not fundamentally concerned with how late nineteenth-century print culture championed a particular reform movement or promoted a particular novelist. Rather, the book asks how print culture did the work of social welfare provision.

83 McHenry, *Forgotten Readers*, 5.

84 Nelson, "The Origins of the Two-Channel Welfare State"; Gordon, "The New Feminist Scholarship on the Welfare State"; Gordon, *Pitied but Not Entitled*; Kornbluh, *The Battle for Welfare Rights*; Federici, *Wages against Housework*.

85 In Nikhil Singh's gloss, racial capitalism refers to the "tightly woven connections between racism, war, and liberalism in the development of capitalist accumulation." Singh, *Race and America's Long War*, 29. Peter James Hudson writes in a similar vein that racial capitalism refers to "the simultaneous emergence of racism and capitalism in the modern world and their mutual dependence." Hudson, *Bankers and Empire*, 13.

86 Lowe, "History Hesitant," 86. Today, this agenda is implicit in the very word *welfare*. What once described a panoply of supportive programs, from mothers' pensions to the GI Bill, is now a racialized pejorative, the vicious caricatures it conjures serving to obscure and justify a host of disciplinary policies. A century ago, social welfare practices furthered the ends of racial

capitalism by means of outright exclusion or segregation but also by supporting the convict lease, vagrancy ordinance, Black industrial education, and imperial expansion.

87 Du Bois, *Darkwater*, 98–99, 102.

88 Erevelles and Minear, "Unspeakable Offenses," 357.

89 See, among many others, Belt, "Contemporary Voting Rights Controversies"; Adams, *Sideshow U.S.A.*; Jarman, "Dismembering the Lynch Mob"; Marshall, "Crippled Speech"; Mitchell and Snyder, "The Eugenic Atlantic"; Wu, *Chang and Eng Reconnected*; Schweik, "Lomax's Matrix"; Piepzna-Samarasinha, *Dirty River*.

90 As scholars such as Rosemarie Garland-Thomson, Jasbir Puar, David Mitchell, and Sarah F. Rose have shown, the history of disability is thus marked by enduring forms of both economic disenfranchisement and compulsory productivity. Garland-Thomson, *Extraordinary Bodies*; Puar, *The Right to Maim*; Rose, *No Right to Be Idle*.

91 In accounting for this formal give-and-take, *Work Requirements* parts ways with literary scholarship that focuses on narrative, figural, and allegorical linkages of race and disability. The chapters to follow are thus indebted to important studies on the cultural codes of sensation, abjection, overcoming, and fantasy by which race and disability are linked in literary and cultural production. See in particular Pickens, *Black Madness*; Schalk, *Bodyminds Reimagined*; Wu, *Chang and Eng Reconnected*; Adams, *Sideshow U.S.A.* The particularity of my archive, however, calls for a recalibration of method. The book does not chart the overlapping representational economies of race and disability in memoir, speculative fiction, or literary realism. Instead, *Work Requirements* attends to the ephemeral modes of intersectionality created by the institutional genres and documentary protocols that emerged in the late nineteenth century to police the economic category of disability.

1. The Pensioner's Claim

1 Neither military invalid pensions nor the fundamentals of bureaucratic record keeping were new with the Civil War. Veterans of every US war since the Revolutionary War had received compensation for injuries received in the line of duty (or as specified by the particular regulations then in effect). What was new with the Civil War invalid pension system was the amount of public scrutiny to which the claims review process was subjected and hence the prominence (and then notoriety) to which the genre of the pension claim rose (or fell). Indeed, it may make sense to think of the Civil War invalid pension claim as a genre today only because the public then did so. On the history of US pension policy and Civil War pension policy in particular,

see Glasson, *Federal Military Pensions in the United States*; Skocpol, *Protecting Soldiers and Mothers*; Oliver, "History of the Civil War Military Pensions"; Marten, *Sing Not War*, 16.

2   Costa, *The Evolution of Retirement*, 161.

3   United States Pension Bureau, *A Treatise on the Practice of the Pension Bureau*, 94.

4   Skocpol, *Protecting Soldiers and Mothers*, 128.

5   Skocpol, *Protecting Soldiers and Mothers*, 151, emphasis added.

6   Linker, *War's Waste*, 2–3.

7   Pretchel-Kluskens, "Anatomy of a Civil War Pension File," 42.

8   To be sure, in the waning decades of the nineteenth century, US culture was still coming to terms with the war's carnage and with the physical violence visited upon the bodies of thousands of injured veterans. See, for instance, Faust, *This Republic of Suffering*. Whenever Americans engaged with the bureaucracy of federal pension policy, however, as an ever-increasing number of veterans and their dependents did, they learned to approach disability strategically not as a measure of bodily injury or incapacitation but as a set of narrative conventions governing a body's eligibility for social support.

9   Couser, *Signifying Bodies*, 2. Couser's term for this particular subset of the "some body narrative" is "autosomatography." It is paired with "somatography," a category that includes life writing "about living *with*, loving, or knowing intimately someone with such a body."

10 Brown, *States of Injury*; Puar, *The Right to Maim*; Weheliye, *Habeas Viscus*.

11 Berlant, "The Epistemology of State Emotion."

12 Twain, *Mark Twain's Civil War*, 96, emphasis in original. Skocpol's careful scholarship backs up Twain's intuition and clearly documents the role that patronage politics played in the expansion of the pension system. See Skocpol, *Protecting Soldiers and Mothers*.

13 Glasson, *Federal Military Pensions in the United States*, 164.

14 Trumbull, "Pensions for All," 729.

15 Christopher Hager writes eloquently about the use of physical language to describe writing, a practice which he takes to illuminate the paucity of our understanding of writing as such (and not just writing situated in the bureaucratic context examined here). "Science surely has more to reveal about the mysteries of written literacy's cognitive workings," Hager notes, "but it may never yield a complete understanding. Our frequent reliance on physical language to describe writing—*grabbing* our pencils, *sitting down* to write, *filling up* or *cranking out* pages—compensates for our incomprehension of the inward process." Hager, *Word by Word*, 17–18.

16 The Pension Bureau continued to use this system of folding and bundling pension claims well past the advent of the letter and drawer file cabinets that allowed materials to lie flat. As the Taft Commission on Economy and Efficiency reported in 1912, there was historically little interest in upgrading the Pension Bureau's filing system because of the "large expense which would necessarily be incurred and the absence of any accruing future benefits or economies." With increasingly elderly claimants dying, in other words, and public opinion squarely against pensioning disabled veterans of future wars, it seemed easiest to leave things as they were. United States President's Commission on Economy and Efficiency, *Economy and Efficiency in the Government Service*, 551. Late in 1913, however, the Pension Bureau did gradually begin to convert from folded to flat filing. Glenn, "The Taft Commission and the Government's Record Practices," 297.

17 Gitelman, *Paper Knowledge*, 49.

18 William W. Eastman to Ziba Roberts, December 30, 1890, box 45, Ziba Roberts Collection, 1861, William L. Clements Library, University of Michigan, Ann Arbor.

19 United States Pension Bureau, *A Treatise on the Practice of the Pension Bureau*, 12.

20 Britton, *A Traveling Court*, 50.

21 "Having been acquainted with said soldier for about 21 years, and that on the 15th day of April 1890 I carefully examined said claimant and found him suffering from general debility and nervous prostration [and] abnormal condition of the heart.... In my opinion, said claimant is totally disabled for the performance of manual labor." Nathan Smyth, "Nathan Smyth Ledger, James S. Schoff Civil War Collection, 1890–1893," box 1, William L. Clements Library, University of Michigan, Ann Arbor.

22 United States Pension Bureau, *General Instructions to Special Examiners*, 19.

23 The ambiguous status of narrative that shaped public perception of the pension system turned on many of the same anxieties about fraud that beset popular culture in the era of P. T. Barnum and a host of well-publicized literary hoaxes. As Lara Langer Cohen has written, across the nineteenth century, fraudulence became at once "indissociable from American literature and even definitive of it." Among antebellum readers, literature was at once similar to other modes of cultural speculation—from inflated currencies to land bubbles and quack medicine—and an absolutely unique tradition of subterfuge, imposture, and plagiarism. If the invalid pension claim was shaped in part by the bureaucratic vicissitudes of postbellum institutional life, the ill repute into which the genre fell also reflected these older anxieties about the literary as such. Cohen, *The Fabrication of American Literature*, 1.

24 Smalley, "The United States Pension Office," 430. There is no way of knowing how many pensions were granted to duplicitous applicants, as Theda Skocpol writes: "After poring over *Annual Reports* of the Commissioners of Pensions to find any possible systematic statistics, I have reluctantly concluded that nothing exact can be said about the proportions of illegitimate pensioners or expenditures." But it does seem plain that cultural anxieties about pension fraud were at root anxieties about narrative in general and the genre's ability to ensure that pensioned veterans had earned what they were given. Skocpol, *Protecting Soldiers and Mothers*, 145.

25 Warner, "Half a Million Dollars a Day for Pensions," 447. Nor did critics of the bureau differentiate between the lay evidence given by fellow soldiers and the medical evidence provided by physicians. Both could be easily fabricated. As one observer complained, "Any system that permitted claims to be established upon affidavits prepared in secret by the claimants and their friends and upon the certificate of the neighborhood physician, is an injustice to honest pensioners and the government." Oliver, "History of the Civil War Military Pensions," 43. For their part, claimants also feared that the bureau had "play[ed] into the hands of the pension-shark" by placing a premium on narrative evidence. "You insist on affidavits," one veteran wrote. "Affidavits? They are his [the lawyer's] stock in trade. He can furnish affidavits by the dozens, swearing anything to anybody. But without his aid the honest soldier is at a loss." Bardeen, *Little Fifer's War Diary*, 318–19.

26 As Cheryl Harris has famously argued, the legal construction of whiteness hinges on the question of reputation. "The reputation of being white," Harris notes, "was treated as a species of property, or something in which a property interest could be asserted." As I explore in what follows, the cultural notoriety of the pension claim—and the threat its alleged fraudulence posed to the reputation of respectable veterans—was indeed bound up with the social value of whiteness and the reputational injury posed by blackness. Harris, "Whiteness as Property," 1734.

27 George, *William Newby*.

28 Quoted in Glasson, *Federal Military Pensions in the United States*, 175–76.

29 See United States Pension Bureau, *General Instructions to Special Examiners*.

30 Britton, *A Traveling Court*, 57–58.

31 See Reid, "Government Policy, Prejudice, and the Experience"; Logue and Blanck, "'Benefit of the Doubt.'"

32 Shaffer, *After the Glory*, 206–7.

33 Quoted in Shaffer, *After the Glory*, 130.

34 United States Pension Bureau, *General Instructions to Special Examiners*, 28. Because marriages among enslaved people were rarely documented, moreover, agents were advised to consult local opinion about whether a

given relationship should be recognized as a marriage: "A marriage may be presumed upon the testimony of two or more credible witnesses who know that the parties lived together as husband and wife for a number of years, acknowledged each other as such, and were so received by reputable persons in the community in which they resided." United States Pension Bureau, *A Treatise on the Practice of the Pension Bureau*, 55.

35 United States Pension Bureau, *General Instructions to Special Examiners*, 28.

36 See Silber, *The Romance of Reunion*.

37 Fleming, *Around the Capital with Uncle Hank*, 202.

38 *New York Times*, "A Pension Fraud Exposed," 10.

39 *New York Times*, "A Pension Fraud Exposed," 10.

40 If a story Paul Laurence Dunbar published in *Collier's Weekly* in 1902 is any indication, Black writers also looked to plantation nostalgia to defuse white anxieties about African American mutual aid societies. "The Promoter" describes how Jane Callender is awarded a pension shortly after her husband's death. Jane dies herself, however, before the first check arrives—though not before she can sign her pension over to Dicey Fairfax to prevent the money from "go[ing] back to the white folks." Dicey thus decides to adopt "Jane Callender" as a "bus'ness name," for the purposes of drawing the pension, while remaining "Dicey Fairfax at home." It is not long, of course, before the special examiners catch wind and Dicey is charged with fraud. The proceedings begin poorly for the defendant, who plainly answers "Dicey Fairfax" rather than "Jane Callender" when asked to state her name for the record. Pressed further, Dicey simply explains why she uses the pseudonym. Ultimately, however, she objects to identifying herself one way or the other. The prosecutor, it turns out, is the son of Dicey's old mistress; before the end of slavery, she would have been known to him as simply "Aunt Dicey." With the intimacy between white child and Black mammy reestablished, the charges against Dicey are dismissed on the condition that she return the ill-gotten money. "No longer a wealthy woman and a capitalist," Dicey resumes her duties in the kitchen, where she bakes "golden-brown biscuits for a certain young attorney and his wife." Dunbar's winking admiration for her manipulation of the pension system notwithstanding, Dicey is thus ultimately reinserted into the paternalist order of the old South and made an object of ridicule. "These were the days of benefit societies that only benefited the shrewdest man," Dunbar writes, "of mutual insurance associations, of wild building companies, and of gilt-edged land schemes wherein the unwary become bogged." The implication, of course, is that the mutual aid societies are also a scam, particularly as they create an incentive for Black Americans to misrepresent themselves. Dunbar, "The Promoter," 10.

41 Quoted in Zimmerman, *Alabama in Africa*, 48.

42 Spivey, *Schooling for the New Slavery*.

43 Bentley, *Frantic Panoramas*, 25.

44 Andrews, "The Representation of Slavery."

45 Washington, *Up from Slavery*, 155.

46 See Rusnak, *Walter Hines Page and the World's Work*.

47 Walter Hines Page to Booker T. Washington," July 15, 1896, Walter Hines Page letters from various correspondents, American period, HOU B MS Am 1090 box 28, Houghton Library, Harvard University.

48 Hale, "The Pension Carnival," 13486–87.

49 Hale, "The Pension Carnival," 13488.

50 Hale, "The Pension Carnival III," 13734.

51 See Mirzoeff, "The Shadow and the Substance."

52 Stone, *The Disabled State*, 23. See also Samuels, "From Melville to Eddie Murphy"; Schweik, *The Ugly Laws*.

53 Washington, "Chapters from My Experience," 13521.

54 Washington, "Chapters from My Experience (II)," 13635.

55 Washington, "Chapters from My Experience (II)," 13636.

56 Washington, "Chapters from My Experience (II)," 13638.

57 On the Black woman's club movement, see Higginbotham, *Righteous Discontent*. On the conservativism and elitism of the uplift project more generally, see Gaines, *Uplifting the Race*.

58 A decade before "Chapters from My Experience" appeared in the *World's Work*, in fact, Washington himself became something of a special examiner—tracking down and discrediting an unlikely political rival by outing him as the recipient of a Civil War invalid pension. On Washington's rivalry with veteran William Hannibal Thomas, the Black author of a popular anti-Black screed titled *The American Negro* (1901), see Carmody, "In Spite of Handicaps." Tuskegee became far more amenable to disabled veterans after Washington's passing in 1915 and with the advent of federal rehabilitation programs during World War I. With the creation of a segregated veterans' hospital at Tuskegee in 1921, moreover, misgivings about the shirking veteran gave way to anxieties about the rise of Black medical professionals. When the Black doctors and nurses hired by the Veterans Bureau arrived for their first day of work, they were met by Klansmen draped in bedsheets taken from the hospital storeroom. Daniel, "Black Power in the 1920s."

59 Best and Hartman, "Fugitive Justice," 1–2.

60 Kelley, "'A Day of Reckoning,'" 205.

61 Weheliye, *Habeas Viscus*, 15. For two other ways of understanding reparations outside of strictly legal and strictly economic paradigms, see also Tillet, *Sites of Slavery*; Laski, *Untimely Democracy*.

62 Vaughan, *Vaughan's "Freedmen's Pension Bill,"* 125.

63 Vaughan, *Vaughan's "Freedmen's Pension Bill,"* 29.

64 Vaughan, *Vaughan's "Freedmen's Pension Bill,"* 32, 29.

65 See Bureau of Pensions, "Washington D.C., Ex-Slave Pension Correspondence"; Berry, *My Face Is Black Is True*, 80.

66 Quoted in Berry, *My Face Is Black Is True*, 44.

67 Bureau of Pensions, "Washington D.C., Ex-Slave Pension Correspondence."

68 A similarly elastic argument is made in an 1898 "Petition to Congress" that lists five ostensibly unrelated resolutions in favor of pensioning ex-slaves. Not only had "generation after generation of Colored people served this country as slaves," but pension policy also neglected the "unknown and deceased Colored soldiers" whose dependents were now "destitute and starving." The pension system itself, moreover, was unthinkable without slave labor: "It is a precedent established by the patriots of this country to relieve its distressed citizens … and millions of our deceased people, besides those who still survive, worked as slaves for the development of the great resources and wealth of this country." Bureau of Pensions, "Washington D.C., Ex-Slave Pension Correspondence."

69 Fleming, "Ex-Slave Pension Frauds," 129.

70 J. B. Stinson, "'Jes' Hurry Up de Penshun': The Old Time Darkey's Appeal for a Pension," 1903, box 147, item 149, Lester S. Levy Sheet Music Collection, Sheridan Libraries, Johns Hopkins University. Stinson's doggerel presents a minstrel plea for Senator Mark Hanna to forget about "dat ol' steamship bill" and push the ex-slave pension legislation through Congress. Hanna did indeed introduce Vaughan's bill to the Senate in February 1903, but he was hardly a champion of the ex-slave cause. Hanna made it clear to his colleagues, in fact, that he had proposed the pension legislation as a favor to Vaughan; he even included the words "by request" on the title page of the bill itself. Hanna's lukewarm endorsement did little to strengthen the proposal's chances, and Vaughan's bill once again failed to reach the floor. But as the *New York Times* noted, the senator's name and prominence could not help but galvanize interest in the ex-slave pension bill, whatever his own thoughts on the matter: "Heretofore the bills have been introduced by members of Congress not so well known as Senator Hanna. The placing of his name upon the bill will undoubtedly have a greater effect than ever upon the ignorant negroes who are supporting the scheme with their little earnings." *New York Times*, "Hanna Aids Ex-Slaves," 3.

71 Berry, *My Face Is Black Is True*, 131. As the *Colored American* of Washington, DC, wrote in 1900: "Despite the widespread warnings of the press, both

white and colored, there are still some people foolish enough to pay over their hard cash to sundry confidence sharks who run up and down the country pretending that Congress is about to grant pensions to ex-slaves. No such thing will be done in this or any other generation and who ever asserts the contrary is a knave, a humbug or worse." *Colored American*, "No Pensions for Ex-Slaves"; quoted in Berry, *My Face Is Black Is True*, 131.

72 Dickerson's conviction was eventually overturned, but House served time in the Jefferson City, Missouri, penitentiary from November 1917 to August 1918. Berry, *My Face Is Black Is True*, 107.

73 As the author of one such letter phrased it: "This Bureau would appreciate any information which you may be able to furnish as to the name and whereabouts of any person who has thus impersonated an officer of the Government in connection with this matter." Letter from the Department of the Interior, Bureau of Pensions, November 20, 1897, to Rev. Thomas Parker, in Bureau of Pensions, "Washington D.C., Ex-Slave Pension Correspondence."

74 Kazanjian, *The Brink of Freedom*, 50, emphasis in original.

75 Bureau of Pensions, "Washington D.C., Ex-Slave Pension Correspondence."

76 Bureau of Pensions, "Washington D.C., Ex-Slave Pension Correspondence."

77 Bureau of Pensions, "Washington D.C., Ex-Slave Pension Correspondence."

78 Bureau of Pensions, "Washington D.C., Ex-Slave Pension Correspondence."

79 Bureau of Pensions, "Washington D.C., Ex-Slave Pension Correspondence."

80 Bureau of Pensions, "Washington D.C., Ex-Slave Pension Correspondence."

81 Bureau of Pensions, "Washington D.C., Ex-Slave Pension Correspondence."

82 Bureau of Pensions, "Washington D.C., Ex-Slave Pension Correspondence."

83 Bureau of Pensions, "Washington D.C., Ex-Slave Pension Correspondence."

84 Goux, *Symbolic Economies*, 58.

85 Liebman, "The Definition of Disability," 838.

86 Diller, "Entitlement and Exclusion," 379.

87 TenBroek and Matson, "The Disabled and the Law of Welfare," 820.

88 Diller, "Entitlement and Exclusion," 383.

89 See Kornbluh, *The Battle for Welfare Rights*.

90 Temporary Aid to Needy Families, a block grant that created work-related benchmarks for states and individuals, was part of Clinton-era welfare reform. It replaced Aid to Families with Dependent Children, a cash assistance program that began with the Social Security Act of 1935. Falk, "Temporary Assistance for Needy Families."

91 Kelley, "'A Day of Reckoning,'" 204–5.

2. The Beggar's Case

1   As in this book's introduction, I use the words *beggar* and *begging* with full recognition of the stigma they have long carried but also with a desire to acknowledge the centrality of begging to disability history and culture. As Rosemarie Garland-Thomson notes, however, "The history of begging is virtually synonymous with the history of disability." For this reason, I omit quotation marks in the rest of the chapter to leave space for the vagaries of self-identification, contestation, and critique that coalesce around the term. Garland-Thomson, *Extraordinary Bodies*, 35.

2   Schweik, *The Ugly Laws*; Fabian, *The Unvarnished Truth*.

3   Across these genres, Schweik notes, mendicant writing tended to the non-fictional and autobiographical. This was "a literature of contestation. In it, marginalized disabled historians wrote about marginalized disability history." Schweik, *The Ugly Laws*, 260.

4   See Hack, *The Material Interests of the Victorian Novel*; Langan, *Romantic Vagrancy*; Sandage, *Born Losers*; Lutz, *Doing Nothing*; Fabian, *The Unvarnished Truth*; Schweik, *The Ugly Laws*; Garland-Thomson, *Extraordinary Bodies*; Samuels, "From Melville to Eddie Murphy."

5   At the turn of the century, *social science* referred not to a set of academic disciplines but to the conviction among social reformers that the methods of natural science should be applied to social problems. If society was an organism, the Spencerian logic went, the rules governing its efficient operation could be established and, with this knowledge, dysfunction easily eliminated. Bernard and Bernard, *Origins of American Sociology*; Turner and Turner, *The Impossible Science*.

6   Becker and Clark, *Little Tools of Knowledge*.

7   Weber, *Sociological Writings*, 79.

8   Hurwitz, "Form and Representation in Clinical Case Reports," 218.

9   See Ragin, "Introduction."

10   Berlant, "On the Case," 664, 663.

11   Jolles, *Einfache Formen*.

12   For historian of science John Forrester, the tension between the particular and the universal in the case can be traced back to Aristotle's efforts to distinguish knowledge from practice. Aristotle argued that we can only know the universal and the necessary, not the contingent or the particular. We certainly deal with the latter in our everyday lives, but these encounters yield practical wisdom rather than real knowledge. It is like playing in the dark: we can feel our way around but never know exactly where we are. Aristotle's distinction between universal knowledge and practical wisdom remained influential for later philosophers, but it also sparked a tradition of dissent.

John Stuart Mill, for instance, turns the tables on Aristotle by arguing that knowledge proceeds only from the inductive study of particulars. Not only is the distinction between practical wisdom and universal knowledge moot, in other words, but the latter does not exist in the first place. Forrester, *Thinking in Cases*, 4–6. For his part, Michel Foucault answers what he takes to be Aristotle's question—"Is a science of the individual possible?"—by pointing to the historical record: the individual became an object of knowledge in the eighteenth century, when the clinical sciences created the genre of the case. This "network of writing" was tasked with documenting the "individual as he may described, judged, measured, and compared with others, in his individuality" but also "the individual who has to be trained or corrected, classified, moralized, excluded." Foucault, *Discipline and Punish*, 191–92, 194. The Aristotelian cleft between the universal and the particular, Foucault thus concludes, collapses in the modern era. But as individuals entered the field of knowledge, they also became subjects of discipline.

Foucault's genealogy of the case in *Discipline and Punish* has been taken up by scholars in fields as disparate as the history of medicine, sociology, and law. But this expansive body of writing has tended to overlook how the case for Foucault is shaped not only by the history of clinical science but also by the vagaries of literary history and the genre of biography. "For a long time," Foucault observes by way of glossing the case, "ordinary individuality— the everyday individuality of everybody—remained below the threshold of description." Only a privileged few were "looked at, described in detail, followed from day to day by an uninterrupted writing." These texts fêted kinship groups, recorded heroic triumphs, or cast the exemplary life as "a monument for future memory." Such honorific modes, however, gradually lost their monopoly on the genre of biography. With the rise of the case, "chronicle[s] of kings or the adventures of the great bandits" were replaced by "the carefully collated lives of mental patients or delinquents." Biography was no longer "a procedure of heroization" but one "of objectification and subjection." It aimed not to preserve "the individuality of the memorable man" but to reproduce the individuality of "the calculable man." Foucault, *Discipline and Punish*, 191–92, 194. This distinction between heroization and subjection might seem absolute, so forcefully does Foucault underscore the novelty of the case. But in the generic evolution he traces, continuity matters as much as rupture. Not a clean break with what came before, that is, the case exists on a continuum with the chronicle, the legend, and the saint's life. Tracking how the individual enters the field of knowledge thus means grappling with how the memorable shades into the calculable and vice versa— and to what ends.

Foucault's idiosyncratic genealogy suggests a more nuanced understanding of why the case became so crucial to turn-of-the-century scientific charity. To be sure, reformers valued the genre as an objective means of assessing and passing judgment on an applicant's work ethic. But they also believed that casework yielded a more accurate portrait of individual circumstances and needs than the charged in-person exchanges promoted by begging. Armed with social casework, in other words, charity agents, social workers, and philanthropists hoped to commit the individual life to paper without clouding their judgment with sentiment or relying on catchall solutions. This perspective is not without appeal today. In a foundational study of gender and the US welfare state, for instance, the historian Linda Gordon also champions social casework as an exacting genre of life writing. For Gordon, casework is "specific rather than universal, grounded rather than abstract, tailored rather than generalized." Gordon, *Pitied but Not Entitled*, 178. In contrasting the "individualizing" methods of charity reformers with the actuarial methods favored by backers of social insurance, Gordon may overstate matters. Her admiration for turn-of-the-century casework risks obscuring the ambivalence these historical practices share with theoretical explications of the case. The writing produced under the sign of scientific charity, after all, was put to decidedly deindividualizing ends, labeling applicants as deserving or undeserving. As such, casework was both individualizing and deindividualizing—a paradoxically irresolute genre of life writing that bears out the contradictions inherent in the broader print culture of social welfare.

13 As economic historians tell us, what we often take to be a self-evident distinction between private giving and public provision is, historically speaking, anything but. See Levy, "Altruism and the Origins of Nonprofit Philanthropy."

14 Skocpol, *Protecting Soldiers and Mothers*, 527.

15 On effective altruism, see Singer, *The Most Good You Can Do*.

16 Berlant, *The Queen of America Goes to Washington City*; Adams, *Sideshow U.S.A.*; Wilderson, "Gramsci's Black Marx"; Moten, *In the Break*; Sharpe, *In the Wake*. For an overview of this corner of affect studies, see Carmody and Love, "Try Anything."

17 Tompkins, *Sensational Designs*.

18 The first American COS was founded in Buffalo in 1877 by the Reverend S. Humphreys Gurteen, an episcopal clergyman who had been active in the London Charity Organization Society. Seeking to address the impoverishment and mendicancy he encountered in his new ministerial post, Gurteen suggested that Buffalo follow London's example. To that end, he gave a series of sermons called "Phases of Charity" and systematized the work of his parish guild so that each application for assistance was promptly and thoroughly investigated. Woodroofe, *From Charity to Social Work*, 90. Gurteen founded the Buffalo Charity Organization Society soon thereafter, an institution whose goals and methods he described in *A Handbook of Char-*

ity Organization. Begun in part as a response to the countless inquiries he received "asking for information with regard to the new plan of dealing with Pauperism and Poverty," Gurteen's book became a practical guide for dozens of coses springing up across the country. Gurteen, *A Handbook of Charity Organization*, iii. The most prominent among these was the New York Charity Organization Society, founded in 1882 by Josephine Shaw Lowell, who was to become a guiding figure in the movement in her own right. Indeed, if Gurteen wrote the first primer in the methods of charity organization in the United States, Lowell's *Public Relief and Private Charity* (1884) was the first American statement on the philosophy of scientific charity. Katz, *In the Shadow of the Poorhouse*, 68. In this influential study, Lowell sought above all to parse the "fundamental difference in mental attitude" separating indiscriminate almsgiving from organized charity. Whereas proponents of conventional "dolegiving" considered it "a natural condition of things that a certain part of the community should not be self-supporting," modern reformers such as Lowell "regard[ed] each case of poverty as a wrong, an unnatural evil and one which they should use every effort to eradicate." Such eradication would not happen by means of relief alone. In many cases, relief actually "prevent[ed] the energetic action required on the part of the sufferers themselves to lift themselves out of their difficulties." It was only by carefully investigating all applicants and coordinating measured and appropriate responses to their needs that charity workers could hope to foster habits of self-reliance and self-help. Lowell, *Public Relief and Private Charity*, 95.

19   Paine, *How to Repress Pauperism and Street Begging*, 2.

20   As reformer Josephine Lowell noted, "The task of dealing with the poor and the degraded has become a science, and it has well defined principles, recognized and conformed to, more or less closely, by all who really give time and thought to the subject." Lowell, *Public Relief and Private Charity*, n.p.

21   Charity Organization Society of New York, *Fifth Annual Report*, 29; quoted in Olasky, *The Tragedy of American Compassion*, 78.

22   Katz, *In the Shadow of the Poorhouse*, 59.

23   Lubove, *The Professional Altruist*, 20. Robert H. Bremner comes to much the same conclusion: "During most of the nineteenth century the prevailing theory was that if an individual failed to obtain competence, the fault lay in some weakness or defect in his own character. The experience of the last quarter of the century, however, produced ample evidence to bring this thesis into disrepute. By 1900 there was widespread conviction that the causes of failure were to be found, in most cases, in circumstances outside and beyond the control of individual personality." Bremner, *From the Depths*, 131.

24   Abel, "Valuing Care," 34.

25   Lubove, *The Professional Altruist*, 12–13; Huyssen, *Progressive Inequality*, 72.

26 Lowell, "Charity Organization," 83. Though the overlap in terminology may have been coincidental, organized charity's fantasy of comprehensive record keeping shares a great deal with the work of Pension Bureau special examiners explored in chapter 1. A more direct source of inspiration came from the new genres of internal communication that emerged with the managerial revolution in US business. As JoAnne Yates has shown, commercial interactions that had previously taken place in person were increasingly facilitated by circulars, reports, and manuals—documents designed to improve the efficiency of a given firm. Were that firm in "the business of charity," as COS reformers described their work, these documents would be used to streamline the vetting process. Yates, *Control through Communication*.

27 Richmond, *Social Diagnosis*, 50.

28 If nine cases of need were brought before the board, Richmond observed, nine different strategies would emerge. Social caseworkers might decide, for instance, to "make a loan to one, send another to the woodyard to work for all he gets, stave off the landlord's eviction notice for a third, find a chance of work outside for a fourth, place the fifth in a hospital, send the sixth and his whole family to the country, provide cash for the exceptionally provident buyer who is the seventh, relieve the improvident eighth sparingly with supplies plus a work-test and, instead of doing work twice over, turn the ninth over to the charity that is already caring for him." Richmond, *What Is Social Case Work?*, 209–10.

29 See Abel, "Valuing Care."

30 Quoted in Byington, *What Social Workers Should Know*, 35.

31 Quoted in Byington, *What Social Workers Should Know*, 35.

32 Byington, *What Social Workers Should Know*, 35–36.

33 Success stories like that of the amputee shoemaker suggest something of a consensus among charity workers that physically disabled applicants could easily reenter the labor force. Such optimism, however, was tempered by the equally widespread belief that many disabled people would not benefit from scientific charity and would be better served by institutionalization or even sterilization. Social workers generally reserved this sort of pessimistic biological determinism for the "feeble-minded," in what might be read as a concession to social Darwinist critics. Lubove, *The Professional Altruist*, 68–69. These latter charged the COS movement with "promoting the survival of the unfit." Amos Warner mounted an influential defense in *American Charities: A Study in Philanthropy and Economics* (1894) by questioning not the validity of social Darwinism as such but rather the consequences of following its dictates too closely in the present. Warner argued that the instinct for solidarity and sympathy was itself necessary for human survival and progress. Only by allowing this instinct to follow its course would society eventually develop more ef-

ficient means of relieving and finally of preventing poverty and dependence. The alternative, to implement social Darwinist policies in response to the problems of the moment, was thus shortsighted at best and detrimental to the course of human evolution at worst. "Some talk as though extermination would be a remedy for pauperism," Warner noted. "Possibly, but it would be a costly remedy biologically; and if we allow our instincts to compel us to forego the use of it, we shall eventually find something better." Like many of his peers, Warner thus did not think that organized charity was incompatible with eugenics in the long run, or even in all cases in the present. Indeed, Warner conceded that "incapables" who could not be rehabilitated by scientific charity were best dealt with by means of eugenic marriage laws, sexual sequestration, and "the permanent isolation of the essentially unfit." Such measures were in humanity's best interest, both in the present and in the future. "Certain it is," Warner concluded, "that while charity may not cease to shield the children of misfortune, it must, to an ever increasing extent, reckon with the laws of heredity, and do what it can to check the spreading curse of race deterioration." Warner, *American Charities*, 119, 128, 135.

34 Huyssen, *Progressive Inequality*, 76.

35 Abel, "Valuing Care," 34–35, 43–44.

36 Abel, "Valuing Care," 43–44.

37 Huyssen, *Progressive Inequality*, 74.

38 Zunz, *Philanthropy in America*, 1. As an adviser to John D. Rockefeller recalled, "I gradually developed and introduced into all his charities the principles of scientific giving, and he found himself in no long time laying aside retail giving almost wholly, and entering safely and pleasurably into the field of wholesale giving." Quoted in Fosdick, *The Story of the Rockefeller Foundation*, 7. "About the year 1890," Rockefeller himself wrote, "I was still following the haphazard fashion of giving here and there as appeals presented themselves. I investigated as I could, and worked myself almost to a nervous breakdown in groping my way, without sufficient guide or chart, through this ever-widening philanthropic endeavor." Rockefeller, *Random Reminiscences of Men and Events*, 156.

39 As Atticus G. Haygood, a Methodist bishop and the author of works nonfiction like *Our Brother in Black* (1881), recalled of an early meeting of the fund's board: "A few ideas seem to be agreed upon. Help none but those who help themselves. Educate only at schools which provide in some form for industrial education." Quoted in Finkenbine, "Law, Reconstruction, and African American Education," 170, 169.

40 Anderson and Moss, *Dangerous Donations*, 4.

41 The GEB was founded in 1902 at the suggestion of Rockefeller's son, John D. Rockefeller Jr. After visiting several prominent Black industrial schools, the

latter initiated a series of conferences in New York where plans were laid "for an organization that would deal in a comprehensive way with the backward and baffling problem of education." The younger Rockefeller consulted with his father and then conceived of a "Negro Education Board, whose activities would be confined to that race." Fosdick, *The Story of the Rockefeller Foundation*, 9. Discovering that such an organization would not be tolerated by white Southerners, the Rockefellers and their allies agreed on a more conciliatory mission statement. The GEB was thus founded with the goal of fostering "*the promotion of education within the United States without distinction of race, sex or creed.*" Fosdick, *Adventure in Giving*, 7–8, emphasis in original. In practice, this meant developing initiatives to foster interest in public education among both white and Black Southerners, from farming demonstrations to hookworm education programs. Endowed with $33 million in Rockefeller gifts in the first decade of its operation, the GEB acquired a virtual monopoly over educational philanthropy in the South and for Black schools across the country. Anderson and Moss, *Dangerous Donations*, 4; Harlan, *Separate and Unequal*, 87.

42 Finkenbine, "Law, Reconstruction, and African American Education," 167–69.

43 Zunz, *Philanthropy in America*, 18.

44 For many institutions, these shortcomings were due to lack of resources or mismanagement, or simply to bad luck. Other schools, however, were alleged to be industrial schools in name only. Recognizing that the GEB only funded industrial education, institutions with academic curricula often strained to present themselves in the best light or even lied outright about their qualifications. As a trusted GEB adviser, Washington and his staff routinely carried out investigations of "fake industrial schools" intended to prevent the misappropriation of GEB funds. Washington's collaboration, of course, was not altogether selfless. He clearly had a great deal to gain by ensuring that the boundaries of what counted as industrial education were properly policed and that anyone who did not play by his rules encountered financial precarity if not also bankruptcy. Anderson, *The Education of Blacks in the South*, 117–18.

45 Many schools continued to solicit donations in person, whether on the "northern trips" that principals and hired agents made to consult with civic groups, churches, and individual donors or by following the example of the Fisk Jubilee Singers and sending student groups on tour.

46 Wexler, *Tender Violence*; Field, *Uplift Cinema*.

47 Harlan, *Booker T. Washington*, 134.

48 Dixon, *The Sins of the Father*, 137; quoted in Anderson and Moss, *Dangerous Donations*, 57.

49 In *Up from Slavery*, Washington addressed the increasingly common criticism of his fundraising practices—that he did little more than beg from

overly sentimental Northerners—with coy evasiveness masquerading as forthrightness. Where ally Walter Hines Page defended Washington's promotional endeavors as effecting a "transfiguration of the begging method," Washington himself preferred to speak of "the science of what is called begging." With this strange phrase, Washington would seem to embrace two more or less strictly opposed stances on the dreaded figure of the beggar. On the one hand, with the "science of what is called begging" Washington conjures the taxonomies of mendicant performance that were a mainstay of the popular press and among readers at once scandalized and titillated. His own strategies of rhetoric, gesture, and comportment, it would seem, whether at the podium or on a cold call, thus had a great deal in common with the efforts of street operators to convince passersby to reach for their wallets. In this regard, Washington's counsel to an imagined interlocutor who asks for fundraising advice is particularly revealing. Among other things, Washington tells the latter to "keep under the body." Washington, *Up from Slavery*, 88. As Daniel Leverenz notes, this phrase cites 1 Corinthians. See Leverenz, *Paternalism Incorporated*, 166. But this phrase also recalls that most notorious ploy of the "sham cripple," hiding one leg so as to be mistaken for an amputee. If Washington's "science of what is called begging" playfully embraces mendicant practice, however, the phrase also clearly recalls the doctrine of scientific charity and the efforts of Washington's friends and colleagues in the world of organized charity to eliminate begging. From this vantage, Washington would seem to be affirming membership in this reformist club. Like the charity workers who sought to abolish indiscriminate giving, Washington believed in the scientific investigation of all claims and above all in finding solutions that promote the ethic of self-help.

That these two ways of understanding "the science of what is called begging" would be so directly at odds speaks to Washington's ambivalence about the seemingly ceaseless fundraising work he was called on to do. Ultimately, however, his musings on the subject in *Up from Slavery* gravitate toward scenarios that allow Washington to distinguish his efforts from the practices of mendicancy by recasting fundraising as a form of employment. Early in his discussion of "the science of what is called begging," for instance, Washington reverses the affective polarity of the charitable exchange by asking readers to sympathize not with needy petitioners but with the wealthy donors they petition. "Very few persons have any idea of the large number of applications for help that rich people are constantly being flooded with," he writes, perhaps with Rockefeller or Carnegie in mind. Some received as many as twenty calls per day, "to say nothing of the applications received in the mails." The implication is that these wealthy men and women had no choice but to entertain their callers and attend to the piles of letters they received daily. Such responsibility transforms what might seem a chance act of benevolence into a regular mode of employment. The private salon becomes a place of business. And as a partner in the transactions conducted there, Washington was by extension also on the job. *Up from Slavery* drives this point home with an anecdote that finds Washington calling on a man in Boston who, with very little prodding, writes a check for a "generous sum." Before Washington can rise to thank his patron, he is beaten to the punch. "I am so grateful to you Mr. Washington," the donor says, "for the opportunity to help a good cause.... We in Boston are constantly indebted to you for doing our work." Washington, *Up from Slavery*, 89. With this narrative sleight of hand, Washington is once again an employee rather than a beggar. Less clear is what kind of labor Washington performs and for whom. The paternalist echoes in the phrase "our work" would suggest that wealthy Bostonians have subcontracted to Washington the arduous labor of meeting the "white man's burden." But Washington also acts as a social caseworker employed by a COS, his investigatory work meant to allow potential donors to make informed decisions about how best to disburse their gifts. Leverenz pushes this reading further, suggesting that Washington's labor in this scene is more specifically that of a white-collar middle manager.

50 Edwards, "Uplifting the Submerged Masses," 225. A handwritten document titled "Obituary of W.J. Edwards," unsigned and undated in the William J. Edwards papers at the Amistad Research Center, provides what may be the fullest and presumably most objective account of Edwards's illness.

> Notwithstanding the devotion and tender care of this aunt, he fell victim of a disease that nearly robbed him of his eyesight and crippled him in one of his feet and one of his arms. For months at a time he was too cripple [*sic*] to get out of doors to run and play as other normal children. Under these conditions attending school was impossible. After years of suffering he was observed one day on the roadside by a kind and sympathetic physician, who urged his Aunt to bring the boy to his office for an examination.... After weeks of treatment and general operations on his crippled foot, Edwards was allowed to come home. His health greatly improved and his sight partially restored, he attempted to study and learn something from his more fortunate playmates who attended school.... [After much work] he found he was far in advance of the boys and girls who regularly attended school and had no handicap. One of the local ministers recognized something unusual in this crippled boy, so he told him about the Tuskegee Institute and the wonderful opportunities it was offering to Negro youths. This fired Edwards' imagination and he was determined to go to Tuskegee. His health had now improved to the point where he could do some work such as chopping and picking cotton, pulling corn and other farm work. There was plenty of this type of work to be done and altho the pay was small Edwards never turned down any call that came his way.... Finally he saved enough to buy himself a few clothes and enough cash to pay for his railroad fare to Tuskegee. So

on January 1 1888 he took his leave for Tuskegee. He arrived at Tuskegee with only 50 cents in money. He was admitted as a work student. He was still greatly handicapped by his early affliction for he had not fully recovered nor did he ever fully recover. But he did not allow these handicaps to stand in his way or block his path to a higher and better life. ("Obituary of W.J. Edwards," n.d., folder 4, William J. Edwards Papers, ca. 1893–1985, Amistad Research Center, New Orleans, LA, 1–3)

51 Indeed, Edwards was not the first to raise money with his story. That honor fell to Washington, who began speaking about his former student on fundraising trips to the North not long after Edwards graduated from Tuskegee in 1893. Edwards occasionally joined his mentor on stage, though the records of these events are scarce. The earliest published account of Edwards's life is an article that Washington placed in *Century* magazine in 1900 and had reprinted in regional newspapers across the country. In "Signs of Progress among the Negroes," Edwards's rehabilitation becomes exemplary of the transformative power of Black industrial education but also serves as a model for "what may be done in Cuba and Porto Rico." Washington's imperial fable opens on the rural South with an encounter between a former slave owner and an unsightly beggar: "Some years after the war, a young Black boy, who seemed to have 'rained down,' was discovered on the plantation of Mr. S——, the owner. In daily rides through the plantation Mr. S—— saw this boy sitting by the roadside, and his condition awakened his pity, for, from want of care, he was covered from head to foot with sores, and Mr. S——soon grew into the habit of tossing him a nickel or a dime as he rode by." Shortly thereafter, Edwards, the young beneficiary of Mr. S——'s almsgiving, learns of Tuskegee and resolves to make the long journey on foot. When he runs into financial difficulty at school, Edwards turns once again to Mr. S——, this time for a loan. The latter obliges with fifteen dollars but holds out no hope of being repaid. When Edwards returns after graduation, however, he does make good on his debt, and with interest. Thus reunited and seeing eye to eye on the virtue of labor, Edwards and Mr. S——go on to found Snow Hill Institute together, now partners in the revitalization of the South.

It should not surprise us that Washington takes liberties with Edwards's biography. It is difficult to miss, for instance, how closely R. O. Simpson, a white veteran of the Confederate army who is less crucial in Edwards's version of events, resembles Washington's own mentor, General Samuel Chapman Armstrong of Hampton Institute. Perhaps more surprising is the static quality of Washington's before-and-after portrait. Where we might expect Edwards to have been completely changed by his rehabilitative experience at Tuskegee, here the unsightly beggar of Edwards's youth shares a great deal with the industrious graduate. Both are dependent on white generosity, whether alms or loans. To be sure, the parallel between Edwards before and after would have served to placate white Southerners concerned that education of any kind would disrupt the delicate racial hierarchy of the New South. Such, it would seem, were the only terms on which Washington was willing to embrace the resemblance between street mendicancy and institutional fundraising. For his part, though, Edwards would take this comparison as the basis for underscoring the productive nature of his own literary labor rather than celebrating the generosity of the donors to whom he appealed. Washington, "Signs of Progress among the Negroes," 472.

52 *Some Results of the Snow Hill Normal and Industrial Institute*, 2, Snow Hill, Alabama, Normal and Industrial Institute, Pamphlet box, Educ 8530.15.7, Widener Library, Harvard College.

53 *Some Results of the Snow Hill Normal and Industrial Institute*, 3.

54 Washington and Scott, *Tuskegee and Its People*, 266.

55 See Enck, "Black Self-Help in the Progressive Era." Washington's enthusiasm for Snow Hill had begun to wane over the years, in part because the GEB and other philanthropic foundations gradually shifted resources away from private industrial schools to lobbying efforts on behalf of public education in the South. But Edwards also brought Washington's disdain upon himself. Not only did Edwards join a symposium organized by W. E. B. Du Bois and Oswald Garrison Villard for the Association of Negro Industrial and Secondary Schools, an organization hostile to Washington's methods, but recent inspectors from Tuskegee had also found Edwards offering two-year courses in Latin and German "for those planning to take up higher work in the professions." Cooper, *Between Struggle and Hope*, 42; Enck, "Black Self-Help in the Progressive Era," 86.

56 Edwards's papers in the Harvard University archive suggest that Edwards had developed an extensive network of donors during summers spent at Harvard's Summer School.

57 On the genre of the carte de visite featuring African American figures before and after Emancipation, see Willis, *Envisioning Emancipation*; Wallace, "Framing the Black Soldier." Wallace situates these before-and-after images in the broader history of the Black soldier portrait: "Photography, in the popularity and proliferation of the Black soldier portrait, participated in nothing less than the genesis of African American manhood as a coherent category of civil identity and experience in the postbellum political imaginary" (247). In many instances, however, given the popularity of photographs that purported to show slaves becoming soldiers in the blink of an eye, this iconography could also be used to "conscript" Black soldiers into images that capture "coerced agency" and "simulated contentment" (259). Wallace is here drawing on Hartman, *Scenes of Subjection*. Jacqueline Fear-Segel describes the use of before-and-after photography at Carlisle in similar terms. "Before the first contingent of pupils had arrived in Pennsylvania from Dakota

Territory, Pratt had already enlisted the services of local photographer J.N. Choate. Choate brought his mobile studio onto campus to ensure their 'before' images were captured the very same day. Pratt's objective was double stranded: firstly, to Americanize Native children in preparation for assimilation into mainstream society; secondly, to convince white Americans that this project to transform Native youth from 'savagery' into 'civilization' was both desirable and possible." Fear-Segel, "Facing the Binary," 156. On before-and-after photography in the context of Bookerite industrial education, see Field, *Uplift Cinema*; Baker, "Missionary Positions."

58 Before-and-after photographs, Jordan Bear and Kate Palmer Albers write, "often obtain their special identity from the ways in which the photographs relate both to one another, and, most intriguingly, to a third, generally unseen, event. This missing pivot is the implicit source of the development whose outer markers are imaged in the before-and-after pair." Bear and Albers, "Photography's Time Zone," 2. See also Sidlauskas, "Before-and-After." I am grateful to Susan Sidlauskas and Kathleen Pierce for encouraging me to think more about the genre of the before-and-after photograph and for introducing me to this literature.

59 Sekula, "The Body and the Archive."

60 Yates, *Control through Communication*, 78. While we most often think of the report as a fundamentally mediated mode of communication, moreover, Oz Frankel notes that the genre originally connoted physical presence. The first reports were submitted by functionaries who could not appear in person or "report for duty." Frankel, *States of Inquiry*, 36.

61 The GEB did fund Snow Hill early in the twentieth century but gradually withdrew its support. This change of heart was likely due to reports of the school's inefficiency that reached the GEB from its field officers, but also Washington's increasing ambivalence about Edwards could not have helped. The GEB's ultimate decision to cease funds to Snow Hill was certainly not due to any lack of effort on Edwards's part. The beleaguered principal maintained a nearly unbroken stream of correspondence with officials at the GEB into the 1920s, always an adamant champion of the work being done at Snow Hill and (nearly) always comporting himself according to the bureaucratic standards of foundation philanthropy.

62 William J. Edwards to Wallace Buttrick, October 3, 1911, box 2, folder 17a, ALA 8 Snow Hill 1906–1914, General Education Board Records, Rockefeller Archive Center.

63 Edwards, *Twenty-Five Years in the Black Belt*, 11.

64 Edwards, *Twenty-Five Years in the Black Belt*, 13.

65 Edwards, *Twenty-Five Years in the Black Belt*, 14.

66 Guyer, *Kant and the Claims of Taste*, 139–47, 162–64.

67 Thank you to Barbara Mennel for helping me to think through this scene. On the history of Micheaux's film, which was for many years thought lost and whose intertitles were translated back into English after the discovery of a Spanish-language version, see Gaines, *Fire and Desire*.

68 Purcell, *Miracle in Mississippi*, 89; Harrison and Freeman, *Piney Woods School*, 61–62. One of Jones's weekly addresses to the student body suggests a sense of camaraderie across this mixed-ability community, even if these inspirational anecdotes are not without a certain note of pathos or pity: "When you are out with the shovel and pick, building roads, when you are out making brick—even these one-armed boys and the boy without any hands who shovels sand; when you are doing carpentry, feeding the pigs, milking the cows, caring for the poultry, running the dynamo, hoeing in the garden, or plowing on the farm, we want you to be able to say, 'I did something too, didn't I, Piney Woods?'" Jones, *The Spirit of Piney Woods*, 55. Like Edwards, Jones was a committed but not rigidly orthodox proponent of industrial education. Unlike Edwards, Jones had no connection to Tuskegee or to Booker T. Washington and was thus left to establish his own network of philanthropic connections. Jones's earliest efforts were sporadic and ad hoc, but fundraising at Piney Woods soon became a well-oiled machine. Ultimately, these efforts provided for Piney Woods the institutional longevity Snow Hill never achieved. Snow Hill closed in 1873, after decades of financial hardship.

69 Quoted in Anderson and Moss, *Dangerous Donations*, 200. This officer, the Rosenwald Fund's Edwin Embree, did concede that at Piney Woods and elsewhere "there are picturesque personalities who are sincerely trying to do their best." But he ultimately concluded that these personalities frequently only made matters worse. Philanthropist George Foster Peabody agreed, although he acknowledged "differing points of view on Mr. Jones" and gradually came to respect the ambitious principal. "I think he is an exceptional man and some aspects of his work prove this," Peabody wrote. "He has a publicity faculty, undoubtedly—something too much in evidence—but he is the one Negro of ability whom I know who goes through the West and stirs up money." George Foster Peabody to Walter B. Hill, October 22, 1931, box 96, folder 864 GEB, Miss 58 Piney Woods School 1909–30, Rockefeller Archive Center, Sleepy Hollow, NY. Peabody was more ambivalent on this point in a letter to Leo M. Favrot on November 16 of that same year. "Opinions differ so much with regard to the Piney Woods Country Life School in Mississippi," Peabody wrote to the GEB general field agent, "that I hesitate to express an opinion with any assurance." box 96, folder 864 GEB, Miss 58 Piney Woods School 1909–30.

70 The idea for the school took root in conversations with the Black residents of Braxton shortly after Jones's arrival in May 1909. Having brought with him nothing in the way of funding or savings, Jones initially met his expenses

with the donations collected weekly on his behalf by several area churches. Harrison and Freeman, *Piney Woods School*, 31. Nights found Jones drumming up support for the idea of a new school among his new neighbors, but his days were spent under a cedar tree with an ever-growing number of students who took lessons "without the formality of buildings and desks and blackboards." Jones, *Piney Woods and Its Story*, 67.

71 Bailey, "The Cotton Blossom Singers."

72 Jones's unconventional methods bordered on the presumptuous. In 1909, for example, he sent Wallace Buttrick of the GEB a peculiar letter of introduction. After first outlining his school's mission and needs, Jones submitted paperwork for Edwards's erstwhile interlocutor to complete: "May I anticipate your kindness in filling out the enclosed blank and returning the same at your earliest convenience[?]" He asked when the board would meet to discuss the following year's budget and requested the names of the committee members in charge. With this information, of course, Jones hoped to better navigate the funding process. But he also meant to signal his familiarity with modern philanthropy. Predictably, Jones's request was declined.

73 Longmore, *Telethons*, 1.

74 The letter writer continues: "The people receiving them are affected by them according to their temperaments. Some are stirred to respond, others are irritated, but all feel, I think, that they would like to know something about the school. If the school is not good, people should know it. If it is good, Mr. Jones should in some way be told that his method of raising money is not a wise one." Miss Marian Homans to the General Education Board, November 22, 1923, box 96, folder 863 GEB, Miss 58 Piney Woods School 1909–30. Homans revisited the issue a few days later, after receiving a reply to her letter. "I think it is a great pity," she wrote to her correspondent at the GEB, "that they should use such means for raising money as the begging letters sent out by children who are students there. People are becoming prejudiced against the school for this reason, and I feel for the good of the school that Mr. Jones should know of the feeling." Miss Marian Homans to the General Education Board, November 27, 1923, box 96, folder 863 GEB, Miss 58 Piney Woods School 1909–30. In response to Homans's letters, H. J. Thorkelson of the GEB noted a report in the board's files on Piney Woods stating that "Mr. Jones, the Principal, is able and highly thought of by the people of Mississippi. He has built up the school entirely by his own efforts. It is a small school doing the work of some of our county training schools." When pressed further by Homans about whether the GEB would be in a position to share with Jones her concerns about his methods, Thorkelson replied, "I am quite sure that any suggestion to the authorities of Piney Woods School regarding questionable methods of soliciting funds will come with greater force from the recipients of such letters than from any of the officers

of our board. This is particularly true in this case, as we have not contributed to this school."

75 Jones did propose his own life story as a representative case, though he did so by invoking the far more prominent figure of Booker T. Washington. Many educators before him, of course, had sought to take advantage of Washington's popularity and influence with donors. But although Jones had no relationship with Washington, he nonetheless encouraged donors to draw the comparison for themselves. Around 1911, for example, Jones solicited donations on letterhead that reprinted in full a two-hundred-word article published by the *Literary Digest*. Running the length of the page's left margin with its title prominently displayed—"Young Booker Washington"—the article-as-illustration effectively claims the founder of Tuskegee as a Piney Woods booster. There is no indication that Washington ever supported Jones's school, but so positioned the article also hints that Washington's story is more relevant to the history of Piney Woods and its deservingness than was the biography of the school's founder. Although his was likewise a story of hardship and accomplishment, Jones sought to make the case for Piney Woods without making himself the focus of attention in any particular way. Rather, he was a kind of case; his story could be generalized as the story of Washington. Box 96, folder 863 GEB, Miss 58 Piney Woods School 1909–30.

76 Box 96, folder 863 GEB, Miss 58 Piney Woods School 1909–30.

77 Shed's name is spelled differently in one of the earliest histories of Piney Woods to be widely published. But his story is recounted in language that closely resembles that used in the school's fundraising materials: "Charles Shedd, class of 1918, has charge of the printing shop and supervises the boys interested in pursuing the graphic arts.… Shedd has had one son graduate from Piney Woods and go on to Tuskegee, and another young son is a senior at Piney Woods and a member of the high school Honor Society. The second-generation youngsters are giving a good account of themselves.… Shedd himself is an example of a handicapped student who has more than made good." Purcell, *Miracle in Mississippi*, 115–16.

78 Dean Carter to Wallace Buttrick, March 30, 1925, box 96, folder 863 GEB, Miss 58 Piney Woods School 1909–30.

79 The response Carter received was brief and negative: "I regret to say that there are no funds at the disposal of this Board that can be contributed for the purpose you suggest." But though Buttrick's refusal was direct and to the point, the fact that Carter's letter and others like it were preserved by the GEB raises questions about how these documents were actually read. On the one hand, it is clear that Carter's letter was held onto as evidence of how the "notorious beggars" of Piney Woods emotionally manipulated unsuspecting

donors. But on the other hand, the letters produced en masse by members of the student aid department might also have been flagged for the routineness of their production. Indeed, GEB officials may have suspected Jones of having learned the lessons of organized charity too well. If the student aid department was created with the goal of streamlining and rationalizing the writing of case studies, that is, the letters it produced bore their provenance rather too openly: they were standardized and even interchangeable narrative histories and as such potentially devoid of any truly personal content. Carter's letter and others like it thus give the lie to the antisentimental project of foundation philanthropy while also exemplifying the practices adopted by Black industrial schools in order to square this circle. Need was still to be earnestly expressed, it seemed, no matter how putatively objective the evaluations process. The corollary was also true. As students at Piney Woods understood, strategically sentimental appeals that purposefully confused the case and the stock figure would only find success by also showing the work involved in doing so. Wallace Buttrick to Dean Carter, April 28, 1925, box 96, folder 863 GEB, Miss 58 Piney Woods School 1909–30.

80 *Collier's Weekly*, "For Ten Cents." On the elusive history of Lincoln's check, see Carr, "The Mysteries of Lincoln's Bank Accounts."

81 Tarbell, *The Life of Abraham Lincoln*, 150–52.

82 Thomas, *Abraham Lincoln*, 483.

83 This distinction holds even if we speculate that the Black amputee was himself a soldier, a likely conclusion given that he also meets Lincoln in the park between the White House and the War Department. Even as a veteran, that is, the Black amputee must tell a "pitiful story" in order to receive the generosity that the white soldiers receive on sight.

84 Ultimately, then, "colored man with one leg" is best understood as an economic rather than a sentimental sign. Lincoln's designation for the Black amputee, in fact, operates much like the check on which it is written. Just as the check stands in for cash or goods deposited with a bank, so too is "colored man with one leg" a sign that indexes, and effectively replaces, the material referent to which it is conventionally bound. In both cases, however, this relationship holds only as long as the sign in question remains in circulation. Like the check, which becomes worthless once redeemed, "colored man with one leg" loses all economic value outside of the charitable exchange in which it originated. When he is no longer the "bearer" of the check—once he cashes it—the Black amputee ceases to be the "colored man with one leg." He is instead the possessor of five dollars, wages earned for a command performance of deservingness before the president.

85 Philip, *Zong!*, 191.

86 Philip, *Zong!*, 199.

87 Wilkinson, "Review of *The Work-Shy*"; see also Bancroft, "Someone Was Looking for Me." My understanding of outsider literature is particularly indebted to Eli P. Mandel's reading of *The Work-Shy*. See Mandel, "Review."

88 Philip, *Zong!*, 200, emphasis in the original.

89 Blunt Research Group, *The Work-Shy*, 65.

3. The Work of the Image

1 As Charles Musser notes, the early Edison demonstration films, produced a year before commercial production began, depict worlds in which work, pleasure, and socializing are integrated. In *Blacksmithing Scene* (1893), for instance, three blacksmiths (played by Edison employees), hammer a heated metal rod that has been removed from a fire and placed on an anvil. One of the men then pulls out a bottle of beer, and each worker takes a drink before then resuming their labors. By 1893, work and socializing were increasingly separated, and drinking on the job was considered part of a more or less bygone era. As such, *Blacksmithing Scene* is a nostalgic enterprise. In the film, as Musser concludes, "the newest and most modern technology is used to prop up and document a past that it is quickly making obsolete." Musser, "At the Beginning," 17.

2 Tosi, *Cinema before Cinema*, 33.

3 Cartwright, "'Experiments of Destruction,'" 129.

4 Cartwright, "'Experiments of Destruction,'" 130–31.

5 Gunning, "In Your Face," 142–43.

6 In this regard, photography was an extension of Marey's earlier work with graphic inscription. Drawing on his training as a physician, Marey had invented a number of mechanical devices to measure minute physiological movements like the beating of the heart, the firing of a nerve, or the contracting of a muscle. These devices involved complex systems of wires, India-rubber tubing, and pneumatic sensors that were connected directly to the experimental subject. See Marey, *Movement*, 1–14. Once isolated, the physiological mechanism under study caused a stylus to move across the recording surface such that the body itself was the direct source of the tracing. This principle was the basis for Marey's sphygmograph and myograph, which measured blood pressure and muscular contraction, but also for the systems he designed to chart the human gait, the flapping of insect wings, and the flight of birds. Doane, *The Emergence of Cinematic Time*, 47–48. Marey hoped to find in Muybridge's methods a means of recording movements in cases where the direct connections required of graphic inscription were impractical.

7 Muybridge's images were produced by a battery of cameras, each of which was activated by a wire as the horse ran past. The resultant photographs show

the general trajectory of the horse's movement. But each image was taken from a different vantage and the time between exposures could not be determined with any accuracy, precluding precise measurements after the fact. There are many scholarly accounts of the evolution of Marey's chronophotography. Marta Braun's remains authoritative. Braun, *Picturing Time*, 42–57. See also Auerbach, *Body Shots*; Cresswell, *On the Move*. Popular conflations of these two figures notwithstanding, as Marta Braun has noted, Marey and Muybridge thus held vastly different commitments. Muybridge was more interested in photography than in science. For Marey, on the other hand, photography was ultimately only a means to an end. His principal concern was with the "objective, measurably accurate, analytic, and systematic" study of movement as such. Braun, *Picturing Time*, 229.

8   Quoted in Rabinbach, "The European Science of Work," 486.

9   Quoted in Daston and Galison, "The Image of Objectivity," 81. For Daston and Galison, Marey's research typifies the new paradigm of objectivity that emerged in the late nineteenth century. Previously, scientists associated objectivity with a process of active selection or curation—in the case of the scientific atlas, for instance—that ensured representativeness by weeding out the idiosyncrasies of nature. The goal was "to make nature safe for science; to replace raw experience—the accidental, contingent of specific individual objects—with digested experience" (85). By the late nineteenth century, a new mode of objectivity took hold that sought to suppress any such intervention. The scientist's goal was now to eliminate "suspect mediation" of any kind and "to foreswear judgment, interpretation, and even the testimony of one's own senses" in favor of allowing the phenomena at hand to speak for themselves. Scientific objectivity, in other words, had come to be opposed to the subjectivity of the scientist.

10 Marey, *Movement*, 139.

11 Rabinbach, *The Human Motor*.

12 See Rabinbach, "The Body without Fatigue."

13 Rabinbach, *The Human Motor*, 25.

14 Marey, "The Work of the Physiological Station at Paris," 406.

15 Rabinbach, "The European Science of Work," 491.

16 Marey, "The Work of the Physiological Station at Paris," 406, 409.

17 Marey's methods of graphic inscription had been in use at the Salpêtrière since the late 1870s to record the movements of patients diagnosed with hysteria and epilepsy. The first photographic studies of hysteria began not long thereafter, furthering a tradition of clinical photography established by Guillaume-Benjamin-Amand Duchenne, Charcot's mentor. When Albert Londe took over the photography department at the Salpêtrière in 1884, he quickly realized the potential of chronophotography for studying the movements of

patients with a range of diagnoses. After consulting with Marey, Londe built a series of multiple-lens cameras with which to study hysteria, pathological gaits, tremors, and epileptic seizures. The resultant images were both a departure from and a continuation of the often eroticized photography of hysteria that filled the pages of *Iconographie photographique de la Salpêtrière*. Just a year after Londe began at the Salpêtrière, the University of Pennsylvania hired Muybridge to carry out an ambitious study of human and animal locomotion. In addition to horses ambling and women ascending stairs, Muybridge captured the lumbering gait of a man with "a history of long-standing and increasing ataxia" and the "crouching shuffle" of a laborer diagnosed with "stuporous melancholia" after being "constantly exposed [to] fine particles of dust mixed with lead." As Tim Creswell notes, the differences between Marey's and Muybridge's studies of pathological locomotion concern matters of spectacle in addition to those of narrative. "While Muybridge gave us pictures of naked people moving as best they could, Marey gives us a distillation of their movement with bodies removed. In Muybridge's images it is hard to read the movement between the frames, in Marey's it is all there is." Cresswell, *On the Move*, 81. See also Mayer, *Wissenschaft vom Gehen*, 187; Aubert, "From Photography to Cinematography," 262; Dercum, "A Study of Some Normal and Abnormal Movements," 121.

18 *Western Electrician*, "Analysis of Movements by Photography and the Incandescent Lamp," 205. See also Braun and Whitcombe, "Marey, Muybridge, and Londe," 220.

19 Marey, *Movement*, 77.

20 Mayer, *Wissenschaft vom Gehen*, 187.

21 Braun and Whitcombe, "Marey, Muybridge, and Londe," 220.

22 Quoted in Braun and Whitcombe, "Marey, Muybridge, and Londe," 220.

23 Canguilhem, *The Normal and the Pathological*, 13. Canguilhelm writes:

> The end result of this evolutionary process is the formation of a theory of the relations between the normal and the pathological, according to which the pathological phenomena found in living organisms are nothing more than quantitative variations, greater or lesser according to corresponding physiological phenomena. Semantically, the pathological is designated as departing from the normal not so much by *a-* or *dys-* as by *hyper-* or *hypo-*. While retaining the ontological theory's soothing confidence in the possibility of technical conquest of disease, this approach is far from considering health and sickness as qualitatively opposed, or as forces joined in battle. The need to reestablish continuity in order to gain more knowledge for more effective action is such that the concept of disease would finally vanish. The conviction that one can scientifically restore the norm is such that in the end it annuls the pathological. Disease

is no longer the object of anguish for the healthy man; it has become instead the object of study for the theorist of health. (13)

24 Braun and Whitcombe, "Marey, Muybridge, and Londe," 220.

25 Dujardin-Beaumetz, "New Therapeutic Agencies."

26 Mayer, *Wissenschaft vom Gehen*, 187.

27 Mayer, *Wissenschaft vom Gehen*, 187.

28 Schwartz, "Torque." Marey's most immediate contribution to this field was the technical advance that his methods represented over the largely theoretical approach favored by previous researchers such as Ernst, Wilhelm, and Eduard Weber. The German Weber brothers mapped out the position of the body at fourteen different moments in a single gait cycle and used mathematical calculation to conclude that walking is a physiological falling-forward arrested momentarily by the pendulum-like swing of each leg. Kirtley, *Clinical Gait Analysis*, 183. Marey's practical studies helped later researchers debunk the so-called pendulum theory and also helped develop new devices and techniques of motion capture. Rather than using electric bulbs, for instance, Otto Fischer and Christian Wilhelm Braune strapped Geisel tubes, a predecessor to neon lights, to the joints of their research subjects. The images they produced were the first three-dimensional analyses of human locomotion. Baker, "The History of Gait Analysis before the Advent of Modern Computers," 334. The "interrupted light studies" conducted in the 1950s by Howard Eberhart and Verne Inman at the University of California, Berkeley, for instance, used "small ophthalmic electric bulbs attached to the subject at estimated joint centers of the leg, iliac crest, and heel and toe of the shoe." These studies were of greatest value, the authors conclude, in "improv[ing] the locomotor system in individuals who have suffered damage to it." Eberhart and Inman, "An Evaluation of Experimental Procedures," 1216, 1213.

29 The division of labor between Frank and Lillian Gilbreth is far from clear in their extensive oeuvre. Although Frank was clearly the public face of the business they ran together, Lillian was arguably the more accomplished of the two. One of the first women to earn a PhD in engineering, Lillian may well have written most of the articles and perhaps even the books attributed only to Frank. As Melissa Gregg elaborates, "Because Lillian Gilbreth was the wife of the more publicly known management consultant Frank Gilbreth, her position as a founder of human factors engineering and workplace psychology is often overlooked in conventional academic accounts." Gregg, *Counterproductive*, 11. Rather than endeavoring to determine who wrote (or did) what, I simply refer to the Gilbreths collectively wherever possible in what follows.

30 Giedion, *Mechanization Takes Command*, 106.

31 Marta Braun, for instance, does indeed find candid acknowledgment of Marey's outsized influence on the Gilbreths in unpublished writings and in private correspondence. In a typescript of a management seminar, for instance, Frank confided that Marey was "the man I wish had never been born" (quoted in *Picturing Time*, 347). Frank made a similar point in the same playful tone when writing to Lillian in 1919: "Prof. Jevon's book is wonderful. He anticipated many of your best ideas. He is your Marey." Frank Gilbreth to Lillian Gilbreth, January 5, 1919, box 101, folder 1, Frank and Lillian Gilbreth Papers, ca. 1869–2000, Purdue University Special Collections. The Gilbreths had far less to say about the French savant, however, in published writings and public talks. Although Taylor's influence could be safely acknowledged and adequately qualified, Marey was mentioned only in passing. Marey plays just a bit part, in fact, in the intellectual genealogy sketched out in *Applied Motion Study* (1916). There the groundbreaking inventor becomes an admirably talented but overcommitted dilettante: "Marey, with no thought of motion study in our present use of the term in his mind, developed, as one line of his multitudinous activities, a method of recording paths of motion, but never succeeded in his efforts to record the direction of motions photographically." Gilbreth and Gilbreth, *Applied Motion Study*, 62. The narcissism of small differences is worth flagging here. But if the Gilbreths downplay the usefulness of Marey's devices and the value of his studies, they also set the stage for a heroic tale of the achievement of specialists—like themselves—narrowly focused on industrial efficiency:

> The problem that presented itself, then, to us who needed and desired instruments of precision, applicable to our motion study and to our time study, was to invent, design, and construct devices that would overcome lacks in the early and existing methods. We needed devices to record the direction as well as the path or orbits of motions, and to reduce the cost of obtaining all time study and motion study data. These were needed not only from the scientific standpoint, but also from the standpoint of obtaining full cooperation of the mechanics and other workers. Many of these had, as a class, become suspicious of time study taken secretly by those who, they thought, did not know enough about the practical features of the trade to take the time study properly, and could not prove that the items were right after putting them on paper. Here was absolute pioneer work to be done in inventing devices that would record times, paths, and directions of motions simultaneously. (63)

While neither figure is specifically mentioned, readers of *Applied Motion Study* would have recognized a familiar critique of Taylor and of scientific management. And because Marey was not a household name in the United States, few would have doubted that the devices Gilbreth "invent[ed], design[ed], and construct[ed]" were indeed a real advance over "the early and existing methods." Crucial to such an advance, Gilbreth argues, was adapting physiological motion study to industry's needs; Taylor's approach thus corrects for Marey's lack of practical focus. But these new methods were also useful "from the standpoint of obtaining full cooperation of the mechanics and other workers" generally reluctant to accommodate efficiency experts. Finding themselves part of a profession suspected of ruthlessly maximizing productivity at workers' expense, the Gilbreths thus presented themselves as the "good exception" to the Taylorist rule. Writing to Lillian from Germany in 1914, Frank argued, *"We must have our own organization and we must have our own writing so made that the worker thinks we are the good exception."* Quoted in Price, "Frank and Lillian Gilbreth," 5, emphasis in original. In order to differentiate themselves from Taylor, the Gilbreths borrowed wholesale from Marey, generally without attribution of any kind. Not only did the Gilbreths present many of Marey's devices as their own inventions, but they also mimicked many of the experimental techniques developed by the French savant.

32 Gilbreth, *Bricklaying System*, xi.

33 Gilbreth and Gilbreth, *Applied Motion Study*, 114.

34 The Gilbreths soon began placing a finely graduated clock in the corner of every film they produced, which allowed them to determine the time required for each of the worker's motions to be determined precisely as well. A comparable device similarly placed was, only a few years earlier, widely regarded as Marey's trademark. Rabinbach, "The European Science of Work," 489. Always willing to repackage a modest improvement as a conceptual game changer, the Gilbreths argued that their "micro-chronometer" far surpassed its predecessors because it could "determine the speed of a motion down to the one-millionth of an hour." *Popular Science Monthly*, "Two and a Half Miles a Minute," 227. This unlikely unit suggests just how anxious the Gilbreths were to distinguish themselves from Marey. The lesson they learned from Marey's clock, however, was also about self-promotion. For just as Marey had done with his own name years earlier, the Gilbreths ensured that the face of the micro-chronometer that appeared in each of their films bore the GILBRETH logo in large block letters. Beyond its role in self-promotion, the GILBRETH logo also helps us to understand the pedagogical shortcomings of micromotion studies. Itself an image, the GILBRETH logo functions differently from the images produced with the devices on which it is inscribed. The logo stands as an image of labor accomplished; it makes visible at a glance the work that has gone into creating and sustaining the GILBRETH brand. At the same time, the logo requires no exegetical work from the viewer; its meaning is intuitively clear. The images produced by micromotion study, on the other hand, are images of labor in both senses of the word. They capture scenes of work and, by isolating individual moments or gestural phrases, make these scenes available for closer scrutiny. But the

images produced by micromotion study do demand work from the viewer, namely frame-by-frame analysis and calculation. Rather than speaking in what Marey called "the language of the phenomena themselves," these images require mediation. Indeed, for micromotion studies to have pedagogical value, they had first to be translated into written instructions. It was only by looking to Marey's electric light bulb method that the Gilbreths developed a mode of image production that realized the aspirations of self-evidence inscribed in the GILBRETH logo. On images and the labor of mediation, see Latour, "What Is Iconoclash?"; Latour, "Drawing Things Together."

35 Colvin, "The Latest Development in Motion Study," 938.

36 The micro-chronometer method, while more accurate, required completing and comparing different images after the fact.

37 On chart junk, see Tufte, *The Visual Display of Quantitative Information*.

38 In a series of experiments that would come to shape the field of fatigue research, Mosso recorded the movements of a single finger performing a simple, repetitive motion over a finite period of time using a graphic inscription apparatus. A battery of physiological tests made it clear that the decline in muscular performance evident in the downward arc of inscription was dependent not on the proportion of work done but rather on the production of toxic substances in the muscles. Ioteyko, *The Science of Labour and Its Organization*; Vatin, "Arbeit und Ermüdung."

39 S. Edgar Whitaker, note on "Fatigue," November 16, 1915, box 36, folder 1, Gilbreth Library of Management Papers Msp8, Purdue University Libraries.

40 Gilbreth and Gilbreth, *Fatigue Study*, 41.

41 Gilbreth and Gilbreth, *Fatigue Study*, 4. This scene, of course, resembles nothing so much as the Lumières' *Employees Leaving the Lumiere Factory* (1895).

42 In addition to human factors and ergonomics, the Gilbreths also anticipate what Aimi Hamraie calls the "disability neutral" aspect of Universal Design, where there is no mention of disability but rather an emphasis on all users. See Hamraie, *Building Access*.

43 Brown, *The Corporate Eye*, 28.

44 Mayer, *The Science of Walking*, 137.

45 Rony, *The Third Eye*, 35.

46 Rony, *The Third Eye*, 48.

47 Tosi, *Cinema before Cinema*, 162–63.

48 Bloom, *French Colonial Documentary*, 22.

49 Bloom, *French Colonial Documentary*, 19.

50 Quoted in Mayer, *Wissenschaft vom Gehen*, 199–200.

51   The chronophotographic studies of colonial subjects carried out by Regnault under Marey's tutelage find an unlikely echo in the work of sociologist Marcel Mauss, whose investigations into the "techniques of the body"
touch on the pathology of primitive locomotion and on the pedagogy of the
military march. At first glance, Mauss's famous essay would seem to have
little concern with the methods developed by Regnault and Marey, just as his
findings appear to repudiate the conclusions they reach. Whereas Regnault
and Marey use chronophotography to determine the most natural mode
of human locomotion, Mauss rejects essentialist ideas of this sort out of
hand. There is no such thing as the natural body or a natural movement, he
contends; the body is rather a product of social, psychological, and biological
processes that vary across different eras and cultures. What can be observed
of the simple act of walking is for Mauss but the clearest manifestation
of a truth that applies to bodily comportment of all kinds: how one walks
depends on where one grew up, what one does, and how one thinks. On
closer inspection, however, it becomes clear that Mauss does in fact share
with Marey and Regnault a commonality of both means and ends. For if
Marey promised to capture the hidden complexity of everyday movements,
Mauss sought to rescue the body from the conceptual catchall of the "miscel-
laneous," a category of phenomena that we often presume to be self-evident
but that are actually understood only casually, if at all. Mauss's tripartite
approach—the body as social, psychological, and biological construct—is
thus shaped by the same revelatory impulse that informs the chronophotography of human locomotion. Nor is Mauss's antiessentialism absolute.
After ruminating on the blind spots created by academic specialization and
reminiscing fondly about his own experience drilling French cadets, Mauss
concludes by positing a more or less fundamental difference between primitive and civilized gaits:

> I believe that this whole notion of the education of races selected on
> the basis of a determinate efficiency is one of the fundamental moments
> of history itself: education of the vision, education in walking, ascend-
> ing, descending, running. It consists especially of education in compo-
> sure. And the latter is, above all, a retarding mechanism, a mechanism
> inhibiting disorderly movements; this retardation subsequently allows a
> coordinated response of coordinated movement setting off in the direc-
> tion of a chosen goal. This resistance to emotional seizure is something
> fundamental in social and mental life. It separates, it even classifies, the
> so-called primitive societies according to whether they display more bru-
> tal, unreflected, unconscious reaction or, on the contrary more isolated,
> precise actions governed by the clear consciousness. (Mauss, "Techniques
> of the Body," 474–75)

Mauss's earlier contention that there is no bodily comportment prior to
or distinct from the social, psychological, and biological forces that consti-

tute the body is here turned on its head. He equates the primitive body with a physiological ground zero, its movements with a mode of behavior that preexists the educative and "retarding mechanism[s]" of modernity. The latter are the techniques by which the primitive subject's "brutal, unreflected, unconscious reaction" to the world is inhibited, and "disorderly movements" and "emotional seizure[s]" are replaced by the habits of restraint and composure. Mauss thus translates into descriptive prose the visual syntax of pathological locomotion established some thirty years earlier by Marey and his collaborators. The wayward trajectories and irregular patterns traced across the dark surface of the chronophotographic image find a parallel here in the jerky, uncontrolled movements of the primitive subject, just as the gradually arcing curves and evenly spaced repetitions that mark the horizon of rehabilitation become the "coordinated response of coordinated movement setting off in the direction of a chosen goal" typical of the modern or civilized subject.

52 Rabinbach, *The Human Motor*, 183.

53 Camiscioli, *Reproducing the French Race*, 60. See also Frader, *Breadwinners and Citizens*.

54 Camiscioli, *Reproducing the French Race*, 63. As Camiscioli observes, Amar's preference for Kabyles over other North African populations had to do with long-standing beliefs that members of that group were whiter and more assimilable than other immigrants from the Maghreb.

55 Amar, *The Physiology of Industrial Organisation*, 210.

56 Amar, *The Physiology of Industrial Organisation*, v.

57 Musser, *The Emergence of Cinema*, 261.

58 Whissel, *Picturing American Modernity*, 22. Recently scholars have illuminated the broadly therapeutic nature of the Spanish-American War, the conflict that first brought the United States onto the imperial stage. For a generation of men who had never taken up arms, this war offered the opportunity to repair a sense of masculinity injured not by enemy fire but by the many indignities of modern life. This is not to say that the United States did not go to war in 1898 for political or economic reasons. Of these there is no shortage. As Kristin Hoganson has written, historians cite as motivating factors "economic ambitions, annexationist aspirations, strategic concerns, partisan posturing, humanitarian sympathy for the Cubans, a desire to avenge the *Maine*, a psychic crisis, and Darwinian anxieties." If there is a single thread to be drawn through this list of plausible explanations, Hoganson argues, it is that gender functions in each as "a motivating ideology and a political posture." To simplify a richly nuanced argument, the felt need to shore up Anglo-American masculinity against the threats of overcivilization, the New Woman, the closing of the frontier, and the social progress of African Americans dovetailed with a pro-imperialist agenda that championed

the benefits of empire for colonizer and colonized alike. Those benefits, to be sure, were not evenly distributed. If for the colonizer war promised to restore masculine prerogative, the colonized were often figured as effete and helplessly in need of rescue. The rewards were no more certain for the African American soldiers who took up arms in Cuba and the Philippines. If pro-war advocates hoped that Black participation would earn respect and win social concessions at home, the martial ideal on which such thinking relied was often kept out of the Black soldier's reach. Hoganson, *Fighting for American Manhood*, 7, 9. Gatewood, *"Smoked Yankees" and the Struggle for Empire*, 4.

59 See Banta, *Taylored Lives*.

60 Musser, *The Emergence of Cinema*, 244–53; Whissel, *Picturing American Modernity*, 14.

61 Gunning, "Before Documentary," 54.

62 Edison Manufacturing Co., "War Extra Catalogue." Addressing the formal malleability of the actuality, film historian Stephen Bottomore has differentiated three subgenres. The "conflict-zone actuality" is shot on location and shows military activity of one sort or another. The "arranged actuality" is shot in the conflict zone with real troops, but the action has been set up specifically for the purpose of being filmed. Finally, the "war-related actuality" is not shot in the conflict zone but is thematically related to war and represents military action, as in films of charging troops shot elsewhere. Bottomore, "Filming, Faking and Propaganda," xxvi.

63 Martha Banta argues that the 1890s and the Spanish-American War more particularly brought about a shift in masculine ideals represented in the gradual replacement of "barbaric" narratives of martial heroism to systems and stories of efficiency: "Eventually the inventor, the manager, and the technocrat—systematizers represented by Thomas Edison, Henry Ford, and Herbert Hoover—would become cultural heroes, displacing military leaders and old-time entrepreneurs, men more appropriate to cruder times when Americans still honored 'the archaic traits' of overtly predatory methods." Banta, *Taylored Lives*, 55.

64 Edison Manufacturing Co., "War Extra Catalogue."

65 Edison Manufacturing Co., "War Extra Catalogue."

66 Edison Manufacturing Co., "War Extra Catalogue."

67 Edison Manufacturing Co., "War Extra Catalogue."

68 Edison Manufacturing Co., "War Extra Catalogue."

69 Edison Manufacturing Co., "War Extra Catalogue."

70 Edison Manufacturing Co., "War Extra Catalogue."

71 Edison Manufacturing Co., "War Extra Catalogue."

72 Gilbreth and Gilbreth, *Motion Study for the Handicapped*, 33.

73 Gilbreth and Gilbreth, "The Engineer, the Cripple, and the New Education," 52, 54.

74 Frank Gilbreth to Lillian Gilbreth, January 5, 1919, box 101, folder 1, Frank and Lillian Gilbreth Papers, ca. 1869–2000.

75 Frank Gilbreth to Lillian Gilbreth, January 5, 1919. And even if things did not work out, Frank continued, he could still "probably sell them a clock … with a nice case for $200 to $150.00."

76 Frank Gilbreth to Lillian Gilbreth, January 5, 1919.

77 Gilbreth and Gilbreth, "Motion Study of Epilepsy and Its Relation to Industry," 1, MSP 8 box 120, folder 6, 0843, 1920, Frank and Lillian Gilbreth Library of Management Research and Professional Papers, Purdue University Special Collections.

78 Gilbreth and Gilbreth, "Motion Study of Epilepsy and Its Relation to Industry," 1.

79 Gilbreth and Gilbreth, "Motion Study of Epilepsy and Its Relation to Industry," 4–5.

80 Gilbreth and Gilbreth, "Motion Study of Epilepsy and Its Relation to Industry," 8.

81 Frank Gilbreth to Lillian Gilbreth, May 16, 1920.

82 Samuels, "My Body, My Closet," 234.

83 Langan, *Romantic Vagrancy*, 2–3.

4. Institutional Rhythms

1 Jackson, "Worksong," 848.

2 Jackson, "Worksong," 848; Titon, "North America/Black America," 154. Though familiar enough to pass for common sense, Jackson's definition of the work song, which he shared with John and Alan Lomax, has not been universally embraced. Marek Korczynski, Michael Pickering, and Emma Robertson argue that Jackson's "functionalist" approach is too limiting. Endeavoring to loosen the "conceptual straitjacket of the work song," the authors offer a broader history of "singing at work" that encompasses moves beyond the use of song to coordinate movements to consider how even "background" music—like that pumped into factories—has impacted the cultural history of work. Korczynski, Pickering, and Robertson, *Rhythms of Labour*, 22–23.

3 Winick, "Folklore and/in Music," 469. Winick usefully elaborates on Jackson's skeletal definition:

In many cultures, laborers use *work songs and work music* in the performance of daily tasks. In this context music serves the function of coordinating the efforts of a group of people who need to do things at the same time or at the same speed. In hauling a heavy yard, up the mast of a square-rigged ship, or moving a section of railroad track a quarter-inch to the right, using nine-pound hammers to tap on the rails, a single man would have no effect at all. But a group of men, pulling or tapping at the same time, can get the job done, and music can be used to keep them in time with one another. Music used to coordinate labor takes many forms, including fife-and-drum bands or bagpipes for soldiers on the march, drumming for oarsmen on large galleys, and women singing rhythmic "waulking song" while they beat on the fibers of newly-woven cloth in order to shrink it. (469, emphasis in original)

For an early discussion of the importance of the sea shanty to the work song genre, see Hugill, *Shanties from the Seven Seas.*

4 Jackson, *Wake Up Dead Man*, 30.

5 Lomax, *The Land Where the Blues Began*, 261. As John Lomax wrote, he and Alan collected "the old Negro tunes the Texas prison system has kept alive, while the prisoners died." Lomax, *Negro Folk Songs as Sung by Lead Belly*, 93.

6 Jackson, "Worksong," 849.

7 Brown, "Negro Folk Expression," 116. For Brown, the work songs performed in Southern penitentiaries are also defined by the candor of their desperation: "From these men—long termers, lifers, three-time losers—come songs brewed in bitterness. This is not the double-talk of the slave seculars, but the naked truth of desperate men telling what is on their brooding minds. Only to collectors who have won their trust—such as the Lomaxes, Lawrence Gellert, and Josh White—and only when the white captain is far enough away, do the prisoners confide these songs. Then they sing not loudly but deeply their hatred of the brutality of the chain-gang" (117).

8 Debates about the social value of prison labor were a cornerstone of the prison reform movement in the 1880s and 1890s. As historian Rebecca McLennan has shown, productive work was central to US penal practices from the early republic through the 1930s. But the system confronted by late nineteenth-century reformers was rooted more particularly in the turn-of-the-century Auburn system of penal management. Whereas in the competing Pennsylvania model inmates worked silently in single cells at tasks like cobbling and harness making, prisoners in the Auburn system were isolated by night and put to congregate labor for private contractors by day. Auburn prisoners were likewise subject to strict oversight that combined military-style discipline with industrial management. As the Auburn system was expanded and refined over the years, three dominant modes of contract prison labor emerged. In the "prison factory system," outside contractors set up shop

in the prison itself; in the "piece-price system," contractors supplied raw materials and paid the state for the goods that prisoners produced; in the "convict lease system," contractors took full possession of inmates they employed beyond the prison walls. In a fourth and less widespread system, the "public account system," prisoners worked for the state, which sold the products they manufactured on the free market. Facing arguments from labor unions who contended that prison labor unfairly competed with free laborers and thus drove down wages beyond the prison walls, reformers and prison administrators soon advocated the "state-use system." This system mandated that prison labor could only be used to produce goods for the state, thus in principle avoiding any harmful incursion into the free market. The rationalization of contract prison labor continued apace through the postbellum years, despite the efforts of Reconstruction-era reformers to reign in abuses and to abolish contract prison labor outright. By the 1880s, nearly every state prison in the country used contract prison labor of some sort. McLennan, *The Crisis of Imprisonment*, 103–4, 134; Ayers, *Vengeance and Justice*, 191–92.

The exploitation and abuse to which contract prison labor in all its forms inevitably led garnered most attention in the case of the convict lease system. As historian Blake McKelvey has written, after the Civil War penal practices in the North and South began to take separate paths. If the North witnessed a burst of interest in reforming contract prison labor during Reconstruction, the necessity of rebuilding public infrastructure and accommodating the ever-growing number of prisoners dominated all other concerns in the South. The convict lease system was adopted as the best solution to both problems. Not only did this system allow prisoners to be managed without the necessity of building expensive prison facilities, but convict labor could also be used to bridge the yawning chasm between the agricultural slave economy of the past and a postbellum present in the earliest stages of industrial development. The convict lease thus "served as an entering wedge, as the only labor force capitalists investing in the South knew they could count on to penetrate dangerous swamps and to work in deadly primitive mines." Given, moreover, that a disproportionate number of Southern prisoners were African American—due to the passage of the black codes and the rise of Jim Crow, among other reasons—the lease was also a tool of racial discipline. Neither the states nor contractors made much of an effort to hide this fact, or to claim that the work performed by prisoners of any race was of rehabilitative value. As W. E. B. Du Bois decried, "In no part of the modern world has there been so open and conscious a traffic in crime for deliberate social degradation and private profit as in the South since slavery." McKelvey, "Penal Slavery and Southern Reconstruction," 178–79; Du Bois, *Black Reconstruction in America*, 698.

9   See Rose, *No Right to Be Idle*; Trent, *Inventing the Feeble Mind*.

10 See Jackson, *The Negro and His Folklore in Nineteenth-Century Periodicals.*

11 On the Port Royal Experiment, see Rose, *Rehearsal for Reconstruction*; Foner, *Reconstruction*; McPherson, *The Struggle for Equality*; Saville, *The Work of Reconstruction*; Ochiai, "The Port Royal Experiment Revisited"; Franke, *Repair*; Carmody, "Rehearsing for Reconstruction."

12 McKim, "Songs of the Port Royal 'Contrabands'"; Higginson, *Army Life in a Black Regiment.* See also Pearson, *Letters from Port Royal*; French, *Slavery in South Carolina and the Ex-Slaves*; Cohen, *The Social Lives of Poems*; Southern, *The Music of Black Americans*; Johnson, preface.

13 Allen, Ware, and Garrison, *Slave Songs of the United States*, xix.

14 Radano, *Lying Up a Nation*, 223. See also Hochman, *Savage Preservation*, 93.

15 Cruz, *Culture on the Margins*, 5. As Cruz goes on to argue, the effect of this mode of interpretation was ultimately to depoliticize the spiritual by extolling the virtues of a preferred and idealized notion of the culturally expressive and performing subject. "This perspective had a dual function: it provided the recognition and admission of a specifiable Black culture, and it granted Black culture admission into the larger and certainly contentious domain of 'American' culture. Muted, indeed eclipsed, in the process were the argumentative, critical, and elaborate Black voices that had already emerged in the slave narratives. These voices had preceded the discovery of the Negro spiritual, but were overshadowed by the larger, newer, aesthetic appreciation of the preferred black culture" (7).

16 Brooks, *Bodies in Dissent*, 298–99. This historical emphasis on the cultural specificity and emotional universalism of the spirituals, however, also obscures how these religious songs were actually used in far worldlier ways. Indeed, the spirituals were often performed during work and might generally be thought of as work songs, were that terrestrial or mundane context not counter to the religious perspective that reformers, missionaries, and educators on the Sea Islands sought to promote. We need look no further, in fact, than to the ubiquity of boat songs in the writing on Black song that emerged from Port Royal. While often religious in content, these songs captured the interest of the Northerners in the Sea Islands less for their imagery or devotional sentiments than for their relation to the working body. As one member of the first group of teachers and superintendents to arrive at Port Royal in March 1862 noted, "Our rowers sing as they row, their own songs—some impromptu and all religious—about the Saviour and the kingdom. Their oars dip in the sparkling water, keeping time to the song." Quoted in Epstein, *Sinful Tunes and Spirituals*, 171. Even as the editors of *Slave Songs in the United States* lamented the seeming paucity of secular songs among the former slaves, they noted that "the same songs are used for rowing as for [religious] shouting" and gave as an example of "Michael Row the Boat Ashore," at once "a real spiritual—it being the archangel Michael that is

addressed" and the only "pure boat-song" yet to be identified. Allen, Ware, and Garrison, *Slave Songs of the United States*, xvi. This song also came to the attention of Higginson and Charlotte L. Forten, both of whom remarked on how the singers describe the movements of their bodies and the demands of their labor in the language of metaphysical conceit: "O I wheel to de right and I wheel to de left." Of this line, which for Higginson demarcates the gulf separating heaven from hell, Forten supposes that "some peculiar motion of the body formed the original accompaniment of the song, but has now fallen into disuse." Quoted in Krehbiel, *Afro-American Folksongs*, 49–50. As a later commentator noted, though, "If the rowing singer meant 'hold' or 'stop' or 'back' on my right and catch on my left, even a novice at the oars would have understood the motion as a familiar one in steering." Krehbiel, *Afro-American Folksongs*, 50.

17 See Pierce, "The Freedmen at Port Royal."

18 Stanley, "Beggars Can't Be Choosers," 1287.

19 Stanley, "Beggars Can't Be Choosers," 1275.

20 American Social Science Association, *Constitution, Address, and List of Members*, 3.

21 Quoted in Brackett, "Supervisory and Educational Movements," 520.

22 Today, the conference proceeding belongs to a category of writing that scholars of library and information studies call gray literature. Broadly defined as everything but peer-reviewed journal articles, monographs, and commercially published books, gray literature includes reports of various kinds, memoranda, technical documentation, and official documents, among many other genres. Bonato, *Searching the Grey Literature*, 159. In science studies, the conference proceeding—like the conference papers it includes—is considered a "research process document" somewhere between what Bruno Latour and others describe as the often speculative discussions that happen in the laboratory as an experiment is conducted and the final publication, with its streamlined and often sanitized methods section. Rowley-Jolivet, "The Pivotal Role of Conference Papers," 9. See also Latour, *Laboratory Life*.

23 Document and monument: theorists from Jacques Le Goff to Michel Foucault have troubled routine distinctions between the empirical objectivity of the one and the ideological coerciveness of the other. The NCCC *Proceedings* blur these lines as a matter of course. Not only were the discussions the *Proceedings* claim passively to record actively shaped by the appeal of having one's words recorded for the ages, but these volumes were probably never widely read. The NCCC's monumental aims notwithstanding, that is, the *Proceedings* in all likelihood did little more in the real world than take up shelf space in public libraries and private archives next to similar publications from countless other organizations. Indeed, shelf life is an apt metaphor

for the overlapping temporalities of the monument and the document at stake in the *Proceedings*. On the one hand, these volumes appear to illustrate how conversations that seem pressing and immediately relevant in the moment become outdated ephemera as soon as they are filed away. On the other hand, however, they also suggest that such transformations are never complete. Indeed, the *Proceedings* pursue the work of institution building by holding the competing claims of intercession and preservation in productive tension. See Guillory, "Monuments and Documents."

24 Stenographers were available to record extemporaneous talks, but speakers were invited to edit these documents as well.

25 Many of these transcripts were printed with apologetic caveats, as if to preempt complaints. Stenographers no doubt also had their complaints about the speakers whose speeches they were tasked with transcribing. As one stenographer observes of his work at "scientific and professional meetings," the speakers "do not take the same amount of care in preparing their addresses that they used to do" and frequently forget "that a mere flow of words will never constitute true eloquence." Petrie, "Review of the Shorthand Year," 267.

26 The voice of the writer who played perhaps the greatest role in crafting the *Proceedings*, moreover, is nowhere to be heard. An accomplished activist, essayist, and physician, Isabelle C. Barrows served as conference stenographer and editor for more than a decade but finds only brief acknowledgment in polite asides here and there. Almost certainly by design, this omission was probably intended to preserve the appearance of institutional authorship.

27 Barrows, preface.

28 Wright, "Employment in Poorhouses," 198–99.

29 Barrows, "Minutes and Discussions, Seventh Session," 366–67. These sentiments were echoed the next year by the director of a juvenile reformatory who called on his colleagues to "quit turning our institutions into money-making machines. The object of all our labor should be instructive, *not* productive." Barrows, "Discussion on Industrial Training," 381.

30 Cable, "The Convict Lease System in the Southern States," 266. Prison reformer Eugene Smith took a similar position, arguing that inmate labor could only be called toil when isolated from the market. Ensuring that didn't happen was easy enough: rather than providing for inmates' material needs and recouping these costs through coerced labor, administrators should charge inmates directly for everything they received, from meals to uniforms and medical care. Only by "impos[ing] on him the necessity of working for his living," Smith asserted, could the prisoner be placed "on precisely the same footing as that occupied by every working man in a free society." Smith, "Labor as a Means of Reformation," 268. No one represented the fantasy of reconciling profitable and educational labor more prominently than Zebulon

Brockway, warden of the New York State Reformatory at Elmira. Though Brockway himself rarely spoke at the conference, his success at Elmira was a touchstone in all but four volumes of the *Proceedings* between 1875 and 1914. Aside from brief mention of Brockway's piece-price system or support for indeterminate sentencing, however, these references were usually superficial. Indeed, *Elmira* soon became a rhetorical shibboleth; instead of clarifying the intellectual project of charity and corrections, it served only to strengthen consensus. Like the fantasy that profitable institutional labor might also be educational, Elmira named a foregone conclusion masquerading as a site of inquiry.

31 The "disappearance" of Native Americans, Sanborn suggested, from what was "practically an unoccupied continent," cleared the way for the march of American progress. Slavery and its aftermath, by contrast, posed a far more intractable problem—how to "hasten the advancement of a savage race towards civilization." Sanborn, "Education of the African Race," 172. The answer, Sanborn offered, was to let evolution run its course. In light of mistakes and missteps made during Reconstruction, the conference should adopt a gradualist approach and ensure that any effort made to inculcate the work ethic proper to productive citizenship among Black Americans did not rush the larger processes already in motion. The conference could only help in the most modest of ways to facilitate these developments. According to Sanborn's civilizationist argument, lynching and anti-Black violence were likewise part of the process and should be tolerated as but temporary aberrations. "It is in the providence of God," Sanborn observed, "to carry forward the education and elevation of the whole human race by broad methods; and a broad movement, like the tide of the ocean, pays no particular regard to the eddies and ebbs here and there" (172). A third speaker in this session, "African and Indian Races," took an altogether different tack, endeavoring to disentangle the "humanitarian" or "benevolent" arguments offered by the likes of Sanborn and Armstrong from the "utilitarian" purposes these arguments served. Philip C. Garrett made no effort to give either the humanitarian or utilitarian angle priority. His own approach to the "tutelary debt" owed "the Africans whom we dragged in chains and slavery from their native land" was rather "both and." Garrett sought to underscore how industrial training was at once spiritually uplifting for African Americans and economically advantageous to everyone involved. In explaining the benevolent point of view, Garrett suggests that it is enough to recall that "every son of Adam is interested in a humane treatment of all other sons of Adam." Such humane treatment, however, involves not only good intentions but also, and perhaps even more importantly, a level economic playing field on which Black Americans would have "an equal chance and perfect opportunity to prove their fitness to compete with Caucasians." If, after the competition had been allowed to run its course, Black Americans had become "hewers of wood

and drawers of water" in disproportionate numbers, Garrett would concede the matter settled. "Our skirts will at least be clear," he wrote. The utilitarian perspective, on the other hand, was less concerned with assuaging white guilt than with reaping the benefits thus won. "It cannot be other than the interest of the country," Garrett went on, "to make them self-dependent, to educate them, to elevate them, and to place them on as high a plane as they can be made to attain. As serfs or hostiles, they are a constant burden; as respectable citizens, an accession to the power and producing capacity of the country." Garrett, "Our Duty to the African and Indian Races," 164, 165–66.

32 Armstrong, "The Future of the American Negro," 167.

33 Benson, "The Prevention of Crime among Colored Children," 261.

34 Acknowledging that not all work is transformative and, by extension, that Black industrial education was often little more than drudge work, Benson made his case for educating young Black people in the liberal arts tradition and preparing them for both university studies and the professions. Nor did Washington miss the subtle criticism that Kowaliga's curriculum represented. An early booster of Benson's, Washington later pulled his support and encouraged others to do the same. The number of African Americans invited to speak before the conference remained small for the greater part of the organization's early years. World War I was something of a watershed, as the lauded contributions of Black soldiers abroad gave what James Weldon Johnson called "the changing status of Negro labor" pride of place on the domestic reform agenda. Fiery papers at the conference by Johnson (1918), Robert Moton of Tuskegee (1917), and Richard R. Wright Jr. of the *Christian Recorder* (1919) drew a bright line between pre- and postwar-era ideas about racial uplift. "Once it was popular," Johnson observed, "to discuss theoretically whether the Negro is capable of advancement. The very shifting of the ground of controversy concerning the race renders any such discussion obsolete." Johnson, "The Changing Status of Negro Labor," 383. For Wright Jr., the answer to the question on the lips of white reformers of the day—"what does the Negro want?"—was simple enough: "The Negro wants a *democracy* not a 'whiteocracy.'" Wright, "What Does the Negro Want in Our Democracy?," 539.

35 His main instructors were Wagner, Schmoller, Wilhelm Steida, and Bücher, but he also studied the works of Roscher and Albert Schäffle and in private wrote of the latter as his principal teacher. Schäfer, *American Progressives and German Social Reform*, 164.

36 "Charles Richmond Henderson," 1915, box 7, folder 3, Charles Richmond Henderson Papers, University of Chicago Special Collections. Across this sizable body of work, Henderson was guided by a deep religious faith. Henderson believed that "God has providentially wrought for us the social sciences and placed them at our disposal" in order "to assist us in the difficult

task of adjustment to new situations." Quoted in Bulmer, *The Chicago School of Sociology*, 35. Students and more secular colleagues grew to find Henderson's moralism unsettling, if not antithetical to objective or properly scientific social research. A similar indifference characterizes most departmental histories of sociology at Chicago, which tend to treat Henderson as a joke of sorts—"pious, ministerial, boring, and a poor substitute for Jane Addams." Turner, "A Life in the First Half-Century of Sociology," 120. Nonetheless, Henderson was the best-known and most published member of the Chicago faculty for many years. Both his standing in the reform world and status as a minister, moreover, allowed Henderson the sociologist to voice opinions and make recommendations that might otherwise have been dismissed as radical. Turner, "A Life in the First Half-Century of Sociology," 120–21. Turner concludes, in fact, that "Chicago sociology, in short, needed Henderson far more than he needed Chicago sociology" (121).

37 Henderson, *Introduction to the Study of the Dependent, Defective, and Delinquent Classes*, 78. Work was the best—if not also the only—means of rehabilitating the deviant individual. This perspective is evident in early studies like Henderson's *Social Elements: Institutions, Characters, Progress* (1898) that move seamlessly between social science and the social gospel. In a chapter titled "Social Misery, Pauperism, and Crime," Henderson lays out in impressionistic language the worldview that later publications would supplement with quantitative and comparative statistical research. His point is simple: anyone who does not heed the imperative to work must be brought back into the fold by one means or another. While it is a well-established fact, Henderson notes, that industrial development has helped "the great majority of the population to gain an increasing share in advancing civilization," there is also "a large class, composed of many elements, which appear to hang like a millstone about the neck of society—miserable, dangerous, parasitic." Henderson, *Social Elements*, 209. These "social dependents" are a mixed lot. But whether one targets "tramps, thieves, beggars, robbers, parasites, gamblers, the idle rich, and all the drones" or "the imbecile, the feeble, and the untrained," work remains the only feasible solution (116, 210). Those who are able but choose not to compete on equal footing with other "citizens in industry" should be forced to do so. Those who cannot are to be placed in institutions that can fit them for the occupations to which they are best suited or, as necessary, simply keep them busy. In this regard, Henderson shared the confidence common among his conference peers. "Thousands of persons can work well enough under command," he noted, "who cannot find work in a competitive market" (225). It is the role of sociologists and social welfare organizations to help these latter to become as productive as possible.

38 Henderson, "Introduction," ix. Each of the essays in *Outdoor Labor for Convicts*, first given before the International Prison Congress in 1905, arrives at the same conclusion. In order to be "as lucrative to the state as possible"

while also preparing "the convict for a rational and useful career in freedom," wardens should contract convicts to work beyond the prison walls, preferably "in the open air." The mode of labor almost uniformly advocated by Henderson's panel is agricultural work, and *Outdoor Labor for Convicts* reads as a catalog of successful experiments in this vein. Perhaps the clearest point of reference for American readers, the convict lease system in the Southern states, was for Henderson and his colleagues merely the exception that proved the rule. Such was the message of Frederick H. Wines's contribution to *Outdoor Labor for Convicts*, a portrait of Louisiana prison labor that serves as an ambivalent coda to the otherwise upbeat and self-congratulatory volume. From hard labor on the parish road crew to the drudgery of clearing "heavily timbered swamp[s]" in the state farm prison, the labor demanded of these largely African American prisoners was purely exploitative. As Wines observes, "except insofar as it involves compulsory labor, regularity of life, and discipline, it is not reformatory." Wines, "Farm Prisons of Louisiana," 152. But nor is Wines's report—much less the other moments of skepticism that flicker throughout *Outdoor Labor for Convicts*—grounds for rethinking the consensus that provides the volume's point of departure and its conclusion, the notion that work is necessarily rehabilitative.

39 Henderson, "The Relation of Philanthropy to Social Order and Progress," 7.

40 It was thus that Henderson reconciled the rehabilitationist imperative of charity and correction with a commitment to eugenics. As he counseled the delegates gathered in Cincinnati, "education and selection" should become the conference mantra. On the one hand, every effort should be made to train the "dependent members of society" to participate in an ever-progressing industrial society. But on the other, the conference should also isolate and eliminate "the depressing influence and the propagation of those who cannot be fitted for competitive life." Extermination was too harsh a word, Henderson suggested, to account for the benevolent ends served by sequestering the unfit and preventing them from having offspring. Nor were the lives they led in seclusion to be unproductive in any absolute sense. Rather, custodial institutions were to become spaces of reformative and uplifting work—work that would not, of course, ever sufficiently prepare or qualify clients to take up their place in industrial society. The work they performed would instead simply be make-work. Henderson, "The Relation of Philanthropy to Social Order and Progress," 14.

41 Henderson, "The Relation of Philanthropy to Social Order and Progress," 14.

42 See Wagner-Hasel, *Die Arbeit des Gelehrten*.

43 Bücher, *Arbeit und Rhythmus*, 6th ed., 17. All translations from *Arbeit und Rhythmus* are my own.

44 Backhaus, "Non-market Exchanges in Healthcare," 338. See also Polanyi, "Karl Bücher"; Campbell, *Joy in Work, German Work*.

45 Bücher, *Industrial Evolution*, 82.

46 On Bücher's "general theory of economic development from primitive to modern times," see Pearson, "The Secular Debate on Economic Primitivism."

47 Bücher, *Arbeit und Rhythmus*, 6th ed., 463.

48 Casalis, *The Basutos*, 134; quoted in Bücher, *Arbeit und Rhythmus*, 2nd ed., 201.

49 Casalis, *The Basutos*, 134; Bücher, *Arbeit und Rhythmus*, 2nd ed., 202.

50 Bücher, *Arbeit und Rhythmus*, 2nd ed., 203.

51 Lipschutz and Rasmussen, "Samori Toure." Samori Toure, also known as Samory Touré and Alamany Samore Lafiya Toure, was the founder and leader of the Wassoulou Empire and among the most effective native challengers to the French.

52 See Korczynski, Pickering, and Robertson, *Rhythms of Labour*.

53 See Paul, "Cultural Mobility between Boston and Berlin."

54 Johnson, "O Black and Unknown Bards," 74; Bücher, *Arbeit und Rhythmus*, 6th ed., 248.

55 Bücher, *Arbeit und Rhythmus*, 6th ed., 262.

56 Bücher, *Arbeit und Rhythmus*, 6th ed., 262.

57 A similar emphasis on how the work song becomes an instrument of discipline is at stake in the transcriptions and commentaries by two African American informants, G. W. Henderson and Richard C. Harrison. The latter, readers learn, performed regularly as a folk singer in Chicago, which is presumably where Henderson met him. G. W. Henderson may well have been George Washington Henderson, a former slave who graduated from Yale and studied at the University of Berlin, as had Charles Richmond Henderson. Rather than adding a differently nuanced understanding of the traditional work song, however, almost certainly the point Bücher hoped to make in stressing that these two men were African American was that Harrison and Henderson brought the disciplinary function of the work song even more spectacularly to the fore. One of the songs they contributed to *Arbeit und Rhythmus* was performed by a group of roustabouts on the Mississippi River. In their commentary, Harrison and Henderson focus on the division of labor that the musical performance creates. Freed from physical labor, the leader "directs the work of the entire crew" according to the beat of his own song. Others join in the refrain to maintain an even pace at their own tasks. But much as his song keeps the others in line, the leader is also an overseer, carrying with him a stick with which to strike the "slow and lazy fellows." Bücher, *Arbeit und Rhythmus*, 6th ed., 259. As such, the leader's role literalizes the disciplinary force attributed to the African American work song. In the reformist context from which these transcriptions originated, moreover, the

leader's role also blurs the conference's tenuous distinction between rehabilitative labor and labor that was merely profitable.

58 Bücher, *Arbeit und Rhythmus*, 6th ed., 261.

59 Bücher, *Arbeit und Rhythmus*, 6th ed., 261.

60 On MacLean, see Deegan, *Annie Marion MacLean and the Chicago School of Sociology*.

61 "A semi-romantic interest is often attached by those away in the distance to the girl who guides a machine or banters her comrades the while," MacLean noted in a 1910 collection of ethnographic sketches. "When the truth is known, she leads a very unromantic life, full of grim realities which she meets often enough with heroism." MacLean, *Wage-Earning Women*, 1–2. In *Women Workers and Society* (1916), MacLean bemoans the strict division between work and leisure industrial labor demanded. If not nostalgic for the cult of domesticity, MacLean does regret the loss of the kind of sociality created when women worked at home. "When industry was carried on in the home," she notes, "it was social. There was always time for chatter and laughter while work was in process; but not so in our modern era, where, ordinarily, in the up-to-date factory, there are stringent regulations against the chatter and laughter that help to make youth pleasant." There can be no doubt, MacLean concedes, that the prohibition of "chatter and laughter" along with song in the factory is reasonable enough. But still she asks "that a little interest be injected into the long day of arduous toil." Many employers, MacLean continues, "are doing what they can to extend educational or recreational features for this very purpose. And if we can only wait long enough, we shall probably see a much more complete socialization." Although MacLean does not herself make the connection, the collegiality and support she anticipates with the coming of corporate "welfare work" resembles the sociality created by the washerwomen whose songs she transcribed for *Arbeit und Rhythmus*. MacLean, *Women Workers and Society*, 116; Bücher, *Arbeit und Rhythmus*, 6th ed., 243.

62 In "A Town in Florida," MacLean recounted in deliberate, pedestrian prose the history and future prospects of three Black churches in Deland, Florida. In a later essay titled "Where the Color Lines Are Drawn," on the other hand, MacLean turned to the lives of Black migrants in the North. Her analysis shares much with her understanding of the problems facing white working women but also with her earlier commentary on Black work songs in *Arbeit und Rhythmus*. Of the difficulties of "industrial adjustment" encountered by Black migrants, for instance, MacLean writes:

> Besides this, the difference between plantation labor in the South and industrialism in the North was too great for the negro to compass in a short time. 'Dat time clock sho' give me a shell shock,' said Tom Jamison, called Jimmison for short, as he came reeling out of a button factory.

Being a man with a hoe was more to his liking, for a hoe is a prop to the wary, and dinner time is the only time heeded where he came from. To tend a machine that cut buttons from bone looked like silly work to Tom when he started, but he soon felt himself a prisoner with all the restrictions placed upon him. No song, no merry laughter as he toiled, only the roar of the machines. (MacLean, *Our Neighbors*, 102)

As in her discussion of work songs in Bücher's volume, the juxtaposition that MacLean draws here between rural Black labor in the South and "industrialism in the North" turns on the question of rhythm. MacLean's ethnographic subject, Tom Jamison, experiences the chiming of the bell that standardizes industrial time not as a benign click-track but as a source of psychological injury. It paces his day according to a rhythm of production all but divorced from the rhythms of his body. Nor does singing itself offer a viable means of reorganizing his days; the "roar of the machines" makes it impossible to hear his own voice or to share with his coworkers a moment of "merry laughter." In place of the machine, Jamison finds himself longing for a hoe, an implement he values less for the kind of work one might do with it than for how it conjoins work and leisure. A hoe, he observes, is both a tool and a "prop"; but it is also a time-keeping device that allows the possessor to establish the pace and the variety of their working day.

63 Bücher, *Arbeit und Rhythmus*, 6th ed., 243.

64 Bücher, *Arbeit und Rhythmus*, 6th ed., 249.

65 In early autobiographies such as the pseudonymously published *Cheero* (1918), MacLean takes on the medical establishment's commitment to reducing people with disabilities to their disabilities. "The queerest thing about wheel-chair residence," MacLean notes, "is the mental attitude of non-residents toward the occupant. They look on him indulgently as on a child, but they do not really take him seriously." MacLean, *Cheero*, 50. MacLean's protagonist Jane moved from one hospital to the next sanitarium and received any number of treatments and devices. Once back home, Jane became a prominent "wheel-chair academic" on returning to public speaking after a long absence: "Once Jane went forth to a public banquet where twelve hundred working-women sat down to celebrate. She thought then that the mere fact that they were able to work was worth celebrating. That was the reason she promised to lift up her voice in public once more. She had had a long vacation from after-dinner speaking and was anxious to know if she could prattle acceptably. But she never knew because the morning papers devoted their space to her crutches! 'Invalid Heroine of Banquet,' they said. 'Women who had not walked for years got out of bed to attend. Carried on shoulders of girls!'" (50). Less travesty than farce, the scene that MacLean describes is one of misdirected or mistaken praise. Whereas Jane feels that the everyday lives of the twelve hundred women assembled at the banquet

deserve celebration, those women and the media believe that the simple fact of her appearance is the larger accomplishment. Indeed, the everyday achievements that brought each of these women to the table—"the mere fact that they were able to work"—is precisely the kind of ordinariness to which Jane aspires. Her return to the after-dinner circuit is motivated, we learn, by a desire less to achieve the rhetorical heights than to "prattle acceptably." And if it was her body that initially removed Jane from carrying on the everyday work that had once occupied her days, her body now prevents her from rejoining the workaday world. The curiosity and near-prurient attention she garners would seem to promise anything but the resumption of business as usual.

66 MacLean, "Twenty Years of Sociology by Correspondence," 464–65.

67 MacLean, "Twenty Years of Sociology by Correspondence," 468.

68 MacLean, "Twenty Years of Sociology by Correspondence," 471–72.

69 MacLean, "This Way Lies Happiness," 24.

70 MacLean, "This Way Lies Happiness," 24.

71 See MacLean, "This Way Lies Happiness":

> Even though one is shut within four walls there are people all about; they come on the printed page, and fill up the lonely places. One can keep a suffering body under by listening to the friends in books. All the enthusiasms of life are there. There is interest, too, in the people who pass. They go their more or less mysterious ways, and I am off in interested speculation. Freed from the emotions born of competitive life, child-like, I look upon all people as my friends. And the cultivation of friends is, I believe, the main business of Life. It is the extension of the friendly spirit alone that can save the world from greed. And in this the physically handicapped can participate.... Through friends, I keep grip on the great world. I participate through them in its joys and sorrows. Through friends my horizon widens. And I feared when I was stricken that it would narrow to intellectual suffocation. Stereotyped forms of happiness have us in their grip till some cataclysm gives us a glimpse of new patterns. By an exercise of will beauty can be read into new combinations. (27–28)

72 Odum and Johnson, *The Negro and His Songs*, 2.

73 Jackson, foreword, vii.

74 Blackburn, "State Programs of Public Welfare in the South," 6. Outdoor relief and the poorhouse, two mainstays of charities and corrections, were of particular concern. As sociologist Robert W. Kelso noted, the "chain of ideation" set in motion by the former was far from positive: "a dreary room with grimy windows; a railing worn smooth by the supplicating caresses of many palms; a bench and upon it a row of figures, some stooped with age and the miseries of life; ... some children, thin and old before their time—these the

beggars of the public bounty, ready to avow their poverty and accept their certificate of pauperization in the form of an order on the village store." The poorhouse was no better: "a barn-like room where the aged sit and rock away the hours, while children go in and out among them, grinning and making sport of the senile or scampering out of reach of the cross old lady with the dusting cap who mutters to herself and will shake folks if they bother her." Kelso, "Recent Advances in the Administration of Poor Relief," 90.

75 As one contributor to the institute's house journal *Social Forces* noted, social work "was not in general use at the opening of the present century. Two or three decades ago, such terms as philanthropy, charity, correction, outdoor relief, care of dependents, defectives, and delinquents were commonly employed by those at work in these fields." Steiner, *Education for Social Work*, 1.

76 Odum, *An Approach to Public Welfare and Social Work*, 7. These various "disadvantaged folks," Odum concluded, were "lost, misplaced, misfits in the game of life." Nonetheless, for all but the most "aged and infirm," productive labor was the crux of any solution modern social work might offer. The same was true for prisoners, for whose rehabilitation society was also responsible. As Odum saw matters, social workers should endeavor to make institutions more or less self-sustaining; to help prisoners support their families; and to institute "educational and corrective measures, including vocational guidance and direction, and physical rejuvenation" (153). These were largely the same goals, of course, with which previous generations of reformers had sought to reshape the public institutions of social welfare in the image of redemptive labor. Like earlier reformers, moreover, Odum and his colleagues were drawn in particular to the Southern peculiarity of the chain gang. To be sure, the abuse of the convict lease system was widely recognized when the Institute for Social Research was founded in 1920. Nor would the conclusions that Odum drew in studies like *An Approach to Public Welfare and Social Work* or *Systems of Public Welfare* have been considered altogether surprising. Odum's primary concern was that prisoners be granted sanitary working conditions and proper medical treatment. He also argued that the practice of leasing convicts to private concerns should be replaced with a well-coordinated plan for employing prisoners on county and state projects, an argument that Charles Richmond Henderson had made thirty years earlier. Odum, *An Approach to Public Welfare and Social Work*, 155.

But if Odum paid greater attention to the capricious violence of the lease in these works than in *The Negro and His Songs*, all of these books toe what emerged as the institute line—an unwillingness to demand the abolition of existing practices in favor of returning the convict lease system to its rehabilitationist roots. This consensus finds fullest articulation in *The North Carolina Chain Gang: A Study of County Convict Road Work* (1927) by Jesse Steiner and Roy Brown. The authors begin by acknowledging that convict labor, far from redemptive, was most often plain and simple drudgery. The "average county official" in charge of a road gang—the most common use of convict labor in North Carolina—had little regard for any "corrective or reformatory value in such methods of penal treatment." Steiner and Brown, *The North Carolina Chain Gang*, 6. The conclusion to be drawn is bleak: "The idea of reformation was far in the background and still apparently is not thought of as one of the purposes of this method of penal treatment. No one expects the prisoners to leave the chain gang improved in character or better prepared for citizenship" (174).

77 Odum and Willard, *Systems of Public Welfare*, 4.

78 Odum, "Religious Folk-Songs of the Southern Negroes," 267.

79 Odum, "Religious Folk-Songs of the Southern Negroes," 265. As such, attending to Black religious expression is a potent resource with which to address the "problem of the relations between the whites and blacks." As Odum writes further:

> Social conditions are changing and it is of paramount importance that every step taken shall be well founded and in the right direction. The political, social, and economical position of the negro, his education, his religion, his tendencies—these are themes that demand definite and accurate comprehension above all else. Truths have too often been assumed. Passion and prejudice have often hindered the attainment of noble ends which were earnestly sought. A true knowledge of actual conditions, if properly set forth, must convince the sincere observer as to the proper relation which should exist between the two races. Nothing else should do it, nothing else can do it. And any evidences that will assist in fixing the real status of the negro should be welcomed by both the whites and the blacks; progress may then be encouraged from the proper stand point. (267)

80 Odum and Johnson, *The Negro and His Songs*, 148.

81 Odum, "Folk-Song and Folk-Poetry as Found in the Secular Songs of the Southern Negroes (Concluded)," 379.

82 Odum, "Folk-Song and Folk-Poetry as Found in the Secular Songs of the Southern Negroes (Concluded)," 378.

83 Odum, "Folk-Song and Folk-Poetry as Found in the Secular Songs of the Southern Negroes (Concluded)," 378.

84 Odum, "Folk-Song and Folk-Poetry as Found in the Secular Songs of the Southern Negroes (Concluded)," 393.

85 Odum and Johnson, *The Negro and His Songs*, 265.

86 Odum, "Folk-Song and Folk-Poetry as Found in the Secular Songs of the Southern Negroes (Concluded)," 391. As such, "any popular song may be adapted to become a work song. Themes are freely mingled; verses, disjointed and inconsequential, are sung to many tunes and variations." Odum,

"Folk-Song and Folk-Poetry as Found in the Secular Songs of the Southern Negroes," 268.

87 Metfessel, *Phonophotography in Folk Music*, 22. As Brenton J. Malin notes, phonophotography was at root "an enhanced version of [Seashore's voice] tonoscope," a device Seashore used as early as 1902 to create a graphic representation of the sound waves produced by vocal performances. Malin, *Feeling Mediated*, 117.

88 Hochman, *Savage Preservation*, 77, 99–100. Indeed, Metfessel's renderings of African American folk songs visually resemble the transcriptions of Hopi songs that Gilman published two and a half decades earlier using his own "phonographic" method. Gilman's method was essentially to compare each note of phonographic recording with the notes of a finely graduated harmonium in order to establish the pitch as exactly as possible: "This comparison always had one or other of two results: either there was one harmonium note which at once impressed me as the nearest, or what struck me was the divergence of the note of the song from any harmonium note, even the one which finally appeared nearer the others." Gilman, *Hopi Songs*, 53. As described below, Metfessel's method, adapted from Seashore, followed much the same tack, though he compared measurements of luminosity. Metfessel's method was indebted perhaps most of all to his mentor at the University of Iowa, the psychologist Carl Seashore, who specialized in audiology and the psychology of the arts. Seashore claimed that the inspiration for phonophotography first came when a Smithsonian specialist in Native American music visited his lab "to have her ears certified with reference to the degree of reliability for the transcribing of phonograph records." Instead of using his audiology equipment to certify a given researcher's capacity for objective analysis, Seashore soon realized, he could use that same equipment to transcribe musical performances directly—essentially sidestepping the fallibility of even the best-trained human ears with the technical objectivity of phonophotography. Seashore, "Phonophotography in the Measurement of the Expression of Emotion," 471.

89 Johnson, preface, 30; quoted in Metfessel, *Phonophotography in Folk Music*, 21. If "the charm and distinctiveness of the singing of Negroes lies in [the] queer pranks of their voices," Metfessel argued, the "twists and turns [that] occur too quickly" for the human ear could easily be captured using the phonophotographic method. Metfessel, *Phonophotography in Folk Music*, 20. In addition to preserving, collecting, and analyzing folk music, as Steve J. Wurtzler notes, Seashore and his acolytes also believed phonophotography allowed researchers to analyze the expression of emotion in music and to quantify aesthetic value. Wurtzler, *Electric Sounds*, 236. As Seashore wrote, "There is no character of music, no musical change, or meaning, or expression of emotion, or art, or skill, manifested in music that is not represented physically and math-

ematically in the sound wave; and in terms of these waves we can describe (within the limits of instrumental errors) every character of music, from the crudest efforts to the most refined exhibition of esthetic emotion." Seashore, "Three New Approaches to the Study of Negro Music," 191.

90   Odum and Johnson, *Negro Workaday Songs*, 253.

91   Odum and Johnson, *Negro Workaday Songs*, 257.

92   Metfessel's interest in measuring innate musical ability bears the influence of both his mentor, Carl Seashore, and Odum's collaborator Guy Benton Johnson. The latter's doctoral research at UNC involved administering the so-called Seashore test to over 3,500 Black students to assess "the musical talent of the American Negro." Johnson, "A Study of the Musical Talent of the American Negro."

93   Metfessel, *Phonophotography in Folk Music*, 85–87.

94   Metfessel, *Phonophotography in Folk Music*, 92.

95   Metfessel, *Phonophotography in Folk Music*, 96.

96   Sanders, *Howard W. Odum's Folklore Odyssey*, 127.

97   Woofter, *Black Yeomanry*, 6.

98   Woofter, *Black Yeomanry*, 243.

99   Woofter, *Black Yeomanry*, 248.

100   Johnson, *A Social History of the Sea Islands*, 155.

101   Quoted in Johnson, *A Social History of the Sea Islands*, 156.

102   Johnson, *A Social History of the Sea Islands*, 199.

103   Pearson, *Letters from Port Royal*, 297; quoted in Johnson, *A Social History of the Sea Islands*, 199.

104   Du Bois, *The Souls of Black Folk*, 208.

105   *Liberator*, "Gen. Howard, at Edisto Island," 198.

106   Another omission on Du Bois's part is equally telling. On Edisto Island, evidently grieved to hear the dissenting freed men and women object to his proclamation "in such an unchristian spirit," General Howard provided one final justification for their dispossession. "He himself professed to be a follower of Christ," another eyewitness recalled, "who taught us to forgive our enemies and said that he had been in twenty-two battles, had lost his arm, and been severely wounded many times; he was willing to suffer more, if necessary, and yet he forgave them, from the bottom of his heart." *Liberator*, "Gen. Howard, at Edisto Island," 198. Unable to convince the freed men and women to accept that their labor would never be redemptive on terms of their choosing, Howard flips the script. No longer a sign of rehabilitative potential, disability is once again a marker of white sacrifice and ultimately of white prerogative. Soldiers under Howard's command roundly praised

the bravery with which the amputee general fought, his missing arm clearly becoming a sign of martial value. Writes cavalryman John L. Collins, for instance, "He was in the middle of the road and mounted, his maimed arm embracing a stand of colors that some regiment had deserted, while with his sound arm he was gesticulating to the men to make a stand by their flag. With a bared head he was pleading with his soldiers, literally weeping as he entreated the unheeding horde.... Maimed in person and sublime in his patriotism, he seemed worthy to stand by, and out of pure compliment to his appearance I hooked up my saber and fell in the line that gathered about him." Quoted in Johnson and Buel, *Battles and Leaders of the Civil War*, 3:45.

Coda

1 Lipsky, *Street-Level Bureaucracy*.

2 Zacka, *When the State Meets the Street*, 10–11.

3 Brodkin, "Work and the Welfare State," 4.

4 King, *Where Do We Go from Here*, 172.

5 Benner, "Building a Real Sharing Economy."

6 Pateman, "Another Way Forward," 53. Pateman quotes Gutmann and Thompson, *Democracy and Disagreement*, 303.

7 Pateman, "Another Way Forward," 55.

8 Kabir, *Raisa Kabir*.

BIBLIOGRAPHY

Abel, Emily K. "Valuing Care: Turn-of-the-Century Conflicts between Charity Workers and Women Clients." *Journal of Women's History* 10, no. 3 (1998): 32–52.

Adams, Rachel. *Sideshow U.S.A.: Freaks and the American Cultural Imagination.* Chicago: University of Chicago Press, 2001.

Allen, William Francis, Charles Pickard Ware, and Lucy McKim Garrison, eds. *Slave Songs of the United States.* New York: A. Simpson, 1867.

Amar, Jules. *Le rendement de la machine humaine.* Paris: Baillière, 1909.

Amar, Jules. *The Physiology of Industrial Organisation and the Re-employment of the Disabled.* New York: Macmillan, 1919.

American Social Science Association. *Constitution, Address, and List of Members of the American Association for the Promotion of Social Science, with the Questions Proposed for Discussion: To Which Are Added Minutes of the Transactions of the Association. July, 1866.* American Social Science Association. Document Published by the Association, with an Abridgment of the Transactions. Part I. 1865–66. Boston: Wright and Potter, 1866.

Anderson, Eric, and Alfred A. Moss Jr. *Dangerous Donations: Northern Philanthropy and Southern Black Education, 1902–1930.* Columbia: University of Missouri Press, 1999.

Anderson, James D. *The Education of Blacks in the South, 1860–1935.* Chapel Hill: University of North Carolina Press, 1988.

Andrews, William L. "The Representation of Slavery and the Rise of Afro-American Literary Realism." In *Slavery and the Literary Imagination,* edited by Arnold Rampersad and Deborah E. McDowell, 62–80. Baltimore: Johns Hopkins University Press, 1989.

Armstrong, Gen. S. C. "The Future of the American Negro." In *Proceedings of the National Conference of Charities and Correction, at the Fourteenth Annual Session Held in Omaha, Neb., August 25–31, 1887,* edited by Isabel C. Barrows, 167–70. Boston: Press of Geo. H. Ellis, 1887.

Ascher, Ludwig. "Der Einfluss Technischer Verbesserungen auf die Gesundheit des Menschen, Insbesondere des Arbeiters." *Resoconti del Congresso,* vol. 2: *IIIo Congresso del Internazionale di Organizzazione Scientifica del Lavoro* (Rome, 1927), 563–70.

Aubert, Geneviève. "From Photography to Cinematography: Recording Movement and Gait in a Neurological Context." *Journal of the History of the Neurosciences* 11, no. 3 (September 2002): 255.

Auerbach, Jonathan. *Body Shots: Early Cinema's Incarnations.* Berkeley: University of California Press, 2007.

Ayers, Edward L. *Vengeance and Justice: Crime and Punishment in the 19th Century American South.* New York: Oxford University Press, 1984.

Backhaus, Ursula. "Non-market Exchanges in Healthcare: Lessons from Karl Bücher." In *Karl Bücher: Theory, History, Anthropology, Non Market Economies*, edited by Jürgen G. Backhaus, 337–63. Marburg, Germany: Metropolis-Verlag, 2000.

Bagenstos, Samuel R. "Disability, Universalism, Social Rights, and Citizenship." *Cardozo Law Review* 39, no. 2 (2017): 413–36.

Bailey, Ben E. "The Cotton Blossom Singers: Mississippi's Black Troubadours." *Black Perspective in Music* 15, no. 2 (October 1987): 133–52.

Baker, Lee D. "Missionary Positions." In *Globalization and Race: Transformations in the Cultural Production of Blackness*, edited by Kamari Clarke and Deborah A. Thomas, 37–54. Durham, NC: Duke University Press, 2006.

Baker, Richard. "The History of Gait Analysis before the Advent of Modern Computers." *Gait and Posture* 26, no. 3 (2007): 331–42.

Bancroft, Christian. "Someone Was Looking for Me: A Review of Blunt Research Group's *The Work-Shy.*" *Gulf Coast: A Journal of Literature and Fine Arts.* Accessed April 19, 2021. http://ftp.gulfcoastmag.org/art-and-reviews/reviews-and-interviews/the-work-shy/.

Banta, Martha. *Taylored Lives: Narrative Productions in the Age of Taylor, Veblen, and Ford.* Chicago: University of Chicago Press, 1995.

Bardeen, C. W. *A Little Fifer's War Diary, with 17 Maps, 60 Portraits, and 246 Other Illustrations.* Syracuse, NY: C. W. Bardeen, 1910.

Barrows, Isabel C. "Discussion on Industrial Training." In *Proceedings of the National Conference of Charities and Correction, at the Fifteenth Annual Session Held in Buffalo, N.Y. July 5–11, 1888*, edited by Isabel C. Barrows, 379–82. Boston: Press of Geo. H. Ellis, 1888.

Barrows, Isabel C. "Minutes and Discussions, Seventh Session. Thursday Morning, Oct. 16." In *Proceedings of the National Conference of Charities and Correction, at the Eleventh Annual Session, Held at St. Louis, October 13–17, 1884*, edited by Isabel C. Barrows, 363–70. Boston: Press of Geo. H. Ellis, 1884.

Barrows, Isabel C. Preface to *Proceedings of the National Conference of Charities and Correction, at the Eighteenth Annual Session Held in Indianapolis, Ind., May 13–20, 1891*, edited by Isabel C. Barrows. Boston: Press of Geo. H. Ellis, 1891.

Bear, Jordan, and Kate Palmer Albers. "Photography's Time Zone." In *Before-and-After Photography: Histories and Contexts*, edited by Jordan Bear and Kate Palmer Albers, 1–11. London: Bloomsbury, 2017.

Becker, Peter, and William Clark. *Little Tools of Knowledge: Historical Essays on Academic and Bureaucratic Practices.* Ann Arbor: University of Michigan Press, 2001.

Beckett, Katherine, and Bruce Western. "Governing Social Marginality: Welfare, Incarceration, and the Transformation of State Policy." *Punishment and Society* 3, no. 1 (2001): 43–59.

Beckwith, Ruthie-Marie. *Disability Servitude: From Peonage to Poverty.* New York: Palgrave Macmillan, 2016.

Beech, Dave. *Art and Value: Art's Economic Exceptionalism in Classical, Neoclassical and Marxist Economics.* Boston: Brill, 2015.

Belt, Rabia. "Contemporary Voting Rights Controversies through the Lens of Disability." *Stanford Law Review* 68, no. 6 (2016): 1491–550.

Beniger, James R. *The Control Revolution: Technological and Economic Origins of the Information Society.* Cambridge, MA: Harvard University Press, 1986.

Benner, Chris. "Building a Real Sharing Economy." Othering and Belonging Institute, April 18, 2018. https://haasinstitute.berkeley.edu/building-real-sharing -economy.

Benson, Wm. E. "The Prevention of Crime among Colored Children. Manual Training as a Preventive of Delinquency." In *Proceedings of the National Conference of Charities and Correction, at the Thirty-First Annual Session Held in the City of Portland, Maine, June 15–22, 1904,* edited by Isabel C. Barrows, 170–72. Columbus, OH: Press of Fred J. Heer, 1904.

Bentley, Nancy. *Frantic Panoramas: American Literature and Mass Culture, 1870–1920.* Philadelphia: University of Pennsylvania Press, 2009.

Bentley, Nancy. "Mass Media and Literary Culture at the Turn of the Twentieth Century." In *A Companion to American Literary Studies,* edited by Caroline F. Levander and Robert S. Levine, 191–207. Malden, MA: John Wiley and Sons, 2015.

Berardi, Franco. *The Soul at Work: From Alienation to Autonomy.* Semiotext(e) Foreign Agents Series. Los Angeles: Semiotexte, 2009.

Berlant, Lauren. "The Epistemology of State Emotion." In *Dissent in Dangerous Times,* edited by Austin Sarat, 46–78. Ann Arbor: University of Michigan Press, 2005.

Berlant, Lauren. "On the Case." *Critical Inquiry* 33, no. 4 (June 2007): 663–72.

Berlant, Lauren. *The Queen of America Goes to Washington City: Essays on Sex and Citizenship.* Durham, NC: Duke University Press, 1997.

Bernard, Luther L., and Jessie Bernard. *Origins of American Sociology: The Social Science Movement in the United States.* New York: Russell and Russell, 1965.

Bernes, Jasper. *The Work of Art in the Age of Deindustrialization.* Stanford, CA: Stanford University Press, 2017.

Berry, Mary Frances. *My Face Is Black Is True: Callie House and the Struggle for Ex-Slave Reparations.* New York: Vintage, 2006.

Best, Stephen, and Saidiya Hartman. "Fugitive Justice." *Representations* 92, no. 1 (November 2005): 1–15.

Best, Stephen M. *The Fugitive's Properties: Law and the Poetics of Possession.* Chicago: University of Chicago Press, 2004.

Blackburn, Burr. "State Programs of Public Welfare in the South." *Journal of Social Forces* 1, no. 1 (1922): 6–11.

Bloom, Peter J. *French Colonial Documentary: Mythologies of Humanitarianism.* Minneapolis: University of Minnesota Press, 2008.

Blunt Research Group. *The Work-Shy.* Wesleyan Poetry. Middletown, CT: Wesleyan University Press, 2016.

Bonato, Sarah. *Searching the Grey Literature: A Handbook for Searching Reports, Working Papers, and Other Unpublished Research.* Lanham, MD: Rowman and Littlefield, 2018.

Bottomore, Stephen. "Filming, Faking and Propaganda: The Origins of the War Film, 1897–1902." PhD diss., Utrecht University, 2007.

Brackett, Jeffrey R. "Supervisory and Educational Movements." *Charities: A Weekly Review of Local and General Philanthropy* 7, no. 23 (December 1901): 514–22.

Braun, Marta. *Picturing Time: The Work of Etienne-Jules Marey.* Chicago: University of Chicago Press, 1995.

Braun, Marta, and Elizabeth Whitcombe. "Marey, Muybridge, and Londe: The Photography of Pathological Locomotion." *History of Photography* 23, no. 3 (1999): 218–24.

Bremner, Robert H. *From the Depths: The Discovery of Poverty in the United States.* New York: New York University Press, 1972.

Britton, Wiley. *A Traveling Court. Based on Investigation of War Claims.* Kansas City, MO: Smith-Grieves, 1926.

Brodhead, Richard H. "The American Literary Field, 1860–1890." In *The Cambridge History of American Literature,* vol. 3: *Prose Writing 1860–1920,* edited by Sacvan Bercovitch, 11–62. Cambridge: Cambridge University Press, 2005.

Brodkin, Evelyn Z. "Work and the Welfare State." In *Work and the Welfare State: Street-Level Organizations and Workfare Politics,* edited by Evelyn Z. Brodkin and Gregory Marston, 3–16. Washington, DC: Georgetown University Press, 2013.

Bromell, Nicholas K. *By the Sweat of the Brow: Literature and Labor in Antebellum America.* Chicago: University of Chicago Press, 1993.

Brooks, Daphne A. *Bodies in Dissent: Spectacular Performances of Race and Freedom, 1850–1910.* Durham, NC: Duke University Press, 2006.

Brouillette, Sarah. "Academic Labor, the Aesthetics of Management, and the Promise of Autonomous Work." *Nonsite.org* (blog), May 1, 2013. https://nonsite.org/academic-labor-the-aesthetics-of-management-and-the-promise-of-autonomous-work/.

Brouillette, Sarah. *Literature and the Creative Economy.* Stanford, CA: Stanford University Press, 2014.

Brown, Elspeth H. *The Corporate Eye: Photography and the Rationalization of American Commercial Culture, 1884–1929.* Baltimore: Johns Hopkins University Press, 2005.

Brown, Matthew P. "Blanks: Data, Method, and the British American Print Shop." *American Literary History* 29, no. 2 (2017): 228–47.

Brown, Matthew P. "Document." *Early American Studies: An Interdisciplinary Journal* 16, no. 4 (Fall 2018): 643–47.

Brown, Sterling. "Negro Folk Expression: Spirituals, Seculars, Ballads, and Work Songs." In *By These Hands: A Documentary History of African American Humanism*, edited by Anthony B. Pinn, 103–22. New York: New York University Press, 2001.

Brown, Wendy. *States of Injury: Power and Freedom in Late Modernity.* Princeton, NJ: Princeton University Press, 1995.

Bruyère, Susanne M., ed. *Disability and Employer Practices: Research across the Disciplines.* Ithaca, NY: Cornell University Press, 2016.

Bücher, Karl. *Arbeit und Rhythmus.* 2nd ed. Leipzig, Germany: B. G. Teubner, 1899.

Bücher, Karl. *Arbeit und Rhythmus.* 6th ed. Leipzig, Germany: E. Reinicke, 1924.

Bücher, Karl. *Industrial Evolution.* Translated by S. Morley Wickett. New York: Henry Holt, 1907.

Bulmer, Martin. *The Chicago School of Sociology: Institutionalization, Diversity, and the Rise of Sociological Research.* Chicago: University of Chicago Press, 1986.

Burden, Chris. *Chris Burden: A Twenty-Year Survey.* Newport Beach, CA: Newport Harbor Art Museum, 1988.

Bureau of Pensions. "Washington D.C., Ex-Slave Pension Correspondence and Case Files, 1892–1922." n.d. Microfilm M2110. National Archives and Records Administration, Washington, DC.

Byington, Margaret Frances. *What Social Workers Should Know about Their Own Communities; an Outline.* 4th ed. New York: Charity Organization Department, Russell Sage Foundation, 1924.

Cable, George Washington. "The Convict Lease System in the Southern States." In *Proceedings of the Tenth Annual National Conference of Charities and Corrections, Held at Louisville, Ky., September 24–30, 1883*, edited by A. O. Wright, 265–301. Boston: Press of Geo. H. Ellis, 1884.

Camiscioli, Elisa. *Reproducing the French Race: Immigration, Intimacy, and Embodiment in the Early Twentieth Century.* Durham, NC: Duke University Press, 2009.

Campbell, Joan. *Joy in Work, German Work: The National Debate, 1800–1945.* Princeton, NJ: Princeton University Press, 2014.

Canguilhem, Georges. *The Normal and the Pathological.* Translated by Carolyn R. Fawcett. New York: Zone, 1991.

Carmody, Todd. "In Spite of Handicaps: The Disability History of Racial Uplift." *American Literary History* 27, no. 1 (Spring 2015): 56–78.

Carmody, Todd. "Rehearsing for Reconstruction: The Archipelagic Afterlives of the Port Royal Experiment." *American Literature* 92, no. 2 (June 2020): 281–307.

Carmody, Todd, and Heather Love. "Try Anything." *Criticism* 50, no. 1 (Winter 2008): 133–46.

Carr, Roland T. "The Mysteries of Lincoln's Bank Accounts." *Bankers Magazine* 148, no. 1 (1965): 18–23.

Cartwright, Lisa. "'Experiments of Destruction': Cinematic Inscriptions of Physiology." *Representations*, no. 40 (October 1992): 129–52.

Casalis, Eugene Arnaud. *The Basutos: Or, Twenty-Three Years in South Africa*. London: James Nisbet, 1861.

Chamberlain, James A. *Undoing Work, Rethinking Community: A Critique of the Social Function of Work*. Ithaca, NY: Cornell University Press, 2018.

Charity Organization Society of New York. *Fifth Annual Report*. New York: Charity Organization Society of New York, 1887.

Chen, Mel Y. *Animacies: Biopolitics, Racial Mattering, and Queer Affect*. Durham, NC: Duke University Press, 2012.

Ciulla, Joanne B. *The Working Life: The Promise and Betrayal of Modern Work*. New York: Times Books, 2000.

Cohen, Lara Langer. *The Fabrication of American Literature: Fraudulence and Antebellum Print Culture*. Philadelphia: University of Pennsylvania Press, 2011.

Cohen, Michael C. *The Social Lives of Poems in Nineteenth-Century America*. Philadelphia: University of Pennsylvania Press, 2015.

Collier's Weekly. "For Ten Cents." March 21, 1908.

Colored American. "No Pensions for Ex-Slaves." April 21, 1900.

Colvin, Fred H. "The Latest Development in Motion Study." *American Machinist* 38 (June 5, 1913): 937–39.

Cooper, Arnold. *Between Struggle and Hope: Four Black Educators in the South, 1894–1915*. Ames: Iowa State University Press, 1989.

Costa, Dora L. *The Evolution of Retirement: An American Economic History, 1880–1990*. Chicago: University of Chicago Press, 1998.

Couser, G. Thomas. *Signifying Bodies: Disability in Contemporary Life Writing*. Ann Arbor: University of Michigan Press, 2009.

Cresswell, Tim. *On the Move: Mobility in the Modern Western World*. New York: Routledge, 2006.

Cruz, Jon. *Culture on the Margins: The Black Spiritual and the Rise of American Cultural Interpretation*. Princeton, NJ: Princeton University Press, 1999.

Daniel, Pete. "Black Power in the 1920s: The Case of Tuskegee Veterans Hospital." *Journal of Southern History* 36, no. 3 (August 1970): 368–88.

Daston, Lorraine, and Peter Galison. "The Image of Objectivity." *Representations* 40 (Fall 1992): 81–128.

Day, Iyko. *Alien Capital: Asian Racialization and the Logic of Settler Colonial Capitalism*. Durham, NC: Duke University Press, 2016.

Deegan, Mary Jo. *Annie Marion MacLean and the Chicago Schools of Sociology, 1894–1934*. New Brunswick, NJ: Transaction, 2014.

Dercum, Francis Xavier. "A Study of Some Normal and Abnormal Movements Photographed by Muybridge." In *Animal Locomotion: The Muybridge Work at the University of Pennsylvania*, 103–33. Philadelphia: J. B. Lippincott, 1888.

Diller, Matthew. "Entitlement and Exclusion: The Role of Disability in the Social Welfare System." *UCLA Law Review* 44 (1996): 361–466.

Dixon, Thomas. *The Sins of the Father: A Romance of the South*. Lexington: University Press of Kentucky, 2004.

Doane, Mary Ann. *The Emergence of Cinematic Time: Modernity, Contingency, the Archive*. Cambridge, MA: Harvard University Press, 2002.

Du Bois, W. E. B. *Black Reconstruction in America*. New York: Simon and Schuster, 1999.

Du Bois, W. E. B. *Darkwater*. New York: Harcourt, Brace and Howe, 1920.

Du Bois, W. E. B. *The Souls of Black Folk*. New York: Penguin Classics, 1996.

Du Bois, W. E. B. "Worlds of Color." *Foreign Affairs* 3, no. 3 (April 1925): 423–44.

Dujardin-Beaumetz. "New Therapeutic Agencies." *Therapeutic Gazette* 5, no. 9 (September 16, 1889): 577–85.

Dunbar, Paul Laurence. "The Promoter." *Collier's Weekly*, February 1, 1902.

Eberhart, Howard D., and Verne T. Inman. "An Evaluation of Experimental Procedures Used in a Fundamental Study of Human Locomotion." *Annals of the New York Academy of Sciences* 51, no. 7 (January 1951): 1213–28.

Edison Manufacturing Co. "War Extra Catalogue (May 20, 1898)." In *Motion Picture Catalogs by American Producers and Distributors, 1894–1908: A Microform Edition*, edited by Charles Musser. Frederick, MD: University Publications of America, 1985.

Edwards, William J. *Twenty-Five Years in the Black Belt*. Westport, CT: Negro Universities Press, 1970.

Edwards, William J. "Uplifting the Submerged Masses." In *Tuskegee and Its People: Their Ideals and Achievements*, edited by Booker T. Washington and Emmett J. Scott, 224–52. New York: D. Appleton, 1905.

Enck, Henry S. "Black Self-Help in the Progressive Era: The 'Northern Campaigns' of Smaller Southern Black Industrial Schools, 1900–1915." *Journal of Negro History* 61, no. 1 (January 1976): 73–87.

Epstein, Dena J. *Sinful Tunes and Spirituals: Black Folk Music to the Civil War*. Urbana: University of Illinois Press, 1977.

Erevelles, Nirmala, and Andrea Minear. "Unspeakable Offenses: Untangling Race and Disability in Discourses of Intersectionality." In *The Disability Studies Reader*, edited by Lennard J. Davis, 4th ed., 354–68. New York: Routledge, 2013.

Fabian, Ann. *The Unvarnished Truth: Personal Narratives in Nineteenth-Century America*. Berkeley: University of California Press, 2000.

Falk, Gene. "Temporary Assistance for Needy Families (TANF): Welfare-to-Work Revisited." Washington, DC: Congressional Research Service, October 2, 2012.

Faust, Drew Gilpin. *This Republic of Suffering*. New York: Vintage, 2008.

Fear-Segal, Jacqueline. "Facing the Binary: Native American Students in the Camera's Lens." In *Before-and-After Photography: Histories and Contexts*, edited by Jordan Bear and Kate Palmer Albers, 153–73. London: Bloomsbury, 2017.

Federici, Silvia. *Wages against Housework*. London: Power of Women Collective, 1975.

Field, Allyson Nadia. *Uplift Cinema: The Emergence of African American Film and the Possibility of Black Modernity*. Durham, NC: Duke University Press, 2015.

Finkenbine, Roy E. "Law, Reconstruction, and African American Education in the Post-Emancipation South." In *Charity, Philanthropy, and Civility in American History*, edited by Lawrence Jacob Friedman and Mark D. McGarvie, 161–78. Cambridge: Cambridge University Press, 2003.

Fisher, Laura R. *Reading for Reform: The Social Work of Literature in the Progressive Era*. Minneapolis: University of Minnesota Press, 2019.

Fleming, Thomas. *Around the Capital with Uncle Hank, Recorded Together with Many Pictures*. New York: Nutshell, 1902.

Fleming, Walter L. "Ex-Slave Pension Frauds." *South Atlantic Quarterly* 9, no. 2 (April 1910): 123–36.

Florida, Richard L. *The Rise of the Creative Class and How It's Transforming Work, Leisure, Community and Everyday Life*. New York: Basic Books, 2002.

Foner, Eric. *Reconstruction: America's Unfinished Revolution, 1863–1877*. New York: Harper Perennial Modern Classics, 2002.

Forrester, John. *Thinking in Cases*. Oxford: Polity, 2016.

Fosdick, Raymond B. *Adventure in Giving: The Story of the General Education Board, a Foundation Established by John D. Rockefeller*. New York: Harper and Row, 1962.

Fosdick, Raymond B. *The Story of the Rockefeller Foundation*. Philanthropy and Society. New York: Harper and Brothers, 1952.

Foucault, Michel. *Discipline and Punish: The Birth of the Prison*. Translated by Alan Sheridan. New York: Pantheon, 1977.

Frader, Laura Levine. *Breadwinners and Citizens: Gender in the Making of the French Social Model*. Durham, NC: Duke University Press, 2008.

Frank and Lillian Gilbreth Library of Management Research and Professional Papers, ca. 1845–1959. Purdue University Special Collections.

Frank and Lillian Gilbreth Papers, ca. 1869–2000. Purdue University Special Collections.

Franke, Katherine. *Repair: Redeeming the Promise of Abolition*. Chicago: Haymarket, 2019.

Frankel, Oz. *States of Inquiry: Social Investigations and Print Culture in Nineteenth-Century Britain and the United States*. Baltimore: Johns Hopkins University Press, 2006.

French, Austa Malinda. *Slavery in South Carolina and the Ex-Slaves, or, The Port Royal Mission*. New York: Winchell M. French, 1862.

Frizot, Michel. *A New History of Photography*. Cologne, Germany: Konemann, 1999.

Fromm, Erich. *Marx's Concept of Man*. Milestones of Thought in the History of Ideas. New York: Fungar, 1961.

Fülöp-Miller, René. *The Mind and Face of Bolshevism: An Examination of Cultural Life in Soviet Russia*. New York: Harper and Row, 1965.

Gaines, Jane M. *Fire and Desire: Mixed-Race Movies in the Silent Era*. Chicago: University of Chicago Press, 2001.

Gaines, Kevin Kelly. *Uplifting the Race: Black Leadership, Politics, and Culture in the Twentieth Century*. Chapel Hill: University of North Carolina Press, 1996.

Garland-Thomson, Rosemarie. "Disability Studies: A Field Emerged." *American Quarterly* 65, no. 4 (2013): 915–26.

Garland-Thomson, Rosemarie. *Extraordinary Bodies: Figuring Physical Disability in American Culture and Literature.* New York: Columbia University Press, 1997.

Garrett, Philip C. "Our Duty to the African and Indian Races." In *Proceedings of the National Conference of Charities and Correction, at the Fourteenth Annual Session Held in Omaha, Neb., August 25–31, 1887,* edited by Isabel C. Barrows, 163–66. Boston: Press of Geo. H. Ellis, 1887.

Gatewood, Willard B. *"Smoked Yankees" and the Struggle for Empire: Letters from Negro Soldiers, 1898–1902.* Urbana: University of Illinois Press, 1971.

General Education Board Records. Rockefeller Archive Center, Sleepy Hollow, NY.

George, G. J. *William Newby, Alias "Dan Benton," Alias "Rickety Dan," Alias "Crazy Jack," or The Soldier's Return; a True and Wonderful Story of Mistaken Identity.* Cincinnati, OH: Press of C. J. Krehbiel, 1893.

Gibson, James Jerome. "The Theory of Affordances." In *The Ecological Approach to Visual Perception,* 127–37. Hillsdale, NJ: Lawrence Erlbaum Associates, 1986.

Giedion, Sigfried. *Mechanization Takes Command: A Contribution to Anonymous History.* Minneapolis: University of Minnesota Press, 1948.

Gilbert, James Burkhart. *Work without Salvation: America's Intellectuals and Industrial Alienation, 1880–1910.* Baltimore: Johns Hopkins University Press, 1977.

Gilbreth, Frank. *Bricklaying System.* New York: Myron C. Clark, 1909.

Gilbreth, Frank Bunker, and Lillian Moller Gilbreth. *Applied Motion Study: A Collection of Papers on the Efficient Method to Industrial Preparedness.* New York: Macmillan, 1919.

Gilbreth, Frank B., and L. M. Gilbreth. "The Engineer, the Cripple, and the New Education." *Journal of the American Society of Mechanical Engineers* 40 (January 1918): 51–61.

Gilbreth, Frank B., and Lillian M. Gilbreth. *Fatigue Study: The Elimination of Humanity's Greatest Unnecessary Waste.* New York: Macmillan, 1916.

Gilbreth, Frank B., and Lillian Moller Gilbreth. *Motion Study for the Handicapped.* London: G. Routledge and Sons, 1920.

Gilman, Benjamin Ives. *Hopi Songs.* Boston: Houghton Mifflin, 1908.

Gilmore, Michael T. *American Romanticism and the Marketplace.* Chicago: University of Chicago Press, 1988.

Gitelman, Lisa. *Paper Knowledge: Toward a Media History of Documents.* Durham, NC: Duke University Press, 2014.

Glasson, William H. *Federal Military Pensions in the United States.* New York: Oxford University Press, 1918.

Glenn, Bess. "The Taft Commission and the Government's Record Practices." *American Archivist* 21, no. 3 (1958): 277–303.

Glenn, Evelyn Nakano. *Unequal Freedom: How Race and Gender Shaped American Citizenship and Labor.* Cambridge, MA: Harvard University Press, 2002.

Goldberg, Chad Alan. *Citizens and Paupers: Relief, Rights, and Race, from the Freedmen's Bureau to Workfare*. Chicago: University of Chicago Press, 2008.

Gordon, Linda. "The New Feminist Scholarship on the Welfare State." In *Women, the State, and Welfare*, edited by Linda Gordon, 9–35. Madison: University of Wisconsin Press, 1990.

Gordon, Linda. *Pitied but Not Entitled: Single Mothers and the History of Welfare, 1890–1935*. New York: Free Press, 1994.

Gorz, André. *Farewell to the Working Class: An Essay on Post-industrial Socialism*. London: Pluto, 1982.

Goux, Jean-Joseph. *Symbolic Economies*. Translated by Jennifer C. Gage. Ithaca, NY: Cornell University Press, 1990.

Gregg, Melissa. *Counterproductive: Time Management in the Knowledge Economy*. Durham, NC: Duke University Press, 2018.

Grillo, Trina, and Stephanie M. Wildman. "Obscuring the Importance of Race: The Implication of Making Comparisons between Racism and Sexism (or Other Isms)." In *Critical Race Feminism: A Reader*, edited by Adrien Katherine Wing, 44–50. New York: New York University Press, 1997.

Guillory, John. "The Memo and Modernity." *Critical Inquiry* 31, no. 1 (Autumn 2004): 108–32.

Guillory, John. "Monuments and Documents: Panofsky on the Object of Study in the Humanities." *History of Humanities* 1, no. 1 (Spring 2016): 9–30.

Gunning, Tom. "Before Documentary: Early Nonfiction Films and the 'View' Aesthetic." In *The Documentary Film Reader: History, Theory, Criticism*, edited by Jonathan Kahana, 52–63. New York: Oxford University Press, 2016.

Gunning, Tom. "In Your Face: Physiognomy, Photography, and the Gnostic Mission of Early Film." In *The Mind of Modernism: Medicine, Psychology, and the Cultural Arts in Europe and America, 1880–1940*, edited by Mark Micale, 141–71. Stanford, CA: Stanford University Press, 2003.

Gurteen, S. Humphreys. *A Handbook of Charity Organization*. Buffalo, NY: Courier, 1882.

Gutmann, Amy, and Dennis F. Thompson. *Democracy and Disagreement*. Cambridge, MA: Harvard University Press, 1996.

Guyer, Paul. *Kant and the Claims of Taste*. Cambridge, MA: Harvard University Press, 1979.

Hack, Daniel. *The Material Interests of the Victorian Novel*. Charlottesville: University of Virginia Press, 2005.

Hager, Christopher. *Word by Word: Emancipation and the Act of Writing*. Cambridge, MA: Harvard University Press, 2013.

Hale, William Bayard. "The Pension Carnival." *World's Work* 20, no. 6 (October 1910): 13485–504.

Hale, William Bayard. "The Pension Carnival III: Capitalizing the Nation's Gratitude." *World's Work* 21, no. 2 (December 1910): 13731–47.

Hamraie, Aimi. *Building Access: Universal Design and the Politics of Disability*. Minneapolis: University of Minnesota Press, 2017.

Hanass-Hancock, Jill, and Sophie Mitra. "Livelihoods and Disability: The Complexities of Work in the Global South." *Disability in the Global South: The Critical Handbook*, edited by Shaun Grech and Karen Soldatic, 133–49. Cham, Switzerland: Springer International, 2016.

Handler, Joel F. *The Poverty of Welfare Reform*. New Haven, CT: Yale University Press, 1995.

Harlan, Louis R. *Booker T. Washington: The Wizard of Tuskegee, 1901–1915*. New York: Oxford University Press, 1983.

Harlan, Louis R. *Separate and Unequal: Public School Campaigns and Racism in the Southern Seaboard States, 1901–1915*. Chapel Hill: University of North Carolina Press, 1958.

Harris, Cheryl I. "Whiteness as Property." *Harvard Law Review* 106, no. 8 (1993): 1707–91.

Harrison, Alferdteen, and Roland Freeman. *Piney Woods School: An Oral History*. Jackson: University Press of Mississippi, 2006.

Hartman, Saidiya V. *Scenes of Subjection: Terror, Slavery, and Self-Making in Nineteenth-Century America*. New York: Oxford University Press, 1997.

Hatton, Erin. *Coerced: Work under Threat of Punishment*. Berkeley: University of California Press, 2020.

Henderson, Charles Richmond. "Introduction." In *Outdoor Labor for Convicts: A Report to the Governor of Illinois*, edited by Charles Richmond Henderson, vii–xv. Chicago: University of Chicago Press, 1907.

Henderson, Charles Richmond. *Introduction to the Study of the Dependent, Defective, and Delinquent Classes, and of Their Social Treatment*. Boston: D. C. Heath, 1906.

Henderson, Charles Richmond. "The Relation of Philanthropy to Social Order and Progress." In *Proceedings of the National Conference of Charities and Correction, at the Twenty-Sixth Annual Session Held in the City of Cincinnati, Ohio, May 17–23, 1899*, edited by Isabel C. Barrows, 1–15. Boston: Press of Geo. H. Ellis, 1900.

Henderson, Charles Richmond. *Social Elements: Institutions, Character, Progress*. New York: Scribner, 1898.

Higginbotham, Evelyn Brooks. *Righteous Discontent: The Women's Movement in the Black Baptist Church, 1880–1920*. Cambridge, MA: Harvard University Press, 1994.

Higginson, Thomas Wentworth. *Army Life in a Black Regiment*. Cambridge, MA: Riverside Press, 1900.

Hirschmann, Nancy J., and Beth Linker. "Disability, Citizenship, and Belonging: A Critical Introduction." In *Civil Disabilities: Citizenship, Membership, and Belonging*, edited by Nancy J. Hirschmann and Beth Linker, 1–21. Philadelphia: University of Pennsylvania Press, 2014.

Hochman, Brian. *Savage Preservation: The Ethnographic Origins of Modern Media Technology*. Minneapolis: University of Minnesota Press, 2014.

Hoganson, Kristin L. *Fighting for American Manhood: How Gender Politics Provoked the Spanish-American and Philippine-American Wars*. New Haven, CT: Yale University Press, 1998.

Hudson, Peter James. *Bankers and Empire: How Wall Street Colonized the Caribbean*. Chicago: University of Chicago Press, 2017.

Hugill, Stan. *Shanties from the Seven Seas: Shipboard Work-Songs and Songs Used as Work-Songs from the Great Days of Sail*. London: Routledge and Kegan Paul, 1961.

Hurwitz, Brian. "Form and Representation in Clinical Case Reports." *Literature and Medicine* 25, no. 2 (2006): 216–40.

Huyssen, David. *Progressive Inequality*. Cambridge, MA: Harvard University Press, 2014.

Ioteyko, Josefa. *The Science of Labour and Its Organization*. London: George Routledge and Sons, 1919.

Jackson, Bruce. Foreword to *American Negro Folk-Songs*, by Newman I. White. Hatboro, PA: Hatboro Folklore Associates, 1965.

Jackson, Bruce. *The Negro and His Folklore in Nineteenth-Century Periodicals*. Austin: University of Texas Press, 1969.

Jackson, Bruce. *Wake Up Dead Man: Hard Labor and Southern Blues*. Athens: University of Georgia Press, 1999.

Jackson, Bruce. "Worksong." In *Folklore: An Encyclopedia of Beliefs, Customs, Tales, Music, and Art*, edited by Thomas A. Green, 2:848–49. Santa Barbara, CA: ABC-CLIO, 1997.

Jaffe, Sarah. *Work Won't Love You Back: How Devotion to Our Jobs Keeps Us Exploited, Exhausted, and Alone*. New York: Bold Type, 2021.

Jakobsen, Janet R. "Queers Are Like Jews, Aren't They? Analogy and Alliance Politics." In *Queer Theory and the Jewish Question*, edited by Daniel Boyarin, Daniel Itzkovitz, and Ann Pellegrini, 64–89. New York: Columbia University Press, 2003.

Jameson, Fredric. *Representing "Capital": A Reading of Volume One*. London: Verso, 2011.

Jarman, Michelle. "Dismembering the Lynch Mob: Intersecting Narratives of Disability, Race, and Sexual Menace." In *Sex and Disability*, edited by Robert McRuer and Anna Mollow, 89–107. Durham, NC: Duke University Press, 2012.

Johnson, Guion Griffis. *A Social History of the Sea Islands, with Special Reference to St. Helena Island, South Carolina*. Chapel Hill: University of North Carolina Press, 1930.

Johnson, Guy Benton. "A Study of the Musical Talent of the American Negro." PhD diss., University of North Carolina, 1927.

Johnson, Guy Benton. *Folk Culture on St. Helena Island, South Carolina*. Chapel Hill: University of North Carolina Press, 1930.

Johnson, James Weldon. "The Changing Status of Negro Labor." In *Proceedings of the National Conference of Social Work, at the Forty-Fifth Annual Session Held in Kansas City, Missouri, May 15–22, 1918*, 383. Chicago: Rogers and Hall, 1918.

Johnson, James Weldon. "O Black and Unknown Bards." In *Book of American Negro Poetry*, edited by James Weldon Johnson, 73–74. New York: Harcourt, Brace, 1922.

Johnson, James Weldon. Preface to *The Book of American Negro Spirituals*, edited by James Weldon Johnson and J. Rosamond Johnson. New York: Viking, 1925.

Johnson, Robert Underwood, and Clarence Clough Buel, eds. *Battles and Leaders of the Civil War, Being for the Most Part Contributions by Union and Confederate Officers. Based upon "The Century War Series."* Vol. 3. New York: Century, 1887.

Johnson, Walter. "To Remake the World: Slavery, Racial Capitalism, and Justice." *Boston Review*, February 20, 2018. https://bostonreview.net/forum/walter-johnson-to-remake-the-world.

Jolles, André. *Einfache Formen: Legende, Sage, Mythe, Rätsel, Spruch, Kasus, Memorabile, Märchen, Witz.* Tübingen, Germany: Max Niemeyer, 1999.

Jones, Laurence C. *Piney Woods and Its Story.* New York: Fleming H. Revell, 1922.

Jones, Laurence C. *The Spirit of Piney Woods.* New York: Fleming H. Revell, 1931.

Kabir, Raisa. *Raisa Kabir.* Accessed April 28, 2021. https://lids-sewn-shut.typepad.com/blog/.

Kaestle, Carl F., and Janice A. Radway. "A Framework for the History of Publishing and Reading in the United States." In *Print in Motion: The Expansion of Publishing and Reading in the United States, 1880–1940*, edited by Carl F. Kaestle and Janice A. Radway, 7–21. History of the Book in America, vol. 4. Chapel Hill: University of North Carolina Press, 2009.

Kafer, Alison. *Feminist, Queer, Crip.* Bloomington: Indiana University Press, 2013.

Kafka, Ben. "Paperwork: The State of the Discipline." *Book History* 12, no. 1 (2009): 340–53.

Katz, Michael B. *In the Shadow of the Poorhouse: A Social History of Welfare in America.* New York: Basic Books, 1986.

Kazanjian, David. *The Brink of Freedom: Improvising Life in the Nineteenth-Century Atlantic World.* Durham, NC: Duke University Press, 2016.

Keller, Helen. *The Story of My Life.* New York: Doubleday, Page, 1903.

Kelley, Robin D. G. "'A Day of Reckoning': Dreams of Reparations." In *Redress for Historical Injustices in the United States: On Reparations for Slavery, Jim Crow, and Their Legacies*, edited by Michael T. Martin and Marilyn Yaquinto, 203–21. Durham, NC: Duke University Press, 2007.

Kelso, Robert W. "Recent Advances in the Administration of Poor Relief." *Journal of Social Forces* 1, no. 2 (January 1923): 90–92.

Kerber, Linda K. *No Constitutional Right to Be Ladies: Women and the Obligations of Citizenship.* New York: Hill and Wang, 1999.

Kessler-Harris, Alice. *In Pursuit of Equity: Women, Men, and the Quest for Economic Citizenship in 20th-Century America.* Oxford: Oxford University Press, 2001.

King, Martin Luther, Jr. *Where Do We Go from Here: Chaos or Community?* Boston: Beacon, 2010.

King, Tiffany Lethabo. *The Black Shoals: Offshore Formations of Black and Native Studies.* Durham, NC: Duke University Press, 2019.

Kirtley, Christopher. *Clinical Gait Analysis: Theory and Practice.* Amsterdam: Elsevier Health Sciences, 2006.

Kleege, Georgina. *Blind Rage: Letters to Helen Keller.* Washington, DC: Gallaudet University Press, 2006.

Korczynski, Marek, Michael Pickering, and Emma Robertson. *Rhythms of Labour: Music at Work in Britain.* New York: Cambridge University Press, 2013.

Kornbluh, Felicia. *The Battle for Welfare Rights: Politics and Poverty in Modern America.* Philadelphia: University of Pennsylvania Press, 2007.

Krehbiel, Henry Edward. *Afro-American Folksongs: A Study in Racial and National Music.* New York: G. Schirmer, 1914.

La Berge, Leigh Clare. *Wages against Artwork: Decommodified Labor and the Claims of Socially Engaged Art.* Durham, NC: Duke University Press, 2019.

Langan, Celeste. *Romantic Vagrancy: Wordsworth and the Simulation of Freedom.* Cambridge: Cambridge University Press, 1995.

Larsen, Neil, Mathias Nilges, Josh Robinson, and Nicholas Brown, eds. *Marxism and the Critique of Value.* Chicago: MCM', 2014.

Laski, Gregory. *Untimely Democracy: The Politics of Progress after Slavery.* New York: Oxford University Press, 2018.

Latour, Bruno. "Drawing Things Together." In *Representation in Scientific Practice,* edited by Michael Lynch and Steve Woolgar, 19–68. Cambridge, MA: MIT Press, 1990.

Latour, Bruno. *Laboratory Life: The Social Construction of Scientific Facts.* Beverly Hills, CA: Sage, 1979.

Latour, Bruno. "What Is Iconoclash? Or Is There a World beyond the Image Wars?" In *Iconoclash: Beyond the Image Wars in Science, Religion, and Art,* edited by Peter Weibel and Bruno Latour, 16–40. Cambridge, MA: MIT Press, 2002.

Leiby, James. *A History of Social Welfare and Social Work in the United States.* New York: Columbia University Press, 1978.

Letchworth, William Pryor. *Care and Treatment of Epileptics.* New York: G. P. Putnam's Sons, 1900.

Leverenz, David. *Paternalism Incorporated: Fables of American Fatherhood, 1865–1940.* Ithaca, NY: Cornell University Press, 2004.

Levine, Caroline. *Forms: Whole, Rhythm, Hierarchy, Network.* Princeton, NJ: Princeton University Press, 2015.

Levy, Jonathan. "Altruism and the Origins of Nonprofit Philanthropy." In *Philanthropy in Democratic Societies: History, Institutions, Values,* edited by Rob Reich, Chiara Cordelli, and Lucy Bernholz, 19–43. Chicago: University of Chicago Press, 2016.

Liberator. "Gen. Howard, at Edisto Island, S.C." December 15, 1865.

Liebman, Lance. "The Definition of Disability in Social Security and Supplemental Security Income: Drawing the Bounds of Social Welfare Estates." *Harvard Law Review* 89, no. 5 (1976): 833–67.

Linker, Beth. *War's Waste: Rehabilitation in World War I America.* Chicago: University of Chicago Press, 2011.

Lipschutz, Mark R., and R. Kent Rasmussen, eds. "Samori Toure (Samory)." In *Dictionary of African Historical Biography*, 203–4. Berkeley: University of California Press, 1989.

Lipsky, Michael. *Street-Level Bureaucracy: Dilemmas of the Individual in Public Services.* New York: Russell Sage Foundation, 1980.

Logue, Larry M., and Peter Blanck. "'Benefit of the Doubt': African-American Civil War Veterans and Pensions." *Journal of Interdisciplinary History* 38, no. 3 (Winter 2008): 377–99.

Lomax, Alan. *The Land Where the Blues Began.* New York: Pantheon, 1993.

Lomax, John A. *Negro Folk Songs as Sung by Lead Belly, "King of the Twelve-String Guitar Players of the World," Long-Time Convict in the Penitentiaries of Texas and Louisiana.* New York: Macmillan, 1936.

Longmore, Paul K. *Telethons: Spectacle, Disability, and the Business of Charity.* Oxford: Oxford University Press, 2015.

Longmore, Paul K. *Why I Burned My Book and Other Essays on Disability.* Philadelphia: Temple University Press, 2003.

Lowe, Lisa. "History Hesitant." *Social Text* 33, no. 4 (2015): 85–107.

Lowe, Lisa. *Immigrant Acts: On Asian American Cultural Politics.* Durham, NC: Duke University Press, 1996.

Lowell, Josephine Shaw. "Charity Organization." *Lend a Hand* 3, no. 2 (February 1888): 81–87.

Lowell, Josephine Shaw. *Public Relief and Private Charity.* New York: G. P. Putnam's Sons, 1884.

Lubove, Roy. *The Professional Altruist: The Emergence of Social Work as a Career, 1880–1930.* Cambridge, MA: Harvard University Press, 1965.

Lutz, Tom. *Doing Nothing: A History of Loafers, Loungers, Slackers and Bums in America.* New York: Farrar, Straus and Giroux, 2006.

Lye, Colleen. *America's Asia: Racial Form and American Literature, 1893–1945.* Princeton, NJ: Princeton University Press, 2005.

MacLean, Annie Marion. *Cheero.* New York: Womans Press, 1918.

MacLean, Annie Marion. *Our Neighbors.* New York: Macmillan, 1922.

MacLean, Annie Marion. "This Way Lies Happiness." *Open Court,* January 1923.

MacLean, Annie Marion. "A Town in Florida." In *The Negro Church: Report of a Social Study Made under the Direction of Atlanta University; Together with the Proceedings of the Eighth Conference for the Study of the Negro Problems, Held at Atlanta University, May 26th, 1903,* edited by W. E. B. Du Bois, 64–68. Atlanta, GA: Atlanta University Press, 1903.

MacLean, Annie Marion. "Twenty Years of Sociology by Correspondence." *American Journal of Sociology* 28, no. 4 (1923): 461–72.

MacLean, Annie Marion. *Wage-Earning Women.* New York: Macmillan, 1910.

MacLean, Annie Marion. *Women Workers and Society.* Chicago: A. C. McClurg, 1916.

Malin, Brenton J. *Feeling Mediated: A History of Media Technology and Emotion in America.* Critical Cultural Communication. New York: New York University Press, 2014.

Mandel, Eli P. "Review: The Work-Shy by Blunt Research Group." *Make Literary Magazine,* May 1, 2017. https://www.makemag.com/review-the-work-shy/.

Marey, E.-J. *Movement.* Translated by Eric Pritchard. New York: D. Appleton, 1895.

Marey, E.-J. "The Work of the Physiological Station at Paris." In *Smithsonian Institution Annual Report, 1895,* 391–412. Washington, DC: Smithsonian Institution, 1896.

Marshall, Caitlin. "Crippled Speech." *Postmodern Culture* 24, no. 3 (2014): n.p.

Marshall, T. *Citizenship and Social Class, and Other Essays.* Cambridge: Cambridge University Press, 1950.

Marten, James Alan. *Sing Not War: The Lives of Union and Confederate Veterans in Gilded Age America.* Chapel Hill: University of North Carolina Press, 2011.

Marx, Karl. *Capital: A Critique of Political Economy.* Vol. 1. Translated by Ben Fowkes. New York: Penguin Classics, 1990.

Marx, Karl. *Capital: A Critique of Political Economy.* Vol. 3. Translated by David Fernbach. New York: Penguin Classics, 1993.

Marx, Karl. *Karl Marx: Selected Writings.* New York: Oxford University Press, 2000.

Mauss, Marcel. "Techniques of the Body." In *Incorporations,* edited by Jonathan Crary and Sanford Kwinter, 455–77. New York: Zone, 1992.

Mayer, Andreas. *The Science of Walking: Investigations into Locomotion in the Long Nineteenth Century.* Translated by Tilman Skowroneck and Robin Blanton. Chicago: University of Chicago Press, 2020.

Mayer, Andreas. *Wissenschaft vom Gehen.* Frankfurt am Main: S. Fischer, 2013.

McClanahan, Annie. "Introduction: The Spirit of Capital in an Age of Deindustrialization." *Post45.* Accessed April 27, 2020. http://post45.org/2019/01/introduction-the-spirit-of-capital-in-an-age-of-deindustrialization/.

McCoy, Terrence. "Disabled and Disdained." *Washington Post,* July 21, 2017. http://www.washingtonpost.com/sf/local/2017/07/21/how-disability-benefits-divided-this-rural-community-between-those-who-work-and-those-who-dont/.

McHenry, Elizabeth. *Forgotten Readers: Recovering the Lost History of African-American Literary Societies.* Durham, NC: Duke University Press, 2002.

McKelvey, Blake. "Penal Slavery and Southern Reconstruction." *Journal of Negro History* 20, no. 2 (1935): 153–79.

McKim, Lucy. "Songs of the Port Royal 'Contrabands.'" *Dwight's Journal of Music* 21 (November 8, 1862): 254–55.

McLennan, Rebecca M. *The Crisis of Imprisonment: Protest, Politics, and the Making of the American Penal State, 1776–1941.* New York: Cambridge University Press, 2008.

McPherson, James M. *The Struggle for Equality: Abolitionists and the Negro in the Civil War and Reconstruction.* Princeton, NJ: Princeton University Press, 2014.

Meek, Ronald L. *Studies in the Labor Theory of Value.* New York: Monthly Review Press, 1976.

Menafee, Martin A. "A School Treasurer's Story." In *Tuskegee and Its People: Their Ideals and Achievements,* edited by Booker T. Washington and Emmett J. Scott, 152–63. New York: D. Appleton, 1905.

Metfessel, Milton. *Phonophotography in Folk Music: American Negro Songs in New Notation.* Chapel Hill: University of North Carolina Press, 1928.

Mirzoeff, Nicholas. "The Shadow and the Substance: Race, Photography, and the Index." In *Only Skin Deep: Changing Visions of the American Self,* edited by Coco Fusco and Brian Wallis, 111–27. New York: International Center of Photography, 2003.

Mitchell, David T., and Sharon L. Snyder. *The Biopolitics of Disability: Neoliberalism, Ablenationalism, and Peripheral Embodiment.* Ann Arbor: University of Michigan Press, 2015.

Mitchell, David, and Sharon L. Snyder. "The Eugenic Atlantic: Race, Disability, and the Making of an International Eugenic Science, 1800–1945." *Disability and Society* 18, no. 7 (2003): 843–64.

Mitchell, David T., and Sharon L. Snyder. *Narrative Prosthesis: Disability and the Dependencies of Discourse.* Ann Arbor: University of Michigan Press, 2001.

Mittelstadt, Jennifer. *From Welfare to Workfare: The Unintended Consequences of Liberal Reform, 1945–1965.* Chapel Hill: University of North Carolina Press, 2005.

Molesworth, Helen, ed. *Work Ethic.* State College: Pennsylvania State University Press, 2003.

Moran, James. *Printing Presses: History and Development from the Fifteenth Century to Modern Times.* Berkeley: University of California Press, 1978.

Moten, Fred. *In the Break: The Aesthetics of the Black Radical Tradition.* Minneapolis: University of Minnesota Press, 2003.

Musser, Charles. "At the Beginning." In *The Silent Cinema Reader,* edited by Lee Grieveson and Peter Krämer, 15–30. New York: Routledge, 2004.

Musser, Charles. *The Emergence of Cinema: The American Screen to 1907.* Berkeley: University of California Press, 1994.

Nadasen, Premilla, Jennifer Mittelstadt, and Marisa Chappell, eds. *Welfare in the United States: A History with Documents, 1935–1996.* New York: Routledge, 2009.

Nelson, Barbara J. "The Origins of the Two-Channel Welfare State: Workmen's Compensation and Mother's Aid." In *Women, the State, and Welfare,* edited by Linda Gordon, 92–122. Madison: University of Wisconsin Press, 1990.

New York Times. "Hanna Aids Ex-Slaves." February 1903.

New York Times. "A Pension Fraud Exposed." January 21, 1900.

Ochiai, Akiko. "The Port Royal Experiment Revisited: Northern Visions of Reconstruction and the Land Question." *New England Quarterly* 74, no. 1 (March 2001): 94–117.

Odum, Howard W. *An Approach to Public Welfare and Social Work.* Chapel Hill: University of North Carolina Press, 1926.

Odum, Howard W. "Folk-Song and Folk-Poetry as Found in the Secular Songs of the Southern Negroes." *Journal of American Folklore* 24, no. 93 (1911): 255–94.

Odum, Howard W. "Folk-Song and Folk-Poetry as Found in the Secular Songs of the Southern Negroes (Concluded)." *Journal of American Folklore* 24, no. 94 (1911): 351–96.

Odum, Howard W. "Religious Folk-Songs of the Southern Negroes." *American Journal of Religious Psychology and Education* 3, no. 3 (July 1909): 265–365.

Odum, Howard W., and Guy B. Johnson. *The Negro and His Songs: A Study of Typical Negro Songs in the South.* Chapel Hill: University of North Carolina Press, 1925.

Odum, Howard W., and Guy B. Johnson. *Negro Workaday Songs.* Chapel Hill: University of North Carolina Press, 1926.

Odum, Howard W., and D. W. Willard. *Systems of Public Welfare.* Chapel Hill: University of North Carolina Press, 1925.

Olasky, Marvin N. *The Tragedy of American Compassion.* Washington, DC: Regnery Gateway, 1992.

Oliver, John William. "History of the Civil War Military Pensions, 1861–1885." *Bulletin of the University of Wisconsin*, no. 844. History Series, no. 1 (1917): 1–120.

Oliver, Michael. *The Politics of Disablement: A Sociological Approach.* London: Palgrave Macmillan, 1990.

Paine, Robert Treat. *How to Repress Pauperism and Street Begging.* New York: Charity Organization Society, 1883.

Pateman, Carole. "Another Way Forward: Welfare, Social Reproduction, and a Basic Income." In *Welfare Reform and Political Theory*, edited by Lawrence M. Mead and Christopher Beem, 34–63. New York: Russell Sage Foundation, 2006.

Paul, Heike. "Cultural Mobility between Boston and Berlin: How Germans Have Read and Reread Narratives of American Slavery." In *Cultural Mobility: A Manifesto*, edited by Stephen Greenblatt, 122–71. Cambridge: Cambridge University Press, 2009.

Pearson, Elizabeth, ed. *Letters from Port Royal 1862–1868.* New York: Arno Press and the *New York Times*, 1969.

Pearson, Harry W. "The Secular Debate on Economic Primitivism." In *Trade and Market in the Early Empires: Economies in History and Theory*, edited by Karl Polanyi, Conrad M. Arensberg, and Harry W. Pearson, 3–11. New York: Free Press, 1957.

Petrie, J. G. "Review of the Shorthand Year." *Shorthand: A Scientific and Literary Magazine* 3 (1889): 259–67.

Philip, M. NourbeSe. *Zong!* Middletown, CT: Wesleyan University Press, 2011.

Pickens, Therí Alyce. *Black Madness: Mad Blackness*. Durham, NC: Duke University Press, 2019.

Piepzna-Samarasinha, Leah Lakshmi. *Care Work: Dreaming Disability Justice*. Vancouver: Arsenal Pulp, 2018.

Piepzna-Samarasinha, Leah Lakshmi. *Dirty River: A Queer Femme of Color Dreaming Her Way Home*. Vancouver: Arsenal Pulp Press, 2016.

Pierce, Edward L. "The Freedmen at Port Royal." *Atlantic Monthly* 12, no. 71 (September 1863): 291–315.

Polanyi, Karl. "Karl Bücher." In *International Encyclopedia of the Social Sciences*, edited by David L. Sills, 2:163–65. New York: Macmillan, 1968.

Popular Science Monthly. "Two and a Half Miles a Minute." August 1917.

Postone, Moishe. *Time, Labor, and Social Domination: A Reinterpretation of Marx's Critical Theory*. Cambridge: Cambridge University Press, 1993.

Pretchel-Kluskens, Claire. "Anatomy of a Civil War Pension File." *NGS Newsmagazine* 34, no. 3 (September 2008): 42–47.

Price, Brian. "Frank and Lillian Gilbreth and the Manufacture and Marketing of Motion Study, 1908–1924." *Business and Economic History* 18 (1989): 88–98.

Puar, Jasbir K. *The Right to Maim: Debility, Capacity, Disability*. Durham, NC: Duke University Press, 2017.

Purcell, Leslie Harper. *Miracle in Mississippi: Laurence C. Jones of Piney Woods*. New York: Comet Press, 1956.

Rabinbach, Anson. "The Body without Fatigue: A Nineteenth-Century Utopia." In *Political Symbolism in Modern Europe: Essays in Honor of George L. Mosse*, edited by George L. Mosse, Seymour Drescher, David Warren Sabean, and Allan Sharlin, 42–62. New Brunswick, NJ: Transaction, 1982.

Rabinbach, Anson. "The European Science of Work: The Economy of the Body at the End of the Nineteenth Century." In *Work in France: Representations, Meaning, Organization, and Practice*, edited by Steven L. Kaplan and Cynthia J. Koepp, 475–512. Ithaca, NY: Cornell University Press, 1986.

Rabinbach, Anson. *The Human Motor: Energy, Fatigue, and the Origins of Modernity*. Berkeley: University of California Press, 1992.

Radano, Ronald. *Lying Up a Nation: Race and Black Music*. Chicago: University of Chicago Press, 2003.

Ragin, Charles C. "Introduction: Cases of 'What Is a Case?'" In *What Is a Case? Exploring the Foundations of Social Inquiry*, edited by Charles C. Ragin and Howard Saul Becker, 1–17. Cambridge: Cambridge University Press, 1992.

Reid, Richard M. "Government Policy, Prejudice, and the Experience of Black Civil War Soldiers and Their Families." *Journal of Family History* 27, no. 4 (October 2002): 374–98.

Rembis, Michael. "Disability Studies." *The Year's Work in Critical and Cultural Theory* 25, no. 1 (2015): 211–30.

Richmond, Mary Ellen. *Social Diagnosis*. New York: Russell Sage Foundation, 1917.

Richmond, Mary Ellen. *What Is Social Case Work? An Introductory Description*. New York: Russell Sage Foundation, 1922.

Riles, Annelise. "Introduction: In Response." In *Documents: Artifacts of Modern Knowledge*, edited by Annelise Riles, 1–38. Ann Arbor: University of Michigan Press, 2006.

Ritchie, Codie. "Local Incident Goes Viral." *Russell County Free Press*, November 24, 2016. https://www.facebook.com/RussellFreePress/posts /672438152933722:0.

Robinson, Cedric J. *Black Marxism: The Making of the Black Radical Tradition*. Chapel Hill: University of North Carolina Press, 2000.

Rockefeller, John D. *Random Reminiscences of Men and Events*. New York: Doubleday, Page, 1909.

Rockman, Seth. *Welfare Reform in the Early Republic: A Brief History with Documents*. Boston: Bedford/St. Martin's, 2003.

Rodgers, Daniel T. *The Work Ethic in Industrial America, 1850–1920*. Chicago: University of Chicago Press, 1979.

Rodríguez, Dylan. "Multiculturalist White Supremacy and the Substructure of the Body." In *Corpus: An Interdisciplinary Reader on Bodies and Knowledge*, edited by Monica J. Casper and Paisley Currah, 39–60. New York: Palgrave Macmillan, 2011.

Rony, Fatimah Tobing. *The Third Eye: Race, Cinema, and Ethnographic Spectacle*. Durham, NC: Duke University Press, 1996.

Rose, Sarah F. *No Right to Be Idle: The Invention of Disability, 1840s–1930s*. Chapel Hill: University of North Carolina Press, 2017.

Rose, Willie Lee. *Rehearsal for Reconstruction: The Port Royal Experiment*. Indianapolis: Bobbs-Merrill, 1964.

Rothman, David J. *The Discovery of the Asylum: Social Order and Disorder in the New Republic*. Boston: Little, Brown, 1990.

Rowley-Jolivet, Elizabeth. "The Pivotal Role of Conference Papers in the Network of Scientific Communication." *ASp: La Revue du GERAS* 23–26 (March 1999): 179–96.

Rusnak, Robert J. *Walter Hines Page and the World's Work, 1900–1913*. Washington, DC: University Press of America, 1982.

Russell, Marta. *Capitalism and Disability*. Edited by Keith Rosenthal. Chicago: Haymarket, 2019.

Ryan, Susan M. "Reform." In *Keywords for American Cultural Studies*, edited by Bruce Burgett and Glenn Hendler, 196–99. New York: New York University Press, 2007.

Samuels, Ellen. *Fantasies of Identification: Disability, Gender, Race*. New York: New York University Press, 2014.

Samuels, Ellen. "From Melville to Eddie Murphy: The Disability Con in American Literature and Film." *Leviathan* 8, no. 1 (2006): 61–82.

Samuels, Ellen. "My Body, My Closet: Invisible Disability and the Limits of Coming-Out Discourse." *GLQ* 9, nos. 1–2 (2003): 233–55.

Sanborn, F. B. "Education of the African Race." In *Proceedings of the National Conference of Charities and Correction, at the Fourteenth Annual Session Held in Omaha, Neb., August 25–31, 1887*, edited by Isabel C. Barrows, 170–72. Boston: Press of Geo. H. Ellis, 1887.

Sandage, Scott A. *Born Losers: A History of Failure in America.* Cambridge, MA: Harvard University Press, 2005.

Sanders, Lynn Moss. *Howard W. Odum's Folklore Odyssey: Transformation to Tolerance through African American Folk Studies.* Athens: University of Georgia Press, 2003.

Saville, Julie. *The Work of Reconstruction: From Slave to Wage Laborer in South Carolina, 1860–1870.* Cambridge: Cambridge University Press, 1996.

Schäfer, Axel R. *American Progressives and German Social Reform, 1875–1920: Social Ethics, Moral Control, and the Regulatory State in a Transatlantic Context.* Stuttgart, Germany: Franz Steiner Verlag, 2000.

Schalk, Sami. *Bodyminds Reimagined: (Dis)Ability, Race, and Gender in Black Women's Speculative Fiction.* Durham, NC: Duke University Press, 2018.

Schalk, Sami. "Reevaluating the Supercrip." *Journal of Literary and Cultural Disability Studies* 10, no. 1 (2016): 71–86.

Schwartz, Hillel. "Torque: The New Kinaesthetic of the Twentieth Century." In *Incorporations*, edited by Jonathan Crary, 70–127. New York: Zone, 1995.

Schweik, Susan. "Lomax's Matrix: Disability, Solidarity, and the Black Power of 504." *Disability Studies Quarterly* 31, no. 1 (2011). http://dsq-sds.org/article/view /1371.

Schweik, Susan M. *The Ugly Laws: Disability in Public.* New York: New York University Press, 2010.

Seashore, Carl E. "Phonophotography in the Measurement of the Expression of Emotion in Music and Speech." *Scientific Monthly* 24, no. 5 (1927): 463–71.

Seashore, Carl E. "Three New Approaches to the Study of Negro Music." *Annals of the American Academy of Political and Social Science* 140 (1928): 191–92.

Sekula, Allan. "The Body and the Archive." *October* 39 (Winter 1986): 3–64.

Sennett, Richard. *The Craftsman.* New Haven, CT: Yale University Press, 2008.

Serpell, C. Namwali. *Seven Modes of Uncertainty.* Cambridge, MA: Harvard University Press, 2014.

Shaffer, Donald Robert. *After the Glory: The Struggles of Black Civil War Veterans.* Lawrence: University Press of Kansas, 2004.

Shapiro, Joseph P. *No Pity: People with Disabilities Forging a New Civil Rights Movement.* New York: Times Books, 1993.

Sharpe, Christina. *In the Wake: On Blackness and Being.* Durham, NC: Duke University Press, 2016.

Shell, Marc. *The Economy of Literature.* Baltimore: Johns Hopkins University Press, 1978.

Shklar, Judith N. *American Citizenship: The Quest for Inclusion.* Cambridge, MA: Harvard University Press, 1991.

Sidlauskas, Susan. "Before-and-After: The Aesthetic as Evidence in Nineteenth-Century Medical Photography." In *Before-and-After Photography: Histories and Contexts*, edited by Jordan Bear and Kate Palmer Albers, 15–41. London: Bloomsbury, 2017.

Silber, Nina. *The Romance of Reunion: Northerners and the South, 1865–1900.* Chapel Hill: University of North Carolina Press, 1997.

Singer, Peter. *The Most Good You Can Do: How Effective Altruism Is Changing Ideas about Living Ethically.* New Haven, CT: Yale University Press, 2015.

Singh, Nikhil Pal. *Race and America's Long War.* Berkeley: University of California Press, 2017.

Skocpol, Theda. *Protecting Soldiers and Mothers: The Political Origins of Social Policy in the United States.* Cambridge, MA: Harvard University Press, 1995.

Smalley, Eugene V. "The United States Pension Office." *Century Illustrated Magazine* 28, no. 3 (July 1884): 427–34.

Smith, Adam. *An Inquiry into the Nature and Causes of the Wealth of Nations.* Vol. 1. Edited by R. H. Campbell, A. S. Skinner, and W. B. Todd. The Glasgow Edition of the Works and Correspondence of Adam Smith, University of Glasgow. Oxford: Clarendon, 1976.

Smith, Eugene. "Labor as a Means of Reformation." In *Proceedings of the National Conference of Charities and Correction, at the Twelfth Annual Session Held in Washington, D.C., June 4–10, 1885*, edited by Isabel C. Barrows, 265–73. Boston: Press of Geo. H. Ellis, 1885.

Smith, Jason E. *Smart Machines and Service Work: Automation in an Age of Stagnation.* Field Notes. London: Reaktion, 2020.

Southern, Eileen. *The Music of Black Americans: A History.* 2nd ed. New York: Norton, 1983.

Spivey, Donald. *Schooling for the New Slavery: Black Industrial Education, 1868–1915.* Westport, CT: Greenwood, 1978.

Spratling, William P. "Industrial Education for Epileptics." In *Proceedings of the National Conference of Charities and Correction at the Twenty-Fourth Annual Session Held in Toronto, Ontario, July 7–14, 1897*, edited by Isabel C. Barrows, 69–75. Boston: Press of Geo. H. Ellis, 1898.

Stanley, Amy Dru. "Beggars Can't Be Choosers: Compulsion and Contract in Postbellum America." *Journal of American History* 78, no. 4 (March 1992): 1265–93.

Steiner, Jesse Frederick. *Education for Social Work.* Chicago: University of Chicago Press, 1921.

Steiner, Jesse Frederick, and Roy Melton Brown. *The North Carolina Chain Gang: A Study of County Convict Road Work.* University of North Carolina Social Study Series. Chapel Hill: University of North Carolina Press, 1927.

Stone, Deborah. *The Disabled State.* Philadelphia: Temple University Press, 1984.

Stone, Deborah. "Welfare Policy and the Transformation of Care." In *Remaking America: Democracy and Public Policy in an Age of Inequality*, edited by Joe

Soss, Jacob S. Hacker, and Suzanne Mettler, 183–202. New York: Russell Sage Foundation, 2007.

Svendsen, Lars. *Work*. New York: Routledge, 2016.

Tarbell, Ida Minerva. *The Life of Abraham Lincoln*. New York: Lincoln History Society, 1908.

Taylor, Sunny. "The Right Not to Work: Power and Disability." *Monthly Review* (blog), March 1, 2004. https://monthlyreview.org/2004/03/01/the-right-not-to-work-power-and-disability/.

tenBroek, Jacobus. "The Right to Live in the World: The Disabled in the Law of Torts." *California Law Review* 54, no. 2 (May 1966): 841–919.

tenBroek, Jacobus, and Floyd Matson. "The Disabled and the Law of Welfare." *California Law Review* 54, no. 2 (May 1966): 809–40.

Thomas, Benjamin P. *Abraham Lincoln: A Biography*. Carbondale: Southern Illinois University Press, 2008.

Tillet, Salamishah. *Sites of Slavery: Citizenship and Racial Democracy in the Post–Civil Rights Imagination*. Durham, NC: Duke University Press, 2012.

Titon, Jeff Todd. "North America/Black America." In *Worlds of Music: An Introduction to the Music of the World's Peoples*, 5th ed., edited by Jeff Todd Titon and Timothy J. Cooley, 144–210. Belmont, CA: Schirmer Cengage Learning, 2009.

Tompkins, Jane P. *Sensational Designs: The Cultural Work of American Fiction, 1790–1860*. New York: Oxford University Press, 1985.

Tosi, Virgilio. *Cinema before Cinema: The Origins of Scientific Cinematography*. London: British Universities Film and Video Council, 2005.

Trent, James W. *Inventing the Feeble Mind: A History of Intellectual Disability in the United States*. New York: Oxford University Press, 2017.

Trumbull, General M. M. "Pensions for All." *Popular Science Monthly*, October 1889.

Tufte, Edward R. *The Visual Display of Quantitative Information*. Cheshire, CT: Graphics Press, 1983.

Turner, Stephen. "A Life in the First Half-Century of Sociology: Charles Ellwood and the Division of Sociology." In *Sociology in America: A History*, edited by Craig J. Calhoun, 115–54. Chicago: University of Chicago Press, 2007.

Turner, Stephen P., and Jonathan H. Turner. *The Impossible Science: An Institutional Analysis of American Sociology*. Sage Library of Social Research, vol. 181. London: Sage, 1990.

Twain, Mark. *Mark Twain's Civil War*. Edited by David Rachels. Lexington: University Press of Kentucky, 2007.

United States Pension Bureau. *General Instructions to Special Examiners of the United States Pension Office*. Washington, DC: US Government Printing Office, 1881.

United States Pension Bureau. *A Treatise on the Practice of the Pension Bureau Governing the Adjudication of the Army and Navy Pensions*. Washington, DC: US Government Printing Office, 1898.

United States President's Commission on Economy and Efficiency. *Economy and Efficiency in the Government Service: Message of the President of the United States Transmitting Reports of the Commission on Economy and Efficiency.* Washington, DC: US Government Printing Office, 1912.

Vatin, Francois. "Arbeit und Ermüdung: Entstehung und Scheitern der Psycho-physiologie der Arbeit." In *Physiologie und industrielle Gesellschaft: Studien zur Verwissenschaftlichung des Körpers im 19. und 20. Jahrhundert,* edited by Philipp Sarasin and Jakob Tanner, 347–68. Frankfurt am Main: Suhrkamp Verlag, 1998.

Vaughan, Walter Raleigh. *Vaughan's "Freedmen's Pension Bill."* Freeport, NY: Books for Libraries Press, 1971.

Vismann, Cornelia. *Files: Law and Media Technology.* Stanford, CA: Stanford University Press, 2008.

Wagner-Hasel, Beate. *Die Arbeit des Gelehrten: Der Nationalökonom Karl Bücher (1847–1930).* Frankfurt: Campus Verlag, 2011.

Wallace, Maurice O. "Framing the Black Soldier: Image, Uplift, and the Duplicity of Pictures." In *Pictures and Progress: Early Photography and the Making of African American Identity,* edited by Maurice O. Wallace and Shawn Michelle Smith, 244–66. Durham, NC: Duke University Press, 2012.

Wallis, Brian, and Deborah Willis, eds. *African American Vernacular Photography: Selected from the Daniel Cowin Collection.* New York: Steidl/ICP, 2006.

Wang, Jackie. *Carceral Capitalism.* South Pasadena, CA: Semiotext, 2018.

Warner, Amos Griswold. *American Charities: A Study in Philanthropy and Economics.* New York: Crowell, 1894.

Warner, John De Witt. "Half a Million Dollars a Day for Pensions." *Forum* 15 (June 1893): 439–51.

Washington, Booker T. "Chapters from My Experience." *World's Work* 20, no. 6 (October 1910): 13505–22.

Washington, Booker T. "Chapters from My Experience (II)." *World's Work* 21, no. 1 (November 1910): 13627–40.

Washington, Booker T. "Signs of Progress among the Negroes." *Century Magazine,* January 1900.

Washington, Booker T. *Up from Slavery.* Edited by William L. Andrews. New York: Oxford University Press, 2000.

Washington, Booker T., and Emmett J. Scott, eds. *Tuskegee and Its People: Their Ideals and Achievements.* New York: D. Appleton, 1905.

Weber, Max. *The Protestant Ethic and the Spirit of Capitalism.* Translated by Talcott Parsons. London: Routledge, 2001.

Weber, Max. *Sociological Writings.* German Library, vol. 60. New York: Continuum, 1994.

Weeks, Kathi. *The Problem with Work: Feminism, Marxism, Antiwork Politics, and Postwork Imaginaries.* Durham, NC: Duke University Press, 2011.

Weheliye, Alexander G. *Habeas Viscus: Racializing Assemblages, Biopolitics, and Black Feminist Theories of the Human.* Durham, NC: Duke University Press, 2014.

Western Electrician. "Analysis of Movements by Photography and the Incandescent Lamp." April 2, 1892, 205.

Wexler, Laura. *Tender Violence: Domestic Visions in an Age of U.S. Imperialism.* Chapel Hill: University of North Carolina Press, 2000.

Whissel, Kristen. *Picturing American Modernity: Traffic, Technology, and the Silent Cinema.* Durham, NC: Duke University Press Books, 2008.

White, Alfred T. "Labor Tests and Relief in Work in the United States." In *The Organization of Charities, Being a Report of the Sixth Section of the International Congress of Charities, Corrections, and Philanthropy, Chicago, June, 1893,* edited by Daniel C. Gilman, 87–98. Baltimore: Johns Hopkins University Press, 1894.

Wiebe, Robert H. *The Search for Order, 1877–1920.* New York: Macmillan, 1967.

Wilderson, Frank. "Gramsci's Black Marx: Whither the Slave in Civil Society?" *Social Identities* 9, no. 2 (June 2003): 225–40.

Wilkinson, John. "Review of *The Work-Shy.*" *Critical Inquiry* 44, no. 3 (2018): 615–17.

Willis, Deborah. *Envisioning Emancipation: Black Americans and the End of Slavery.* Philadelphia: Temple University Press, 2013.

Wines, F. H. "Farm Prisons of Louisiana." In *Outdoor Labor for Convicts: A Report to the Governor of Illinois,* edited by Charles Richmond Henderson, 152–53. Chicago: University of Chicago Press, 1907.

Winick, Stephen D. "Folklore and/in Music." In *A Companion to Folklore,* edited by Galit Hasan-Rokem and Regina F. Bennd, 464–82. New York: Wiley-Blackwell, 2012.

Wong, Edlie L. *Racial Reconstruction: Black Inclusion, Chinese Exclusion, and the Fictions of Citizenship.* New York: University Press, 2015.

Woodroofe, Kathleen. *From Charity to Social Work in England and the United States.* London: Routledge and Keegan Paul, 1962.

Woofter, Thomas Jackson. *Black Yeomanry: Life on St. Helena Island.* New York: Henry Holt, 1930.

Wright, A. O. "Employment in Poorhouses." In *Proceedings of the National Conference of Charities and Correction, at the Sixteenth Annual Session, Held in San Francisco, Cal., September 11–18, 1889,* edited by Isabel C. Barrows, 197–203. Boston: Press of Geo. H. Ellis, 1889.

Wright, R. R., Jr. "What Does the Negro Want in Our Democracy?" In *Proceedings of the National Conference of Social Work, at the Forty-Sixth Annual Session Held in Atlantic City, New Jersey, June 1–8, 1919,* 539–44. Chicago: Rogers and Hall, 1919.

Wu, Cynthia. *Chang and Eng Reconnected: The Original Siamese Twins in American Culture.* Philadelphia: Temple University Press, 2012.

Wurtzler, Steve J. *Electric Sounds: Technological Change and the Rise of Corporate Mass Media.* New York: Columbia University Press, 2008.

Yates, JoAnne. *Control through Communication: The Rise of System in American Management.* Baltimore: Johns Hopkins University Press, 1989.

Zacka, Bernardo. *When the State Meets the Street: Public Service and Moral Agency.* Cambridge, MA: Belknap, 2017.

Zatz, Noah D. "Welfare to What." *Hastings Law Journal* 57, no. 6 (2006): 1131–88.

Zatz, Noah D. "What Welfare Requires from Work." *UCLA Law Review* 54, no. 2 (2007): 373–464.

Zimmerman, Andrew. *Alabama in Africa: Booker T. Washington, the German Empire, and the Globalization of the New South.* Princeton, NJ: Princeton University Press, 2012.

Zunz, Olivier. *Philanthropy in America: A History.* Princeton, NJ: Princeton University Press, 2012.

personal
exp of difficulty
getting accommodations
filing claims

intersectionality of print
culture - excluded blackest w/race
the uneducated dynamics & disability
reasons for distancing race

moral layer of the economy -
uniquely American

How much there are throughlines to today?
where can value come from in the US if not
from work? will anything of value turn into work?

ch 3: visual representation/performance of work
"universality of il laboring bodies
"the ideal perfection" 148